On Transactional
Concurrency Control

Synthesis Lectures on Data Management

Editor
H.V. Jagadish, *University of Michigan*

Founding Editor
M. Tamer Özsu, *University of Waterloo*

Synthesis Lectures on Data Management is edited by H.V. Jagadish of the University of Michigan. The series publishes 80–150 page publications on topics pertaining to data management. Topics include query languages, database system architectures, transaction management, data warehousing, XML and databases, data stream systems, wide scale data distribution, multimedia data management, data mining, and related subjects.

On Transactional Concurrency Control
Goetz Graefe
2019

Answering Queries Using Views, Second Edition
Foto Afrati and Rada Chirkova
2019

Transaction Processing on Modern Hardware
Mohammad Sadoghi and Spyros Blanas
2019

Data Management in Machine Learning Systems
Matthias Boehm, Arun Kumar, and Jun Yang
2019

Non-Volatile Memory Database Management Systems
Joy Arulraj and Andrew Pavlo
2019

Scalable Processing of Spatial-Keyword Queries
Ahmed R. Mahmood and Walid G. Aref
2019

On Transactional Concurrency Control

Goetz Graefe

ISBN: 978-3-031-00745-3   paperback
ISBN: 978-3-031-01873-2   ebook
ISBN: 978-3-031-00100-0   hardcover

DOI 10.1007/978-3-031-01873-2

A Publication in the Springer series
SYNTHESIS LECTURES ON DATA MANAGEMENT

Lecture #59
Series Editor: H.V. Jagadish, *University of Michigan*
Founding Editor: M. Tamer Özsu, *University of Waterloo*
Series ISSN
Print 2153-5418   Electronic 2153-5426

On Transactional Concurrency Control

Goetz Graefe

SYNTHESIS LECTURES ON DATA MANAGEMENT #59

ABSTRACT

This book contains a number of chapters on transactional database concurrency control. A two-sentence summary of the volume's entire sequence of chapters is this: traditional locking techniques can be improved in multiple dimensions, notably in lock scopes (sizes), lock modes (increment, decrement, and more), lock durations (late acquisition, early release), and lock acquisition sequence (to avoid deadlocks). Even if some of these improvements can be transferred to optimistic concurrency control, notably a fine granularity of concurrency control with serializable transaction isolation including phantom protection, pessimistic concurrency control is categorically superior to optimistic concurrency control, i.e., independent of application, workload, deployment, hardware, and software implementation.

KEYWORDS

concurrency, concurrency control, database, update, transaction, serializability, phantom protection, locking, index, b-tree, key-range locking, key-value locking, deadlock avoidance, lock acquisition sequence, pessimistic concurrency control, optimistic concurrency control, validation, timestamps, snapshot isolation, versioning, multi-version storage, write buffer, distributed systems, mirroring, replication, log shipping, two-phase commit, three-phase commit, controlled lock violation, deferred lock acquisition, deferred lock enforcement, weak lock enforcement, reserved locks, pending locks, orthogonal key-range locking, orthogonal key-value locking, partitioning

Contents

Goetz Graefe
Hewlett–Packard Laboratories

2   Hierarchical Locking in B-Tree Indexes 45

Goetz Graefe
Hewlett–Packard Laboratories

4 Controlled Lock Violation 129

Goetz Graefe, Mark Lillibridge, Harumi Kuno, Joseph Tucek, and Alistair Veitch
Hewlett–Packard Laboratories

7 Serializable Timestamp Validation 251

Goetz Graefe

10　A Problem in Two-Phase Commit **321**

Goetz Graefe

11　Deferred Lock Enforcement **327**

Goetz Graefe

PART IV   The End of Optimistic Concurrency Control 367

12 The End of Optimistic Concurrency Control 369

Goetz Graefe

On Transactional Concurrency Control

This volume contains a number of chapters on transactional database concurrency control. A two-sentence summary of the volume's entire sequence of chapters is this: traditional locking techniques can be improved in multiple dimensions, notably in lock scopes (sizes), lock modes (increment, decrement, and more), lock durations (late acquisition, early release), and lock acquisition sequence (to avoid deadlocks). Even if some of these improvements can be transferred to optimistic concurrency control, notably a fine granularity of concurrency control with serializable transaction isolation including phantom protection, pessimistic concurrency control is categorically superior to optimistic concurrency control, i.e., independent of application, workload, deployment, hardware, and software implementation.

Most of the chapters assume that there is another layer of concurrency control that coordinates threads to protect in-memory data structures. In contrast, transactional concurrency control coordinates transactions to protect logical database contents. For most chapters, the survey of B-tree locking techniques contains sufficient background information. Among all chapters, included in this volume, the most important ones are found in Chapters 1, 4, 5, 11, and 12. Two short chapters with practical significance are found in Chapters 9 and 10. The techniques of Chapters 6, 7, and 8 improve optimistic concurrency control but cannot overcome its inherent limitations. If a reader wants to take time for just one chapter, let that be Chapter 11.

LOCK MANAGEMENT

Many of the chapters refer to transaction managers and lock managers. A transaction manager is a software module around an array representing active transactions. Each transaction has an identifier that might simply be its index (or address) in this array. Transaction identifiers may be reused, but many systems do not reuse transaction identifiers because log records usually include transaction identifiers. The minimal information about each transaction includes its state, e.g., inactive, working, preparing to commit, committing, or hardening. Hardening refers to write-ahead logging, specifically to flushing the system's recovery log up to and including the transaction's commit log record to stable storage.

A database lock manager is a software module around a data structure representing a many-to-many relationship between transactions and database objects, e.g., tables, indexes, pages, records, key values, or index entries. Each instance of this relationship is a requested (and perhaps granted) lock. While lock acquisition requires access by database object, lock release at end-of-transaction requires access by transaction. A typical implementation uses a hash table to search by object identifier, a doubly-linked list of database objects per slot in the hash table, a doubly-linked list of lock requests per database object, and a doubly-linked list of lock requests per slot in the transaction manager.

Figure 1 shows the typical data structures of a lock manager. At the bottom is the transaction manager with an array of transaction descriptors; many of those are inactive here. On the left is a hash table showing here only a single hash bucket along the top. Each element in that linked list represents an item in the database. Each item has one or more lock requests attached. Lock requests by the same transaction form a linked list for efficient lock release at end-of-transaction. For example, transaction 1 (second from left at the bottom) has locks or lock requests on the left and the right items within this hash bucket of the lock manager.

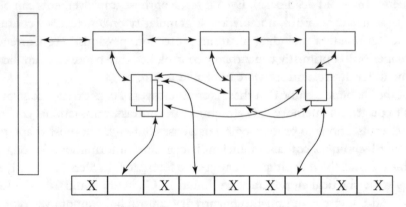

Figure 1: Core data structures of a lock manager.

A transaction manager and its lock manager interact in many ways. For example, lock acquisition must consider a conflicting transaction's state. More specifically, even a high-priority transaction cannot kill a low-priority transaction and preempt its locks if the low-priority transaction is already hardening, i.e., it is waiting for its commit log record to reach stable storage. There are additional states and protections for local transactions participating in a two-phase commit.

Both the transaction manager and the lock manager must serve many threads and therefore require low-level concurrency control in form of latches or, if available, by hardware transactional memory. A single thread offering transaction or lock management as a service to other threads may improve cache behavior but its effect on low-level concurrency is that of a single exclusive latch.

1   PUBLISHED PAPERS

The chapters reprinted in Part I of this volume have already been published. Two of them have been extended substantially since their original publication.

1.1   A SURVEY OF B-TREE LOCKING TECHNIQUES (ACM TODS 2010)

This short survey introduces the separation between low-level concurrency control coordinating threads in order to protect in-memory data structures and high-level concurrency control coordinating transactions in order to protect logical database contents. For example, in parallel query execution, two threads may work for the same query and the same transaction but their accesses to in-memory data structures such as the buffer pool's table-of-contents needs to be coordinated, typically by low-level synchronization mechanisms called latches in the context of database implementations, even if all threads working for the same transaction share locks and thus can (and indeed must) read each other's database updates. The purpose of this chapter is to separate these two levels of concurrency control conceptually such that they can be implemented separately and thus simply.

A little database knowledge is required for this chapter. Basic knowledge of databases, e.g., tables and indexes; of transaction concepts, e.g., the ACID properties atomicity, consistency, isolation, and durability [Härder and Reuter, 1983]; and of B-trees is very helpful, as is some minimal experience writing multi-threaded software. Basic B-tree concepts are readily available in database textbooks as well as in the first two chapters of an earlier volume on "Modern B-tree Techniques" [Graefe, 2011].

1.2   HIERARCHICAL LOCKING IN B-TREE INDEXES (BTW KEYNOTE 2007)

This chapter presages some of the material in the survey but also adds other material, in particular the idea of applying transactional range locks not only in B-tree leaf nodes but also in branch nodes. Thus, the hierarchy of B-tree nodes and their branch keys informs a hierarchy of lock scopes, adapting to the actual key value distribution as naturally as a B-tree structure. The purpose of this chapter is to enable a simple design and implementation of concurrency control for both large queries and small transactions.

1.3   TRANSACTION SUPPORT FOR INDEXED VIEWS (ACM SIGMOD 2004)

The technical report is substantially extended from the conference version, notably with consideration for savepoints and partial rollback, lock escalation and de-escalation, and distributed transactions including two-phase commit. This extended version also discusses the writer's early understanding of commit processing in optimistic concurrency control. The purpose of this chapter is to enable materialized and indexed views not only in read-only business intelligence but also in online transaction processing, with no more concurrency conflicts due to materialized views than due to indexes on base tables and their indexes.

1.4   CONTROLLED LOCK VIOLATION (ACM SIGMOD 2013)

Among the multiple possible dimensions in which traditional pessimistic concurrency control (locking) can be improved, this chapter focuses on lock durations. After one transaction modifies some database contents and while that transaction still waits for all its log records to become persistent on stable storage, controlled lock violation permits other transactions to read and overwrite this database contents, but without the danger of premature publication, which was overlooked in initial ideas for early lock release during transaction commit. The purpose of this chapter is to reduce or avoid lock conflicts in serializable transactions.

1.5   ORTHOGONAL KEY-VALUE LOCKING (BTW 2015 AND EXTENDED DRAFT 2019)

Among the multiple possible dimensions in which traditional pessimistic concurrency control (locking) can be improved, this chapter focuses on lock scopes or sizes, specifically in B-tree leaves. The version included here is substantially extended from the conference version, notably with partitioning of key values within gaps, with more cases studies, and with many new illustrations. The purpose of this chapter is to demonstrate, illustrate, and avoid the large amount of false conflicts in traditional locking in B-tree indexes.

2   OPTIMISTIC CONCURRENCY CONTROL

The following chapters attempt to bring serializability and fine-granularity concurrency control to optimistic concurrency control. In other words, they are attempts to make optimistic concurrency control competitive with advanced modern locking.

Optimistic concurrency control is defined by end-of-transaction validation and conflict detection. Conflicts may be found by comparing multiple transactions' read- and write-sets or by comparing timestamps attached to database contents. The next two chapters focus on these two ways of end-of-transaction conflict detection.

The third chapter in this section recommends a lock manager and controlled lock violation for a correct, simple, and efficient implementation of optimistic transactions and their commit logic. The lock manager enables concurrent validation of multiple optimistic transactions as well as guaranteed compliance by local participants with a global commit decision. Controlled lock violation prevents premature publication of optimistic updates that are validated but not yet hardened.

Figure 2 summarizes the improvements discussed in these chapters.

Dimension	Improvement	Context	Effect
Phantom protection	Gaps in read- and write-sets	Database indexes, phantom protection	Concurrency within a page, even within a gap
	Timestamps for gaps		
Efficiency	Temporary time-stamps	Timestamp concurrency control	Database without timestamps
Simplicity	Lock manager for commit processing	Concurrent validation	Existing designs + imple-mentations
Functionality		Two-phase commit	Guaranteed ability to commit and to abort
Concurrency	Controlled lock violation	Transaction hardening	Weak locks during logging
		Two-phase commit	Weak locks during log-ging, communication, + waiting

Figure 2: Improvements to optimistic concurrency control.

2.1 ORTHOGONAL KEY-VALUE VALIDATION

The original design for optimistic concurrency control and end-of-transaction conflict detection focuses on validating read- and write-sets. For serializable transaction isolation and specifically phantom protection, this chapter focuses on gaps between index keys in such read- and write-sets. The chapter includes case studies comparing optimistic concurrency control with up-to-date pessimistic techniques, i.e., orthogonal key-value locking. The purpose of this chapter is to transfer the benefits of orthogonal locking techniques to traditional optimistic concurrency control.

2.2 SERIALIZABLE TIMESTAMP VALIDATION

Most current implementations of optimistic concurrency control compare timestamp values as observed during data access and during end-of-transaction validation. This chapter adds serializability and phantom protection by assigning timestamps to gaps between index keys. Moreover, it introduces timestamp validation in databases without timestamps plus end-of-transaction validation of hierarchical timestamps. The purpose of this chapter is to transfer the benefits of orthogonal locking techniques to optimistic concurrency control with end-of-transaction timestamp validation.

2.3 REPAIRING OPTIMISTIC CONCURRENCY CONTROL

Optimistic concurrency control suffers from multiple problems this chapter attempts to remedy. First, concurrent validation of multiple transactions requires communication among them in order to detect conflicting database accesses. Second, two-phase commit requires that all local participants prepare themselves to abide by a global coordinator's commit decision, which means that other transactions must not read or write database items in conflict with a local participant of a committing distributed transaction and thus disturbing the local participant's ability to commit or to abort. Third, the danger of premature publication of updates committed but not yet durable requires that the atomic phase at the end of each optimistic transaction must include not only validation and propagation of updates from the transaction-private update buffer to the global buffer pool but also forcing the transaction's commit log record to stable storage.

The remedies proposed for these problems are perhaps radical but definitely simple. They employ locks and a lock manager for commit processing in optimistic concurrency control. Thus, in the parlance of lock management, optimistic concurrency control is a form of deferred lock acquisition. The purpose of this chapter is to identify and overcome some traditional weaknesses of optimistic concurrency control.

3 LOCKING

After multiple chapters above focused on the granularity of concurrency control, the chapters in this part of this volume explore improvements to traditional locking techniques in duration, modes, and acquisition sequence. One of the chapters (on two-phase commit) introduces an oversight in two-phase commit as implemented in many database systems and suggests a solution (based on controlled lock violation); another one modifies the traditional lock acquisition sequence in order to prevent many of the deadlocks from which today's database software suffers. The third chapter in this section exploits non-traditional lock modes to reduce the effective duration of locks.

Figure 3 summarizes the improvements discussed in these chapters.

3.1 AVOIDING INDEX NAVIGATION DEADLOCKS

Most actual deadlocks in database management are, at least partially, due to lock acquisition sequences. A simple technique can avoid these deadlocks. Of course, it cannot prevent all deadlocks, e.g., in database scripts with multiple SQL statements. The purpose of this chapter is to improve pessimistic concurrency control with a simple insight and simple techniques, and to weaken one of the traditional arguments against pessimistic concurrency control.

3.2 TWO-PHASE COMMIT

It turns out that an optimization of two-phase commit that is common in distributed databases just happens to be wrong if multi-version storage is used. Fortunately, the flaw can be fixed

Dimension	Improvement	Context	Effect
Lock scopes	Orthogonal locks	Database indexes, key value vs. gap	Independent lock modes for key value and gap
	Partitioning of index entries	Non-unique indexes	Concurrency within a list
	Partitioning of missing keys	Phantom protection	Concurrency within a gap
Lock modes	Increment/decrement locks	Summary views, rollups	Concurrent relative updates
	Reserved + pending locks	Instead of update locks	Concurrency of reads and updates
	Semantics of shared and exclusive locks	Multi-version storage	Concurrency of reads and version creation + updates
Lock durations	Deferred lock enforcement	"Read" or work phase	Weak exclusive locks, compatible with read locks
	Controlled lock violation	Hardening phase	Weak locks, unconstrained concurrency
		Three-phase commit	
	Lock retention and controlled lock violation	Two-phase commit + multi-version storage	Correct distributed updates + commits
Lock acquisition	Uniform sequence of lock acquisitions	Queries and updates of secondary indexes	Fewer deadlocks

Figure 3: Improvements to pessimistic concurrency control.

and the impact of the correct approach to two-phase commit in databases can be mitigated by controlled lock violation. The purpose of this chapter is to call out a heretoforth overlooked problem with an optimization common in distributed database systems and to repair it nicely using a published technique.

3.3   DEFERRED LOCK ENFORCEMENT

This chapter actually introduces two new techniques, deferred lock acquisition and deferred lock enforcement, with the latter one recommended. It complements controlled lock violation, multi-version storage, and non-volatile memory. Whereas snapshot isolation removes read-only transactions from all lock contention, controlled lock violation and deferred lock enforcement shrink the effective duration of exclusive locks to the bare minimum and thus enable more concurrency among read-write transactions. The purpose of this chapter is to reduce lock conflicts, complement controlled lock violation, and provide a categorical argument for the advantages of locking over optimistic concurrency control.

4   THE END OF OPTIMISTIC CONCURRENCY CONTROL

This chapter collects comparisons of optimistic and pessimistic concurrency control and then issues a recommendation to simply avoid optimistic concurrency control for database transactions, and to remove it wherever it is used today.

		Optimistic Concurrency Control		Pessimistic Concurrency Control (locking)
		Backward Validation	Forward Validation	
Global data structure …	Insertion	On commit	Before each data access	
	Deletion	Delayed by the last concurrent transaction	Commit end	
Conflict	Visibility	2nd commit	Before data access	Before data access
	Detection		1st commit	
	Resolution options	Abort 2nd transaction	Abort 1st or 2nd transaction, delay 1st commit	Wait for lock release, lock de-escalation in 1st or 2nd transaction, abort 1st or 2nd transaction
Related techniques		Track oldest active transaction		Hierarchical locking, "increment" locks, limited wait depth, timeout, commit-lsn

Figure 4: Optimistic vs. pessimistic concurrency control.

Figure 4 summarizes the argument. All methods must find all actual conflicts and should not find any false conflicts; locking finds conflicts as soon as possible whereas end-of-transaction validation runs doomed transactions to completion before rolling them back; early detection of conflicts permit more options for conflict resolution, e.g., waiting rather than immediate transaction abort; even optimistic concurrency control requires locks and a lock manager for concurrent validation and for two-phase commit; and there are many improvements for locking with no equivalent in optimistic concurrency control.

ACKNOWLEDGEMENTS

Wey Guy suggested describing the core data structures of a lock manager.

REFERENCES

Bayer, R. and Schkolnick, M. (1977). Concurrency of operations on B-trees. *Acta Information*, 9, pages 1–21. DOI: 10.1007/bf00263762.

Bayer, R. and Unterauer, K. (1977). Prefix B-trees. *ACM TODS*, 2(1), pages 11–26. DOI: 10.1145/320521.320530.

Berenson, H., Bernstein, P. A., Gray, J., Melton, J., O'Neil, E. J., and O'Neil, P. E. (1995). A critique of ANSI SQL isolation levels. *ACM SIGMOD*, pages 1–10. DOI: 10.1145/223784.223785.

Bernstein, P. A., Hadzilacos, V., and Goodman, N. (1987). *Concurrency Control and Recovery in Database Systems*, Addison-Wesley.

Bornea, M. A., Hodson, O., Elnikety, S., and Fekete, A. (2011). One-copy serializability with snapshot isolation under the hood. *ICDE*, pages 625–636. DOI: 10.1109/icde.2011.5767897.

Cahill, M. J., Röhm, U., and Fekete, A. D. (2009). Serializable isolation for snapshot databases. *ACM TODS*, 34(4). DOI: 10.1145/1620585.1620587.

Carey, M. J. and Muhanna, W. A. (1986). The performance of multi-version concurrency control algorithms. *ACM TODS*, 4(4), pages 338–378. DOI: 10.1145/6513.6517.

Carey, M. J. and Stonebraker, M. (1984). The performance of concurrency control algorithms for database management systems. *VLDB*, pages 107–118.

Cha, S. K., Hwang, S., Kim, K., and Kwon, K. (2001). Cache-conscious concurrency control of main-memory indexes on shared-memory multiprocessor systems. *VLDB*, pages 181–190.

Chamberlin, D. D., Astrahan, M. M., Blasgen, M. W., Gray, J., King III, W. F., Lindsay, B. G., Lorie, R. A., Mehl, J. W., Price, T. G., Putzolu, G. R., Selinger, P. G., Schkolnick, M., Slutz, D. R., Traiger, I. L., Wade, B. W., and Yost, R. A. (1981). A history and evaluation of system R. *Communication of the ACM*, 24(10), pages 632–646. DOI: 10.1145/358769.358784.

Chan, A., Fox, S., Lin, W.-T. K., Nori, A., and Ries, D. R. (1982). The implementation of an integrated concurrency control and recovery scheme. *SIGMOD*, pages 184–191. DOI: 10.1145/582383.582386.

DeWitt, D. J., Katz, R. H., Olken, F., Shapiro, L. D., Stonebraker, M., and Wood, D. A. (1984). Implementation techniques for main memory database systems. *ACM SIGMOD*, pages 1–8. DOI: 10.1145/602260.602261.

Diaconu, C., Freedman, C., Ismert, E., Larson, P., Mittal, P., Stonecipher, R., Verma, N., and Zwilling, M. (2013). Hekaton: SQL Server's memory-optimized OLTP engine. *ACM SIGMOD*, pages 1243–1254. DOI: 10.1145/2463676.2463710.

Faleiro, J. M. and Abadi, D. J. (2015). Rethinking serializable multi-version concurrency control. *PVLDB*, 8(11), pages 1190-1201. DOI: 10.14778/2809974.2809981.

Gawlick, D. and Kinkade, D. (1985). Varieties of concurrency control in IMS/VS fast path. *IEEE Database Engineering Bulletin*, 8(2), pages 3–10.

Graefe, G. (2003). Sorting and indexing with partitioned B-trees. *CIDR*.

Graefe, G. (2004). Write-optimized B-trees. *VLDB*, pages 672–683. DOI: 10.1016/b978-012088469-8/50060-7.

Graefe, G. (2007). Hierarchical locking in B-tree indexes. *BTW*, pages 18–42 (Chapter 2).

Graefe, G. (2010). A survey of B-tree locking techniques. *ACM TODS*, 35(3) (Chapter 1). DOI: 10.1145/1806907.1806908.

Graefe, G. (2011). Modern B-tree techniques. *Foundations and Trends in Databases*, 3(4), pages 203–402. DOI: 10.1561/1900000028. 3

Graefe, G. (2012). A survey of B-tree logging and recovery techniques. *ACM TODS*, 37(1), pages 1:1–1:35. DOI: 10.1145/2109196.2109197.

Graefe, G. (2016). Revisiting optimistic and pessimistic concurrency control. *Hewlett Packard Labs Technical Report HPE-2016-47*, May.

Graefe, G., Bunker, R., and Cooper, S. (1998). Hash joins and hash teams in Microsoft SQL Server. *VLDB Conference*, pages 86–97.

Graefe, G., Kimura, H., and Kuno, H. (2012). Foster B-trees. *ACM TODS*, 37(3). DOI: 10.1145/2338626.2338630.

Graefe, G., Lillibridge, M., Kuno, H. A., Tucek, J., and Veitch, A. C. (2013). Controlled lock violation. *ACM SIGMOD*, pages 85–96 (Chapter 4). DOI: 10.1145/2463676.2465325.

Graefe, G., Volos, H., Kimura, H., Kuno, H. A., Tucek, J., Lillibridge, M., and Veitch, A. C. (2014). In-memory performance for big data. *PVLDB*, 8(1), pages 37–48. DOI: 10.14778/2735461.2735465.

Graefe, G., Guy, W., and Sauer, C. (2016). *Instant recovery with write-ahead logging: Page repair, system restart, media restore, and system failover*, 2nd ed., *Synthesis Lectures on Data Management*, pages 1–113, Morgan & Claypool Publishers. DOI: 10.2200/s00710ed2v01y201603dtm044.

Graefe, G. and Kimura, H. (2015). Orthogonal key-value locking. *BTW*, pages 237–256 (Chapter 5).

Graefe, G. and Zwilling, M. J. (2004). Transaction support for indexed views. *ACM SIGMOD*, pages 323–334 (Chapter 3). DOI: 10.1145/1007568.1007606.

Gray, J. (1978). Notes on data base operating systems. *Advanced Course: Operating Systems*, pages 393-481, Springer. DOI: 10.1007/3-540-08755-9_9.

Gray, J., Lorie, R. A., Putzolu, G. R., and Traiger, I. L. (1975). Granularity of locks in a large shared data base. *VLDB*, pages 428–451. DOI: 10.1145/1282480.1282513.

Gray, J., Lorie, R. A., Putzolu, G. R., and Traiger, I. L. (1976). Granularity of locks and degrees of consistency in a shared data base. *IFIP Working Conference on Modelling in Data Base Management Systems*, pages 365–394.

Gray, J., McJones, P. R., Blasgen, M. W., Lindsay, B. G., Lorie, R. A., Price, T. G., Putzolu, G. R., and Traiger, I. L. (1981). The recovery manager of the system R database manager. *ACM Computer Survey*, 13(2), pages 223–243. DOI: 10.1145/356842.356847.

Gray, J. and Reuter, A. (1993). *Transaction Processing Concepts and Techniques*, Morgan Kaufmann.

Härder, T. (1984). Observations on optimistic concurrency control schemes. *Information Systems*, 9(2), pages 111–120. DOI: 10.1016/0306-4379(84)90020-6.

Härder, T. and Reuter, A. (1983). Principles of transaction-oriented database recovery. *ACM Computer Survey*, 15(4), pages 287–317. DOI: 10.1145/289.291. 3

Johnson, R., Pandis, I., Hardavellas, N., Ailamaki, A., and Falsafi, B. (2009). Shore-MT: A scalable storage manager for the multicore era. *EDBT*, pages 24–35. DOI: 10.1145/1516360.1516365.

Johnson, R., Pandis, I., Stoica, R., Athanassoulis, M., and Ailamaki, A. (2010). Aether: A scalable approach to logging. *PVLDB*, 3(1), pages 681–692. DOI: 10.14778/1920841.1920928.

Jordan, J. R., Banerjee, J., and Batman, R. B. (1981). Precision locks. *ACM SIGMOD*, pages 143–147. DOI: 10.1145/582338.582340.

Jung, H., Han, H., Fekete, A. D., Heiser, G., and Yeom, H. Y. (2013). A scalable lock manager for multicores. *ACM SIGMOD*, pages 73–84. DOI: 10.1145/2463676.2465271.

Jung, H., Han, H., Fekete, A. D., Heiser, G., and Yeom, H. Y. (2014). A scalable lock manager for multicores. *ACM TODS*, pages 29:1–29:29. DOI: 10.1145/2691190.2691192.

Kimura, H., Graefe, G., and Kuno, H. A. (2012). Efficient locking techniques for databases on modern hardware. *ADMS@VLDB*, pages 1–12.

Korth, H. F. (1983). Locking primitives in a database system. *Journal of the ACM*, 30(1), pages 55–79. DOI: 10.1145/322358.322363.

Kung, H. T. and Papadimitriou, C. H. (1979). An optimality theory of concurrency control for databases. *ACM SIGMOD*, pages 116–126. DOI: 10.1145/582095.582114.

Kung, H. T. and Robinson, J. T. (1981). On optimistic methods for concurrency control. *ACM TODS*, 6(2), pages 213–226. DOI: 10.1145/319566.319567.

Lehman, P. L. and Yao, S. B. (1981). Efficient locking for concurrent operations on B-trees. *ACM TODS*, 6(4), pages 650–670. DOI: 10.1145/319628.319663.

Lomet, D. B. (1993). Key range locking strategies for improved concurrency. *VLDB*, pages 655–664.

Lomet, D. B., Fekete, A., Wang, R., and Ward, P. (2012). Multi-version concurrency via timestamp range conflict management. *ICDE*, pages 714–725. DOI: 10.1109/icde.2012.10.

Menascé, D. A. and Nakanishi, T. (1982). Optimistic vs. pessimistic concurrency control mechanisms in database management systems. *Information Systems*, 7(1), pages 13–27. DOI: 10.1016/0306-4379(82)90003-5.

Mohan, C. (1990). ARIES/KVL: A key-value locking method for concurrency control of multiaction transactions operating on B-tree indexes. *VLDB*, pages 392–405.

Mohan, C. (1994). Less optimism about optimistic concurrency control. *RIDE-TQP*, pages 199–204. DOI: 10.1109/ride.1992.227405.

Mohan, C., Lindsay, B. G., and Obermarck, R. (1986). Transaction management in the R* distributed database management system. *ACM TODS*, 11(4), pages 378–396. DOI: 10.1145/7239.7266.

Mohan, C., Haderle, D. J., Lindsay, B. G., Pirahesh, H., and Schwarz, P. M. (1992). ARIES: A transaction recovery method supporting fine-granularity locking and partial rollbacks using write-ahead logging. *ACM TODS*, 17(1), pages 94–162. DOI: 10.1145/128765.128770.

Mohan, C. and Levine, F. E. (1992). ARIES/IM: An efficient and high concurrency index management method using write-ahead logging. *ACM SIGMOD*, pages 371–380. DOI: 10.1145/130283.130338.

Neumann, T., Mühlbauer, T., and Kemper, A. (2015). Fast serializable multi-version concurrency control for main-memory database systems. *ACM SIGMOD*, pages 677–689. DOI: 10.1145/2723372.2749436.

O'Neil, P. A. (1986). The Escrow transactional method. *ACM TODS*, 11(4), pages 405–430. DOI: 10.1145/7239.7265.

O'Neil, P. A., Cheng, E., Gawlick, D., and O'Neil, E. J. (1996). The log-structured merge-tree (LSM-tree). *Acta Information*, 33(4), pages 351–385. DOI: 10.1007/s002360050048.

Peinl, P. and Reuter, A. (1983). Empirical comparison of database concurrency control schemes. *VLDB*, pages 97–108.

Ports, D. R. K. and Grittner, K. (2012). Serializable snapshot isolation in PostgreSQL. *PVLDB*, 5(12), pages 1850–1861. DOI: 10.14778/2367502.2367523.

Ren, K., Thomson, A., and Abadi, D. J. (2012). Lightweight locking for main memory database systems. *PVLDB*, 6(2), pages 145–156. DOI: 10.14778/2535568.2448947.

Skeen, D. (1981). Nonblocking commit protocols. *ACM SIGMOD*, pages 133–142. DOI: 10.1145/582338.582339.

SQLite. (2004). File locking and concurrency in SQLite version 3. `http://sqlite.org/lockingv3.html`

Thomasian, A. (1997). A performance comparison of locking methods with limited wait depth. *IEEE TKDE*, 9(3), pages 421–434. DOI: 10.1109/69.599931.

Thomasian, A. (1998). Performance analysis of locking methods with limited wait depth. *Performance Evaluation*, 34(2), pages 69–89. DOI: 10.1016/s0166-5316(98)00025-x.

Weikum, G. (1991). Principles and realization strategies of multilevel transaction management. *ACM TODS*, 16(1), pages 132–180. DOI: 10.1145/103140.103145.

Weikum, G. and Vossen, G. (2002). *Transactional Information Systems: Theory, Algorithms, and the Practice of Concurrency Control and Recovery*, Morgan Kaufmann.

PART I

Published Papers

CHAPTER 1

A Survey of B-Tree Locking Techniques

Goetz Graefe, *Hewlett–Packard Laboratories*

ABSTRACT

B-trees have been ubiquitous in database management systems for several decades, and they are used in other storage systems as well. Their basic structure and basic operations are well and widely understood including search, insertion, and deletion. Concurrency control of operations in B-trees, however, is perceived as a difficult subject with many subtleties and special cases. The purpose of this survey is to clarify, simplify, and structure the topic of concurrency control in B-trees by dividing it into two subtopics and exploring each of them in depth.

1.1 INTRODUCTION

B-tree indexes [Bayer and McCreight, 1972] have been called ubiquitous more than a quarter of a century ago [Comer, 1979], and they have since become ever more ubiquitous. Gray and Reuter [1993] asserted that "B-trees are by far the most important access path structure in database and file systems." In spite of many innovative proposals and prototypes for alternatives to B-tree indexes, this statement remains true today.

As with all indexes, their basic function is to map search keys to associated information. In addition to exact-match lookup, B-trees efficiently support range queries and they enable sort-based query execution algorithms such as merge join without an explicit sort operation. More recently, B-tree indexes have been extended to support multidimensional data and queries by using space-filling curvers, for example, the Z-order in UB-trees [Bayer, 1997, Ramsak et al., 2000].

The basic data structure and algorithms for B-trees are well understood. Search, insertion, and deletion are often implemented by college students as programming exercises, including split and merge operations for leaves and interior nodes. Accessing B-tree nodes on disk storage using a buffer pool adds fairly little to the programming effort. Variable-length records within fixed-length B-tree nodes add moderate complexity to the code, mostly book-keeping for lengths, offsets, and free space. It is far more challenging to enable correct multithreaded execution and even transactional execution of B-tree operations.

Database servers usually run in many threads to serve many users as well as to exploit multiple processor cores and, using asynchronous I/O, many disks. Even for single-threaded applications, for example, on personal computing devices, asynchronous activities for database maintenance and index tuning re- quire concurrent threads and thus concurrency control in B-tree indexes.

The plethora of terms associated with concurrency control in B-trees may seem daunting, including row-level locking, key value locking, key range locking, lock coupling, latching, latch coupling, and crabbing, the last term applied to both root-to-leaf searches and leaf-to-leaf scans. A starting point for clarifying and simplifying the topic is to distinguish protection of the B-tree structure from protection of the B-tree contents, and to distinguish separation of threads against one another from separation of user transactions against one another. These distinctions are central to the treatment of the topic here. Confusion between these forms of concurrency control in B-trees unnecessarily increases the efforts for developer education, code maintenance, test development, test execution, and defect isolation and repair.

The foundations of B-tree locking are the well-known transaction concept, including multilevel transactions [Weikum, 1991], open nested transactions [Ni et al., 2007, Weikum and Schek, 1992], and pessimistic concurrency control, that is, locking, rather than optimistic concurrency control [Kung and Robinson, 1981]. Multiple locking concepts and techniques are discussed here, including phantom protection, predicate locks, precision locks, key value locking, key range locking, multigranularity locking, hierarchical locking, and intention locks.

No actual system works precisely as described here. There are many reasons for this fact; one is that code for concurrency control is complex and rarely touched, such that many concepts and implementations are years or even decades old.

1.1.1   HISTORICAL BACKGROUND

Although the original B-tree design employed data items and their keys as separators in the nodes above the B-tree leaves, even the earliest work on concurrency control in B-trees relied on all data items being in the leaves, with separator keys in the upper B-tree levels serving only to guide searches without carrying actual information contents.

Bayer and Schkolnick [1977] presented multiple locking (latching) protocols for B*-trees (all data records in the leaves, merely separator or "reference" keys in upper nodes) that combined high concurrency with deadlock avoidance. Their approach for insertion and deletion is based on deciding during a root-to-leaf traversal whether a node is "safe" from splitting (during an insertion) or merging (during a deletion), and on retaining appropriate locks (latches) for ancestors of unsafe nodes. Bernstein et al. [1987] cover this and other early protocols for tree locking. Unfortunately, this definition of safety does not work well with variable-size records and keys.

IBM's System R project explored many transaction management techniques, including transaction isolation levels and lock duration, predicate locking and key locking, multigranularity and hierarchical locking, etc. These techniques have been adapted and refined in many research and product efforts since then. Research into multilevel transactions [Weikum, 1991] and into open nested transactions [Moss, 2006] enables crisp separation of locks and latches, the former protecting database contents against conflicts among transactions and the latter protecting in-memory data structures against conflicts among concurrent threads.

Mohan's ARIES/KVL design [Mohan, 1990] explicitly separates locks and latches in a similar way as described here, that is, logical database contents versus "structure maintenance" in a B-tree. A key value lock covers both a gap between two B-tree keys and the upper boundary key. In nonunique indexes, an intention lock on a key value permits operations on all rows with the same value in the indexed column. Gray and Reuter's book [1993] describes row-level locking in B-trees based primarily on ARIES/KVL. In contrast, other designs include the row identifier in the unique lock identifier and thus do not need to distinguish between unique and nonunique indexes.

In order to reduce the number of locks required during index-to-index navigation, for instance, searching for a row in a nonclustered index followed by fetching additional columns in a clustered index, a single lock in ARIES/IM [Mohan and Levine, 1992] covers all index entries for a logical row even in the presence of multiple indexes. Srinivasan and Carey [1991] compared the performance of various locking techniques.

Lomet's design for key range locking [Lomet, 1993] attempts to adapt hierarchical and multigranularity locking to keys and half-open intervals but requires additional lock modes, such as a "range insert" mode, to achieve the desired concurrency. Graefe's design [2007] applies traditional hierarchical locking more rigorously to keys and gaps (open intervals) between keys, employs ghost (pseudodeleted) records during insertion as well as during deletion, and achieves more concurrency with fewer special cases. The same paper also outlines hierarchical locking in B-tree structures (key range locking on separator keys) and in B-tree keys (key range locking on fixed-length prefixes of compound keys).

Numerous textbooks on database systems cover concurrency control in index structures, with various degrees of generality, completeness, and clarity. Weikum and Vossen's book [2002] comes closest to our perspective on the material, focusing on a page layer and an access layer. The discussion here resonates with their treatment but focuses more specifically on common implementation techniques using latching for data structures and key range locking for contents protection.

Some researchers have used "increment" locks as examples for general lock- ing concepts, for example, Korth [1983]. Others have argued that increment locks, differently than write locks, should enable higher concurrency as increment operations commute. In fact, techniques very similar to increment locks have been used in real high-performance systems [Gawlick and Kinkade, 1985] and described in a more general and conceptual way with additional "escrow" guarantees [O'Neil, 1986]. A more recent effort has focused on integrating increment locks with key range locking in B-tree indexes including maximal concurrency during creation and removal of summary records [Graefe and Zwilling, 2004].

In spite of these multiple designs and the many thoughtful variants found in actual implementations, we agree with Gray and Reuter [1993] that "the last word on how to control concurrency on B-trees optimally has not been spoken yet."

1.1.2   OVERVIEW

The following two short sections clarify assumptions and define the two forms of B-tree locking that are often confused. The next two sections cover these two forms of locking in depth, followed by detailed discussions of a variety of locking techniques proposed for B-tree indexes. Future directions, summary, and conclusions close this chapter.

1.2   PRELIMINARIES

Most work on concurrency control and recovery in B-trees assumes what Bayer and Schkolnick [1977] call B*-trees and what Comer [1979] calls B+-trees, that is, all data records are in leaf nodes and keys in nonleaf or "interior" nodes act merely as separators enabling search and other operations but not carrying logical database contents. We follow this tradition here and ignore the original design of B-trees with data records in both leaves and interior nodes.

We also ignore many other variations of B-trees here. This includes what Comer [1979], following Knuth, calls B*-trees, that is, attempting to merge an overflowing node with a sibling rather than splitting it immediately. We ignore whether or not underflow is recognized and acted upon by load balancing and merging nodes, whether or not empty nodes are removed immediately or ever, whether or not leaf nodes form a singly or doubly linked list using physical pointers (page identifiers) or logical boundaries (fence keys equal to separators posted in the parent node during a split), whether suffix truncation is employed when posting a separator key [Bayer and Unterauer, 1977], whether prefix truncation or any other compression is employed on each page, and the type of information associated with B-tree keys. Most of these issues have little or no bearing on locking in B-trees, with the exception of sibling pointers, as indicated in the following where appropriate.

Most concurrency control schemes distinguish between reading and writing, the latter covering any form of update or state change. These actions are protected by shared and exclusive locks, abbreviated S and X locks hereafter (some sections also use N as a lock mode indicating no lock). For these, the standard lock table is shown in Figure 1.1.

One axis indicates the lock already held by one thread or transaction and the other axis indicates the lock requested by another thread or transaction. Some systems employ nonsymmetric lock tables; if in doubt, the left column indicates the lock already held and the top row indicates the lock requested. Obviously, if no lock is held yet on a resource, any lock request may succeed.

	S	X
N	✓	✓
S	✓	–
X	–	–

Figure 1.1: Minimal lock table.

1.3 TWO FORMS OF B-TREE LOCKING

B-tree locking, or locking in B-tree indexes, means two things. First, it means concurrency control among concurrent database transactions querying or modifying database contents and its representation in B-tree indexes. Second, it means concurrency control among concurrent threads modifying the B-tree data structure in memory, including in particular images of disk-based B-tree nodes in the buffer pool.

These two aspects have not always been separated cleanly. Their difference becomes very apparent when a single database request is processed by multiple parallel threads. Specifically, two threads within the same transaction must "see" the same database contents, the same count of rows in a table, etc. This includes one thread "seeing" updates applied by the other thread. While one thread splits a B-tree node, however, the other thread must not observe intermediate and incomplete data structures. The difference also becomes apparent in the opposite case when a single execution thread serves multiple transactions.

1.3.1 LOCKS AND LATCHES

These two purposes are usually accomplished by two different mechanisms, locks and latches. Unfortunately, the literature on operating systems and programming environments usually uses the term locks for the mechanisms that in database systems are called latches. Figure 1.2 summarizes their differences.

Locks separate transactions using read and write locks on pages, on B-tree keys, or even on gaps (open intervals) between keys. The latter two methods are called key value locking and key range locking. Key range locking is a form of predicate locking that uses actual key values in the B-tree and the B-tree's sort order to define predicates. By default, locks participate in deadlock detection and are held until end-of-transaction. Locks also support sophisticated scheduling, for example, using queues for pending lock requests and delaying new lock acquisitions in favor of lock conversions, for example, an existing shared lock to an exclusive lock. This level of sophistication makes lock acquisition and release fairly expensive, often thousands of CPU cycles, some of those due to cache faults in the lock manager's hash table and its linked lists.

Latches separate threads accessing B-tree pages cached in the buffer pool, the buffer pool's management tables, and all other in-memory data structures shared among multiple threads.

	Locks	Latches
Separate ...	User transactions	Threads
Protect ...	Database contents	In-memory data structures
During ...	Entire transactions	Critical sections
Modes ...	Shared, exclusive, update, intention, escrow, schema, etc.	Read, writes, (perhaps) update
Deadlock ...	Detection and resolution	Avoidance
... by ...	Analysis of the waits-for graph, time-out, transaction abort, partial rollback, lock de-escalation	Coding discipline, "lock leveling"
Kept in ...	Lock manager's hash table	Protected data structure

Figure 1.2: Locks and latches.

Since the lock manager's hash table is one of the data structures shared by many threads, latches are required while inspecting or modifying a database system's lock information. With respect to shared data structures, even threads of the same user transaction conflict if one thread requires a write latch. Latches are held only during a critical section, that is, while a data structure is read or updated. Deadlocks are avoided by appropriate coding disciplines, for example, requesting multiple latches in carefully designed sequences. Deadlock resolution requires a facility to roll back prior actions, whereas deadlock avoidance does not. Thus, deadlock avoidance is more appropriate for latches, which are designed for minimal overhead and maximal performance and scalability. Latch acquisition and release may require tens of instructions only, usually with no additional cache faults since a latch can be embedded in the data structure it protects. For images of disk pages in the buffer pool, the latch can be embedded in the descriptor structure that also contains the page identifier, etc.

The difference between locking and latching also becomes apparent in concurrency control for nonclustered indexes, that is, redundant indexes that point into nonredundant storage structures. Data-only locking makes no attempt to separate transactions using the nonclustered index and its keys. All intertransaction concurrency control is achieved by locks on nonredundant data items, for example, record identifiers in the table's heap structure. Latches, on the other hand, are required for any in-memory data structure touched by multiple concurrent threads, including of course the nodes of a nonclustered index.

1.3.2 RECOVERY AND B-TREE LOCKING

The difference between latches and locks is important not only during normal transaction processing but also during recovery from a system crash. Considering the requirements for latching and locking during crash recovery may further illuminate their difference.

Latches and locks also differ both during system recovery and while waiting for the decision of a global transaction coordinator. While waiting, no latches are required, but retaining locks is essential to guarantee a local transaction's ability to abide by the global coordinator's final decision. During recovery without concurrent execution of new transactions, locks are not required, because concurrency control during forward processing prior to the system crash already ensured that active transactions do not conflict. Latches, however, are as important during recovery as during normal forward processing if recovery employs multiple threads and shared data structures such as the buffer pool.

The separation of locks and latches does not determine whether an operation must be logged for recovery purposes. Logging is required if disk contents change, whether or not the logical database contents changes.

Locks must be retained during transaction rollback, although they could be released incrementally, for example, during a partial rollback to a transaction savepoint. During recovery from a system failure, lock acquisition during log analysis permits resuming transaction processing while repeating logged actions and applying compensating actions of aborted transactions. These locks need not be the same ones acquired during the original transactions. For example, if hierarchical locking (see the following) is supported in the system, locks during recovery may be smaller or larger, as long as they cover the actions performed by the transaction. If lock escalation and deescalation are supported, these techniques can be employed even by transactions currently in recovery. Similarly, lock escalation and deescalation may be invoked while a local transaction waits for a global decision by a transaction coordinator.

The operations protected by latches only (and not by locks) are those that modify a B-tree's structure without modifying its logical contents. Typical examples are splitting a B-tree node and balancing the load among neighboring B-tree nodes. Examples that affect less than an entire node are creation and removal of ghost records (see what follows). As the logical database contents is the same whether such an operation is completed or not, recovery from a system failure during such an operation may either roll the operation back or complete it. Completion or "forward recovery" of such operations may be faster and require less log volume than rollback. In order to prepare an operation for forward recovery, preallocation of all required resources is essential, most notably of sufficient disk space. In general, forward recovery seems more promising for deletion or deallocation operations, for example, dropping a B-tree index or erasing a ghost record, than for creation or allocation operations.

1.3.3   LOCK-FREE B-TREES

Occasionally, one sees claims or descriptions of database indexes implemented "lock-free." This might refer to either of the two forms of B-tree locking. For example, it might mean that the in-memory format is such that pessimistic concurrency control in form of latches is not required. Multiple in-memory copies and atomic updates of in-memory pointers might enable such an implementation. Nonetheless, user transactions and their access to data must still be coordinated, typically with locks such as key range locking on B-tree entries.

On the other hand, a lock-free B-tree implementation might refer to avoidance of locks for coordination of user transactions. A typical implementation mechanism would require multiple versions of records based on multiversion concurrency control. However, creation, update, and removal of versions must still be coordinated for the data structure and its in-memory image. In other words, even if conflicts among read transactions and write transactions can be removed by means of versions instead of traditional database locks, modifications of the data structure still require latches.

In the extreme case, a lock-free implementation of B-tree indexes might avoid both forms of locking in B-trees. Without further explanation, however, one has no way of knowing what specifically is meant by a lock-free B-tree implementation.

1.3.4   SUMMARY

In summary, latching and locking serve different functions for B-tree indexes in database systems. Accordingly, they use different implementation primitives. The difference is starkly visible not only during normal transaction processing but also during "offline" activities such as crash recovery.

1.4   PROTECTING A B-TREE'S PHYSICAL STRUCTURE

If multiple threads may touch an in-memory data structure, their concurrent accesses must be coordinated. This is equally true whether these data structures always reside in memory, such as the look-up table in a buffer pool or pages in an in-memory database, or reside in memory only temporarily, such as images of disk pages in a buffer pool. Multiple threads are required if multiple concurrent activities are desired, for example, in a traditional shared-memory machine or in a modern many-core processor.

The simplest form of a latch is a "mutex" (mutual exclusion lock). Any access precludes concurrent access. For data structures that change constantly, this might be an appropriate mechanism; for disk pages that remain unchanged during query processing, exclusion of all concurrent activities should be reserved for updates. Latches with shared and exclusive (read and write) modes are common in database systems.

Since latches protect in-memory data structures, the data structure representing the latch can be embedded in the data structure being protected. Latch duration is usually very short and amenable to hardware support and encapsulation in transactional memory [Larus and Rajwar, 2006]. This is in contrast to locks, discussed in Section 1.5, that protect the logical database contents. Since locks often protect data not even present in memory, and sometimes not even in the database, there is no in-memory data structure within which the data structure representing the lock can be embedded. Thus, database systems employ lock tables. Since a lock table is an in-memory data structure accessed by multiple concurrent execution threads, access to the lock table and its components is protected by latches embedded in the data structures.

1.4.1   ISSUES

Latches ensure the consistency of data structures when accessed by multiple concurrent threads. They solve several problems that are similar to each other but nonetheless lend themselves to different solutions. All these issues are about the consistency of in-memory data structures, including images of disk pages in the buffer pool.

First, a page image in the buffer pool must not be modified (written) by one thread while it is interpreted (read) by another thread. This issue does not differ from other critical sections for shared data structures in multithreaded code, including critical sections in a database system protecting the lock manager's hash table or the buffer pool's table of contents.

Second, while following a pointer (page identifier) from one page to another, for example, from a parent node to a child node in a B-tree index, the pointer must not be invalidated by another thread, for instance, by deallocating a child page or balancing the load among neighboring pages. This issue requires more refined solutions than the first issue given earlier because it is not advisable to retain a latch (or otherwise extend a critical section) while performing I/O (e.g., to fetch a child page into the buffer pool).

Third, "pointer chasing" applies not only to parent-child pointers but also to neighbor pointers, such as, in a chain of leaf pages during a range scan or while searching for the key to lock in key range locking (see the following). Concurrent query execution plans, transactions, and threads may perform ascending and descending index scans, which could lead to deadlocks. Recall that latches usually rely on developer discipline for deadlock avoidance, not on automatic deadlock detection and resolution.

Fourth, during a B-tree insertion, a child node may overflow and require an insertion into its parent node, which may thereupon also overflow and require an insertion into the child's grandparent node. In the most extreme case, the B-tree's old root node overflow must split, and be replaced by a new root node. Going back from the leaf toward the B-tree root works well in single-threaded B-tree implementations, but it introduces the danger of deadlocks between root-to-leaf searches and leaf-to-root B-tree modifications, yet latches rely on deadlock avoidance rather than deadlock detection and resolution.

For the first issue given before, database systems employ latches that differ from the simplest implementations of critical sections and mutual exclusion only by the distinction between read-only latches and read-write latches, that is, shared or exclusive access. As with read and write locks protecting database contents, starvation needs to be avoided if new readers are admitted while a writer already waits for active readers to release the latch. Update latches (similar to update locks) may be used, but the other modes well-known for lock management are usually not adopted in database latches.

1.4.2   LOCK COUPLING

The second issue given earlier requires retaining the latch on the parent node until the child node is latched. This technique is traditionally called "lock coupling" but a better term is "latch coupling" in the context of transactional database systems. The look-up operation in the buffer pool requires latches to protect the buffer manager's management tables, and proper "lock leveling" (latch leveling) is required to guarantee that there can be no deadlock due to latches on data pages and the buffer pool.

If the child node is not readily available in the buffer pool and thus requires relatively slow I/O, the latch on the parent node should be released while reading the child node from disk. Lock coupling can be realized by holding a latch on the descriptor of the needed page in the buffer pool. Otherwise, the I/O should be followed by a new root-to-leaf traversal to protect against B-tree changes in the meantime. Restarting the root-to-leaf traversal may seem expensive but it is often possible to resume the prior search after verifying, for example, based on the log sequence number on each page, that ancestor pages have not been modified while the needed page was fetched into the buffer pool.

The third issue explained before is similar to the second, with two differences. On the positive side, asynchronous read-ahead may alleviate the frequency of buffer faults. Deep read-ahead in B-tree indexes usually cannot rely on neighbor pointers but requires prefetch based on child pointers in leaves' parent nodes or even the grandparent nodes. On the negative side, deadlock avoidance among scans in opposite directions requires that latch acquisition code provides an immediate failure mode. A latch acquisition request can return a failure immediately rather than waiting for the latch to become available. If such a failure occurs during forward or backward index traversal, the scan must release the leaf page currently latched to let the conflicting scan proceed, and reposition itself using a new root-to-leaf search.

The fourth issue given before is the most complex one. It affects all updates, including insertion, deletion, and even record updates, the latter if length changes in variable-length records can lead to nodes splitting or merging. The most naïve approach, latching an entire B-tree with a single exclusive latch, is not practical in multithreaded servers, and all approaches that follow latch individual B-tree nodes.

One approach latches all nodes in exclusive mode during the root-to-leaf traversal while searching for an affected leaf. The obvious problem with this approach is that it can create a concurrency bottleneck, particularly at a B-tree's root page. Another approach performs the root-to-leaf search using shared latches and attempts an upgrade to an exclusive latch when necessary. When the upgrade can be granted without the danger of deadlock, this approach works well.

Since it might fail, however, it cannot be the only method in a B-tree implementation. Thus, it might not be implemented at all in order to minimize code volume and complexity. A third approach reserves nodes using "update" or "upgrade" latches in addition to traditional shared and exclusive latches. Update locks or latches are compatible with shared locks or latches and thus do not impede readers or B-tree searches, but they are not compatible with each other and thus a B-tree's root node can still be a bottleneck for multiple updates.

A refinement of the three earlier approaches retains latches on nodes along its root-to-leaf search only until a lower, less-than-full node guarantees that split operations will not propagate up the tree beyond the lower node. Since most nodes are less than full, most insertion operations will latch no nodes in addition to the current one. On the other hand, variable-length B-tree records and variable-length separator keys seem to make it difficult or impossible to decide reliably how much free space is required for the desired guarantee. Interestingly, this problem can be solved by deciding, before releasing the latch on the parent, which separator key would be posted in the parent if the child were to split as part of the current insertion. If it is desirable to release the parent latch before such inspection of the child node, a heuristic method may consider the lengths of existing separators in the parent, specifically their average and standard deviation.

A fourth approach splits nodes proactively during a root-to-leaf traversal for an insertion. This method avoids both the bottleneck of the first approach and the failure point (upgrading from a shared to an exclusive latch) of the second approach. Its disadvantage is that it wastes some space by splitting earlier than truly required, and more importantly that it may be impossible to split proactively in all cases in B-trees with variable-length records and keys.

A fifth approach protects its initial root-to-leaf search with shared latches, aborts this search when a node requires splitting, restarts a new one, and upon reaching the node requiring a split, acquires an exclusive latch and performs the split. This approach can benefit from resuming a root-to-leaf traversal rather than restarting it at the root, as mentioned earlier.

1.4.3   B^{link}-TREES

An entirely different approach relaxes the data structure constraints of B-trees and divides a node split into two independent steps, as follows. Each node may have a high fence key and a pointer to its right neighbor, thus the name B^{link}-trees [Lehman and Yao, 1981]. If a node's high fence and pointer are actually used, the right neighbor is not yet referenced in the node's parent. In other words, a single key interval and its associated child pointer in the parent node really refer to two nodes in this case. A root-to-leaf search, upon reaching a node, must first compare the sought key with a node's high fence and proceed to the right neighbor if the sought key is higher than the fence key. The first step (splitting a node) creates the high fence key and a new right neighbor. The second, independent step posts the high fence key in the parent. The second step can be made a side effect of any future root-to-leaf traversal, should happen as soon as possible, yet may be delayed beyond a system reboot or even a crash and its recovery without data loss or inconsistency of the on-disk data structures. The advantage of B^{link}-trees is that allocation of a new node and its initial introduction into the B-tree is a local step, affecting only one preexisting node. The disadvantages are that search may be a bit less efficient, a solution is needed to prevent long linked lists among neighbor nodes during periods of high insertion rates, and verification of a B-tree's structural consistency is more complex and perhaps less efficient.

Figure 1.3 illustrates a state that is not possible in a standard B-tree but is a correct intermediate state in a B^{link}-tree. "Correct" here means that search and update algorithms must cope with this state and that a database utility that verifies correct on-disk data structures must not report an error. In the original state, the parent node has three children. Note that these children might be leaves or interior nodes, and that the parent might be the B-tree root or an interior node. The first step is to split a child, resulting in the intermediate state shown in Figure 1.3. The second step later places a fourth child pointer into the parent and abandons the neighbor pointer, unless neighbor pointers are required in a specific implementation of B-trees. In fact, it might be left to a third step to erase the neighbor pointer value from the child node.

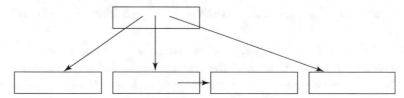

Figure 1.3: Intermediate state in a B^{link}-tree.

This process can be reversed in order to enable removal of B-tree nodes [Lomet, 2004]. The first step creates a neighbor pointer, the second step erases the child pointer in the parent node, and the third step merges the removal victim with its neighbor node.

Long linked lists due to multiple splits can be prevented by restricting the split operation to nodes pointed to by the appropriate parent node. These and further details of B^{link}-trees have recently been described in a detailed paper [Jaluta et al., 2005].

1.4.4   LOAD BALANCING AND REORGANIZATION

In many implementations, removal of nodes, load balancing among nodes, etc., are omitted in user transactions and left to asynchronous facilities. These may be invoked immediately after a user transaction, guided to a specific B-tree node by information left behind by the user transaction, or they may be invoked occasionally to scan and optimize an entire B-tree, index, table, or database. Actually, even node splits could be organized in this way, ensuring that user transactions can always add one more entry to any B-tree node.

All these operations are contents-neutral; the logical database contents does not change, only its representation. Thus, once the affected database pages are present in the buffer pool, these changes require concurrency control merely for the data structures. In other words, these operations require latches but no locks. Of course, since subsequent user transactions may log changes that refer to changes due to such B-tree optimizations, these optimizations must be reflected in the recovery log.

As an aside, there are corresponding optimizations in logging and recovery. One can avoid logging the page contents by careful write ordering [Gray and Reuter, 1993], and one can employ "forward recovery" to complete a reorganization action after system restart instead of rollback [Zou and Salzberg, 1996].

1.4.5   SUMMARY

In summary, latches coordinate multiple execution threads while they access and modify database contents and its representation. While cached in the database buffer pool, these data structures require the same coordination and protection as data structures representing server state, for example, the table of contents of the buffer pool, the list of active transactions, or the hash table in the lock manager.

The implementation of latches is optimized for their frequent use. In particular, modes beyond shared and exclusive are avoided, and deadlock avoidance is favored over deadlock detection. In complex data structures such as B-trees, careful designs such as B^{link}-trees combine high concurrency and deadlock avoidance.

Latches should be held only for very short periods. None should be held during disk I/O. Thus, all required data structures should be loaded and pinned in the buffer pool before a latched operation begins.

In the following, we focus on coordination among transactions and assume that the required data structures have the necessary coordination and protection by latches.

1.5   PROTECTING A B-TREE'S LOGICAL CONTENTS

Locks separate transactions reading and modifying database contents. For serializability, read locks are retained until end-of-transaction. Write locks are always retained until end-of-transaction in order to ensure the ability to roll back all changes if the transaction aborts. Weaker retention schemes exist for both read locks and write locks. Shorter read locks lead to weak transaction isolation levels; shorter write locks may lead to cascading aborts among transactions that read and modify the same database item.

In addition, serializability requires locking not only the presence but also the absence of data. For example, if a range scan finds 10 rows, a second execution of the same range scan must again find 10 rows, and an insertion by another transaction must be prevented. In B-tree indexes, this is usually enforced by key range locking, that is, locks that cover a key value and the gap to the next key value.

Modern designs for key range locking are based on hierarchical or multigranularity locking. Multigranularity locking is often explained and illustrated in terms of pages and files but it can be applied in many other ways. If the granules form a strict hierarchy, not a directed acyclic graph, the term hierarchical locking can be used. In modern B-tree implementations and their locks on keys, hierarchical locking is used to protect individual B-tree entries, the gaps or open intervals between existing B-tree keys, and half-open intervals comprising a B-tree entry and one adjoining open interval.

A fine granularity of locking is required most often at hot spots, for example, "popular" insertion points such as the high end of a time-organized B-tree. Coarse locks such as intention locks on a database, table, or index may be retained from one transaction to another. Requests for conflicting locks may employ an immediate notification or commit processing of the holding transaction may verify that the wait queue for the lock remains empty.

A useful implementation technique separates the "test" and "set" functions within lock acquisition, that is, verification that a certain lock could be acquired and insertion of a lock into the lock manager's hash table. Test without set is equivalent to what has been called "instant locks," for instance, by Gray and Reuter [1993]; set without test is useful during lock deescalation, lock reacquisition during system recovery, and other situations in which lock conflicts can be ruled out without testing.

1.5.1   KEY RANGE LOCKING

The terms key value locking and key range locking are often used interchangeably. Key range locking is a special form of predicate locking [Eswaran et al., 1976]. Neither pure predicate locking nor the more practical precision locking [Jordan et al., 1981] has been adopted in major products. In key range locking, the predicates are defined by intervals in the sort order of the B-tree. Interval boundaries are the key values currently existing in the B-tree. The usual form are half-open intervals including the gap between two neighboring keys and one of the end points, with "next-key locking" perhaps more common than "prior-key locking." The names describe the key to be locked in order to protect the gap between two neighboring keys. Next-key locking requires the ability to lock an artificial key value "$+\infty$." Prior-key locking gets by with locking the NULL value, assuming this is the lowest possible value in the B-tree's sort order.

In the simplest form of key range locking, a key and the gap to the neighbor are locked as a unit. An exclusive lock is required for any form of update of this unit, including modifying nonkey fields of the record, deletion of the key, insertion of a new key into the gap, etc. Deletion of a key requires a lock on both the old key and its neighbor; the latter is required to ensure the ability to reinsert the key in case of transaction rollback.

Figure 1.4 summarizes the possible scopes in key range locking in a B-tree leaf containing three records within the key range 1170–1180. A lock on key value 1174 might have any of the ranges indicated by arrows. The first arrow illustrates traditional next-key locking. The second arrow indicates prior-key locking. The third arrow shows a lock limited to the key value itself, without coverage of either one of the neighboring gaps. Thus, this lock cannot guarantee absence of a key for a transaction's duration, for instance, absence of key value 1176, and it therefore cannot guarantee serializability. The fourth lock scope complements the key value lock; it can guarantee absence of a key without locking an existing key. While one transaction holds a lock on key value 1174 as shown in the fourth arrow, a second transaction may update the record with key value 1174, except of course the record's key value. The second transaction must not erase the record or the key, however, until the first transaction releases its lock. Figure 1.4 could show a fifth lock scope that covers the gap preceding the locked key; it is omitted because it might confuse the discussion that follows.

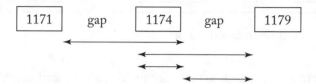

Figure 1.4: Possible lock scopes.

High rates of insertion can create a hotspot at the "right edge" of a B-tree index on an attribute correlated with time. With next-key locking, one solution verifies the ability to acquire a lock on $+\infty$ (infinity) but does not actually acquire or retain the lock. Such "instant locks" violate two-phase locking but work correctly if a single acquisition of the page latch protects both verification of the lock and creation of the new key on the page.

Latches must be managed carefully in key range locking if lockable resources are defined by keys that may be deleted if not protected. Until the lock request is inserted into the lock manager's data structures, the latch on the data structure in the buffer pool is required to ensure the existence of the key value. On the other hand, if a lock cannot be granted immediately, the thread should not hold a latch while the transaction waits. Thus, after waiting for a key value lock, a transaction must repeat its root-to-leaf search for the key.

1.5.2 KEY RANGE LOCKING AND GHOST RECORDS

In many B-tree implementations, the user transaction requesting a deletion does not actually erase the record. Instead, it merely marks the record as invalid, "pseudodeleted," or a "ghost record." For this purpose, all records include a "ghost bit" in their record headers that must be inspected in every query such that ghost records do not contribute to query results. Insertion of a new B-tree key for which a ghost record already exists is turned into an update of that preexisting record. After a valid record has been turned into a ghost record in a user transaction's deletion, space reclamation happens in an asynchronous clean-up transaction. Until then, the key of a ghost record participates in concurrency control and key range locking just like the key of a valid record. During ghost removal, no transaction may hold a lock on the key. Record removal including space reclamation does not require a lock, as it is merely a change in the physical representation of the database, not in database contents.

Figure 1.5 illustrates three records in a B-tree leaf after a user transaction committed the deletion of key 1174 from the logical database contents. Each record carries a ghost bit with the possible values "valid" or "ghost." The ghost bit is not part of the search key in the B-tree. The user transaction commits this state, leaving it to subsequent activities to remove the record and reclaim the space within the leaf page.

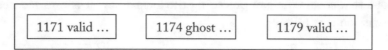

Figure 1.5: Intermediate state in row deletion.

The advantage of ghost records is that they avoid space allocation during transaction rollback and thus eliminate a possible rollback failure. Moreover, the user transaction need not log the deleted record and, with an appropriate implementation (fusing the log records for ghost removal and transaction commit), neither does the clean-up transaction. For B-trees with large records, such as, clustered indexes, this can be a meaningful reduction in log volume. With respect to locking, since a user transaction's deletion is implemented as merely an update, it requires a lock until end-of-transaction only on the key but not on the neighboring gaps.

If a root-to-leaf search has directed an insertion operation to a specific leaf, yet the new key is higher than the highest existing key (in next-key locking; or lower than the lowest existing key in prior-key locking), then the key to be locked must be found on a neighboring leaf node. Chaining leaf pages using page identifiers speeds up this process. Nonetheless, the latch on the current page must be released while fetching the neighbor page, in order to avoid holding the latch a long time as well as creating a deadlock among multiple page latches. Alternatively, each B-tree node may include the lowest and highest possible keys. These keys are copies of the separator keys posted in the parent page during leaf splits. One of these two "fence" keys, say the highest possible key, is always a ghost record. The other fence key can be a ghost record or it can be a valid record. Fence keys ensure that in any B-tree operation, the key to be locked can be found on the page affected by the operation. Thus, this design ensures that key range locking never requires navigation to neighbor nodes.

Since ghost records are not part of the logical database contents, only part of the database representation, they can be created and removed even in the presence of locks held by user transactions. For example, if a user transaction holds a key range lock on the half-open interval [10, 20), a new ghost record with value 15 can be inserted. This new key in the B-tree defines a new interval boundary for key range locking, and a range lock on value 10 now covers merely the range [10, 15). Nonetheless, the user transaction must retain its concurrency control privileges. Thus, the same operation that adds the key value 15 to the B-tree data structure must also add a lock for the user transaction on the interval [15, 20).

Inversely, when a ghost record is removed, two intervals are merged and the locks held on the two intervals must also be merged. Obviously, the merged lock set must not include a lock conflict. A ghost record should not be removed while some transaction is still attempting to acquire a lock on the ghost record's key. Merging lock sets can be avoided if ghost records are never removed while some transaction is still holding a lock on the ghost record's key.

In addition to deletions, ghost records can also improve the performance and concurrency of insertions. Initial creation of a ghost record does not require any locks because this operation, invoked by a user transaction but not part of the user transaction, modifies merely the database representation without changing the logical database contents. Once the ghost record is in place, the user transaction merely updates an existing record including its ghost bit. The user transaction requires a lock only on the key value, not on its neighboring gaps. Thus, this two-step insertion can alleviate insertion hotspots for both prior-key locking and next-key locking. If future key values are predictable, for example, order numbers and time values, creation of multiple ghost records at-a-time may further improve performance.

Figure 1.6 shows the intermediate state during a user transaction in need of appending a row with key value 1172. In preparation of future transactions, multiple ghost records are created. As a single key range lock would cover the key range from 1172 to $+\infty$ (infinity) prior to this insertion, testing for conflicting locks is very fast. The user transaction triggering this insertion locks merely the first among the new ghost records, changes the value of the ghost bit to mark the B-tree entry "valid," updates the other fields in the record, and commits. If ghost records are created proactively but never used, removal and space reclamation apply just as for other ghost records.

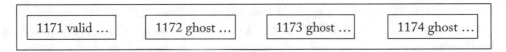

Figure 1.6: Insertion of multiple ghost records.

1.5.3   KEY RANGE LOCKING AS HIERARCHICAL LOCKING

When a serializable transaction locks the absence of a key, for instance, after returning the count of 0 for a query of the type "select count (*) from …where …," one standard design requires key range locking for the interval containing the key. Alternatively, merely the specific key can be locked, possibly after insertion as a ghost record into the appropriate B-tree leaf node or merely into the lock manager's hash table.

Another specific example benefiting from locks on individual key values is key deletion using a ghost record. The user transaction turning a valid record into a ghost record merely needs to lock a key value, not the neighboring gaps to the neighboring keys. Key range locking is required for key removal only to guarantee successful rollback, that is, reinsertion of the key.

These and other cases benefit from the ability to lock a key value without locking an entire half-open interval. There are also cases in which it is desirable to lock the open interval without locking a key value. In the preceding example, two transactions might lock the key value [10] and the open interval (10, 20) without conflict, such as, the query "select count (*) from ...where ...between 16 and 19."

Some operations such as scans, however, need to lock one or more half-open intervals in order to lock a key range much larger than a single interval between neighboring keys in a B-tree index. This could be accomplished by locking the key value and the gap between keys separately, but a single lock would be more efficient.

Hierarchical or multigranularity locking answers this need, even if it was not originally invented for key range locking. Figure 1.7 shows the traditional lock compatibility matrix for intention lock modes IS and IX and absolute lock modes S and X.

	IS	IX	S	X	SIX
IS	✓	✓	✓	–	✓
IX	✓	✓	–	–	–
S	✓	–	✓	–	–
X	–	–	–	–	–
SIX	✓	–	–	–	–

Figure 1.7: Lock table with intention locks.

Any read or write operation requires a shared or exclusive lock at the appropriate granularity of locking. Before any S or IS lock is taken on any item, an IS lock is required on the larger item containing it. For example, before a page can be locked in S mode the file containing the page must be locked in IS mode. X and IX locks work similarly. An IX lock also permits acquiring an S lock. An SIX lock is the combination of an S lock and an IX lock, useful when scanning a data collection searching individual items to update. The SIX lock might also be used within the lock manager to indicate that one transaction holds an S lock and another transaction holds an IX lock.

In key range locking based on hierarchical locking, the large granularity of locking is the half-open interval; the small granularities of locking are either the key value or the open interval. This simple hierarchy permits very precise locks appropriate for the case at hand. The disadvantage of this design is that locking a key (or an open interval) requires two invocations of the lock manager, one for the intention lock on the half-open interval and one for the absolute lock on the key value.

Given that all three locks are identified by the key value, a trade-off is possible between the number of lock modes and the number of lock manager invocations. Additional, artificial lock modes can describe combinations of locks on the half-open interval, the key value, and the open interval. Thus, a system that employs hierarchical locking for half-open interval, key value, and open interval requires no more lock management effort than one that locks only half-open intervals. Without additional effort for lock acquisition and release, such a system permits additional concurrency between transactions that lock a key value and an open interval separately, for example, to ensure absence of key values in the open interval and to update a record's nonkey attributes. A record's nonkey attributes include the property whether the record is a valid record or a ghost record; thus, even logical insertion and deletion are possible while another transaction locks a neighboring open interval.

Specifically, the half-open interval can be locked in S, X, IS, IX modes. The SIX mode is not required because with precisely two resources, more exact lock modes are easily possible. The key value and the open interval each can be locked in S or X modes. The new lock modes must cover all possible combinations of S, X, or N (no lock) modes of precisely two resources, the key value and the open interval. The intention locks IS and IX can remain implicit. For example, if the key value is locked in X mode, the half-open interval is implicitly locked in IX mode; if the key value is locked in S mode and the open interval in X mode, the implicit lock on the half-open interval containing both is the IX mode. Locks can readily be identified using two lock modes, one for the key value and one for the open interval. Assuming previous-key locking, a SN lock protects a key value in S mode and leaves the following open interval unlocked. A NS lock leaves the key unlocked but locks the open interval. This lock mode can be used for phantom protection as required for true serializability.

Figure 1.8 shows the lock compatibility matrix. It can be derived very simply by checking for compatibility of both the first and the second components. For example, XS is compatible with NS because X is compatible with N and S is compatible with S. Single-letter locks are equivalent to using the same letter twice, but there is no benefit in introducing more lock modes than absolutely necessary.

	NS	NX	SN	S	SX	XN	XS	X
NS	✓	–	✓	✓	–	✓	✓	–
NX	–	–	✓	–	–	✓	–	–
SN	✓	✓	✓	✓	✓	–	–	–
S	✓	–	✓	✓	–	–	–	–
SX	–	–	✓	–	–	–	–	–
XN	✓	✓	–	–	–	–	–	–
XS	✓	–	–	–	–	–	–	–
X	–	–	–	–	–	–	–	–

Figure 1.8: Lock table with combined lock modes.

1.5.4   LOCKING IN NONUNIQUE INDEXES

If entries in a nonclustered index are not unique, multiple row identifiers may be associated with each value of the search key. Even thousands of record identifiers per key value are possible due to a single frequent key value or due to attributes with few distinct values. In nonunique indexes, key value locking may lock each value (including its entire cluster of row identifiers) or it may lock each unique pair of value and row identifier. The former saves lock requests in search queries, while the latter may permit higher concurrency during updates. For high concurrency in the former design, intention locks may be applied to values. Depending on the details of the design, it may not be required to lock individual row identifiers if those are already locked in the table to which the nonclustered index belongs.

A hierarchical design might permit locks for both unique values of the userdefined index key and for individual entries made unique by including the record identifier. Key range locking seems appropriate for both levels in the hierarchy, and therefore it seems sensible to use the lock modes of Figure 1.7 for both levels. This is a special case of the hierarchical locking in B-tree keys [Graefe, 2007].

Figure 1.9 shows an example with two distinct key values and seven record identifiers. The key values are sorted in the B-tree ("Shoes" before "Toys"); moreover, each list of record identifiers is also sorted (e.g., "1147" before "4117"). Key range locking can be applied both the key values (e.g,. "Shoes") and to pairs of key value and record identifier (e.g., "Toys 4711"). A lock might thus protect all records with a key value (e.g., "Shoes"), the gap between two key values (e.g., between "Shoes" and "Toys"), a pair of key value and record identifier (e.g., "Shoes 4117"), or a gap between two record identifiers (e.g., between "Toys 4171" and "Toys 4711"). There are really two hierarchies here: the hierarchy of key ranges and a hierarchy of key value, gap, and their combination. Each of these lock levels may be optimal depending on the operation (e.g., "insertion" or "select") and the level of lock contention in the database.

| Shoes: 1147, 4117, 7114, 7411 | Toys: 1174, 4171, 4711 |

Figure 1.9: Records in a nonunique nonclustered index.

The choice whether to lock unique values (and their clusters of row identifiers) or each unique pair of value and row identifier is independent of the choice of representation on disk or in memory. For example, a system may store each key value only once in order to save disk space yet lock individual pairs of key value and row identifier. Conversely, another system may store pairs of key value and record identifier yet lock all such pairs with the same value with a single lock. Representation and granularity of locking are independent of each other whether any form of compression is applied or not.

Even in bitmap indexes, which employ particularly compressed representations for large sets of row identifiers, locks may protect row identifiers one-at-a-time. The same is true for index formats that mix uncompressed bitmaps, compressed bitmaps, traditional lists of record identifiers, and lists of record identifiers compressed by storing distances between "on" bits in bitmaps. Note that bitmaps compressed with run-length encoding are quite similar to lists of record identifiers compressed by storing differences.

Another variety of bitmap indexes employs segmented lists, that is, the domain represented by the bitmap is divided into segments and a bitmap is stored for each nonempty segment. For example, if a record identifier consists of a device identifier, page identifier, and slot number, then the device identifier plus some bytes of the page identifier may be interpreted as a segment identifier. Bitmaps then capture the remaining bytes of the page identifier and the slot number. The search key in the B-tree appends the segment identifier to the search key desired by the user. With respect to concurrency control, a single lock may cover all segments for a search key value or a separate lock may be required for each segment. In the latter case, insertion and deletion of empty segments is quite similar to record insertion and deletion in the simplest form of B-trees, both with respect to concurrency control and recovery.

All these variations on locking in nonunique indexes are special cases of the general orthogonality between the representation (including compression) of data in a data structure and the required concurrency control among user transactions (including locking), which is related, of course, to the separation of latches to protect data structures and locks to protect the logical database contents.

1.5.5   INCREMENT LOCK MODES

In addition to the traditional read and write locks, or shared and exclusive locks, other lock modes have been investigated. Most notable among these is the "increment" lock. Increment locks enable concurrent transactions to increment and decrement sums and counts. This is rarely required in detail tables but can be a concurrency bottleneck in materialized and indexed summary views, also known as "group by" views.

Increment locks are compatible with each other, but they are not compatible with read or write locks. Moreover, increment locks do not imply read permission for the lock holder. In other words, a transaction holding an increment lock cannot determine a current value without also acquiring a read lock. The combination of read lock and increment lock is equivalent to a write lock, because it excludes all other transactions from holding any kind of lock at the same time.

Figure 1.10 shows the compatibility matrix. The increment lock is indicated with the letter E in reference to O'Neil's escrow locks [O'Neil, 1986], although they have more semantics than merely incrementing a sum or count. Here, we assume that any addition or subtraction is permitted, with no concern for valid value ranges. The original escrow locks have such provisions, for example, to prevent a negative account balance.

Increment locks in B-tree indexes are particularly useful for materialized and indexed summary views. Exclusive locks may be sufficient for updates in the base tables but, due to

	S	X	E
S	✓	–	–
X	–	–	–
E	–	–	✓

Figure 1.10: Lock compatibility with increment locks.

fewer rows in the summary view, may lead to unacceptable contention during view maintenance. Very much like reference counts in traditional memory management, records in such views must include a count field. This field serves as a generalization of the ghost bit; when the count is zero, the record is a ghost record not to be included in query results. Holding an increment lock, a user transaction may increment counts and sums thus turning a ghost record into a valid summary row and vice versa.

In grouped summary views, ghost records enable efficient creation and removal of groups [Graefe and Zwilling, 2004]. Upon deletion of the last relevant row in the detail table, the reference count in the corresponding summary row reaches zero and thus turns the record into a ghost. Ghost clean-up can be deferred past end-of-transaction, for instance, until the space is required. When a new group must be created due to a new detail item with a unique group key, a ghost record can be created outside of the user transaction and can turn into a valid record when the user transaction commits an increment in the reference count. Note that no lock is required to insert or remove a new ghost record and key, only a latch for the data structure. Luo et al. [2005] developed an alternative solution for these issues based on special "value-based" latches.

Increment locks on key values immediately permit incrementing counts and sums in the record whose key is locked. Increment locks on large key ranges containing many keys and records permit increment operations in all records in the key range, including ghost records. Increment locks for an open interval between two neighboring key values can be defined, with perhaps surprising semantics and effects. They apply to any new ghost record inserted into the key range, that is, the transaction starting with an increment lock on an open interval ends up holding increment locks on the newly inserted key as well as the two resulting open intervals. Based on the increment lock, the transaction may turn the ghost into a valid record by incrementing its counts and sums. Thus, an increment lock on an open interval permits insertion of new summary records and it prevents all other transactions from obtaining a shared or exclusive lock on the interval.

Figure 1.11 shows the lock compatibility matrix for key range locking with increment locks. The matrix is becoming a bit large, but it can be derived from Figure 1.10, just like Figure 1.8 from Figure 1.7. The derivation could be done by software during code development or during start-up of the database management process. Alternatively, the large lock matrix of

Figure 1.11 may not be stored at all and lock requests test two compatibilities as appropriate. The savings due to combined lock modes are in the number of lock manager invocations including latching and searching the lock manager's hash table; once a lockable resource is found in the hash table, two tests instead of one are a minor overhead.

	NS	NX	NE	SN	S	SX	SE	XN	XS	X	XE	EN	ES	EX	E
NS	✓	–	–	✓	✓	–	–	✓	✓	–	–	✓	✓	–	–
NX	–	–	–	✓	–	–	–	✓	–	–	✓	–	–	–	–
NE	–	–	✓	✓	–	–	✓	✓	–	–	✓	✓	–	–	✓
SN	✓	✓	✓	✓	✓	✓	✓	–	–	–	–	–	–	–	–
S	✓	–	–	✓	✓	–	–	–	–	–	–	–	–	–	–
SX	–	–	–	✓	–	–	–	–	–	–	–	–	–	–	–
SE	–	–	✓	✓	–	–	✓	–	–	–	–	–	–	–	–
XN	✓	✓	✓	–	–	–	–	–	–	–	–	–	–	–	–
XS	✓	–	–	–	–	–	–	–	–	–	–	–	–	–	–
X	–	–	–	–	–	–	–	–	–	–	–	–	–	–	–
XE	–	–	✓	–	–	–	–	–	–	–	–	–	–	–	–
EN	✓	✓	✓	–	–	–	–	–	–	–	–	✓	✓	✓	✓
ES	✓	–	–	–	–	–	–	–	–	–	–	✓	✓	–	–
EX	–	–	–	–	–	–	–	–	–	–	–	✓	–	–	–
E	–	–	✓	–	–	–	–	–	–	–	–	✓	–	–	✓

Figure 1.11: Lock table key range locking and increment locks.

This latter argument becomes even stronger if U lock modes are considered. As pointed out by Korth [1983], there can be many "upgrade" locks from one mode to another. For example, when some set of transactions holds a record in increment mode, some transaction might request an upgrade to a shared lock. In the traditional system based on only shared and exclusive locks, only one upgrade lock mode is useful and is commonly called the "update" lock; if additional basic lock modes are introduced such as the increment lock, the name "update" lock is no longer helpful or appropriate.

1.5.6   SUMMARY

In summary, key range locking is the technique of choice for concurrency control among transactions. It is well understood, enables high concurrency, permits ghost records to minimize effort and "lock footprint" in user transactions, adapts to any key type and key distribution, and prevents phantoms for true serializability. By strict separation of locks and latches, of abstract database contents and in-memory data structures including cached database representation, and of transactions and threads, previously difficult techniques become clear. This clarity enables efficient implementations, correct tuning, and innovation with advanced lock modes and scopes, exemplified by increment locks and key range locking for separator keys in upper B-tree nodes.

1.6   FUTURE DIRECTIONS

Perhaps the most urgently needed future direction is simplification. Functionality and code for concurrency control and recovery are too complex to design, implement, test, debug, tune, explain, and maintain. Elimination of special cases without a severe drop in performance or scalability would be welcome to all database development and test teams.

At the same time, B-trees and variants of B-tree structures are employed in new areas, such as Z-order UB-trees for spatial and temporal information, various indexes for unstructured data and XML documents, and in-memory and on-disk indexes for data streams and as caches of reusable intermediate query results. It is unclear whether these application areas require new concepts or techniques in B-tree concurrency control.

Some implementation techniques need to be revised for optimal use of modern many-core processors. For example, will traditional B-tree primitives be divided into concurrent operations? Could the operations discussed earlier for B^{link}-trees and for ghost records serve as the basis for such highly concurrent primitives? Will these processors offer new hardware support for concurrency control, to be used for critical sections instead of latches? Is transactional memory a suitable replacement for latches? Can the implementation of database management systems benefit from hardware transactions with automatic rollback and restart? Depending on the answers to these questions, high concurrency in B-tree operations may become possible with fairly simple and compact code.

1.7   SUMMARY AND CONCLUSIONS

In summary, concurrency control for B-tree indexes in databases can be separated into two levels: concurrent threads accessing in-memory data structures and concurrent transactions accessing database contents. These two levels are implemented with latches and locks.

Latches support a limited set of modes such as shared and exclusive, they do not provide advanced services such as deadlock detection or escalation, and they can often be embedded in the data structures they protect. Therefore, their acquisition and release can be very fast, which is important as they implement short critical sections in the database system code.

Locks support many more modes than latches and provide multiple advanced services. Management of locks is separate from the protected information, for example, keys and gaps between keys in the leaf page of a B-tree index. The hash table in the lock manager is in fact protected itself by latches such that many threads can inspect or modify the lock table as appropriate.

The principal technique for concurrency control among transactions accessing B-tree contents is key range locking. Various forms of key range locking have been designed. The most recent design permits separate locks on individual key values and on the gaps between key values, applies strict multigranularity locking to each pair of a key and a neighboring gap, reduces lock manager invocations by using additional lock modes that can be derived automatically, enables increment locks in grouped summary views, and exploits ghost records not only for deletions for but also for insertions.

ACKNOWLEDGEMENTS

Helpful feedback and encouragement by Theo Härder, Harumi Kuno, Gary Smith, the anonymous ACM TODS reviewers, and last not least the associate editor Hank Korth are gratefully acknowledged.

1.8   REFERENCES

Bayer, R. (1997). The universal B-Tree for multidimensional indexing: General concepts. In *Proc. of the International Conference on Worldwide Computing and its Applications (WWCA)*, pp. 198–209. DOI: 10.1007/3-540-63343-x_48. 17

Bayer, B. and McCreight, E. M. (1972). Organization and maintenance of large ordered indices. *Acta Informatica*, 1, pp. 173–189. DOI: 10.1007/bf00288683. 17

Bayer, R. and Schkolnick, M. (1977). Concurrency of operations on B-trees. *Acta Informatica*, 9, pp. 1–21. DOI: 10.1007/bf00263762. 18, 20

Bayer, R. and Unterauer, K. (1977). Prefix B-trees. *ACM Transactions on Database Systems*, 2(1), pp. 11–26. DOI: 10.1145/320521.320530. 20

Bernstein, P. A., Hadzilacos, V., and Goodman, N. (1987). *Concurrency Control and Recovery in Database Systems*, Addison-Wesley. DOI: 10.1145/356842.356846. 18

Comer, D. (1979). The ubiquitous B-tree. *ACM Computing Surveys*, 11(2), pp. 121–137. DOI: 10.1145/356770.356776. 17, 20

Eswaran, K. P., Gray, J., Lorie, R. A., and Traiger, I. L. (1976). The notions of consistency and predicate locks in a database system. *Communications of the ACM*, 19(11), pp. 624–633. DOI: 10.1145/360363.360369. 30

Gawlick, D. and Kinkade, D. (1985). Varieties of concurrency control in IMS/VS fast path. *IEEE Database Engineering Bulletim*, 8(2), pp. 3–10. 19

Graefe, G. (2007). Hierarchical locking in B-tree indexes. In *Proc. of the BTW Conference*, pp. 18–42 (Chapter 2). 19, 36

Graefe, G. and Zwilling, M. J. (2004). Transaction support for indexed views. In *Proc. of the ACM SIGMOD International Conference on Management of Data*, pp. 323–334 (Chapter 3). 20, 38

Gray, J. and Reuter, A. (1993). *Transaction Processing: Concepts and Techniques*, Morgan Kaufmann, San Fransisco, CA. 17, 19, 20, 29, 30

Jaluta, I., Sippu, S., and Soisalon-Soininen, E. (2005). Concurrency control and recovery for balanced B-link trees. *VLDB Journal*, 14(2), pp. 257–277. DOI: 10.1007/s00778-004-0140-6. 28

Jordan, J. R., Banerjee, J., and Batman, R. B. (1981). Precision locks. In *Proc. of the ACM SIGMOD International Conference on Management of Data*, pp. 143–147. DOI: 10.1145/582338.582340. 30

Korth, H. F. (1983). Locking primitives in a database system. *Journal of ACM*, 30(1), pp. 55–79. DOI: 10.1145/322358.322363. 19, 39

Kung, H. T. and Robinson, J. T. (1981). On optimistic methods for concurrency control. *ACM Transactions on Database Systems*, 6(2), pp. 213–226. DOI: 10.1145/319566.319567. 18

Larus, J. R. and Rajwar, R. (2006). *Transactional Memory, Synthesis Lectures on Computer Architecture*, Morgan & Claypool Publishers. 25

Lehman, P. L. and Yao, S. B. (1981). Efficient locking for concurrent operations on B-trees. *ACM Transactions on Database Systems*, 6(4), pp. 650–670. DOI: 10.1145/319628.319663. 27

Lomet, D. B. (1993). Key range locking strategies for improved concurrency. In *Proc. of the International Conference on Very Large Databases (VLDB)*, pp. 655–664. 19

Lomet, D. B. (2004). Simple, robust and highly concurrent B-trees with node deletion. In *Proc. of the International Conference on Data Engineering (ICDE)*, pp. 18–28. DOI: 10.1109/icde.2004.1319981. 28

Luo, G., Naughton, J. F., Ellmann, C. J., and Watzke, M. (2005). Locking protocols for materialized aggregate join views. *IEEE Transactions on Knowledge Data Engineering*, 17(6), pp. 796–807. DOI: 10.1109/tkde.2005.96. 38

Mohan, C. (1990). ARIES/KVL: A key-value locking method for concurrency control of multiaction transactions operating on B-tree indexes. In *Proc. of the International Conference on Very Large Databases (VLDB)*, pp. 392–405. 19

Mohan, C. and Levine, F. (1992). ARIES/IM: An efficient and high concurrency index management method using write-ahead logging. In *Proc. of the ACM SIGMOD International Conference on Management of Data*, pp. 371–380. DOI: 10.1145/130283.130338. 19

Moss, J. E. B. (2006). Open nested transactions: Semantics and support. In *Proc. of the Workshop on Memory Performance Issues (WMPI)*. 19

Ni, Y., Menon, V., Adl-Tabatabai, A.-R., Hosking, A. L., Hudson, R. L., Moss, J. E. B., Saha, B., and Shpeisman, T. (2007). Open nesting in software transactional memory. In *Proc. of the ACM SIGPLAN Symposium on Principles and Practice of Parallel Programming (PPoPP)*, pp. 68–78. DOI: 10.1145/1229428.1229442. 18

O'Neil, P. E. (1986). The Escrow transactional method. *ACM Transactions on Database Systems*, 11(4), pp. 405–430. DOI: 10.1145/7239.7265. 20, 37

Ramsak, F., Markl, V., Fenk, R., Zirkel, M., Elhardt, K., and Bayer, R. (2000). Integrating the UB-tree into a database system kernel. In *Proc. of the International Conference on Very Large Databases (VLDB)*, pp. 263–272. 17

Srinivasan, V. and Carey, M. J. (1991). Performance of B-tree concurrency algorithms. In *Proc. of the ACM SIGMOD International Conference on Management of Data*, pp. 416–425. DOI: 10.1145/115790.115860. 19

Weikum, G. (1991). Principles and realization strategies of multilevel transaction management. *ACM Transactions on Database Systems*, 16(1), pp. 132–180. DOI: 10.1145/103140.103145. 18, 19

Weikum, G. and Schek, H.-J. (1992). Concepts and applications of multilevel transactions and open nested transactions. In *Database Transaction Models for Advanced Applications*, pp. 515–553. 18

Weikum, G. and Vossen, G. (2002). *Transactional Information Systems: Theory, Algorithms, and the Practice of Concurrency Control and Recovery*, Morgan Kaufmann, San Fransisco, CA. 19

Zou, C. and Salzberg, B. (1996). On-Line reorganization of sparsely-populated B+-trees. In *Proc. of the ACM SIGMOD International Conference on Management of Data*, pp. 115–124. DOI: 10.1145/233269.233325. 29

CHAPTER 2

Hierarchical Locking in B-Tree Indexes

Goetz Graefe, *Hewlett–Packard Laboratories*

ABSTRACT

Three designs of hierarchical locking suitable for B-tree indexes are explored in detail and their advantages and disadvantages compared.

Traditional hierarchies include index, leaf page, and key range or key value. Alternatively, locks on separator keys in interior B-tree pages can protect key ranges of different sizes. Finally, for keys consisting of multiple columns, key prefixes of different sizes permit a third form of hierarchical locking.

Each of these approaches requires appropriate implementation techniques. The techniques explored here include node splitting and merging, lock escalation and lock de-escalation, and online changes in the granularity of locking. Those techniques are the first designs permitting introduction and removal of levels in a lock hierarchy on demand and without disrupting transaction or query processing.

In addition, a simplification of traditional key range locking is introduced that applies principled hierarchical locking to keys in B-tree leaves. This new method of key range locking avoids counter-intuitive lock modes used in today's high-performance database systems. Nonetheless, it increases concurrency among operations on individual keys and records beyond that enabled by traditional lock modes.

2.1   INTRODUCTION

Since the 1970s, hierarchical locking has served its intended purpose: letting large transactions take large (and thus few) locks and letting many small transactions proceed concurrently by taking small locks. Multi-granularity locking was one of the great database inventions of that decade.

Hierarchical locking is widely used for database indexes. The standard lock hierarchy for B-tree indexes starts by locking the table or view, then locks the index or an index partition, and finally locks a page or individual key. This design is implemented in many database systems where it works reliably and efficiently.

2.1.1   PROBLEM OVERVIEW

With disk sizes approaching 1 TB and with very large databases and indexes, this hierarchy of locking begins to show a flaw. Specifically, the currently common step from locking an index to locking its individual pages or keys might prove too large. There may be millions of pages and billions of keys in an index. Thus, if a lock on an entire index is too large and too restrictive for other transactions, thousands and maybe millions of individual locks are required. If a transaction touches multiple indexes and if there are many concurrent transactions, the count of locks multiplies accordingly.

Each lock structure takes 64–128 bytes in most implementations. This includes a doubly linked list for the transaction and one for the lock manager's hash table, where each pointer nowadays requires 8 bytes. In addition, there is a list for transactions waiting for a lock conversion (e.g., shared to exclusive) and a list of transactions waiting to acquire an initial lock on the resource. Thus, millions of locks take a substantial amount of memory from the buffer pool, from sort operations for index creation and index maintenance, and from query processing.

Acquiring and releasing a single lock costs thousands of CPU cycles, not only for memory allocation but also for searching the lock manager's hash table for conflicting locks, and not only for instructions but also for cache faults and pipeline stalls in the CPU. Thus, millions of locks require billions of CPU cycles, which is why hierarchical locking and automatic lock escalation are very important for commercial workloads.

A single ill-advised lock escalation suffices, however, to reduce the multi-programming level to one. Consider, for example, a transaction that reads some fraction of a B-tree index and updates some selected entries. Depending on the fraction read, tens or hundreds of such transactions operate concurrently on a single B-tree index. If a single one of them exceeds its lock escalation threshold and indeed escalates to an index lock, no other transaction can update even a single B-tree entry, the multi-programming level collapses and server throughput drops accordingly.

2.1.2   SOLUTION OVERVIEW

Neither abandoning hierarchical locking nor partitioning large indexes into small partitions solves this problem satisfactorily. The solution advanced in this research redefines the hierarchy of resources locked. It introduces two new designs with additional lock granularities between an entire index and an individual page or key, and compares strengths and weaknesses of traditional locking hierarchies with the two new designs.

All three designs let large scans lock entire indexes such that no conflict can invalidate a scan when it is almost complete. They also let transaction processing lock individual records or keys. In addition, the two new designs let queries lock index fractions of various sizes. Thus, the original spirit of hierarchical locking is preserved and indeed strengthened by eliminating the dilemma between locking an entire index and acquiring thousands or millions of individual locks.

In contrast to prior lock hierarchies, the two new designs support online changes to the granularity of resources available for locking. Thus, they permit to start with traditional locks on indexes and keys only and to introduce or remove larger locking granules if, when, where, while, and as much as warranted by the workload.

In addition, a new design for key range locking is introduced. Compared to existing methods, it relies on hierarchical locking in a principled way. It is simpler than traditional designs for key range locking as it avoids counterintuitive lock modes such as "RangeI-N" (discussed below). Nonetheless, it permits higher concurrency in B-tree leaves. It requires new lock modes, but eliminates as many, and the new lock modes are based on established sound theory. Due to these advantages, the new design for key range locking has value independent of the proposed techniques for locking large sections of B-trees.

The following sections first review related work and some preliminaries, then describe each of the three alternative designs for hierarchical locking in B-tree indexes and, and finally offer some conclusions from this effort.

2.2   RELATED WORK

Multiple prior efforts have investigated and refined multi-granularity locking as well as key range locking in B-tree indexes. The techniques proposed in subsequent sections do not require understanding of the related work reviewed in this section, and some readers may wish to skip ahead. The details given here are provided for those readers who wish to compare and contrast prior techniques with the present proposals.

2.2.1   RELATED WORK ON MULTI-GRANULARITY LOCKING

Multi-granularity locking has been a standard implementation technique for commercial database system for more than a quarter century [Gray et al., 1975]. Other hierarchical concurrency control methods [Carey, 1983] have not been widely adopted.

Multi-granularity locking is often restricted to hierarchies. The hierarchy levels usually include table, index, partition, page, record, key, or a subset of these. The choice of lock level can be based on explicit directives by the database administrator or by the query developer or it can be based on cardinality estimates derived during query optimization. The theory of multi-granularity locking is not restricted to these traditional hierarchies, however. A premise of this research is that alternative hierarchies deserve more attention than they have received in the past.

A radically different approach has also been advocated in the past. In predicate locking, locks contain query predicates, and conflict detection relies on intersection of predicates [Eswaran et al., 1976]. In precision locking [Jordan et al., 1981], read locks contain predicates whereas write locks contain specific values. Conflict detection merely applies predicates to specific values. Precision locking may be seen as predicate locking without the cost and complexity of predicate intersection.

These techniques target the same problem as hierarchical locking, i.e., locking appropriate large data volumes with little overhead, but seem to have never been implemented and evaluated in commercial systems. The key-prefix locks in Tandem's NonStop SQL product [Gray and Reuter, 1993] might be closest to an implementation of precision locks. Note that Gray and Reuter explain key-range locking as locking a key prefix, not necessarily entire keys, and that "granular locks are actually predicate locks" [Gray and Reuter, 1993].

"In addition to the ability to lock a row or a table's partition, NonStop SQL/MP supports the notion of generic locks for key-sequenced tables. Generic locks typically affect multiple rows within a certain key range. The number of affected rows might be less than, equal to, or more than a single page. When creating a table, a database designer can specify a 'lock length' parameter to be applied to the primary key. This parameter determines the table's finest level of lock granularity. Imagine an insurance policy table with a 10-character ID column as its primary key. If a value of '3' was set for the lock length parameter, the system would lock all rows whose first three bytes of the ID column matched the user-defined search argument in the query" (from Saracco and Bontempo [1997]; see also Bontempo and Saracco [1977]).

Gray [2006] recalls a design in which locking a parent or grandparent node in S mode protects the key range of all leaf nodes underneath. A lock on the root page locks the entire index. IS locks are required on the entire path from root to leaf. A leaf-to-leaf scan locks appropriate parent and ancestor nodes. Exclusive locks work similarly.

At first sight, these locks may seem equivalent to key range locks on separator keys. Both methods adapt gracefully to very large tables and indexes. However, there are important differences. For example, before a leaf page can be locked in S mode, its parent page needs to be locked in IS mode. Both locks are retained until transaction commit. The IS lock prohibits any X lock on that parent node and thus prevents any update there, e.g., splitting a different leaf page under the same parent or splitting the parent itself. While holding IS locks on the root page, user transactions prevent any kind of update of the root node, e.g., splitting a child node or load balancing among the root's child nodes.

In addition, System R had "a graph for physical page locks" [Gray et al., 1975] but no further public documentation seems to exist [Gray, 2006].

2.2.2   RELATED WORK ON KEY RANGE LOCKING

In the final System R design, a lock on a key implicitly locks the gap to the next key value; locking a key and locking the gap to the next key is the same [Blasgen and Gray, 2006]. The conceptual hierarchy applies to fields within a record but does not consider the gap between keys a lockable resource separate from a key.

The Aries family of techniques includes two methods for concurrency control for B-tree indexes, key value locking [Mohan, 1990] and index management [Mohan and Levine, 1992].

The former is quite subtle as it relies not only on locks but also on latches and on instant locks. The latter establishes that a lock on a row in a table can cover the index entries for that row in all the indexes for the table.

Lomet's design for key range locking [Lomet, 1993] builds on Aries [Mohan, 1990, Mohan and Levine, 1992] but leaves multiple opportunities for further simplification and improvement. The present work addresses those pointed out here.

1. Most importantly, multi-granularity locking is considered for general ranges and keys, but is described in detail only for keys in leaf pages.

2. Lock manager invocations are minimized by identifying multiple granules with the same key value and by introducing additional lock modes, but the B-tree level is omitted in the lock identifier which implies that locking key ranges in interior B-tree nodes is not possible.

3. Intention locks (e.g., IS, IX) on the half-open interval (K_{i-1}, K_i) permit absolute locks on the key value K_i, but no provision is made to lock the open interval (K_{i-1}, K_i) separately from the key value, and appropriate concurrency can be achieved only by using unconventional and counter-intuitive lock modes.

4. Protecting a gap between two keys by locking the prior or next key is discussed and next-key locking is chosen, but it seems that prior-key locking is more suitable for B-trees with suffix truncation for separator keys [Bayer and Unterauer, 1977], i.e., half-open intervals of the form $[K_i, K_{i+1})$.

5. Application of key range locking to heap files is mentioned, but not generalized to ranges larger than immediately successive record identifiers.

6. Locking complex objects with sets of components by means of range locks is considered, but neither developed in detail nor related to B-tree indexes.

7. Locking individual pairs of key and record identifier even if the representation stores each distinct key value only once is discussed, but locking such a key value with all its record identifiers is neither appreciated for its beneficial interaction with query predicates nor generalized to locking arbitrary key prefixes in a hierarchy.

8. Finally, deletion using "ghost" records is mentioned, i.e., separating row deletion in a user transaction and key removal in a subsequent clean-up action, but instead of applying this idea symmetrically to insertions, "instant" insertion locks are employed.

Microsoft SQL Server is a sample commercial database system using key range locking [Microsoft, 2006]. Many aspects of the design and its implementation match Lomet's description [Lomet, 1993]. It locks the open interval between two keys together with the interval's high boundary key. This is evident in the "RangeI-N" mode, which is an insertion lock on the open interval with no lock on the boundary.

Each key value identifies locks on both the key value and the gap to the neighboring key such that a single invocation of the lock manager may obtain a combined lock. These savings are enabled by introduction of additional lock modes. This technique is employed in multiple ways, including "schema stability" and "schema modification" locks on tables. Schema stability read-locks a table's catalog information,[1] e.g., during query optimization. In order to save lock manager invocations during query execution, both S and X locks on a table imply a schema stability lock. Schema modification write-locks both the catalogs and the data, e.g., during schema changes. Schema, data, and their combination could be modeled as a hierarchy in the locking protocol. However, while locking the schema without locking the data is useful, e.g., during query optimization, it is not immediately obvious what it means to lock the data without protecting the schema against modifications by other transactions.[2]

In SQL Server's implementation of key range locking, the set of combined lock modes is not equivalent to multi-granularity locking. This is evident in several missing lock combinations, e.g., an exclusive lock on the gap between keys with no lock on the key value, i.e., there is no "RangeX-N" mode. This mode would permit one transaction to delete a key within an interval while another transaction modifies (the non-key portions of) the record at the interval's high boundary. Similarly, a query with an empty result cannot lock the absence of a key without locking at least one existing key value, i.e., there is no "RangeS-N" mode. Finally, due to the missing "RangeS-X" and "RangeS-N" modes, it is not possible that one query inspects a key range and then updates the boundary key while another query merely inspects the key range.

Despite these missing lock modes, SQL Server uses as many as 6 lock modes of the form "RangeP-Q", where P can be S, X, or I, i.e., shared, exclusive, or insertion lock modes, and Q can be S, X, or N, i.e., shared, exclusive, or no lock. In addition, SQL Server employs update locks [Gray and Reuter, 1993, Korth, 1983] on key values but not on ranges. Nonetheless, update locks add another three lock modes of the form "RangeP-U", where P again can be S, X, or I.

SQL Server relies on short-term locks to guard key ranges against insertion of phantom records. Ghost records and system transactions (see below) are used for deletion but not for insertion. SQL Server employs lock escalation from keys or pages to an entire index, based on an initial threshold and an incremental threshold if earlier lock escalation attempts failed. SQL Server does not support lock de-escalation. Rollback to a savepoint does not reverse lock escalation or lock conversion.

---

[1]In a way, schema stability protects an entire complex object with rows in multiple tables and records in multiple indexes. We plan on generalizing this idea to user-defined complex objects in future work.

[2]There are exceptions to this general statement. For example, one transaction's query may continue while another transaction adds a new constraint to a table. We plan on investigating concurrency among schema operations and data operations in future work.

IBM's multi-dimensional clustering [Bhattacharjee et al., 2003, Padmanabhan et al., 2003] is a special implementation of partitioning that includes the ability to lock an entire "block" (partition) or individual records within a block, albeit without lock escalation from record to block. The only commercial database system that supports lock de-escalation seems to be Oracle's (formerly Digital's) RDB product [Joshi, 1991], although only in the special case of "lock caching" within nodes of a shared-disk cluster.

2.3   ASSUMPTIONS

Assumptions about the database environment are designed to be very traditional.

B-tree indexes map search keys to information. This information might represent a row in a table or a pointer to such a row, i.e., B-trees may be clustered or non-clustered indexes. Each B-tree entry fits on a page; for larger objects, B-tree variants with a byte count rather than a search key added to each child pointer [Carey et al., 1989, Srivastava and Lum, 1988] may be an attractive storage format but are not explored further here.

B-tree pages range from 4–64 KB, although the discussion applies to pages of any size. The number of records per page may be in the tens, most likely is in the hundreds, and in extreme cases is in the thousands.

Prefix and suffix truncation [Bayer and Unterauer, 1977] might be applied to leaf entries and to separator keys, but hardly affect the discussion at hand. Other compression methods, e.g., order-preserving run-length encoding or dictionary compression [Antoshenkov et al., 1996], affect the representation of keys and records but do not change the substance of the discussion, neither the techniques nor the conclusions.

The database implementation observes the separation of latches and locks summarized in Figure 2.1. This separation lets a single thread serve multiple transactions and it lets a single transaction use multiple threads in a parallel query or index operation. In-memory data struc-

	Latches	Locks
Separate ...	Threads	Transactions
Protect ...	In-memory data structures	Database contents
Modes ...	Shared, exclusive	Shared, exclusive, update, intention, escrow, etc.
Duration ...	Critical section	Transaction
Deadlock ...	Avoidance	Detection and resolution
... by ...	Coding discipline, "lock leveling"	Lock manager, graph traversal, transaction abort, partial rollback, lock de-escalation

Figure 2.1: Latches and locks.

tures include the in-memory images of database pages. The database contents include only those characteristics observable with ordinary "select" queries. This excludes database pages, distribution of records within pages, existence and contents of non-leaf pages in B-trees, etc. Thus, non-leaf pages do not require locks and are protected by latches only. The remainder of this chapter focuses on locks.

In contrast to user transactions, "system transactions" modify only the database representation but not its contents and therefore permit certain optimizations such as commit without forcing the transaction log. Logging and recovery rely on standard write-ahead logging [Gray, 1978, Gray and Reuter, 1993, Mohan et al., 1992].

A common use of system transactions is to remove ghost records left behind after deletions by user transactions. Separation of logical deletion (turning a valid record into a ghost) and physical removal (reclaiming the record's space) serves three purposes, namely simplified rollback for the user transaction if required, increased concurrency during the user transaction (locking a single key value rather than a range), and reduced overall log volume. If the ghost removal can capture record deletion and transaction commit in a single log record (perhaps even including transaction start), there is never any need to log undo information, i.e., the deleted record's non-key contents.

Lock escalation and de-escalation are required or very desirable due to unpredictable concurrency contention and due to inaccuracy of cardinality estimation during query optimization. Lock escalation, e.g., from locking individual pages to locking an entire index, reduces overhead for queries with unexpectedly large results. It saves both invocations of the lock manager and memory for managing the locks.

Lock de-escalation reduces contention by relaxing locks held by active transactions. It requires that each transaction retain in transaction-private memory the information required to obtain the appropriate fine-grain locks. For example, even if a transaction holds an S lock on an entire index, it must retain information about the leaf pages read as long as de-escalation to page locking might become desirable or required.

Initial large locks combined with on-demand lock de-escalation can improve performance, because detail locks can be acquired without fear of conflict and thus without search in the lock manager's hash table [Gottemukkala and Lehman, 1992]. Also note that management of such locks in transaction-private memory is very similar to management of locks in a shared lock manager's hash table. Therefore, propagation of locks from private memory to the shared lock manager is quite similar to bulk updates of indexes, which has been found to improve fault rates in CPU caches (and in the buffer pool for on-disk indexes) and thus performance and scalability.

For large index-order B-tree scans, interior B-tree nodes guide deep read-ahead. Therefore, accessing those nodes and their separator keys do not incur any extra I/O, and it is conceivable to lock those nodes or their separator keys if desired.

Some operations benefit from fence keys, i.e., when a node is split, copies of the separator key posted in the parent are retained in the two sibling nodes. Fence keys aid B-tree operations in multiple operations, including key range locking and defragmentation [Graefe, 2004]. Prefix and suffix truncation minimize fence key sizes [Bayer and Unterauer, 1977].

All B-tree entries are unique. It is not required that the declared search keys are unique; however, the entries must have identifying information such that a row deletion leads to deletion of the correct B-tree entry. Standard solutions add the row pointer to the sort order of non-clustered indexes or a "uniquifier" number to keys in clustered indexes.

Finally, locks on the low boundary of a gap protect the gap, e.g., against insertion of phantoms [Gray et al., 1976]. In other words, the description below employs "prior-key locking" rather than "next-key locking."

2.4   TRADITIONAL LOCKING HIERARCHIES

Traditional locking in B-tree indexes is the basis with which the two new designs of hierarchical locking will be compared. Locking of units larger than individual B-trees, e.g., databases and tables, is ignored in this discussion, because locking those does not affect hierarchical locking within B-trees. Partitioning is also ignored; if a table or an index is partitioned, the focus is on the B-tree that represents a single partition of a single index. If such a B-tree cannot be locked because it can only be locked implicitly by locking a larger unit such as a table or an index with all its partitions, the other database contents covered by those locks is ignored and the lock is called an index lock nonetheless.

The standard techniques lock the index and then leaf pages, keys, or both. The choice among page and key locks can be built into the software or might be available to database administrators. In the latter case, a change requires a short quiescence of all query and update activity for the affected table or index.

2.4.1   LOCKS ON KEYS AND RANGES

Both proposed methods for hierarchical locking in B-trees depend on key range locking. Therefore, it may be useful to first introduce a simplification for traditional key range locking that relies more directly on traditional multi-granularity locking [Gray et al., 1975, Korth, 1983], avoids irregular complexities such as instant locks and insert locks [Lomet, 1993], and increases concurrency when applied to keys in B-tree leaves. While helpful for hierarchical locking in B-trees discussed in later sections, it also is a simplification and improvement for traditional key range locking applied solely to keys in leaves.

For maximal concurrency and for maximal simplicity, hierarchical lock modes on keys should be designed so that a key and a key range together can be intention-locked and such that the gap between two keys and an individual key value can each be locked separately. In order to optimize performance of lock acquisition and release, it makes sense to implement not two levels of lockable resources (comparable to the standard example with pages and files) but as a single resource with many possible lock modes [Lomet, 1993]. This technique should be an implementation optimization only rather than lead to the introduction of new locking semantics such as range insert locks.

Figure 2.2 shows a traditional lock compatibility matrix. For this discussion, the intention locks apply only to the combination of key value and gap between keys. The absolute locks can apply to the key value, the gap between keys, or their combination.

	S	X	IS	IX
S	✓	–	✓	–
X	–	–	–	–
IS	✓	–	✓	✓
IX	–	–	✓	✓

Figure 2.2: Traditional lock compatibility matrix.

Using the locks in this lock compatibility matrix, the key value, the gap between keys, and the combination of key value and gap are three separate resources that must be locked using different locks and thus separate invocations of the lock manager code. The optimized design exploits the fact that the key value serves as the identifier for each of the three resources in the lock manager's hash table, which permits employing only one resource and one invocation of the lock manager at the expense of additional lock modes.

In the optimized design, which is strictly equivalent to traditional locking for separate resources, an S or X lock covers the combination of key value and gap between keys. The new lock modes in Figure 2.3 lock a key and the gap between two keys separately.

	S	X	SØ	ØS	XØ	ØX	SX	XS
S	✓	–	✓	✓	–	–	–	–
X	–	–	–	–	–	–	–	–
SØ	✓	–	✓	✓	–	✓	✓	–
ØS	✓	–	✓	✓	✓	–	–	✓
XØ	–	–	–	✓	–	✓	–	–
ØX	–	–	✓	–	✓	–	–	–
SX	–	–	✓	–	–	–	–	–
XS	–	–	–	✓	–	–	–	–

Figure 2.3: Lock modes for key values and gaps.

In order to avoid any possible confusion with combination lock modes such as SIX, which really represents two locks on the same resource such as a file, these new lock modes should be thought of and pronounced with the words "key" and "gap" added. For example, SØ should be pronounced "key shared" and SX should be pronounced "key shared, gap exclusive." Intention locks on the combination of key and gap, though implied by these new lock modes in the obvious way, are not part of the name.

The new lock mode SØ locks the combination in IS mode, the key in S mode, and the gap not at all. A ØS lock on key K_i locks the open interval (K_i, K_{i+1}) yet keeps the key value K_i unlocked. SX locks the combination in IX mode, the key in S mode, and the gap in X mode. A lock held in this mode is most likely the result of a lock conversion rather than a single request; as is the XS mode. All other lock modes are defined similarly.

Figure 2.3 shows the lock compatibility matrix for the new lock modes. It is important to stress that these lock modes are merely a straightforward application of the traditional theory of hierarchical locking [Gray et al., 1975, Korth, 1983], and thus less complex and less prone to mistakes by developers during implementation and maintenance than traditional key range locking [Lomet, 1993, Mohan, 1990].

These new lock modes are identified by a key value but they really represent traditional locks on the key value itself, the gap between key values, and the combination of key value and gap. IS and IX modes are not shown because they do not apply to key values in this scheme other than implied by the new lock modes. The derivation of the values in the compatibility matrix follows directly from the construction of the lock modes.

For example, SØ and ØX are compatible because both take intention locks on the combination of key value and gap, and one transaction locks the key value in S mode whereas the other transaction locks the gap in X mode. Similarly, XØ and ØX are compatible, as are SØ and SX. A specific use of the ØS lock is to ensure absence of a key without inhibiting updates on the locked key. An alternative design inserts a ghost key for the absent key and retains a lock only on the specific key value.

New lock modes based on other basic modes, e.g., update locks [Gray and Reuter, 1993, Korth, 1983] or escrow locks [Graefe and Zwilling, 2004, O'Neil, 1986], can be added in a similar way. In fact, it seems promising to integrate automatic derivation of lock modes such as SØ from a basic set of operational lock modes (e.g., S, X) and the set of components identified by the same database item (e.g., key value, gap between keys, and their combination) in a way similar to Korth's lock derivation techniques [Korth, 1983]. Automatic derivation seems far more promising for the lock modes in Figure 2.3 than for the lock modes of traditional key-range locking.

The strict separation of locks on keys and gaps enables concurrency not supported by traditional key range locking. The earlier discussion of lock modes omitted in SQL Server [Microsoft, 2006] includes several examples of concurrent operations that are correct but are not enabled. The new design enables all of them. The essential reason is that the presented design follows the traditional theory for hierarchical locking and thus provides fully independent locks on keys and gaps. Nonetheless, SQL Server and the proposed design require the same number of new lock modes (6) and of lock manager invocations.

2.4.2 KEY INSERTION USING GHOST RECORDS

Insertion of a new key and record can be implemented as a system transaction. This is analogous to key deletion implemented by turning a valid B-tree record into a ghost record with asynchronous ghost removal using a system transaction. The system transaction for key insertion leaves behind a ghost record that the user transaction can lock in key value mode and then turn into a valid record to effect the logical insertion [Graefe and Zwilling, 2004].

The value of using a system transaction for key insertion is that it releases its lock on the gap between preexisting keys when it commits. The user transaction holds a lock only on the new key value, not on the gap. Holding this XØ lock until it commits, the user transaction can modify the record from a ghost to a valid record. In the case of a rollback, the ghost record remains and can be removed like any ghost record, e.g., upon request by a future user transaction that requires more space in the B-tree leaf.[3]

In the meantime, another user transaction or a system transaction may lock the gap defined by the new key. Using a ØX lock on the new key (really locking the gap only), the other transaction may insert yet another key, for example. Thus, this design supports high insertion rates within a page and an index, without any need to introduce irregular complexities such as instant locks and insert locks [Lomet, 1993] that do not fit the traditional theories of two-phase locking and of hierarchical locking [Gray et al., 1975, Korth, 1983].

Moreover, the system transaction locks only the gap into which it inserts the new key; it has no need to lock the pre-existing key value that identifies the gap. Thus, another transaction can concurrently read the record with the pre-existing key. It can update and even delete the record if deletion is implemented by turning the valid record into a ghost record. Neither concurrent readers nor concurrent updates are possible in locking schemes without locks on only the open interval between keys, e.g., traditional key range locking [Lomet, 1993, Microsoft, 2006, Mohan, 1990]. The system transaction inserting a new key into a gap is compatible with any of these actions on the pre-existing key as long as the key is not erased from the B-tree. Thus, interference among neighboring keys is minimized by use of ghost records and system transactions.

This system transaction can be very efficient. Forcing the transaction log on commit is not required [Graefe and Zwilling, 2004], and a single log record can cover transaction start, key insertion, and transaction commit. In workloads that append many B-tree keys with predictable keys, e.g., order numbers in an order-entry application, a single system transaction can create multiple ghost records such that multiple user transactions each can find an appropriate ghost

---

[3]In fact, since a rollback operation never needs to roll back itself, the ghost can be removed as part of rolling back the user transaction, if desired.

record that merely needs updating, without creating a new record or a new lockable resource. Note that this technique applies not only to unique indexes on order numbers but also to indexes with multiple records for each order number, e.g., an index on order details or a merged index holding both orders and order details [Graefe, 2007].

2.4.3   SPLITTING AND MERGING KEY RANGES

Consider a user transaction that first ensures the absence of a key value and then attempts to insert a new record with that key. In the first step, the user transaction obtains a shared lock on a key range. The second step requires an exclusive lock on that range, albeit only briefly. If the second step employs a system transaction, the two transactions and their locks conflict with each other.

One possible solution is to ignore lock conflicts between a system transaction and the transaction that invoked it—this can lead to complex conditions if one or both of the transactions roll back. Another possible solution is to avoid the system transaction in this special case, letting the user transaction perform the entire insertion—this requires complex code to recognize the correct cases.

The preferred solution is to enable inserting a new ghost key into an existing key range even while it is locked. In order to ensure that existing transactions are not materially affected, their locks on the key range must be duplicated such that they cover the two ranges resulting from the split as well as the newly inserted key. In the specific example above, a new ghost record and its key are inserted and all locks on the original key range are duplicated for the newly created key range including the new key itself.

The newly created locks are inserted into the lock manager and into the appropriate transactions' data struc tures, with a few differences to the standard procedures. First, lock conflicts with concurrent transactions are not possible, so there is no need to search the lock manager's hash table for conflicting locks. Second, these locks cannot be released during a partial transaction rollback to a savepoint. Instead, these locks must be retained during rollback, unless the lock on the original range is also released. Third, if locks are recorded in the transaction log for reacquisition during log analysis after a crash, these newly created locks appear at an appropriate point in the recovery log with respect to the locks they protect in the next-lower B-tree level. Thus, the recovery procedure must be augmented to ensure that the lock hierarchy is respected during log analysis and recovery.

While perhaps tempting, the reverse operation is not always correct. A ghost record must not be erased while it is locked, because the lock might indicate that deletion of the key is not yet committed. If, however, only key ranges are locked but the ghost record's key value is not, and if the locks on the ranges below and above the ghost key do not conflict, then the ghost record can be erased and sets of locks combined.

2.4.4   SUMMARY

The presented design is, in a way, "radically old." Its contribution is in combining appropriate existing techniques into a simple and sound design that permits more concurrency than traditional key range locking.

The proposed design applies the theory of multi-granularity and hierarchical locking to keys and gaps in B-tree leaves. By doing so, it permits more concurrency than prior designs, yet it eliminates multiple counter-intuitive lock modes. It then applies a second existing technique to reduce the count of lock manager invocations by introducing derived lock modes. The proposed design benefits from this technique as much as traditional designs for key range locking. Finally, introduction of new B-tree keys using system transactions and ghost records simplifies the implementation of highly concurrent insertions and mirrors a standard implementation technique for key deletion.

2.5   LOCKS ON SEPARATOR KEYS

Key range locking applies more broadly than it is used today. Specifically, in addition to its use in B-tree leaves, it can be used in interior B-tree pages. A lock on a separator key represents the entire key range from one separator key to its next neighbor (at the same B-tree level). Thus, a key range lock at the level of the leaves' parents is similar in some ways with a traditional lock on an entire leaf page. Both intention locks and absolute locks can be employed at that level, again similar to intention locks and absolute locks on B-tree leaf pages in the traditional hierarchy.

Like key range locks on keys in B-tree leaves, key range locks in non-leaf B-tree nodes are special forms of predicate locks [Eswaran et al., 1976]. Arguments and proofs for the correctness of key range locking in non-leaf B-tree nodes are based on established techniques for predicate locks. For example, splitting and merging of nodes and of ranges must ensure that appropriate predicate locks are preserved and protected.

Locking key ranges at the parent level results in locking overhead and concurrency behavior similar to traditional locking of leaf pages. A key range lock at the grandparent level, however, covers a much larger key range. Depending on a node's fan-out, a range lock at the grandparent level may save tens or hundreds of locks at the parent level, just like a key range lock in a parent node covers tens or hundreds of individual keys. For even larger B-tree indexes and queries, locking can start even higher in the tree.

Each level adds some overhead for acquisition and release of intention locks, even for transactions that actually touch only a single key. Fortunately, the B-tree level at which locking starts can be tuned according to the data and the application at hand, from locking keys in the leaves only to locking a key range at every level from the root to the leaves. Mechanisms for changing this level dynamically and online are discussed below.

2.5.1   TECHNIQUES

In contrast to locking in B-tree leaves, it is less useful in interior B-tree nodes to separate locks on key values and locks on gaps between keys. Thus, only standard lock modes (Figure 2.2) apply to those keys, and cover the half-open range from the locked separator key (inclusively) to the next separator key (exclusively).

A "high fence key" in each B-tree node, i.e., a copy of the separator key in the node's parent, may delimit the range protected by a lock on the highest key value in a node. Some B-tree implementations already retain such a fence key, e.g., B^{link}-trees [Lomet and Salzberg, 1997]. Similarly, a "low fence key" may readily provide the key value to lock in order to protect the key range of a node's left-most child. Thus, each node should also retain a "low fence key." Many systems already retain this key [Gray and Reuter, 1993] even if they do not employ fence keys for multiple purposes [Graefe, 2004].

Locks on separator keys in parents are different from locks on keys in leaves, even if the key values are the same. Thus, their identifier in the lock manager includes the index identifier, the key value, and the node level within the B-tree. Node levels are commonly stored in each node's page header, with level 0 assigned to leaves, if for no other reason than for use during physical consistency check of the tree structure. Note that this identification of locks does not refer to physical location, e.g., a page identifier, such that locks remain valid if a separator key migrates when a node splits or when two nodes merge.

2.5.1.1 Splitting and Merging Nodes

When a node splits, a new separator key is inserted in the node's parent. The required steps with respect to existing locks are precisely those necessary to insert a new ghost key into a key range even while it is locked. This procedure permits page splits at all B-tree levels without interrupting the flow of transactions and ensures that no transaction's locked range is modified due to a change in the physical B-tree structure.

When two nodes merge, the opposite procedure applies. As two key ranges merge in the parent node, transactions end up holding locks on the combined range, as if they had locked both original ranges equally. It is required to verify, therefore, that the combined set of locks does not include conflicts, e.g., an S lock on one original range and an IX lock on the other original range.[4] In such cases, the merge operation must be delayed.

Load balancing between two neighboring nodes can be accurate in its locking but fairly complex due to the shift in key ranges, or it can be fairly simple. The accurate method determines the locks needed in the parents from the locks held on child entries that migrate. The simple method models load balancing as a merge operation followed by a split. The actual implementation and manipulation of data structures is, of course, not tied to these steps. The likely result

---

[4]In the instant of merging the two ranges, transactions do not conflict even if their lock modes do. Thus, it might seem safe to permit merge operations even if locks conflict. However, transactions might perform additional operations based on their existing locks on the combined range, and conflicts among these additional operations would remain undetected.

is that some transactions hold more locks than they need. However, given that load balancing operations are rare (if implemented at all) and that the alternative procedure is complex, the simple procedure is preferable.

2.5.1.2 Lock Escalation and De-Escalation

While mechanisms to split and merge key ranges are required, lock escalation and de-escalation are optional, although they add significant value to locks on separator keys.

By default, locking may start with key range locks in the leaves' parents, which is most similar to traditional page locking. Alternatively, it may start at the grandparent level in order to cover larger key ranges and require fewer locks in large range scans. For the discussion here, assume that initially locking starts with intention locks on separator keys at the grandparent level (e.g., IS locks) and continues with absolute locks on separator keys at the parent level (e.g., S locks). In the B-tree sketched in Figure 2.4, this means intention locks (IS or IX) on key ranges in grandparent node a, absolute locks (S or X) on key ranges in parent node c, and no locks in leaf nodes e, f, and g.

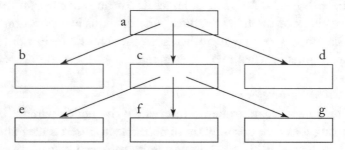

Figure 2.4: Lock escalation and de-escalation.

If so, either lock escalation (to absolute locks in the grandparents) or de-escalation (to intention locks in the parents and absolute locks in the leaves) may be required. Which one is required at what time depends on the workload, and in fact may differ within a single B-tree, e.g., an index on some time attribute in a data warehouse.

For lock escalation, the intention lock at the grandparent must become an absolute lock. In Figure 2.4, the only remaining locks will be absolute locks (S or X) on key ranges in grandparent node a. The locks at the parent level, now obsolete due to the absolute lock at the grandparent level, may be erased. Alternatively, they may be retained in the lock manager or in transaction-private memory for future lock de-escalation, which may be desired due to increasing contention or due to a partial transaction rollback.

For lock de-escalation, the absolute locks at the parent level must become intention locks. In Figure 2.4, intention locks will be used in grandparent node a as well as parent node c, and absolute locks will be used only in the leaves e, f, and g. This requires the opposite procedure and relies on proactive gathering of leaf-level key locks omitted during initial processing. After these leaf-level locks have been propagated from transaction-private memory to the global lock manager's hash table, the lock on the separator key in the parent can be relaxed to an intention lock.

Partial transaction rollback probably should not reverse lock de-escalation because reversal requires upgrading a lock (e.g., from IS to S in node c in Figure 2.4), which might fail due to locks held by concurrent transactions. In fact, after lock de-escalation due to contention by concurrent transactions, it is likely that such a lock upgrade during partial transaction rollback will fail.

2.5.1.3 Granularity Changes

An entirely different kind of locking adjustment is a change in the lock hierarchy. In the case of locking separator keys in a B-tree index, this means changes in the set of B-tree nodes where key ranges are locked. For example, the discussion above assumed locks on separator keys in the leaves' grandparents and parents but not the great-grandparents. This can be adjusted dynamically and online, i.e., without disruption of transaction processing.

Techniques for granularity changes may be useful beyond locking in B-trees. They apply whenever a specific granularity of locking is to be activated or deactivated online. Nonetheless, modifying the granularity of locking is a new notion not used or described elsewhere, as are techniques for doing so online.

Like lock escalation and de-escalation, these techniques are not mandatory for a functional implementation of locks on separator keys. However, these techniques may be required to minimize locking overhead for both online transaction processing and large range queries, in particular for workloads that change over time.

It seems most convenient to augment each interior B-tree node with a label to indicate whether or not keys in that node must be locked. The label applies to each node individually, not to entire B-tree levels. In fact, it even seems possible to label each individual separator key, an idea to be explored in the future.

In Figure 2.4, for example, assume that grandparent node a is not labeled and no locks are taken there, and that parent node c is labeled such that key range locks are taken on separator keys there.

Setting this label on a node, e.g., on grandparent node a in Figure 2.4, can be either immediate or delayed. The advantage of the immediate method is that a transaction may request lock escalation even to a node in which no transaction has acquired locks yet; the advantage of the delayed method is less search in the lock manager.

The immediate method searches in the lock manager's hash table for active transactions that ought to hold intention locks. These transactions can be found by searching for locks on keys in the node's children (e.g., nodes b, c, and d in Figure 2.4). For all such transactions, appropriate intention locks for the appropriate separator keys in the present node are inserted into the lock manager. While the search for such transactions is expensive, acquisition of the new intention locks is fast as there is no need to search for conflicting locks (intention locks never conflict with other intention locks). The correctness of the immediate method relies on its correct acquisition of all intention locks that would have been held already if the label had been set on the node before any of the active transaction began.

The delayed method forces all new transactions to acquire intention locks and prevents acquisition of absolute locks in the node until all older transactions have completed. To do so, it employs two system transactions. The first one labels the node, thus forcing all future transactions to acquire intention locks while descending the B-tree. A second system transaction obtains IX locks on all keys in the node, observes the set of currently active transactions, waits until the last one of those has finished, and then commits. For the duration of these IX locks, no transaction may acquire an absolute lock. The correctness of the delayed method relies on a system transaction holding IX locks on all keys on behalf of all active transactions, whether those transactions require them or not.

When a non-leaf node is split, e.g., grandparent node a or parent node c in Figure 2.4, both resulting nodes inherit the label from the original node. A split operation can proceed even while a granularity change is on-going, whether the immediate or delayed method is employed. For two nodes to merge, they must be labeled equally first, i.e., a modification in the granularity of locking might be needed prior to a merge operation.

Removing a node's label, e.g., on parent node c in Figure 2.4, also employs a system transaction that acquires IX locks on all keys, erases the node's label, and commits. If necessary, it waits for other transactions to release their absolute locks, if any, on those keys. Requesting lock de-escalation by those other transactions permits faster completion; once their absolute locks are relaxed to intention locks, there is no conflict with the desired IX locks.

Both setting and removing a node's label are very local operations that hardly affect data availability. Note that new user transactions can acquire intention locks within a node while a system transaction holds IX locks, because IX locks do not conflict with other intention locks, only with absolute locks.

The set of nodes labeled for locks on separator keys has few restrictions. For example, it is possible that a node is labeled but some of its siblings are not, or that a leaf's parent is not labeled but its grandparent is (skip-level locking). These examples seem counter-intuitive, but they might be appropriate incremental states while an entire B-tree is converted to a different granularity of locking, or they might be permanent states tuned for skew in the data distribution or in the access pattern. Nonetheless, skip-level locking might not be a good idea because it raises the complexity of lock escalation, de-escalation, and granularity changes.

While powerful, these mechanisms require governing policies. For transaction processing systems, an initial policy might start with locking keys in the leaves only and locking separator keys in interior B-tree nodes only inasmuch as necessary for lock escalation. In other words, non-leaf nodes are labeled as described above only on demand. Similarly, labels are removed after their benefit ceases, i.e., nodes remain labeled only during demand. For relational data warehousing, locks in parent and grandparent nodes seem like a reasonable default.

2.5.2   ADVANTAGES

The most salient advantage of locking separator keys in non-leaf B-tree nodes is that the method scales with the size and the height of the index tree. The stepping factor is fairly uniform across all levels of the index, even in an index with a non-uniform key value distribution. Typical values for the stepping factor may be 100 to 1,000; the latter value requiring large pages or very short keys, e.g., due to aggressive prefix and suffix truncation. Thus, the database administrator or the automatic tuning component can adjust the granularity of locking very accurately, much better than in the rigid traditional locking hierarchy of index, page, and key.

In addition, lock escalation and de-escalation permit graceful adjustments to precision and overhead of locking during query execution, even in cases of inaccurate cardinality estimation during query optimization. For unpredictable or time-variant workloads, the nodes at which key range locks are taken can be adjusted with very little disruption of online transaction processing. Thus, there is a real promise that the method can be made automatic, incremental, online, yet robust.

Even if multi-level hierarchies are not exploited and ranges are locked only in leaf nodes and their parent nodes, the method has some advantages over traditional locking of leaf pages and leaf keys. Specifically, there never is any doubt about which lock covers which other lock. Thus, there is no need for lock migration during leaf splits and merges, with the attendant code simplification and performance improvements.

2.5.3   DISADVANTAGES

Despite the advantages over traditional locking for B-tree indexes, some queries and update still suffer with this strategy for hierarchical locking. While simple range queries will likely need only tens or maybe hundreds of locks, or orders of magnitude less than with traditional hierarchical locking, more complex yet common query clauses may still require a thousand locks or more. Consider, for example, an index on columns (a, b) and the query predicate "where a in (3, 9, 15, 21)." There are eight range boundaries to consider in this simple query, and each range boundary requires a choice whether to lock a larger range using few locks or to lock precisely using many fine-grain locks.

2.5.4   OPPORTUNITIES

While the mechanisms described above are reasonably straightforward, their usage is an opportunity for further research, e.g., the number of locks required in average and worst cases. This analysis should cover not only selections but also joins, e.g., not only "between" queries but also "in" queries with lists of values or with nested queries. This evaluation ought to consider page splits near (rather than: at) a full node's center, as already recommended for effective prefix truncation [Bayer and Unterauer, 1977].

Research into policies and automatic self-tuning—starting level, performance metrics to observe, thresholds for lock escalation, lock de-escalation, and changes in the granularity of locking—could speed adoption of the proposed mechanisms in commercial systems. Nonetheless, if there is a global switch to force locking of keys or pages only and to prevent changes in the granularity of locking, the proposed mechanisms can always be restricted to a behavior very similar to current systems, thus providing a safe fall-back if a novel automatic policy fails.

Finally, one might design an alternative concurrency control method in which transactions lock large key ranges by locking interior B-tree pages, i.e., physical pages instead of logical key ranges. During searches and updates of existing pages, this approach is similar to locking separator keys. It is quite different, however, with respect to lock migration during page split and merge operations, during defragmentation, and during write-optimized operation [Graefe, 2004].

2.5.5   SUMMARY

The proposed design for hierarchical locking in indexes exploits the tree structure of B-trees. Traditional absolute locks and intention locks on separator keys in interior B-tree nodes protect all entries in their key ranges. Data skew is considered automatically, just as it is in the insertion, deletion, and search logic of B-trees with respect to concurrency control. Workload skew can be accommodated by lock escalation and lock de-escalation.

In order to minimize locking overhead during transaction processing, locking can be limited to keys in a B-tree's leaf level. Mixed operation, i.e., concurrent large queries and small updates in a real-time data warehouse, can be accommodated by adjusting the locking granularity dynamically. Modifying a database's lock hierarchy online is a novel technique that may seem particularly well suited to key range locking in B-tree indexes but is applicable to any form of hierarchical or multi-granularity locking.

2.6   LOCKS ON KEY PREFIXES

The prior method exploited the tree structure for multi-level hierarchical locking; the second alternative for hierarchical locking in B-tree indexes ignores the tree structure and instead exploits the key structure for the same purpose. Consider, for example, a B-tree index for a multi-column compound key with columns (a, b, c, d) and with specific values (a_0, b_0, c_0, d_0). Any leading prefix such as (a_0, b_0) can serve as a resource that permits locking all index entries with keys starting with these specific values.

The promise of this method is that it matches precisely with query predicates, e.g., a query clause "where a = a_0 and b = b_0." More complex predicates map to only a few very precise locks. For example, a query with the clause "where a in (a_0, a_1, a_2) and b in (b_0, b_1, b_2, b_3)" requires only 12 locks, independent of the sizes of the table and its index. Thus, locking key prefixes may be competitive with predicate locking and precision locking but without any need for predicate evaluation for concurrency control.

At the same time, this method promises efficient locking for single-row updates, because it is possible to lock a single B-tree entry (recall that all B-tree entries are unique in order to permit accurate deletion and maintenance). Thus, hierarchical locking based on key prefixes promises to match very well with both queries and updates in both transaction processing and data warehousing.

Locking key prefixes matches so well with query predicates because it is, in fact, a special form of predicate locking. Thus, arguments and proofs for the correctness of locking key prefixes rely on established techniques for predicate locks [Eswaran et al., 1976].

2.6.1 TECHNIQUES

A lock on a specific value, say the two-column prefix (a_0, b_0), covers all B-tree keys starting with these values. In order to prevent phantom records in serializable transaction isolation, however, non-existent key values also need locking. In order to solve this problem, locks can cover only a specific prefix, the gap between two actual prefix values, or both. As in traditional key range locking in leaf pages, this can be modeled using an additional level in the locking hierarchy, e.g., those shown in Figure 2.2. For a smaller number of lock manager invocations, the actual implementation may use the artificial lock modes and their compatibility matrix shown in Figure 2.3.

Existence of specific key values in a B-tree can be decided only after a B-tree search has found the right index leaf. Thus, key locking starts only after the navigation from the B-tree root to the leaf. As discussed earlier, this navigation is protected by latches, not locks, including the inspection of the current leaf contents.

2.6.1.1 Insertion and Deletion of Values

While exact-match lookup in a B-tree, e.g., during an index nested loops join, benefits from precise locking and thus from key prefixes, insertion and deletion of keys might require key range locking. Specifically, during insertion, if a key prefix needs to be locked, the lock mode depends on the existence of a prior B-tree entry with the same prefix value as the new record. If such a prior B-tree entry exists, a key value lock suffices. If no such entry exists, a range lock on the prior key is needed. Note that this lock only needs to cover the open interval between the two pre-existing actual prefix values; there is no need to lock either of these values.

The initial insertion can be a system transaction that only inserts a ghost record, leaving it to the user transaction to turn that ghost record into a valid record. While the system transaction requires a range lock, the user transaction needs to lock only the new key value, not the gap between keys. Thus, the key range is locked only very briefly.

While this description is very similar to the earlier discussion of key range locking of unique keys in B-tree leaves, it applies here to key ranges defined by key prefixes. For example, if a locked key prefix matches the definition of complex objects clustered in the B-tree by common key prefixes [Graefe, 2007], a new complex object can be in serted without ever locking its neighboring objects or their components.

Deletion follows a similar pattern. A user transaction might simply mark a B-tree entry a ghost, leaving it to a system transaction to erase the record from the B-tree, or a user transaction might immediately erase the record and the key. Erasing a record requires a lock on the record's key in exclusive mode, thus ensuring that no other transaction holds any kind of lock on it. Moreover, the gap between two neighboring keys must remain locked in order to ensure successful transaction rollback if required. Gaps must be locked at all levels in the hierarchy for which a distinct value disappears.

2.6.1.2 Lock Escalation and De-Escalation

Whereas insertion and deletion of values are required, lock escalation and de-escalation are optional, as are granularity changes to be discussed shortly.

While key insertion and deletion are slightly subtle, lock escalation and de-escalation are particularly simple in this design, for two reasons. First, the granularity of locking and the currently active components of the lock hierarchy are uniform across the entire index. Second, structural modifications such as page splits of the B-tree do not affect the set of locks required. Both reasons, of course, are based on the complete separation of physical B-tree structure and locking hierarchy.

The sequence of locking granularities can be defined in very general ways. For example, it is not required that each column in the key defines a lock granularity. Skipping a column might be advisable if the column has only very few distinct values. A column with an extremely large number of distinct values could conceivably be modeled using multiple lock levels, e.g., the first three digits in a zip code or in a social security number can be modeled as a separate level in the locking hierarchy by treating them as a column in their own right, even if only for the purposes of locking.

Given these considerations, lock escalation and de-escalation follow the fairly obvious pattern. For lock escalation, an intention lock is upgraded to an absolute lock for the appropriate short key prefix, and the prior absolute locks can be forgotten or retained for possible subsequent lock de-escalation. For de-escalation, appropriate information must be retained during the transaction's prior activities such that appropriate locks on longer prefixes can be inserted into the lock manager's hash table, and the absolute lock on the short prefix can be downgraded to an intention lock.

2.6.1.3 Granularity Changes

When locking separator keys in interior B-tree nodes, modifying the granularity of locking affects one node at a time. When locking key prefixes, the granularity of locking must be modified uniformly for the entire index. Thus, changes in the granularity of locking affect the entire B-tree, even for very large indexes.

With this exception, the procedure for changing the granularity of locking is quite similar for the two new strategies for hierarchical locking in B-tree indexes. When adding a new granularity of locking, both immediate and delayed methods can be designed.

In the delayed method, a system transaction locks all distinct key values at the new granularity of locking across an entire index. In contrast, hierarchical locking based on separator keys can modify the granularity of locking one B-tree node at a time.

Enumeration of all distinct values for a specific key prefix is a standard problem in relational query processing, e.g., for a query such as "select distinct a from ..." based on an index on columns (a, b). While standard solutions exist under various names, e.g., as multi-dimensional B-tree access [Leslie et al., 1995], the run-time expense seems impractical for adding a granularity of locking to a B-tree index.

The immediate method analyzes existing locks in order to acquire only those locks that are truly needed for specific active transactions. If hierarchical locking based on key prefixes is more precise than alternative locking methods and thus there are fewer locks to consider, this analysis can be faster than in hierarchical locking based on separator keys. An important difference, however, is that granularity changes apply to locking on separator keys one node at a time, whereas they apply to locking key prefixes for an entire index all at once.

Therefore, the delayed method does not seem promising for hierarchical locking based on key prefixes, and only the immediate method seems feasible, albeit not very practical. This is in contrast to hierarchical locking of separator keys, where both methods seem practical and appropriate in different circumstances.

Removal of an existing granularity of locking needs to wait for the release of all absolute locks at that granularity. A possible implementation technique is to wait for an IX lock competing with each such absolute lock held by a user transaction. Identifying all such locks requires search either in the lock manager's hash table or in the index.

To summarize, while it is possible to adjust the granularity of locking when locking key prefixes and when locking separator keys, the implementation mechanisms and tradeoffs are quite different. Whereas locking separator keys only on demand and only during demand appears to be a promising approach, a similarly promising approach is not apparent for locking key prefixes.

2.6.2   ADVANTAGES

Hierarchical locking of key prefixes has several very attractive characteristics. All of them reflect the match between query predicates and key prefixes. One overall advantage is that all of these characteristics are achieved with a single mechanism. This mechanism permits locking large ranges or individual B-tree records, and thus supports equally well decision support, transaction processing, and applications with similar access patterns.

First, this design matches well with equality predicates and "in" predicates, which are very common both in single-table selections and in joins. A single lock can often cover precisely the index entries needed, such that consistency and serializability among such a set of index entries are guaranteed, even in transaction isolation levels weaker than strict serializability. This aspect makes the locking strategy ideal for non-unique indexes including indexes on foreign key columns. If the leading key column is not specified and multiple index probes are required [Leslie et al., 1995], a single lock per probe will suffice.

Second, if master-detail clustering is supported based on equality of search columns in a B-tree [Graefe, 2007], locking key prefixes permits locking complex objects. For example, if orders and order details are co-located within a B-tree index based on equal values in the common column of order numbers, locking an order number locks an entire order object and all its component records. A single lock can also cover a large object, e.g., a customer with multiple orders, shipments, invoices, and payments. Insertion and deletion of one complex object does not require any lock on its neighbors.

Finally, locking key prefixes is a good match for partitioned B-trees [Graefe, 2003b], i.e., B-trees with an artificial leading key column that indicates partitions in indexes and run numbers during sorting. The first granularity of locking is the partition identifier, which permits efficient operations on partitions such as merging partitions, creating a partition during data import, or dropping a partition while purging data from a data warehouse.

2.6.3   DISADVANTAGES

This approach to hierarchical locking in B-tree indexes also has some disadvantages. Their common theme is the difficulty to set good defaults for the granularity of locking.

First, there is the danger of needing thousands of individual locks for thousands of distinct values, e.g., in index nested loops join or other forms of nested iteration. Thus, this locking strategy seems practical only if lock escalation is supported. Even then, a leading column with millions of unique values may be troublesome without dynamic changes in the hierarchy of locks.

Second (and amplifying the first point), the number of unique values may not be known due to old statistics or due to a missing range predicate on the leading index column. The number of unique values may be surprisingly large, leading to many individual locks. It may also be surprisingly small, leading to coarse locks that might restrict concurrency more than anticipated or desired.

Third, the effect of data skew are unclear, yet skew seems ubiquitous in real data.

Finally, there does not seem to be an opportunity to adjust the locking strategy locally to match any skew in the actual data values or in the workload. In order to achieve local adjustments in the granularity of locking similar to those described for key range locking on separator keys, an additional control table is needed that indicates which specific key prefixes should be locked with a granularity different than the default. Introduction of a control table for concurrency control seems like an unacceptable increase in the complexity of implementation, testing, maintenance, tuning, user education, and post-deployment vendor support.

2.6.4   OPPORTUNITIES

Some of the disadvantages above could possibly be addressed by locking not only prefix columns but parts thereof. For example, if a column is a four-byte integer, each individual byte could be interpreted as a column of its own for the purpose of locking. This idea is reminiscent of bit-sliced indexes [O'Neil and Quass, 1997] and, like those, can interact beneficially with range predicates.

This idea might alleviate the problem of key columns with a very large number of unique values, but it does not address data skew. Keys could be compressed, however, e.g., using order-preserving Huffman coding, in order to maximize the entropy of each stored bit. In that case, data skew might be less of a problem, although skew in the access pattern remains an unsolved issue.

Another opportunity based on disassembling a column is to apply hierarchical locking based on key prefixes not only to indexes but also to heap files. Specifically, components of a record identifier including file identifier, page identifier, slot number, and their individual bytes are treated as if they were individual columns in a compound B-tree index. Locks may cover predefined static ranges or dynamic ranges. In the former case, even ranges as yet unused require locks, i.e., files and pages ranges with no pages yet allocated for the relevant heap. In the latter case, the information about actual ranges covered by each lock would need to be inferred from the data structures used for space allocation. While very preliminary, this might be the first proposal for scalable hierarchical locking in heaps.

2.6.5 SUMMARY

Hierarchical locking based on key prefixes is promising because locks match query predicates as well as complex objects in master-detail clustering. Insertion and deletion of unique values can benefit from the lock modes of Figure 2.3. Lock escalation and de-escalation can readily be supported. Adjusting the granularity of locking is not particularly complex if it is applied uniformly to an entire index, which unfortunately seems expensive and thus impractical. Nonetheless, if adjusting the granularity is not required and if lock escalation and de-escalation are sufficient dynamic mechanisms, locking key prefixes seems a viable alternative or complement to other locking strategies.

2.7 SUMMARY AND CONCLUSIONS

Traditional hierarchical locking is starting to fail for very large indexes—the stepping from a single page to an entire index is too large. The dilemma between locking an entire index and locking millions of individual pages or keys demands a resolution.

The two alternative solutions introduced in this research have their distinct advantages and disadvantages when compared with the traditional design or with each other. Both new designs scale more gracefully than the traditional design due to their intermediate incremental stepping between index lock and page or key lock.

Key range locking in interior B-tree nodes scales with additional B-tree levels and adapts to skewed or unpredictable key distributions. The additional stepping levels between index and key eliminate the dilemma between massive overhead due to many individual locks and massive contention due to a single index lock. Moreover, splitting pages at keys that minimize the size of truncated separator keys [Bayer and Unterauer, 1977] matches key ranges in parent and grandparent nodes to clusters of records and complex objects.

Locking prefix values of search keys more obviously matches query predicates and complex objects in masterdetail clustering, in many cases comparably with predicate locks and precision locks. However, it suffers in cases of very few or very many distinct values and in cases of data skew. Moreover, it does not permit efficient local adjustment of the granularity of locking. Thus, key range locking in parent and grandparent nodes is more practical as a general solution than locking prefix values of search keys.

In addition, this research is the first to consider dynamic changes in the lock hierarchy in response to skew in the data or in the workload, and to propose specific algorithms for doing so. In fact, these algorithms are online and incremental such that they minimize disruption to ongoing transaction processing.

These dynamic changes can be exploited in the many ways. For example, to maximize performance and scalability of transaction processing, only keys in leaf nodes are locked by default, with overhead, performance, and scalability comparable to traditional key value locking. If an actual transaction would benefit from a larger granularity of locking, e.g., locking the key range of an entire leaf page, key range locking can be introduced specifically in those parents and grandparents that benefit an actual transaction. When no longer advantageous, that granularity of locking can be abandoned to maximize transaction processing performance again.

For some applications and their indexes, the ideal locking strategy might be a combination of these techniques. Multi-granularity locking permits each element to participate in multiple hierarchies. For example, some readers may lock only keys and key ranges based on leaf records and separator keys, while other readers lock key prefixes. This is permissible if writers acquire appropriate locks in all hierarchies. Such locking strategies might be particularly useful in real-time data warehousing with concurrency among large queries and small incremental "trickle" updates, as well as in partitioned B-trees and their use cases [Graefe, 2003b]. Even other hierarchies not considered in this research might be included, e.g., key ranges based on key ranges with fixed boundary values [Lomet, 1993] or even multi-dimensional ranges in temporal or spatial data and applications.

Finally, this research simplifies and improves key range locking. The presented proposal simply applies the traditional sound theory for hierarchical locking to keys, gaps between keys, and the combination of key and gap. It avoids unconventional lock modes that violate traditional two-phase locking and traditional hierarchical locking. The new lock modes in Figure 2.3 are performance techniques with no new semantics. They ensure the same number of lock manager invocations as used in traditional key range locking. For high concurrency during both key insertions and removals, the proposed design employs system transactions. These transactions can use ordinary lock modes and lock retention to transaction commit. In combination, these techniques simplify key range locking without introducing new overhead. Equally important, they correctly admit more concurrency than traditional key range locking and may thus be useful in all database management systems.

ACKNOWLEDGEMENTS

Jim Gray has been very helpful and encouraging. Phil Bernstein, Barb Peters, and the reviewers contributed helpful suggestions that improved the presentation of the material.

2.8   REFERENCES

Antoshenkov, G., Lomet, D. B., and Murray, J. (1996). Order preserving compression. *ICDE*, pp. 655–663. DOI: 10.1109/icde.1996.492216. 51

Bayer, R. and Unterauer, K. (1977). Prefix B-trees. *ACM TODS*, 2(1), pp. 11–26. DOI: 10.1145/320521.320530. 49, 51, 53, 63, 70

Bhattacharjee, B., Padmanabhan, S., Malkemus, T., Lai, T., Cranston, L., and Huras, M. (2003). Efficient query processing for multi-dimensionally clustered tables in DB2. *VLDB*, pp. 963–974. DOI: 10.1016/b978-012722442-8/50090-2. 51

Blasgen, M. and Gray, J. (2006). Personal communication, March. 48

Bontempo, C. J. and Saracco, C. M. (1977). *Database Management: Principles and Products*, Prentice Hall. 48

Carey, M. J. (1983). Granularity hierarchies in concurrency control. *PODS*, pp. 156–165. DOI: 10.1145/588058.588079. 47

Carey, M. J., DeWitt, D. J., Richardson, J. E., and Shekita, E. J. (1989). Storage management in EXODUS. *Object-Oriented Concepts, Databases, and Applications*, pp. 341–369. 51

Eswaran, K. P., Gray, J., Lorie, R. A., Traiger, I. L. (1976). The notions of consistency and predicate locks in a database system. *Communications of the ACM*, 19(11), pp. 624-633. DOI: 10.1145/360363.360369. 47, 58, 65

Gottemukkala, V. and Lehman, T. J. (1992). Locking and latching in a memory-resident database system. *VLDB*, pp. 533–544. 52

Graefe, G. (2003a). Executing nested queries. *BTW Conference*, pp. 58–77.

Graefe, G. (2003b). Sorting and indexing with partitioned B-trees. *CIDR*. 68, 70

Graefe, G. (2004). Write-optimized B-trees. *VLDB*, pp. 672–683. DOI: 10.1016/b978-012088469-8/50060-7. 53, 59, 64

Graefe, G. (2007). Algorithms for merged indexes. *BTW Conference.* 57, 65, 68

Graefe, G. and Zwilling, M. J. (2004). Transaction support for indexed views. *SIGMOD*, pp. 323–334 (Chapter 3). DOI: 10.1145/1007568.1007606. 55, 56

Gray, J. (1978). Notes on data base operating systems. *Advanced Course: Operating Systems*, pp. 393–481. DOI: 10.1007/3-540-08755-9_9. 52

Gray, J. (2006). Personal communication. March. 48

Gray, J., Lorie, R. A., Putzolu, G. R., and Traiger, I. L. (1975). Granularity of locks in a large shared data base. *VLDB*, pp. 428–451. DOI: 10.1145/1282480.1282513. 47, 48, 53, 55, 56

Gray, J., Lorie, R. A., Putzolu, G. R., and Traiger, I. L. (1976). Granularity of locks and degrees of consistency in a shared data base. *IFIP Working Conference on Modelling in Data Base Management Systems*, pp. 365–394. 53

Gray, J. and Reuter, A. (1993). *Transaction Processing: Concepts and Techniques*, Morgan Kaufman 1993. 48, 50, 52, 55, 59

Jordan, J. R., Banerjee, J., and Batman, R. B. (1981). Precision locks. *SIGMOD*, pp. 143–147. DOI: 10.1145/582338.582340. 47

Joshi, A. M. (1991). Adaptive locking strategies in a multi-node data sharing environment. *VLDB*, pp. 181–191. 51

Korth, H. F. (1983). Locking primitives in a database system. *Journal of the ACM*, 30(1), pp. 55–79. DOI: 10.1145/322358.322363. 50, 53, 55, 56

Leslie, H., Jain, R., Birdsall, D., and Yaghmai, H. (1995). Efficient search of multi-dimensional B-trees. *VLDB*, pp. 710–719. 67, 68

Lomet, D. B. (1993). Key range locking strategies for improved concurrency. *VLDB*, pp. 655–664. 49, 53, 54, 55, 56, 70

Lomet, D. B. and Salzberg, B. (1997). Concurrency and recovery for index trees. *VLDB Journal*, 6(3), pp. 224–240. DOI: 10.1007/s007780050042. 59

Microsoft MSDN on SQL server key-range locking. `http://msdn2.microsoft.com/en-us/library/ms191272.aspx` 49, 55, 56

Mohan, C. (1990). ARIES/KVL: A key-value locking method for concurrency control of multiaction transactions operating on B-tree indexes. *VLDB*, p. 392. 48, 49, 55, 56

Mohan, C., Haderle, D. J., Lindsay, B. G., Pirahesh, H., and Schwarz, P. M. (1992). ARIES: A transaction recovery method supporting fine-granularity locking and partial rollbacks using write-ahead logging. *ACM TODS*, 17(1), pp. 94–162. DOI: 10.1145/128765.128770. 52

Mohan, C. and Levine, F. (1992). ARIES/IM: An efficient and high concurrency index management method using write-ahead logging. *SIGMOD*, pp. 371–380. DOI: 10.1145/130283.130338. 48, 49

O'Neil, P. E. (1986). The escrow transactional method. *ACM TODS*, 11(4), pp. 405–430. DOI: 10.1145/7239.7265. 55

O'Neil, P. E. and Quass, D. (1997). Improved query performance with variant indexes. *SIGMOD*, pp. 38–49. DOI: 10.1145/253260.253268. 69

Padmanabhan, S., Bhattacharjee, B., Malkemus, T., Cranston, L., and Huras, M. (2003). Multi-dimensional clustering: A new data layout scheme in DB2. *SIGMOD*, pp. 637–641. DOI: 10.1145/872757.872835. 51

Saracco, C. M. and Bontempo, C. J. (1997). Getting a lock on integrity and concurrency. *Database Programming and Design.* 48

Srivastava, J. and Lum, V. (1988). A tree based access method (TBSAM) for fast processing of aggregate queries. *ICDE*, pp. 504–510. DOI: 10.1109/icde.1988.105497. 51

CHAPTER 3

Concurrent Queries and Updates in Summary Views and Their Indexes

Goetz Graefe

ABSTRACT

Materialized views have become a standard technique in decision support databases and for a variety of monitoring purposes.[1] In order to avoid inconsistencies and thus unpredictable query results, materialized views and their indexes should be maintained immediately within user transactions just like ordinary tables and their indexes. Unfortunately, the smaller and thus the more effective a materialized view is, the higher the concurrency contention between queries and updates as well as among concurrent updates. Therefore, we have investigated methods that reduce contention without forcing users to sacrifice serializability and thus predictable application semantics. These methods extend escrow locking with snapshot transactions, multi-version concurrency control, multi-granularity (hierarchical) locking, key range locking, and system transactions, i.e., with multiple proven database implementation techniques. The complete design eliminates all contention between pure read transactions and pure update transactions as well as contention among pure update transactions; it enables maximal concurrency of mixed read-write transactions with other transactions; it supports bulk operations such as data import and online index creation; it provides recovery for transaction, media, and system failures; and it can participate in coordinated commit processing, e.g., in two-phase commit.

3.1 INTRODUCTION

Timely business decisions depend on rapid information propagation from business operations to summary views for decision support. For example, productivity gains through inventory reduc-

---

[1]A shorter report on this research appears in Proc. ACM SIGMOD Conf. 2004. Beyond more related work, details, and examples, the present chapter adds coverage of save points and partial rollback (including release of recently acquired or upgraded locks), lock escalation and de-escalation (including their treatment during partial rollback), two-phase commit (in local and distributed systems), and commit processing for optimistic concurrency control (which turns out to be similar to commit processing with escrow locks and virtual log records).

tion depend on just-in-time supply chain management and thus require that e-commerce orders be summarized quickly for business analytics applications. In the ideal case, a single database management system is used for both business operations and decision support, and material-ized views and their indexes summarizing customer orders are maintained immediately as user transactions update base tables and their indexes.

Consider, for example, the *lineitem* table in the well-known TPC-H database [TPC, 1988]. Among others columns, this table includes *orderno*, *lineno*, *partno*, *commitdate*, and *ship-date*, as illustrated in Figure 3.1 with some example values. Assume that a business using such a table wishes to monitor or audit its current and recent adherence to shipping deadlines and thus defines the view *select commitdate, shipdate, count (*) as shipments from lineitem where shipdate > '2000-01-01' group by commitdate, shipdate*, as illustrated in Figure 3.2 using some example val-ues. For efficiency of both queries and updates, this view might be materialized and a clustered B-tree index may be constructed for the view with the grouping columns as search key, i.e., *com-mitdate, shipdate*, and all other columns as payload, i.e., *shipments*. While the main table might contain 100,000,000 rows, the materialized summary view might contain only 10,000 rows; and while insertions and updates in the table might affect different rows such that traditional lock-ing is entirely adequate, most of the update activity in the view is focused on only a few rows.

Order No	Line No	...	Part No	Commit Date	Ship Date
4922	...	...	...	2003-11-29	2003-11-27
4922	...	...	...	2003-11-29	2003-11-27
4939	...	...	...	2003-11-29	2003-11-27
4956	...	...	...	2003-12-31	2003-12-28
4961	...	...	...	2003-12-31	2003-12-29

Figure 3.1: Fact table with detail rows.

Commit Date	Ship Date	Shipments
2003-11-29	2003-11-27	3
2003-12-31	2003-12-28	1
2003-12-31	2003-12-29	1

Figure 3.2: Materialized summary view.

Moreover, in the assumed business scenario as in any real-time monitoring cases, much of the query activity also focuses on the part of the view that includes the rows with the most updates.

3.1.1   SERIALIZABLE VIEW MAINTENANCE

A premise of our research is that indexes should improve performance but should not alter the semantics of queries and updates. Thus, we believe that all indexes should be maintained immediately as part of user transactions, such that there is never a possibility that a transaction or query has different semantics depending on the query optimizer's plan choices. Even if some users and some businesses are willing and able to accept query results that are somewhat out-of-date, i.e., accept asynchronous maintenance of materialized views, a general-purpose database management system should at least offer instant maintenance of views. This is contrary to designs that only support deferred view maintenance and thus force the user or application developer to trade off high performance against stale or even inconsistent data. Strict serializability of concurrent transactions provides users and businesses by far the most predictable application semantics, and we therefore believe that database management systems should provide efficient and correct implementations of serializable queries and updates for indexed views.

If maintenance of materialized views is deferred, i.e., materialized views are permitted to "fall behind" the base tables and are brought up-to-date only at convenient times, e.g., during nights or other periods of low system activity, it might seem that the techniques presented here are not required. However, if there is any activity at all against those views, concurrency and consistency must be considered. Such activity can result from sporadic queries due to around-the-clock or around-the-world operations, or it can result from concurrent updates because view maintenance is split into multiple concurrent batches. In all those cases, the techniques described in the present research can guarantee serializability, consistency, and high concurrency.

In fact, unless materialized views and their indexes are maintained immediately as part of user transactions, their existence can alter the semantics of queries and thus applications. For example, assume a view is indexed in support of some important, frequent query, and that a second query also happens to use this view, but with only moderate gain. After some updates, an automatic utility refreshes histograms and other statistics, whereupon the query optimizer recompiles the second query into a plan that does not employ the materialized view. The question now is: Did the automatic statistics refresh modify the transaction semantics and affect the query results? If the indexes on the materialized view are maintained immediately just like indexes on traditional tables, the answer is "no," and indexes on materialized views are purely a choice in physical database design just like traditional indexes on tables. On the other hand, if maintenance of materialized views is deferred or delegated to future maintenance transactions, the answer is "yes," since the query optimizer's choice affects which data are produced as query result.

If the view is joined with a table that is maintained immediately by all user transactions, even inconsistent query results are easily possible. For example, consider a query that lists orders for which the committed ship date was missed (comparing the *commitdate* and *shipdate* columns in the example table), specifically those orders that were the only ones for a specific ship date. The specific restriction is computed most efficiently using the materialized view; however, if the view is out-of-date, incorrect query results may be presented to the monitoring or auditing application.

Traditional concurrency control methods use shared and exclusive locks on tables, indexes, pages, records, and keys. For any locked data item, these lock modes limit update activity to a single update transaction at a time, which can be too restrictive for indexed views. Escrow locks and other commutative "increment" locks permit multiple concurrent update transactions to lock and modify a single data item, but they have their own restrictions. First, modification operations must be commutative with each other; fortunately, most summary views rely on counts and sums that can be incremented and decremented with commutative operations. Second, since multiple concurrent uncommitted updates imply that there is no single definitive current value, escrow locks are incompatible with share locks and therefore with read transactions, thus defeating the benefit of materialized views for monitoring ongoing operations.

3.1.2   CONTRIBUTIONS

Mechanisms for concurrency control and recovery in summary views and their indexes are the primary subject of this chapter. Prior research on materialized views has focused on choosing the views most desirable to materialize, on incremental maintenance of such views, and on query optimization exploiting materialized views. The present research is the first to focus on concurrency control and recovery for materialized and indexed views. Thus, it complements prior research on materialized views.

A second subject is integration of concurrency control and recovery with the entire operation of a database management system, e.g., multi-granularity locking, lock escalation and de-escalation, transaction save points, distributed two-phase commit, and online index creation of materialized views. The latter cover not only creating an index for a view that is already materialized but specifically creating the view's initial materialization and thus its first index while permitting concurrent update transactions against the tables over which the view is defined.

In a side note, we also explore parallels between commit processing in optimistic concurrency control and commit processing with delayed transaction steps, e.g., in IBM's IMS/FastPath product, in difficult-to-reverse traditional index operations such as a drop operation, and in our design for concurrent updates of materialized and indexed views.

Since the proposed design originated in a product development organization, its goals are completeness of coverage, exploiting and complementing existing transaction implementation methods, and simplicity and robustness to the extent possible. It is this reliance on existing techniques that leads us to believe in the correctness and performance of the proposed methods. A complete analysis and sound proof of all aspects of this design seem an unrealistic undertaking.

To the best of our knowledge, our design is the first to address concurrent high read traffic and high update traffic over the same summary rows, to combine concurrent updates permitted by escrow locking and the linear history required for multi-version concurrency control and snapshot isolation, to consider multi-granularity escrow locks as well as concurrent small and large increment transactions using escrow locks, to integrate escrow locking with two-phase commit as well as save points and partial rollback with lock release, or to address concurrent update operations while a view is initially materialized and indexed, i.e., online materialization and index creation for summary views.

3.1.3 OVERVIEW

Building upon a wealth of existing research and experience, the design presented here fundamentally relies on four techniques, three of which are adaptations and extensions of existing research whereas the last one is a new idea that unifies multiple prior techniques. The contribution of our research effort is to combine these techniques into a coherent whole that enables concurrent execution and commit processing for small and large read and update transactions.

The first technique we adapted is to run pure read transactions in snapshot isolation, i.e., their commit point is their start time or logically their position in an equivalent serial transaction schedule. Moreover, we describe a novel design that combines concurrent update transactions with multi-version snapshot isolation, which in its traditional form supports only linear histories with only one update transaction at a time (for each data item).

Second, counts and sums in indexed views are maintained within user transactions using extensions of escrow locks, e.g., multi-granularity (hierarchical) escrow locking. Our extensions support not only small update transactions but also large operations such as bulk import and index creation, both with concurrent small update transactions using escrow locks.

Third, system transactions are employed not only to erase pseudo-deleted or "ghost" records but also to create such records that can then be maintained by user transactions using ordinary increment and decrement operations protected by escrow locks. This implementation technique ensures maximal concurrency when new summary rows are created in materialized views and their indexes.

The fourth component of our design requires that all stored records include a delta count, which unifies the roles of the count of duplicate rows, the size of the group, ghost bit, and anti-matter bit (explained later). Traditional ghost bit and anti-matter bit are no longer required, and an implicit predicate on the delta count in any query supplants today's implicit predicate on the ghost bit. The value of this unification will become apparent later, in particular in the section on online index operations.

After reviewing the wealth of prior research, we consider readers and updaters, multiple updaters, logging and recovery, multi-granularity locking, creation and removal of summary rows, and finally online index creation. We end with arguments about correctness and performance as well as a summary and our conclusions from this research.

3.2   PRIOR WORK

Our research is based on many prior research and development efforts, which we survey now in some depth because our design is primarily a novel combination of those existing techniques. No system has integrated all of them to-date. While some of these techniques might seem unrelated to each other or even to the topic at hand, they all contribute to the design. Knowledgeable readers may prefer to skip this section or refer to specific topics only as needed during later sections.

3.2.1   DELTAS FOR MATERIALIZED VIEWS

Multiple research efforts have focused on deriving the minimal delta needed for incremental maintenance of materialized views, e.g., [Blakeley et al., 1986a], and [Gupta and Mumick, 1999]. While important, those techniques are not reviewed here because they are complementary and orthogonal to our research, which focuses on transaction techniques such as locking and logging while applying such deltas to indexes on materialized views.

We also do not concern ourselves here with concurrency control needs during computation of the delta, e.g., reading additional tables while computing the delta for a join view. Concurrent updates of multiple tables contributing to the same join view may lead to contention in traditional locking system. Some of that contention may be mitigated by multi-version concurrency control, which is discussed below.

3.2.2   CONCURRENCY CONTROL FOR MATERIALIZED VIEWS

Other research also started with the importance of serializability of tables and materialized views, but assumed that instant maintenance imposes unacceptable overhead on update transactions, and then derived theories for detecting inconsistencies as part of read operations and resolving them using a postulated operation that brings a single row in the summary view up-to-date [Kawaguchi et al., 1997]. In contrast, we assume that indexes on views are maintained as part of user update transactions just like indexes on ordinary tables.

Instead of locking rows, records, key ranges, and keys in materialized views and their indexes, it is possible to always lock the underlying tables, their rows and their indexes, even if the chosen query execution plan does not employ them at all [Luo et al., 2005]. The advantage of this approach is that no special lock modes are needed; in fact, no locks are needed at all for the views and their rows. The disadvantage, however, is that a single row in a materialized view might derive from tens, hundreds, or thousands of rows in an underlying table, forcing a choice to either acquire that many individual row locks or lock that table in its entirety.

We are aware of only one prior effort that specifically focuses on the same problems as our research. This prior design [Luo et al., 2003] employs special V and W locks that are, in a first approximation, equivalent to escrow locks and to short-term exclusive locks. In fact, the W locks and their duration are similar to our design choice of running system transactions that create ghost records, including their key-range locking behavior. In a follow-on publication [Luo et al., 2005], the same authors introduce multi-granularity or intention locks (IV locks) and replace the W locks with latches, i.e., short-term concurrency control mechanisms that do not participate in deadlock detection and thus impose other restrictions. In the specific design, these latches are allocated in a fixed-size pool, with each individual key value mapped to a specific latch using a hash function; in other words, these latches are somewhat detached from the views being updated. The authors argue that the appropriate size of the lock pool depends on the number of concurrent updates rather than their size or the size of the views. Transaction rollback is not discussed, e.g., whether transaction rollback erases records created under the protection of such a latch or what happens if another transaction has acquired a V lock on such a row right after it had been created.

For small update transactions, the performance effects reported in Luo et al. [2003, 2005] and the design here are quite comparable, primarily because V locks and our E locks are very similar. The main difference in the two designs is that our design integrates concurrency control for materialized views with write-ahead logging and recovery as well as with multi-version snapshot isolation, transaction save points, partial rollback, and two-phase commit; and that our design covers additional application scenarios including readers concurrent with writers as well as bulk load and online index operations for materialized views.

3.2.3   MULTI-LEVEL TRANSACTIONS AND ARIES

Prominent among the prior work are multi-level transactions [Weikum et al., 1990, Weikum and Schek, 1984] as well as the Aries family of techniques [Mohan et al., 1992], including appropriate logging and recovery techniques, e.g., Lomet [1992]. The essence of multi-level transaction *undo* is that a higher-level action can be compensated in multiple ways. In fact, it is often not even possible to undo the precise physical actions invoked during the original forward processing. For example, if inserting a new key into a B-tree requires inserting a new record into a specific leaf page, undoing the key insertion might remove a record from a different leaf page, since the original leaf page was split or merged between the initial insertion and its compensation during transaction rollback.

Another important characteristic of multi-level transactions and Aries is that *redo* and *undo* of higher-level actions are not necessarily idempotent. The logging and recovery protocol guarantees that a higher-level action is redone only if none of its effects are reflected in the database, and it is undone only if all of its effects are captured in the database. Lowest-level actions are undone or redone as in traditional recovery methods; higher-level actions rely on the fact that lower-level actions provide transaction semantics in their own right: higher-level actions are never redone (only the lowest-level actions are redone after a system restart), and they are undone by logical compensation.

When a transaction starts and invokes another transaction, that other transaction can commit its locks and its results either into the invoking transaction or to the system at large. The former case is a classic nested transaction. The latter case is called a "nested top-level action" in the Argus language [Liskov and Scheifler, 1982] and in Aries, and a "restructuring operation" elsewhere [Shasha, 1985]; we call it a "system transaction" because it is a transaction invoked by the system itself for its own purposes. A typical example splits or recombines a page within a B-tree index. For those transactions, special commit optimizations apply, as discussed later. Moreover, a system transaction can be lock-compatible with its invoking transaction, which usually does not resume processing the user transaction until the system transaction commits.

3.2.4   CONCURRENT UPDATE TECHNIQUES

The second very important foundation of our work is escrow locking [O'Neil, 1986]. As originally defined, escrow locks imply not only concurrent increment and decrement operations but also holding minimum values in escrow. However, we ignore this second aspect of escrow locks here and use the name generically for the family of locking schemes that exploit the commutativity of operations such as increment and decrement. Alternative commutative sets of actions could also be supported based on escrow locks, but incrementing and decrementing are the prototypical operations for escrow locking.

By definition, multiple concurrent, uncommitted update transactions imply that there is no single correct current value. Hence, an escrow lock does not permit reading the value or to set it to a specific value, and an escrow lock ("E" locks from now) implies neither a traditional "share" ("S") nor an "exclusive" ("X") lock. If a transaction holds an E lock on a data item and then needs to read the item, it must also acquire an S lock, which can only be granted after all other transactions have released their E locks and thus resolved all uncertainty about the correct current value.

Interestingly, the combination of S and E lock is practically equivalent to an X lock, not because it ensures the same privileges but because it has the same lock conflicts. Thus, we assume that the combination of S+E is not explicitly modeled; instead, E locks are upgraded to an X lock when read privileges are required in addition to increment privileges.

The original recovery scheme for escrow locks is quite complex, and multi-level transactions or Aries can be employed for a significantly simpler one [Mohan et al., 1992]. The essence of this simplification is that recovery actions need not be idempotent—specifically, in a multi-level recovery scheme, *undo* actions at higher levels are not necessarily idempotent in their effects at lower levels. Specifically, *undo* actions are invoked only for data items that reflect the effect of the original *do* action, and *redo* actions are invoked only for data items that do not. Thus, *undo* and *redo* actions are increment and decrement actions practically equal to the original *do* actions. Log records must carry increment values, not the *before* and *after* images well known from traditional exclusive locking that permits setting a specific value but restricts update activity to a single uncommitted transaction at a time.

Somewhat similar to escrow locks are the concurrency and recovery techniques of IBM's IMS/FastPath product [Gawlick and Kinkade, 1985]. During forward processing, conditions and increment operations are collected in an intention list associated with a transaction; during commit processing, the intention list is processed and values in the database are updated, using traditional after-image logging for durability and recovery. Commit processing for multiple transactions is serialized using the single latch synchronizing access to the recovery log. Careful optimization of the code path executed while holding the latch ensures that serial commit processing does not restrict overall system throughput [Gawlick, 2003].

Intention lists of deferred actions are often implemented but usually reserved for large destructive operations such as dropping an index or a table. For example, if an index is dropped within a multi-statement transaction, the actual structure is erased on disk only when the entire multi-statement transaction commits, because otherwise transaction rollback could be extremely expensive and might fail, e.g., due to lack of auxiliary disk space while reconstructing an index. Of course, transaction rollback must always be possible and succeed if attempted, or all transaction semantics are in jeopardy. It is not sufficient to deallocate the space allocated by the old index yet keep that space locked until transaction commit. For example, if an online index rebuild operation replaces one copy with a new one (which then has the proper on-disk layout, per-page free space, etc.), the old copy must remain accessible. In fact, it even must be maintained by concurrent update transactions, because otherwise the index would be out-of-date if the index builder aborts and rolls back.

The implementation of such deferred actions attaches an intention list (containing deferred actions) to each uncommitted transaction. Each such action is quite similar to a *redo* action, although there is no need to include such actions in the recovery log on stable storage. Instead, the recovery log on stable storage will document the actual physical actions performed while processing such "virtual" *redo* log records during commit processing, i.e., immediately before writing the transaction's commit record to stable storage, or before the pre-commit record in a distributed transaction.

An interesting aspect is that recovery in multi-level transactions traditionally relies on physical *redo* and logical *undo* (usually called "compensation"), whereas virtual log records employed for deferred actions represent a logical *redo* operation. Note that idempotent *redo* actions are not required, because virtual log records are used only when execution of the *do* action is omitted during ordinary forward processing and because virtual log records are never found in the recovery log on stable storage, i.e., they are never processed during possibly multiple restart attempts.

Alternative to the IMS/FastPath method, conditions can be verified immediately against the entire range of uncertainty of a data value [Reuter, 1982]. For example, if one uncommitted transaction has incremented a data item by 2 and another one has decremented it by 3, given an initial value of 10 the current range of uncertainty is 7 to 12. While it is possible to test a range of uncertainty against a condition, e.g., whether the value is greater than 5, it is not possible to read such a value, e.g., in order to display or print it.

3.2.5   SNAPSHOT ISOLATION AND MULTI-VERSION CONCURRENCY CONTROL

The third foundation for our work is the combination of snapshot isolation [Berenson et al., 1995] and multi-version concurrency control [Bernstein et al., 1987]. Together, they can reduce or eliminate concurrency problems between readers and writers. In a correct serializable transaction schedule, each transaction must "see" for each database item the value most recently committed in any equivalent serial schedule, and a transaction must not overwrite any value other than those that it is permitted to "see." A standard technique is to set the commit point (determining the position in an equivalent serial schedule) of a pure read transaction at the beginning of the transaction's execution and to set the commit point for update transactions to the end of the transaction's execution.

Thus, no matter how long a read transaction runs, the database management system must present a snapshot of the database as it existed at the transaction's start, even if subsequent updates may have overwritten some database items. Read transactions have no need for locks, since they only read committed data that cannot be changed by concurrent or subsequent update transactions. Note that if a read transaction and a write transaction run concurrently, the commit point of the read transaction necessarily precedes the commit point of the write transaction, and the two transactions cannot possibly conflict.

A limitation of this technique affects transactions that both read and write, because a transaction cannot have two commit points in a serial schedule or in a correct serializable schedule. A seemingly clever implementation is to run such a transaction as if it had two commit points, an early one for read actions and a late one for write actions, which of course violates the rules for well-formed transactions in serializable schedules and thus does not result in proper transaction isolation [Berenson et al., 1995].

There are multiple implementation alternatives for snapshot isolation. Without supporting multiple versions, queries must fail rather than read a database value that is "too new." If multiple versions are supported, since the main database reflects the most current state of the information stored in the database, earlier versions can either be retained or recreated on demand.

For the latter choice, i.e., recreating earlier version on demand, the recovery log is the main data source. The buffer pool must be designed to manage multiple versions of the same disk page, and an older version is derived from a newer one (the current one) by rolling back the page image [Bridge et al., 1997]. For efficient navigation within the recovery log, the standard backward chain (linked list) of log records per transaction is not useful, i.e., the traditional mechanism for transaction rollback. In addition, a recovery log may also embed a backward chain per page. In fact, the recovery logs in some commercial systems already do. Thus, it is possible to roll back a single page to an earlier point in time, assuming the transaction log has not been truncated to reclaim space on the log disk.

For the former choice, i.e., retaining earlier images of records or fields, some additional temporary space must be allocated. In a database management system using B-tree indexes, the free space in each B-tree node is a natural place to retain earlier records. Note that the average space utilization in B-tree pages is about 70%, i.e., there is about 30% free space, and that accessing a single record's earlier image within the same page seems less expensive than rolling back an entire page to an earlier time using the recovery log and an auxiliary buffer. If earlier record images must be retained for a long time due to long running queries, spill-over space must be provided. A possible design, in particular if long-running transactions are rare, is to employ node splits in the B-tree using standard mechanisms and code. Alternative designs are possible but might increase code complexity beyond the proposed scheme without improving overall system efficiency. Since multiple commercial database management systems already include support multiple versions, we do not discuss these tradeoffs further.

Interestingly, no data locks are required to prevent premature clean-up of data structures used to support multiple versions. If the system keeps track of the oldest running snapshot transaction, a simple decision suffices to decide whether any active read transaction is currently reading an old version or might need to do so in the future. This idea, its efficiency and its implementation, are quite similar to keeping track of the oldest active update transaction in the *Commit_LSN* method [Mohan, 1990], and have been employed in commercial database systems [Arun and Joshi, 1998].

3.2.6   DERIVED LOCK MODES

The fourth foundation is the derivation of auxiliary lock modes from primitive lock modes, including intention locks, combination locks, and upgrade ("U") locks. Intention locks ("IS," "IU," and "IX") enable multi-granularity or hierarchical locking, e.g., such that one transaction can lock a few individual records individually, another transaction can lock an entire file with all records with one large lock, yet conflicts are detected correctly and reliably. Combination locks bestow the privileges of multiple locks for a locked resource, e.g., an "S+IX" lock on a file provides a shared access to the entire file plus the right to obtain exclusive locks on pages or records within the file.

Upgrade locks reserve exclusive upgrade rights from one lock mode to another, i.e., convert from one lock mode to another one that encompasses the prior one. The upgrade component of the lock does not grant any data access privileges; thus, it can be relinquished prior to transaction completion if lock conversion turns out not to be required. "U" locks are often called "update" locks, because update processing often upgrades traditional "S" locks to "X" locks in order to prevent deadlocks among multiple transactions attempting to convert an "S" lock to an "X" lock [Gray, 1993]. The concept of upgrade locks is much broader, however. In his thesis, Korth developed a comprehensive theory of intention locks, combination locks, and upgrade locks as well as algorithms for designing sets of lock modes and their compatibility matrix [Korth, 1983].

3.2.7   LOCK ESCALATION AND DE-ESCALATION

An entirely different kind of lock upgrade is lock escalation, i.e., replacing a set of fine-granularity locks with a single coarse lock covering all of the original locks. For example, an existing IS lock is converted to an S lock and the S locks acquired at the finer granularity are subsumed by it. The primary reasons for lock escalation are lack of memory for the lock manager [Chang et al., 2002, 2005], excessive run-time overhead for lock acquisition at the finer level, and adaptation after an initial error in choosing the appropriate locking granularity, e.g., after a predicate's selectivity was estimated at 10% during query optimization but turned out to be 90% during query execution.

The opposite of lock escalation is lock de-escalation, e.g., from an S lock at a coarse granularity to an IS lock plus individual S locks at the next finer granularity. The primary reasons for lock de-escalation are errors in anticipated selectivity and unexpected contention for resources. If implemented well, it even seems reasonable to always attempt locking at a coarse granularity but to resort to a finer granularity in case of conflicts, either if lock acquisition fails or if another transaction requests a lock later on.

Lock de-escalation during initial lock acquisition is fairly simple to implement. For lock de-escalation during execution, i.e., after some data access, the needed finer-granularity locks must be recorded from the start [Joshi, 1991, Lehman, 1989]. The difference to locking immediately at the finer granularity is that the finer-granularity locks are guaranteed by the initial coarse-granularity lock. Thus, there is no need to record these locks in a shared lock manager; they can be recorded in threador transaction-private memory. Of course, during lock de-escalation, they must be propagated to the shared lock manager. However, these lock requests are guaranteed to succeed, because they cannot conflict with other transactions while the transaction still holds the initial coarse-granularity lock. In fact, due to fewer searches in the lock manager, recording fine-granularity locks and propagating them later can be faster than acquiring these fine-granularity locks individually [Gottemukkala and Lehman, 1992].

Even in private space, it might be a good idea to organize fine-granularity locks like the hash table in the shared lock manager, in order to avoid acquiring and recording the same detail lock twice. Moreover, it quite possibly simplifies merging these locks into the shared lock manager during lock de-escalation, and it enables in private memory precisely the same operations as are needed in shared memory for efficient lock management, e.g., during rollback to transaction save points.

As a side note, it might be interesting in some cases to perform lock escalation or de-escalation while a prepared transaction is waiting to learn the global transaction outcome. Such escalation and de-escalation are possible and correct, and may be worthwhile if lock contention changes due to other local transactions starting or ending. The essence of the preparation phase in two-phase commit is that the local transaction can abide by the global decision. Thus, the local transaction must retain sufficient locks to maintain that guarantee, but the granularity of locking may be modified at any time.

Similarly, if recovery after a system crash resumes transaction processing immediately after log analysis, i.e., during redo and undo (compensation) processing, then log analysis phase must obtain locks for all transactions that need recovery actions. If forward processing logs the acquisition of locks, lock acquisition during the log analysis pass may be guided by these log entries. Lock escalation and de-escalation during recovery can be employed to replace the locks chosen during pre-crash forward processing with locks more appropriate to the contention during post-crash recovery and concurrent transaction processing.

3.2.8 TRANSACTION SAVE POINTS

When a save point is requested by a user or an application, it is marked in the transaction's chain of locks and possibly in the transaction log. Rollback to a save point, also known as partial rollback of a transaction, means that all database changes since that time are undone or compensated [Kim et al., 1999]. Typical uses of transaction save points include interactive transactions in which a failed statement cleans up all its changes without aborting the entire transaction. Each individual statement execution starts with a new save point implicitly created by the system for the purpose of statement rollback.

An interesting aspect of transaction save points is that locks can be released during partial transaction rollback. Thus, another use case for partial rollback is deadlock resolution. For that to happen correctly and efficiently, the lock manager's data structures must support not only efficient insertion and search but also deletion as well as enumeration of a transaction's locks in the reverse order of lock acquisition.

While aborting a single statement rolls back only the most recent save point, locking and logging must support any sequence of forward processing and partial transaction rollback. Figure 3.3 illustrates a complex transaction. In the first run through the transaction logic, a short rollback to save point 2 is needed, perhaps to abort the current statement. A second attempt of the same logic succeeds, but later a rollback to save point 1 is requested, perhaps to resolve a deadlock with minimal effort for transaction rollback and retry. In third attempt, the entire transaction succeeds and commits. While probably not a typical or frequent case, the locking and logging logic must support complex cases such as this one.

If read locks are kept in a separate lock chain, additional concurrency during one transaction's partial rollback can be gained by releasing read locks immediately (e.g., "S" and "IS"), before rollback of any write locks and update operations. This is quite similar to releasing read locks early in ordinary commit processing and during two-phase commit. In addition, upgrade locks can be downgraded (e.g., "U" to "S") and often released early together with the read locks. For maximal concurrency, write locks can be released incrementally as the rollback progresses.

Lock upgrades are special, e.g., from S or U to X as well as from IS or IU to IX, in particular if initial acquisition and upgrade are separated by a save point. In that case, either lock release during rollback must exclude upgrades and may include only original lock acquisitions,

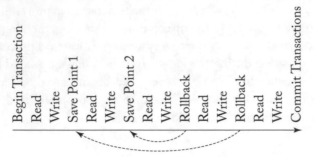

Figure 3.3: Complex partial rollbacks.

or initial lock acquisition and subsequent upgrade are represented as two separate data structures in the lock manager, even if these locks pertain to the same database resource.

Lock escalation, e.g., from an IS lock and multiple dependent S locks to a single S lock, can be rolled back quite readily, because this rollback actually releases locked access rights, namely those implied in the single large S lock but not included in the original small S locks. This assumes, of course, that appropriate detail information has been retained, i.e., the lock escalation was initiated in order to reduce the number of lock requests, not to reduce the amount of memory dedicated to locks and their data structures. Rolling back lock de-escalation, on the other hand, needs to re-acquire locks. If the original lock de-escalation happened upon demand, i.e., due to contention with a new lock request by a concurrent transaction, reacquiring these locks is likely to fail. Moreover, even if rollback succeeds, renewed lock de-escalation is likely to be needed or wanted again soon. Thus, attempting to roll back lock de-escalation may not be worth the effort. Note also that rollback must never fail in such a way that a transaction can go neither forward nor backward; thus, the implementation of rollback must not rely on rolling back lock de-escalation. Fortunately, correctness of transaction rollback and continuation of that transaction do not depend on rolling back escalation and de-escalation, because the database resources required for the transaction will remain locked whether or not such rollbacks succeed.

Incremental lock release applies not only to rollback to a save point but also to rollback of an entire transaction. In fact, rollback of an entire transaction can be modeled and implemented using an implicit save point at the start of every transaction, and thus both rollback situations can use the same code. Neither rollback of lock escalation and nor rollback of lock de-escalation seems worthwhile if the entire transaction is aborted.

3.2.9 LOCAL COMMIT PROCESSING

A transaction's commit point is defined by writing a commit record to the recovery log on stable storage. However, contrary to common belief, traditional shared and exclusive locks can be released prior to that point, and the same is desirable for high-performance transaction processing with materialized and indexed views.

Shared locks can be released immediately after user or application request the transaction commit, i.e., after the transaction reaches its "high point" in two-phase locking. "Precommit" [DeWitt et al., 1984] (not related to preparation or pre-commit in distributed transactions) permits release of write locks to other transactions as soon as commit record has been written to the log buffer, even before it is written to stable storage and before the transaction's durability is truly guaranteed. If a subsequent transaction immediately locks the same resources, that transaction requires only durability if its own commit record is in the log on stable storage, and sequential log writing implies that the first transaction's log record is written earlier or simultaneously. Only notification of user or application must be delayed until the commit record is safely on stable storage.

This sequence of commit activities is used in IBM's IMS/FastPath. IMS/FastPath employs *group commit* and *fast commit* [Gawlick and Kinkade, 1985]. The former attempts to always write full log pages rather than forcing the current log buffer to stable storage; the main mechanism is to introduce small delays with timeouts. The latter completes the commit process including lock release without flushing the log buffer containing the commit record. Correctness is ensured by delaying acknowledgement of the commit to the user (and thus delivery of the transactional durability promise) until the log buffer has indeed been written to stable storage. In other words, IMS/FastPath links user communication to the transaction log and its flush actions. This is quite similar to the link in traditional write-ahead logging between ordinary data pages in the I/O buffer and the transaction log. Both I/O buffer and communication buffer employ the same "high water mark" mechanism.

System transactions and their commit sequence are a special case of this optimization. All locks are released as soon as the transaction commit record is in the log buffer in memory. However, there is no user or application waiting for a notification; thus, there is no need to ever force the commit record to stable storage. Instead, a system transaction becomes durable only after the log buffer containing the transaction's commit record is written to stable storage, e.g., because commit processing forced a log write for a subsequent user transaction.

A system transaction may modify only the physical data representation but not any logical database contents, because its results remain in the database even if the user transaction rolls back. It must be impossible based on the result of an ordinary "select" query to discern whether such a system transaction actually happened. Therefore, users and applications have no need for durability, one of the four traditional ACID properties of transactions [Härder, 1983], so committing a system transaction does not require forcing buffered blocks of the recovery log to stable storage. Thus, committing a system transaction is substantially less expensive than committing an ordinary user transaction.

3.2.10 TWO-PHASE COMMIT

Two-phase commit is needed in many situations, as evidenced by many implementations and optimizations [Samaras et al., 1993]. In addition to distributed query processing, two-phase commit is needed if a single transaction spans multiple databases within a single database server or if a database employs multiple files each with its own transaction log. If two or more transactions logs are involved in a transaction, reliable commit processing requires two-phase commit or an even more advanced technique such as a three-phase commit [Skeen, 1981].

From an observer's point of view, the essence of a two-phase commit is that the commit-or-abort decision is centralized to a single location and a single point in time [Gray, 1993]. From a participant's point of view, the essence of a two-phase commit is the separation of preparation and final commit or abort. During the preparation phase, the participants have a last chance to veto global transaction commit; if they don't veto the commit, they subjugate the outcome of their local transaction to the global decision. Part of this promise is to protect the local transaction from any failure or abort. For example, such a transaction cannot be chosen as the victim in deadlock resolution. Interestingly, in addition to being the initiator, the user or the application also is an important participant that is often overlooked in discussions of commit coordination: in exchange for the user's right to abort as well as the user's promise to accept the transaction outcome whatever it may be, the transaction manager will attempt to commit the transaction as requested.

Write locks can only be released when the final transaction outcome is known and enforced within each participant, including both "X" and "IX" locks. Read locks, on the other hand, including both "S" and "IS" locks, can be released at the start of the preparation phase, without violation of two-phase locking [Gray, 1993]. As a corollary, read-only transaction participants do not need to participate in the second phase of the commit coordination. After receiving the initial request to prepare and vote on the outcome of the global transaction, nothing of the local read-only transaction remains, neither locks nor log records. Traditional "U" and "IU" locks can be downgraded to "S" and "IS," respectively. This relinquishes their implied exclusive permission to upgrade to an X or IX lock, which is no longer needed once the user or application requests transaction commit or abort. Thus, traditional U and IU locks can be released, too, during the preparation phase of two-phase commit.

3.2.11 MANAGING INDIVIDUAL RECORDS AND KEYS

Another important foundation of our research and of our design is found in the implementation mechanisms for key deletion under key-range locking [Lomet, 1992, Mohan, 1990]. When a key is deleted, a witness for the actual key value remains in the index, because this permits retaining the key-value lock until the end of the user transaction. This witness usually is the deleted record with its old search key intact and with a special invalidation marker in the record header. While this idea has been known and used for a long time, e.g., during the System R project [Blasgen, 2003] and in Aries [Mohan, 1990], we call this record a "ghost record" and its marker a "ghost bit." (The term "ghost" for logically deleted records seems to originate from Johnson and Shasha [1989], albeit in a somewhat different meaning.)

Turning a valid record into a "logically deleted" or "pseudo-deleted" or ghost record instead of erasing it immediately from its storage location simplifies not only lock management but also *undo* processing, e.g., because space allocation cannot fail during rollback. After locks have been released during commit processing, the ghost record may be left behind for clean-up by a subsequent transaction, either a future insertion or an asynchronous clean-up utility. If the original transaction does not erase the ghost record during commit processing, all queries and scans must implicitly ignore records marked as ghosts. Thus, the convenience of ghost records implies that all queries have an implied predicate on the "ghost bit" or other marker within each record.

Note that a ghost record remains a resource that can be locked until it is actually erased, and that it defines a key range for the purposes of key range locking. Note also that erasing a ghost record is contents-neutral, that this action therefore is another typical use of system transactions. This system transaction may be part of commit processing for the original transaction, of an asynchronous clean-up utility, or of a future insert transaction that needs to reclaim and reuse record space within the disk page.

3.2.12 ONLINE INDEX OPERATIONS

In addition to the ghost bit in each record header, some database implementations employ an "antimatter" bit during online index creation, i.e., when permitting updates in a table while an index is still being created. There are two basic designs for online index operations, called "side file" and "no side file" [Mohan and Narang, 1992]. The former design builds the new index without regard to concurrent update operations and applies those in a "catch-up" phase guided by a side file that describes the missed updates, typically the recovery log. The latter design requires that concurrent update operations be applied immediately to the index being built, even if the index builder itself is still sorting and thus has not yet inserted any data into the new index. If a concurrent update operation attempts to delete a key in the new index that does not yet exist there, it instead inserts a special marker ("anti-matter") that indicates to the index builder that a key must be suppressed.

Anti-matter is employed only within an index still being built, and all anti-matter is resolved by the index builder. Thus, no anti-matter remains when the index is complete, and no query or scan must ever encounter a record with anti-matter. Note that anti-matter can exist both in valid records and in ghost records due to multiple transactions in sequence deleting and inserting the same key while the index builder is still scanning and sorting. The semantics of the anti-matter bit are that the history of a given key in a given index began with a deletion. Note also that the traditional method using a single Boolean value (a bit) is not sufficient in indexes on views with a "group by" clause, where each record summarizes a group of rows and where multiple deletions might affect a non-existing row in the view.

3.2.13 DUPLICATE RECORDS AND KEYS

A seemingly unrelated seventh foundation are the well-known mechanisms for representing duplicate records in intermediate query results and in stored tables. Duplicates can be represented using multiple records or by a single record with a counter. The former representation is easier to produce as it is the natural output of projection execution, whereas the latter is often desirable for data compression as well as for table operations with multi-set semantics. For example, the SQL "intersect all" clause applied to two input tables with duplicate rows requires finding, for each distinct row, the minimum duplication count between the two input tables. Combinations of the two representations are also possible, i.e., multiple copies each with a counter. Converting from one representation to the other is trivial in one direction and in the other direction requires any one of the well-known algorithms for executing "group by" queries.

Duplicate counts are often used in materialized views and serve a function similar to reference counts in memory management. If the view definition includes a projection that renders the view result without a relational key, the duplicate counts assist in deciding when to remove a row from the view result. In fact, one approach to supporting materialized views in a commercial database management system is to require a key in the view result or a "group by" clause and a "count(*)" expression in the view result. The operation in the update plan maintaining the materialized view must delete the row when the duplicate count is decremented to zero.

Duplicate counts can also be employed in an intermediate result to represent the difference (the "delta stream") that must be applied to a materialized view. Figures 3.4–3.6 show intermediate results in an update execution plan that modifies both the table and the materialized view introduced in Figures 3.1 and 3.2. Figure 3.4 shows the delta stream for the *line item* table upon the request *update lineitem set shipdate = shipdate − 1 day where orderno in (4922, 4956, 4961)*. Moreover, we assume that records in the table are identified by record identifiers (RIDs), which permit fetching any column not included in the delta stream. Figure 3.5 captures the same change preprocessed for maintaining an index on *shipdate*. Large updates can be applied to B-tree indexes more efficiently if the changes are sorted in the index order. Note that value changes for indexed columns imply insertions and deletions in the index, shown as *action* column.

RID	Old Ship Date	New Ship Date
[14:2]	2003-12-27	2003-12-26
[14:3]	2003-12-27	2003-12-26
[15:6]	2003-12-28	2003-12-27
[16:9]	2003-12-29	2003-12-28

Figure 3.4: Delta stream for the details table.

Ship Date	RID	Action
2003-12-26	[14:2]	Insert
2003-12-26	[14:3]	Insert
2003-12-27	[14:2]	Delete
2003-12-27	[14:3]	Delete
2003-12-27	[15:6]	Insert
2003-12-28	[15:6]	Insert
2003-12-28	[16:9]	Insert
2003-12-29	[15:6]	Delete

Figure 3.5: Delta stream for an index on the details table.

3.2.14 INCREMENTAL VIEW MAINTENANCE

Figure 3.6 shows the delta stream for the materialized view and its index. Rows in the view are identified here by their relational key, which might also be the search key in the view's clustered index. A second optimization has the query processor collapse multiple updates to the same row in the materialized view such that the storage engine applies and logs only one update for each record in the view's index. Positive and negative counts represent insertions and deletions and thus generalize the *action* column of Figure 3.5. When multiple changes apply to the same row in the materialized view, positive and negative values are simply added up to a single value (the "delta count"). This applies not only to counts but also to sums. If all counts and sums are zero, insertions and deletions cancel each other out such that no change is required to the stored record in the indexed view. Note that all counts and all sums must be equal to be zero in a delta record; it is not sufficient if only the count is zero, as it is to determine whether a stored record is a ghost record.

Commit Date	Ship Date	Delta Count
2003-12-24	2003-12-27	−2
2003-12-24	2003-12-26	+ 2
2003-12-31	2003-12-27	+ 1
2003-12-31	2003-12-28	± 0
2003-12-31	2003-12-29	−1

Figure 3.6: Delta stream for an index on the view.

Among the standard aggregation functions, only *count*, *sum*, and *avg* can be maintained incrementally using the standard techniques for incremental view maintenance [Blakeley et al., 1986a,b], the last one as *sum/count*. Sums of squares, sums of products, etc., can also be maintained efficiently in order to support variance, standard deviation, covariance, correlation, regression, etc. *Min* and *max* can be maintained incrementally during insertions but not always during updates and deletions, because a new extreme value must be found when the old one is deleted, whereupon summary rows for the affected groups must be recomputed [Quass, 1996]. However, counts can be used to maintain reference counts for the current extreme value, thus ensuring that recomputation is triggered only when truly necessary. Thus, the design presented here applies not only to counts and sums but also in a limited way to indexed views with *min* and *max* expressions.

An alternative to instant maintenance is to mark affected summary rows in the materialized view as "out of date" without recalculating them, and to let queries invoke system transactions that apply all recent changes or recompute individual summary rows for groups marked "out of date." While possibly an interesting alternative, in particular for views with *min* and *max* expressions, we do not explore it here, instead focusing on techniques that incrementally keep all indexes on tables and views completely up-to-date at all times using serializable transactions.

3.2.15 EXPANDED "Group by" CLAUSES

Since escrow locking is not supported in most of today's database management systems, database administrators can work around lock contention among multiple update transactions by enlarging the view, e.g., augmenting the view definition such that multiple records together are equivalent to each summary row in the view of Figure 3.2. Each such record can be locked independently by the update transactions. Queries, however, pay the additional cost of summarizing results across all such records in order to derive a single row of Figure 3.2. Therefore, we consider these methods viable alternatives for database users to avoid contention, but they do not solve the contention problem to the same extent as our design does as described in the following sections.

In the example of Figure 3.2, assume that there is a small set of warehouses and each warehouse has only one process (no concurrent transactions) that set commit dates and ship dates. In that case, the "group by" clause in the view definition for Figure 3.2 can be expanded with a warehouse identifier, such that for each summary row in the unmodified view there is precisely one row for each warehouse in the modified view. Thus, updates can never interfere with each other or wait for record locks in the modified view. Of course, this work-around does not solve the problem of conflicting readers and updaters.

Alternatively, if all update transactions are small, i.e., affect only one or two rows in the base table and therefore only one or two summary rows, the additional grouping column does not have to be a realworld entity but can be the result of a randomizing function. Instead of a warehouse identifier, one could add "hash (OrderKey) % 10" to the view in Figure 3.2. In this case, each summary row in the unmodified view would be represented by up to 10 records, each update transaction would modify and lock typically only one of them, and queries would process them in order to produce the view of Figure 3.2. Unfortunately, this method works only for small update transactions that affect only a few orders; a bulk load operation that affects most summary rows in the original view will probably also affect most rows in the modified view, and thus block all small transactions that capture and summarize the on-going business activity.

Finally, one could invent syntax that directs each transaction to pick just one summary record at random and to increment only that summary row, e.g., "group by ..., rand() %10." Quite obviously, such syntax does not exist in SQL. In fact, such a language extension would violate the spirit of ANSI/ISO SQL, which is designed to be a language about data contents rather than its representation. Just as the SQL standards contain syntax for table definition but not for index creation, such syntax would inappropriately mix information semantics and storage tuning. Moreover, the number of expected concurrent update transactions should determine the number of records per summary row. Unfortunately, the number of concurrent transactions varies quickly and widely in most systems, whereas the modulo calculation above is part of the database schema design and thus fixed.

3.3 MULTI-VERSION SNAPSHOT ISOLATION

Combining and extending these prior techniques enables highly concurrent read and update operations on indexed views with aggregation. Focusing on the separation of readers and writers, let us now consider how pure read transactions and pure update transactions interact.

First, we consider whether running queries with a commit point equal to their start time is a reasonable and justifiable design decision. To do so, let us review whether a database server truly guarantees that query results reflect the most recent database state. The argument here covers multi-statement transactions processed in a single round-trip between client application and server. Interactive transactions with multiple user interactions as well as transactions including both queries and updates will be discussed later, since we believe they are the exception rather than the rule in monitoring applications.

After a query has been submitted to a database server as a single statement running as an implicit transaction, the server parses, compiles, and runs the actual query, and then assembles and sends network packets with result data. In traditional concurrency control schemes (assuming, as always in this chapter, serializability, which implies repeatable read), traditional share locks are held until query execution completes; thus, the commit point is at the end of plan execution.

A user submitting a query and interpreting its result cannot determine the duration of each phase within the entire interaction with the database server. For example, it might be that query execution takes 90% of the time or it might be that 90% of the time is spent returning result data from the database server to the user. Thus, even traditional concurrency control methods guarantee only that a query's commit point is after submission of the query to the server.

Setting a query's commit point consistently at the beginning of query execution provides precisely the same guarantees with respect to currency of the query's result data. Note that query compilation, including insertion of the optimized query plan into a plan cache shared by all users and all transactions, should be a system transaction that does not acquire locks for the user transaction and thus does not affect that transaction's commit point.

Figure 3.7 illustrates the point. A user cannot, except with special performance management tools, distinguish among the three schedules, i.e., determine the time spent in each of the phases. Thus, any execution that is equivalent to one of these schedules is viable and acceptable to a reasonable user. Compilation may be omitted if the database management system employs pre-compiled query evaluation plans, or it may be modeled as very brief because query start-up requires finding a precompiled plan and validating it against the current data, e.g., using a schema version number. Computation might also be very brief if indexed views are readily available, possibly even in the buffer pool such that no physical I/O is required. Our model for concurrency control for read-only queries suggests that a user be presented with query results as if an extreme version of the right schedule in Figure 3.7 had been used.

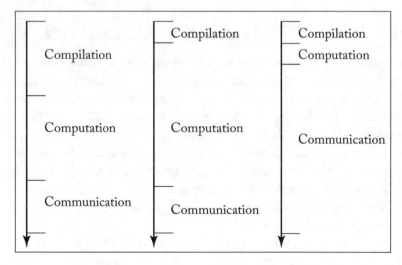

Figure 3.7: Timing in query execution.

The guarantees with respect to resource contention are much improved in this schedule compared to the other schedules. As queries "see" only data already committed before their execution, queries do not require locks. More importantly, the values for items in the database are actually decidable, whereas the outcomes of any uncommitted concurrent update transactions are, by definition, undecided. Thus, we believe that the proposed isolation method for queries is not only reasonable but in fact provides the best possible concurrency of query and update transactions without violating serializability.

It might be tempting to set a read transaction's commit point slightly later than the start of its plan execution. For example, not the query's start of execution but its first lock conflict could set the transaction's commit point. While this scheme might seem appealing, it requires read locks, i.e., items read without lock conflict must be locked in order to prevent subsequent updates that would otherwise undermine "repeatable read" transaction isolation. In other words, this scheme might create precisely the type of lock conflicts in materialized views between read transactions and update transactions that we set out to prevent.

In general, in order to process read transactions in serializable isolation yet without read locks, their commit point must be no later than their first read action. Given that there is practically no time between a query plan's start of execution and its first read action, our choice of commit points for read-only transactions is effectively the best possible to guarantee both serializability and maximal concurrency between read transaction and update transactions.

For transactions that both read and update an indexed view, serializability requires a single commit point, as discussed earlier. If the commit point is chosen as for read-only transactions above, i.e., when a transaction begins, a transaction must abort when attempting to modify an item that has been modified already by another transaction since the first transaction's commit point. If the commit point is chosen as for traditional transactions, i.e., when the transaction actually attempts to commit, all items read must be locked against updates in order to ensure repeatable reads. This dilemma is not avoided by escrow locks or any other standard method for concurrency control; thus, the present design does not offer any new technique for transactions that both read and update an indexed view.

In fact, escrow locks and thus multiple concurrent update transactions are in conflict with traditional multi-version snapshot isolation, because snapshot isolation requires a single linear history, which at first sight requires a single update transaction at a time (for each data item), i.e., traditional exclusive locks. The next section describes our solution to this ostensible contradiction between snapshot isolation and escrow locking.

3.4   CONCURRENT UPDATES AND LINEAR VERSION HISTORY

Prior schemes for snapshot isolation and multi-version concurrency control require a single linear sequence of consecutive values, and that each item's versions thus represent this one history of committed values of a data item. Note that a single history implies that a new version is not created until the most recent one has been committed, i.e., that multiple concurrent updates are not permitted. If multiple updates (to the same item) can be processed yet remain uncommitted at the same time, which is the essential value of escrow locking and of equivalent techniques, the assumption of a single sequential history is not justified.

For example, consider the schedule shown in Figure 3.8 and based on the materialized view of Figure 3.2. The initial state includes one order with CommitDate = 2003-12-31 and ShipDate = 2003-12-29. Transaction 1 inserts two more orders and Transaction 2 inserts one

Step	Transaction 1	Transaction 2	Transaction 3
1	Begin	Begin	
2	Insert two new orders	Insert a new order	
3	E lock, increment by 2		
4		E lock, increment by 1	
5		Commit	
6			Begin
7			Read summary row

Figure 3.8: Sample transaction schedule.

more order with the same dates, and both transactions increment the count of shipments in the appropriate summary row. With its snapshot point set in step 6, Transaction 3 needs to see the value 2 as the current shipment count, but nowhere in the versions generated by the schedule is the value 2 found.

Thus, escrow locking and multi-version concurrency control have an inherent incompatibility, for which this section offers three alternative resolutions. While the first approach is likely easiest to implement, because it actually does not require escrow locks, we recommend the third approach, because it retains all update processing and overhead within update statements and thus will likely result in the best query performance for indexed views and data warehouses.

Following discussion of these three alternative methods, we discuss details and variations of the third method. We introduce new commit-time-only locks, develop appropriate commit processing and transaction abort, and finally integrate escrow locks and commit-time-only locks with transaction save points and with two-phase commit. Subsequent sections complement the third method with logging and recovery, multi-granularity lock, online index operations, etc.

3.4.1 MULTIPLE RECORDS PER SUMMARY ROW

Our first approach employs, when necessary, multiple records to represent a single row in a summary view. Recall that duplicate rows in an intermediate query result can be represented by multiple copies, by a single copy with a duplicate counter, or by multiple copies each with a duplicate counter, and that it is then left to subsequent query operations to interpret these records appropriately. For example, an "intersect all" query might include a preparatory operation that forces multiple copies, with or without counter, into a single copy with a counter.

The same idea applies to aggregation views with counts and sums, because materialized views are quite literally intermediate query results. This approach permits multiple records, each with counts and appropriate partial sums, rather than strictly requiring that a single row in the view is represented by a single record in each index on the view. A query over this kind of index is always obligated to perform the final summation of counts and sums. Note that multiple records for a single summary row are not the default, and that in an ordered index, multiple records contributing to a single row will typically be immediately next to each other, thus reducing the processing burden on queries.

In the example of Figure 3.8, Transaction 1 would X lock and update the shipment count for the existing row in the view, changing the count from 1–3. The old value of 1 remains available as a prior version of that row. Transaction 2 would find the lock held on the row and instead insert a new row with a shipment count of 1. Transaction 3 would then add the shipment counts from the newly inserted row by Transaction 2 and from the original row, i.e., prior to the update by Transaction 1, and produce the correct output value 2.

Update operations for any specific row within the view attempt to lock any one of the existing records for that row, typically the one-and-only existing record. Only if this lock request fails due to concurrency contention, a new record is created and locked. Thus, contention among multiple updaters for any one specific record can always be avoided, even if contention for a specific row within the view is high. Since concurrent increment and decrement operation on the same record are not required, these updates can actually employ traditional X locks; escrow locks are not required. Thus, each record has a single sequential history that can be represented in traditional multi-version concurrency control, and a query can determine a count or sum in a row at a specific time by adding up counts and sums in all records representing that row at that time.

At most times, each row is represented by a single record. When and where this is not the case, system transactions attempt to collapse multiple records into one. This process is reminiscent of traditional ghost clean-up, with comparable and thus overall acceptable overheads. One important difference is that clean-up must distinguish between increments older than the oldest current read transaction and newer ones; it may collapse all value changes due to the older increments but it must preserve the precise history represented in the newer increments because these might still be required in queries. Thus, it might be pragmatic to clean up only records and their versions when they are older than the oldest current read transaction.

To summarize this first approach, multiple records for each row in the summary view are employed for two purposes: sequential histories and concurrent partial counts and sums. This approach eliminates the need for escrow locks and thus is compatible with traditional versioning schemes, enabling snapshot readers and multiple concurrent updaters for any row or all rows in a summary view. Its costs are an additional asynchronous consolidation activity as well as residual consolidation within retrieval queries. The novelty of this approach is that it dynamically adjusts the number of records representing a single summary row in response to increasing or decreasing contention for that specific summary row, and that it thus sidesteps all contention without requiring unconventional lock modes such as escrow locks.

3.4.2   MULTIPLE DELTA RECORDS PER SUMMARY ROW

A second approach to the problem represents each summary row by a single "base record" that holds an absolute value for each count and sum, but relies on an alternative method to capture the actual increments and decrements ("delta records") rather than storing earlier values in the multi-version store. This scheme is similar to the recovery scheme described for the original escrow locks [O'Neil, 1986]. Just as a version store permits clean-up and consolidation when update transactions commit or abort, delta records can be erased after committed changes in the version store have been consolidated into the base record. This consolidation is not required within each user transaction; an asynchronous clean-up process can perform these actions. Queries against the version store must aggregate the base record and all delta records left behind by committed transactions.

Again referring to the example of Figure 3.8, the update by Transaction 1 would leave the prior record (with count 1) in place yet add another delta record with value 2. Similarly, Transaction 2 adds another delta record with value 1. Transaction 3 would read all committed records and adds the counts, producing the correct value 2. Alternatively, a consolidation clean-up after the commit of Transaction 2 and before the start of Transaction 3 might already have combined these two records, making the correct value 2 immediately available to Transaction 3.

3.4.3   DEFERRED ACTIONS AND VIRTUAL LOG RECORDS

A third approach relies on intention lists of deferred actions and serial commit processing applying these deferred actions to guarantee a single linear history of committed values for each row in the view as well as a single linear history for the entire database. Each row in the materialized summary view is represented by a single record in each index on the view. A virtual log record is created when, under the protection of an escrow lock, an increment or decrement operation is permitted but not yet applied. The virtual log record contains the delta by which to increment or decrement counts and sums in a row in the indexed summary view, and is therefore quite similar to a *redo* log record, albeit a *redo* of a logical rather than a physical operation. The increment operation captured in the virtual log record is applied in the commit phase of the transaction—after the application requests the commit but before the final commit record is generated. The virtual log records are applied using ordinary low-level transactions that include writing physical log records. Thus, only commit processing applies increment and decrement operations to records in a materialized view and its indexes.

Using the example schedule of Figure 3.8 for a third time, the stored value for the count remains unchanged in steps 3 and 4, and is incremented from 1–2 only in step 5, during commit processing of Transaction 2. Transaction 3, with its snapshot time set in step 6, will correctly see the value 2 in step 7.

Logic similar to commit processing for a single summary row is required when a transaction upgrades an E lock to an X lock. Recall that this lock upgrade is required if a transaction attempts to read a summary row it just incremented or attempts to overwrite it with a specific new value, i.e., an assignment rather then an increment operation. Upgrading an E lock to an X lock requires applying the change protected by the E lock as well as waiting until any other E locks are released, in either order. In order to speed processing in those cases, each virtual log record should be attached to the data structure representing the associated lock. If this design is employed, it is also possible to ensure that each summary row and each escrow lock has only one associated virtual log record, even if multiple statements within a transaction increment or decrement that summary row.

If commit operations are serial as in IMS/FastPath, increment operations performed during commit processing will give each record as well as the entire database a serial history, which can readily be supported by traditional version stores and which is compatible with multi-version snapshot isolation. The experience of IMS/FastPath [Gawlick and Kinkade, 1985] indicates that serial, one-transaction-at-a-time commit processing is practical and can be implemented extremely efficiently, and in fact can scale to very high transaction rates, assuming the typical FastPath environment in which many small transactions modify only very few records each. If each insert, update, or delete operation affects an individual row in a table underlying a summary view, this assumption is definitely justified. Even updates in the view's grouping columns, which force a decrement operation in one group and an increment operation in another group, still justify this assumption. Even the additional effort imposed by versioning, i.e., copying the pre-increment value to a version record, probably still does not invalidate the assumption. Thus, serial commit processing most likely suffices for many applications, databases, tables, views, and their indexes.

3.4.4 COMMIT-TIME-ONLY LOCKS

Large transactions with many virtual *redo* log records, however, clearly violate the assumption that each transaction modifies only very few records. A typical example is a bulk operation that affects a large fraction of the view, e.g., a large data import (load) into one of the underlying tables. Note that even if the fraction of updated rows in the underlying table is relatively small, the fraction of affected rows in the view might be quite large. Another example is "catching up" a materialized view that has fallen behind due to deferred maintenance, i.e., in systems that fail to keep tables and materialized views over those tables synchronized. If bulk operations were to be supported with many virtual log records, IMS/FastPath could not use the single latch protecting the recovery log and still achieve high transaction throughput. Serial commit processing for a single large transaction would prevent and delay commit processing for many small transactions, which directly contradicts the purpose and value of escrow locking.

In order to support large transactions against indexed summary views, we extend the design above such that multiple transactions can process their commit activities concurrently. To that end, we introduce commit-time-only exclusive locks that permit serializable instead of serial commit processing. Importantly, these commit-time-only locks do not conflict with locks acquired during normal transaction processing, specifically with escrow locks. Thus, transactions not yet in their commit process are not affected by these commit-time-only locks. Serializing data access during normal transaction execution and serializing concurrent commits are two separate concerns with separate locks. Note that these commit-time-only exclusive locks are needed in addition to the escrow locks acquired during normal transaction execution.

Figure 3.9 illustrates the new commit-time-only exclusive locks, labeled "C" in the compatibility matrix. They are compatible with all other locks type except other C locks. Using this definition and compatibility matrix, a transaction must acquire a C lock during commit processing in addition to the E lock acquired while updating the materialized and indexed view.

	S	X	E	C
S	✓	–	–	✓
X	–	–	–	✓
E	–	–	✓	✓
C	✓	✓	✓	–

Figure 3.9: Lock compatibility matrix including E and C locks.

Alternatively, the C lock can be defined as a combination lock, i.e., as E+C in Figure 3.9. This is illustrated in Figure 3.10. Most importantly, C locks remain compatible with E locks. The main difference to the prior lock compatibility matrix is that a transaction avoids adding new locks; instead, it converts existing E locks to C locks. Other than that, semantics are not changed. In particular, concurrency among transactions is not changed. Very importantly, C locks continue to be compatible with E locks, i.e., one transaction may process its commit while other transactions still hold E locks on the same data.

	S	X	E	C
S	✓	–	–	–
X	–	–	–	–
E	–	–	✓	✓
C	–	–	✓	–

Figure 3.10: Lock compatibility with upgrade from E to C.

Upgrading from one lock type to another might benefit from an intermediate upgrade lock, analogous to common "U" lock between S and X locks. While true in general, the upgrade from E to C locks is special, for two reasons. First, C locks are typically held only a short time, and contention for C locks is likely low. Recall that IMS/FastPath has, in effect, only a single C lock for the entire system, i.e., the exclusive latch protecting access to the transaction log.

Second, acquisition of C locks can be organized in such a way that it is guaranteed to be free of deadlocks. This is possible because C locks are acquired only during commit processing, when the set of required C locks is known and can be sorted.

3.4.5   COMMIT PROCESSING

Commit processing proceeds in multiple steps, starting with the user's request to commit. First, all read locks are released as in traditional commit processing. Second, E locks are upgraded to C locks. Third, virtual log records are applied and their effects logged like updates covered by ordinary X locks. Finally, the transaction is truly committed using a traditional commit record in the transaction log, and all remaining locks are released.

These basic steps require some further comments. Most importantly, in order to avoid deadlocks while upgrading E locks to C locks, the existing E locks should be sorted. The sort order does not really matter, as long as it is the same for all transactions trying to commit. The sort key typically will include index identifier and index key, and it might include the hash value with which each lock is stored in the lock manager's hash table. The hash bucket number within the lock manager's hash table could be used as artificial leading sort column, a technique that avoids most of the sort effort by sorting once per hash bucket rather than sorting all necessary lock requests in one large sort.

In addition to sorting the E locks prior to their upgrade to C locks, it might make sense to sort the virtual log records, e.g., by index identifier and index key, and to aggregate multiple virtual log records pertaining to the same summary row, if any, into a single change. This optional sort operation ensures that, if multiple virtual log records apply to the same page or even the same summary row in an indexed view, these changes are applied efficiently with beneficial effect on I/O buffer, the CPU caches, transaction log size, etc. This effect, of course, is quite similar to optimized index maintenance described elsewhere [Gärtner et al., 2001] and also implemented in some products, and not really unique to deferred actions or virtual log records.

Traditionally, acquiring locks during commit processing has been an anathema just like acquiring locks during transaction rollback. However, because deadlocks are avoided due to sorting the required lock requests, it is not required that these commit-time-only locks are full traditional locks, with deadlock detection, etc. Instead, much less expensive latches will suffice. For record-level or key-value latching, these latches can be attached to data structures in the lock manager, namely those used to coordinate escrow locks and other locks for a record or key. Moreover, it is not required to employ record-level locking during commit processing; depending on the desired achievable degree of concurrency, records can be grouped into pages, page extents, key ranges, etc. such that a single latch covers application of multiple virtual log records, although this introduces new challenges.

If commit-time-only exclusive locks are obtained on precisely the same resources as the escrow locks, then absence of deadlocks is guaranteed. If, however, escrow locks are obtained in fine granularity (e.g., individual keys) and commit-time-only exclusive locks are obtained in coarser granularity (e.g., large key ranges), then there might be conflicts, namely if some other transaction holds an X lock within the larger granule. Alternatively, the commit-time-only exclusive lock could be defined and interpreted to cover only those resources for which the transaction also holds an escrow lock, e.g., the individual keys within the large key range. In other words, this case must employ the lock compatibility matrix shown in Figure 3.9, not the one in Figure 3.10.

One might ask what needs to happen if an E lock has been combined with an S lock, i.e., it has been upgraded to an X lock? In that case, the X lock and its traditional commit processing prevail. Note that there shouldn't be any remaining virtual log records for the item upgraded from an E lock to an X lock, because any remaining virtual *redo* log records must be applied at the time of the upgrade to an X lock and no further virtual log records will be generated after the transaction holds an X lock.

Also, can E locks be released after C locks have been acquired? That depends on the compatibility of C locks. If C locks conflict only with other C locks, as shown in Figure 3.9, E locks must be retained. If these C locks imply all conflicts of E locks, as shown in Figure 3.10, then E locks can be upgraded to C locks. Note that deadlocks are still impossible because a transaction holding an E lock guarantees that no other transaction can hold an S or X lock.

3.4.6   TRANSACTION ABORT

If a transaction fails to commit and instead aborts, the sequence of actions is much simpler. Interestingly, E locks can be released immediately together with S locks, because the actions protected by E locks have not been applied to the database yet. Similarly, deferred actions described in virtual log records are simply ignored, because their effect is no longer desired. Only X locks need to be retained and their actions compensated by traditional transaction rollback, including any X lock that resulted from adding an S lock to an E lock. C locks are not required when processing a transaction rollback.

3.4.7   TRANSACTION SAVE POINTS

Rolling back to a save point, however, deserves special attention. Releasing recently acquired locks when rolling back to a save point is an effective technique for improving concurrency and even resolving deadlocks already employed in some commercial database management systems, and should remain possible in the presence of E locks. Rollback of C locks does not make sense, since these exist only during commit processing, i.e., the user or application has already relinquished their right to control the transaction.

Similar to transaction abort, recently acquired S and E locks can be released immediately, recently deferred actions and their virtual log records can be ignored, and recently acquired X locks are rolled back as in traditional partial rollback.

The situation is more complex if an E lock has been augmented with an S lock since the save point, i.e., the E lock has been upgraded to an X lock. In this case, the X lock must be downgraded back to an E lock. This is not strictly required for the purposes of isolation, given that the X lock provides more protection and isolation than the E lock. For the purpose of logging and recovery, however, in particular if the transaction is to support subsequent rollback to even earlier save points as illustrated earlier in Figure 3.3, the increment operations and their virtual log records must be re-established as part of the downgrade from X to E, as will be discussed shortly in the section on logging and recovery.

3.4.8   TWO-PHASE COMMIT

The goal of the preparation phase in two-phase commit is to ensure that the local transaction can abide by the global decision to commit or to abort. In traditional two-phase commit, this implies that all actions are complete except writing the final commit to the transaction log. Shared locks and upgrade locks can be released during the preparation phase, whereas exclusive locks must be retained until the commit record is safely on stable storage.

Applying this logic to the commit processing sequence discussed above, a transaction must retain its X and C locks until the global transaction outcome is confirmed and logged. E locks must be upgraded to C locks or must also be retained, i.e., if the design follows Figure 3.9 rather than Figure 3.10. The C locks are retained until the global transaction outcome is decided and propagated to the participating resource managers. S locks can be released as they are not affected by escrow locking, whether or not escrow locking is employed by a transaction, and X locks must be retained just as in traditional transaction processing and two-phase commit.

In addition to considerations about locks, two-phase commit also affects logging. Thus, the following section about logging and recovery will resume discussion of two-phase commit processing.

3.5   LOGGING AND RECOVERY

The original description of escrow transactions included somewhat complex methods for recovery from failures of individual transactions, storage media, or the entire database management system. In fact, one might surmise that the complexity of logging and recovery prevented the adoption of escrow locking in mainstream database management systems. Fortunately, multi-level transactions and Aries, suitably adapted to E and C locks as described above, can substantially simplify the required protocols and their implementation.

Because transaction abort is simpler than transaction commit, abort and rollback are covered prior to commit processing and recovery from system and media failures, including those that catch a transaction already in commit processing. Two additional sections cover two-phase commit and a side note on optimistic concurrency control.

3.5.1   TRANSACTION ABORT

Rolling back an individual transaction to its beginning is actually less expensive than in traditional update processing using X locks, assuming that the actual application of increment operations is deferred until commit processing using virtual log records. This is because neither *undo* action nor compensation is required for deferred updates. The updates deferred using virtual log records have not been reflected yet in either the transaction log or the database, neither in the buffer pool nor on disk. Thus, no corrective action is required when a transaction aborts. The virtual log records are discarded without further action, quite similar to the corresponding E locks as discussed above.

3.5.2   PARTIAL ROLLBACK FOR SAVE POINTS

Support for partial rollback is a bit more complex. If there are multiple updates to the same row in the summary view and thus the same record in the view's index, and if save points are interspersed with these updates, it is necessary to retain multiple virtual log records. During commit processing, sorting all virtual log records permits aggregating those such that each database record is actually updated and logged only once. Until then, however, aggregation must not cross save points that might still be the target of a partial transaction rollback. Aggregation within each interval between save points is acceptable, and might well be sufficient to capture most of the performance improvement of aggregating virtual log records. Aggregation across anonymous save points is also possible after those save points have become irrelevant. For example, if a save point is established to enable statement abort without transaction abort after, that save point can be ignored after the statement is completed successfully.

Rollback of a lock upgrade from E to X mode needs to consider the case that there might have been multiple save point intervals with increment operations under the E lock in each interval. If so, all those increment operations must be applied when the E lock is upgraded to an X lock, such that a read operation by the current transaction indeed reflects all the updates.

In the discussion so far, it has been implied that the pertinent virtual log records can be dropped once they have been applied to the database. Unfortunately, this would not be correct if subsequent rollback to a save point is to be supported. Recall that after rollback to a save point and subsequent processing, rollback to an even earlier save point might be requested.

If a lock upgrade from E to X is rolled back, the individual increment operations must be reestablished within their original save point intervals, in order to recreate the situation prior to the lock upgrade. Perhaps the simplest implementation retains the virtual log records during the lock upgrade but marks them "already applied," such that rollback can revoke those markings. More precisely, the update that applied the cumulative increment during the lock upgrade is undone or compensated, and the relevant virtual log records are either deleted or their marking is revoked, depending on these virtual log records' time of creation relative to the save point targeted by the current rollback.

3.5.3   TRANSACTION COMMIT

Virtual log records cannot contribute to the durability of transactions after their commit. Instead, they remain attached to the transaction's in-memory data structure when they are created during increment and decrement operations under the protection of E locks, and they are not written into the transaction log on stable storage.

Durability is guaranteed by the log records written while an actual change is applied to the database under the protection of commit-time-only exclusive locks. These C locks, together with the database updates applied during commit processing and their log records, resemble very closely the changes applied in traditional concurrency control and recovery under traditional X locks. The difference is in the locking behavior and in the deferment of actual updates using virtual log records. In other words, the difference is in the timing when these updates are applied, the difference is not in the mechanisms how these updates are applied, logged, and made durable. Thus, the same rules about write-ahead logging, buffer management, etc. apply, with the same effects.

Specifically, the log records created for updates protected by C locks must obey the standard rules of write-ahead logging. They must be written to the transaction log on stable storage before the modified data pages may overwrite old database contents on disk.

For all transactions other than those at the lowest level in the multi-level transaction hierarchy, it is not required that *redo* and *undo* actions be idempotent, since the logging and recovery protocol ensures that a *redo* action is applied only when the database does not contain any effects of the action being redone, and that an *undo* action is applied only when the database contains all effects of the action being undone. As implied earlier in connection with virtual log records, the increment and decrement operations should be higher-level actions that are realized by lower-level transactions that actually assign specific new values within the records on disk. Thus, lowest-level "physical" log records contain absolute values just as in traditional transaction processing using X locks, whereas higher-level "logical" log records contain deltas.

If deemed desirable, it is not even required that entirely new formats for log records be designed. In fact, a traditional log record describing the update of a database field is sufficient for logging and recovery of escrow updates, with only a single bit indicating that the operation is a relative or escrow operation. The old and new values in a traditional log record must be interpreted as a numeric difference, positive or negative, and this difference must be applied when compensating an action during transaction rollback. In fact, formatting a log record of this type could be leveraged twice, first for the virtual log record that defers forward processing and then as for the log record on stable storage while applying the virtual log record during commit processing.

Copying the virtual log records to the persistent transaction log is not required. Logging the virtual log records could, however, enable an interesting optimization, albeit possibly with some risk. As soon as these virtual log records are logged, the entire transaction can be reported completed and committed to the user or application, which therefore do not need to wait until all changes and virtual log records have been applied to the individual records and summary rows in all indexed views affected by the transaction. Should the system fail after reporting completion to the user, the changes can be applied during restart, very similar to a global commit decision by a distributed transaction coordinator. This technique might seem promising, but the implied risks require further research. For example, should a failure occur while the logical log records are applied to the database, what are the appropriate next steps for the transaction and for the database affected?

3.5.4 SYSTEM AND MEDIA RECOVERY

For the most part, checkpoints as well as system and media recovery follow the well-known Aries techniques [Mohan et al., 1992]. Logical *redo* log records are used during recovery only for unfinished distributed transactions. If the recovery log contains a pre-commit or prepare log record but no final log record for that transaction, and if the transaction coordinator logged a commit record, all logical *redo* log records are processed as in normal commit processing, i.e., they are applied to the data records using low-level transactions that write standard physical log records. *Redo* processing for distributed transactions is interleaved with *redo* processing of local transactions based on the sequence in the recovery log, i.e., there is only one *redo* pass even if the system was finishing distributed transactions at the time of the server crash.

Other than that, the *redo* pass relies not on virtual log records but on the physical log records written to the recovery log by low-level transactions while processing virtual log records. The usual recovery optimizations apply: for example, if locks are taken during the analysis pass, new transactions can be accepted and processed concurrently with both the *redo* and *undo* passes. If locks are taken only during the *redo* pass, e.g., because log analysis is integrated and interleaved with the *redo* pass, concurrent transactions must wait until the *redo* pass is complete, i.e., until *undo* or compensation processing has begun. In general, if locks are reacquired before the *undo* pass, transactions can be allowed to enter the system as soon as the *redo* pass is complete.

Checkpoint processing is also not affected by escrow locks, multiple concurrent updates, multiple concurrent commits, deferred updates, or virtual log records. In fact, the techniques discussed in this chapter do not interfere with checkpoints during the analysis, *redo*, and *undo* phases of restart recovery, with fuzzy checkpoints (e.g., second chance checkpoints that write out only those pages that have already been dirty during the prior checkpoint), or with checkpoint intervals (with separate *begin checkpoint* and *end checkpoint* log records, and active transaction processing while taking the checkpoint [Mohan et al., 1992]). In Aries and multi-level trans-actions, checkpoints only affect (i.e., shorten) the *redo* effort to apply traditional physical log records.

Media recovery also employs Aries mechanisms, using fuzzy image copies obtained during active transaction processing, combined with a suitable period of the recovery log. During media recovery, the log is applied to the database restored from the image copy, including transaction *undo* and compensation [Mohan et al., 1992]. Even single-page recovery (e.g., after a "bad block" disk error) or continuous database mirroring ("log shipping") are compatible with escrow locks, multiple concurrent updates, deferred updates, and virtual log records.

3.5.5 FAILURES AND TRANSACTION ABORT DURING COMMIT PROCESSING

If a transaction aborts prior to commit processing, the discussion above applies—escrow locks and virtual log records are not applied to the database and instead are simply ignored, and traditional locks and log records are processed in the traditional way. What wasn't covered above was transaction failure during commit processing, e.g., if lock conversion from E to C locks fails for some unexpected reasons (e.g., out of memory) or logging a change fails for some unexpected reasons (e.g., out of log space).

It turns out that the problem is simpler than perhaps expected, due to the similarity of C locks to traditional X locks and the parallel similarity of logging increment operations during commit processing to logging traditional update operations. If failure occurs during commit processing, some virtual log records have already been applied including generation of traditional log records, and some have not. For the former, abort processing follows the same rules as abort processing described earlier: the virtual log records are ignored and simply deallocated. For the latter, abort processing follows traditional lines: using the traditional log record generated from the virtual log records and applied under protection of a C lock, the update is compensated and the compensation action logged.

In summary, the commit-time-only exclusive locks ensure that any index entry can be updated by only one transaction currently in its commit processing phase. Thus, even if a transaction is forced to roll back after some of its commit processing has completed, it can do so with ordinary transaction mechanisms. Special, non-traditional logging and rollback mechanisms are not required.

3.5.6 TWO-PHASE COMMIT

In addition to upgrading E locks to C locks, two-phase commit needs to apply the changes protected by the C locks and log them. The first or "preparation" phase of two-phase commit performs all operations of commit processing up to yet excluding writing the commit record. Instead, as in ordinary two-phase commit, it writes a "prepared" record to the transaction log. When the global commit coordinator's final commit decision is known, commit processing resumes as discussed above. Alternatively, abort processing takes over as if the local transaction had failed at the end of commit processing, just before the final commit record was to be written—just as in traditional two-phase commit processing.

The notion of virtual log records, which more accurately can be called virtual *logical redo* log records, opens another possible optimization that might improve concurrency as well as response time for the preparation request. In spirit, this optimization is similar to the "vote reliable" optimization implemented in some IBM transaction processing products [Samaras et al., 1993]. In general, an operation is considered durable (in the sense of transactional "ACID" guarantees) when its effects and updates are safely captured in the transaction log (on "stable storage"), whether or not these effects and updates are already reflected in the database. If a failure happens, redoing the actions described in the transaction log will recover their effects and thus ensure their durability.

Thus, it could be argued that capturing the virtual logical redo log records not only in the transaction's in-memory state but also in the transaction log is sufficient to report a local transaction ready to abide by the global decision about transaction commit or abort. In fact, this idea might be applicable in additional situations and cases. Of course, care must be taken to avoid unacceptable additional risks to transaction completion, e.g., out-of-memory or out-of-disk-space errors that might be encountered while performing the actions described in these *logical redo* log records, and that would have caused the local transaction to veto against global transaction commit if these errors had happened during the local transaction's preparation phase.

3.5.7   OPTIMISTIC CONCURRENCY CONTROL

Interestingly, and added here only as a side note, many of the commit processing techniques described above also apply to transactions governed by optimistic concurrency control [Kung and Robinson, 1979, 1981].

A transaction under optimistic concurrency control proceeds with its work even if it might interfere with other active transactions. Employing temporary copies of data or temporarily accepting inconsistent data, end-of-transaction validation ensures that only valid transactions commit, i.e., all transaction schedules are serializable, by comparing a transaction's "read set" and "write set" with other transactions' read sets and write sets. In addition to maintenance of these read sets and write sets, the major downside of optimistic concurrency control is that work might be wasted even after it would have been possible to detect the interference with other transactions and to resolve that interference by waiting or by an earlier transaction abort.

Implementation of end-of-transaction validation uses some form of locks or latches to ensure consistency and validity of the validation step; the original research [Kung and Robinson, 1979] relied on critical sections. However, it could be argued that optimistic concurrency control simply defers lock acquisition until commit processing. A significant difference to pessimistic concurrency control is that the set of required locks is known at commit time in optimistic concurrency control, meaning the lock set can be sorted. As in commit processing for escrow locks above, this knowledge permits avoiding deadlocks with other transactions committing under optimistic concurrency control [Halici, 1991]. Moreover, because commit processing takes only a fraction of the time needed for processing an entire transaction, coarser lock granularity is feasible without excessive contention.

After all locks have been acquired and transaction validation is complete, the transaction can release all read locks immediately, then perform and log the updates, finish by writing the commit record, and finally release the write locks. A transaction under optimistic concurrency control switches into a commit processing mode very much like pessimistic concurrency control and very much like transactions converting escrow locks to exclusive locks during commit processing. In both cases, i.e., optimistic concurrency control and transactions with escrow locks, these exclusive locks are limited to commit time only, and they interfere only with other commit-time-only locks held by transactions equally in their commit processing phase.

Maintenance of the transaction's read set and write set, i.e., maintenance of the set of required locks, can be implemented using a data structure very much like the data structure used in transaction-private memory for possible lock de-escalation as well as like the data structure for the lock manager. Thus, bookkeeping in transactions under optimistic concurrency control is more similar to bookkeeping for transactions under pessimistic concurrency control than usually understood. At least one research effect, however, suggested locks and a lock manager to determine the intersection between read sets and write sets, using a "dummy" lock mode that does not conflict with any other lock and only serves as a witness for a transaction's read operation [Halici, 1991]. A refinement of that approach might employ notification locks [Gray, 1993] instead of dummy locks.

Interestingly, not only concurrency control but also logging and recovery for optimistic concurrency control might be surprisingly similar to the mechanisms discussed above for escrow locks. Specifically, virtual log records seem a promising implementation technique to defer updates until they have been validated during commit processing, with its potential for performance and scalability proven in IMS/FastPath.

Given these similarities, it seems that mixing optimistic concurrency control and pessimistic concurrency control might be easier to realize than one might suspect, and the choice of concurrency control methods can be made for each transaction rather than for the entire system and its implementation. It is even conceivable to choose the concurrency control method for individual resources, if desired. A candidate might be schema stability versus data operations. Protecting a transaction against changes in the database schema or at least the schema of the relevant tables could use traditional locking (with hardly any contention and waiting for locks) whereas queries and updates may employ optimistic concurrency control for the tables' contents. In the extreme, a transaction may lock an individual data items after accessing it repeatedly under optimistic concurrency control; or a database management system may learn which resources to manage with optimistic concurrency control and which ones to manage with pessimistic concurrency control.

Lausen investigated very similar ideas on formal level [Lausen, 1982] and also came to the conclusion that optimistic concurrency control and pessimistic concurrency control can be combined, even to the point that a single transaction locks some resources and validates others at the end of the transaction. Managing an optimistic transaction's read set and write set in transaction-private memory using the same type of data structures employed by a traditional lock manager might be the implementation technique needed to make Lausen's ideas realistic and perhaps address some of the concerns about optimistic concurrency control [Härder, 1984, Mohan, 1992].

Two-phase commit after optimistic concurrency control, i.e., optimistic concurrency control participating in distributed commit coordination, can also benefit from techniques borrowed from pessimistic concurrency control. In particular, the preparation phase requires that the transaction acquire the appropriate locks, such that the local transaction is entirely subjugated to the global commit decision. Read locks can be released at the end of validation and write locks must be retained until the global commit decision is known and reflected in the local database. In other words, in the commit sequence above for optimistic concurrency control, writing the commit record is replaced by writing the pre-commit record, voting, receiving the global decision, and then committing or aborting.

3.6   MULTI-GRANULARITY LOCKING

One of the proven database implementation techniques found in all commercial database management systems is multi-granularity (hierarchical) locking. When updating all rows in a table or all records in an index, rather than taking row locks or key locks for each one, a single "large granularity" lock for the table or index is taken. In order to detect conflicts correctly, a transaction that modifies only a single row (and thus intends to take a row lock) must obtain an "intention" lock at the larger granularity. Note that two intention locks never conflict, because two intention locks indicate that both participating transactions intend to take locks at a smaller granularity where actual concurrency conflicts will be detected if they indeed exist. At least one absolute lock (as opposed to an intention lock) is required for any lock conflict. Note also that a reasonable interpretation of an absolute lock at a larger granularity is equivalent to that same lock on each instance at the smaller granularity, including phantom instances. For example, a large read transaction holding an S lock on a table implicitly holds an S lock on all rows, including ones to be inserted after the initial S lock on the table has been granted—since an insert transaction must hold an X lock on the new row, which is incompatible with the S lock held implicitly by the large read transaction even on the new row, the insert must be prevented, which is why S and IX locks on a table conflict with each other.

For escrow locks and escrow transactions, two obvious questions are: if summary records in an indexed view are usually modified using escrow locks, can other transactions still employ large granularity locks when appropriate? Second, if a large transaction, e.g., a bulk insertion into a table of detail records, modifies practically all summary records in an indexed view, is it possible to obtain a single escrow lock on the entire materialized view or the entire index of the materialized view?

3.6.1   DERIVED LOCK TYPES

Korth has described a fairly straightforward procedure for deriving auxiliary lock modes from a set of basic operational locks [Korth, 1983], including intention locks, combination locks, and upgrade locks. Thus, the answer is "yes" for both questions above. For the first question, we must define a new "intent to escrow" ("IE") lock mode that all escrow transactions must obtain for the materialized view or its index before requesting an escrow lock for a specific row in a summary table or for a specific key in an indexed view. This IE lock does not conflict with other intention locks, but it conflicts with both shared and exclusive locks on the view or index. Similarly, we ought to define a new "intent-to-commit" ("IC") lock mode that permits efficient multi-granularity locking during commit processing.

Figure 3.11 shows a traditional lock compatibility matrix extended with escrow locks ("E"), intent-toescrow ("IE") locks, commit-time-only exclusive locks ("C"), and intent-to-commit locks ("IC"). The assumption in Figure 3.11 is that E locks are upgraded to C locks, i.e., C locks are obtained in place of E locks rather than in addition to E locks.

	S	X	E	C	IS	IX	IE	IC
S	✓	–	–	–	✓	–	–	–
X	–	–	–	–	–	–	–	–
E	–	–	✓	✓	–	–	✓	✓
C	–	–	✓	–	–	–	✓	–
IS	✓	–	–	–	✓	✓	✓	✓
IX	–	–	–	–	✓	✓	✓	✓
IE	–	–	✓	✓	✓	✓	✓	✓
IC	–	–	✓	–	✓	✓	✓	✓

Figure 3.11: Lock compatibility including intention locks.

Note that the extension from S and X locks to S, X, E, and C locks might warrant multiple kinds of upgrade locks. For example, the traditional U lock is an S lock with the exclusive permission to upgrade to an X lock. After the introduction of E locks, there must be two upgrade locks, namely from E to X in addition to the traditional upgrade from S to X. Upgrade from S to E is not required because an E lock does not imply an S lock, and because an S+E combination lock is equivalent to an X lock. Update or upgrade locks ("U" and "IU") are not included to limit size and complexity of the diagram, even if they are a standard technique in commercial database management systems.

Traditional combination locks ("S+IX", etc.) are also not shown in Figure 3.11 as they can easily be inferred: a requested combination lock is compatible with a prior lock if both components of the combination are compatible, and a new lock request is compatible with a prior combination lock if the new lock is compatible with both components of the combination lock. Some combination locks might not increase concurrency and should thus be omitted: just as an S+X lock does not make any sense, an S+E lock is like an X lock in its conflict patterns, and transactions should obtain an X lock rather than separate S and E locks on the same resource or their combination. Similarly, IS+IE is equivalent to IX, which implies that locking a large granularity of locking in IX mode grants permission to lock at the next smaller granularity of locking not only in traditional X, S, IX, and IS modes but also in E or IE modes.

3.6.2 INTERPRETATION OF THE LOCK TABLE

The compatibility matrix of Figure 3.11 shows the usual patterns seen in lock compatibility matrices that include intention locks—no conflicts among intention locks and the same pattern repeated in the three remaining quadrants. Each quadrant is mirrored over the diagonal, as is the entire matrix. The top-left quadrant applies to both larger and smaller granularities in the locking hierarchy, e.g., to both tables and rows or to both indexes and keys. If the lock hierarchy includes more than two granularities, all quadrants apply to multiple granularities. Thus, not only traditional S and X locks but also E and C locks apply to entire tables, views, or indexes.

For example, a bulk insert transaction may update 1% of the rows in a table and thus obtain X locks on individual rows in the table, but it may touch 90% of the rows in a view summarizing the table. Thus, the bulk insert operation can obtain an E lock on an entire materialized view, upgrading to a C lock on the entire materialized view during commit processing. It is even possible that a second, concurrent bulk update transaction also obtains an E lock on the entire view, with both bulk insertions updating the same set of summary rows in the materialized and indexed view concurrently. The results is that these two bulk operations conflict neither in the table nor in the view—the former due to locking disjoint sets of rows or keys in the table, the latter due to escrow locking in the materialized and indexed view. These bulk operations do, however, conflict during commit processing, i.e., they serialize their final updates to the summary rows in the materialized and indexed view.

The matrix also indicates that, even while a large transaction holds an E lock on the entire index (and thus implicitly on all keys in the index), another small transaction may obtain an IE lock on the index and then an E lock on one or more specific keys. This is entirely consistent with the interpretation of large granularity locks given earlier, because the small transaction may increment and decrement counts and sums in existing records. However, another transaction cannot insert or delete keys or records while the entire index is locked in E mode, because those actions would require an IX lock on the index and an X lock on the affected keys or records. Insertion and deletion operations will be discussed shortly.

3.6.3 COMMIT PROCESSING WITH INTENTION LOCKS

In order to avoid deadlocks during commit processing, E locks must be sorted before being upgraded to C locks. Similarly, IE locks must be upgraded to IC locks. In general, the sort cost can be minimized if the sort key begins with the hash bucket number in the lock manager's hash table, i.e., a single large sort operation is replaced by one small sort operation per hash bucket. If intention locks are involved, however, it is imperative that IC locks be acquired before their dependent C locks. Thus, the sort order and its implementation must ensure that IC locks sort earlier than their dependent C locks, and similarly that IE locks sort earlier than their dependent E locks.

It seems impractical to require that all C locks within a given index fall in the same hash bucket as the IC lock for the entire index—thus, the small per-bucket sort operations cannot guarantee that the IC locks sort earlier than their dependent C locks. A better alternative seems to employ either dedicated hash buckets for different granularities, and to ensure the proper sequence of lock upgrades by processing the hash buckets in the appropriate order.

3.7   UPDATE AND UPGRADE LOCKS

Not only intention locks but also upgrade locks are similar yet different with escrow locks. In the original design for "U" locks for relational databases, a U lock implies an S lock and puts the transaction into favorite position to convert to an exclusive X lock [Gray, 1993]. Because a transaction can convert an existing S lock to a U lock without waiting for other readers to finish, converting from S to U is very different from an immediate request for an X lock. Nonetheless, converting the U lock to an X lock will like succeed quickly and without deadlock because no second U lock can exists and because no further S locks can be granted once a U lock is in place.

In a system with escrow locks, not only S locks but also E locks may require conversion to an X lock. In fact, as discussed earlier, adding an S lock to an E lock is tantamount to converting the E lock to an X lock. Similarly, adding an E lock to an S lock does not really make sense and the lock should instead be converted to an X lock.

In the traditional interpretation of lock conversions, upgrade locks are intermediate lock modes between two primary lock modes, e.g., S and X. This interpretation leads to two separate upgrade modes, one from S to X and one from E to X. These two lock modes ought to conflict, because only one transaction can actually obtain the desired X lock. Thus, these two intermediate upgrade locks are more similar than different, and it seems that an alternative interpretation of upgrade locks might be more appropriate.

Rather than tying an intermediate upgrade lock to both the original and the desired lock modes, it might be tied only to the desired lock mode. Thus, it is not really an intermediate lock mode anymore; it is a really a preparatory lock mode. It does not give any rights to access data, it merely gives rights to acquire a desired lock. If such preparatory locks are indicated by P subscripted by the desired lock mode, a traditional U lock must then be written and thought of as $S+P_X$.

Moreover, there is use for a preparatory lock mode even if a transaction does not hold any lock at all on the desired resource, i.e., in situations in which an intermediate lock mode between two other locks modes does not really apply. For example, consider a transaction that employs a non-clustered index to

determine which rows in a table to update, and assume that records in non-clustered indexes and in clustered indexes are locked separately by their respective index identifier and key value. After the initial search, this transaction holds locks in the non-clustered index but no locks yet in the clustered index. It may be beneficial to place preparatory locks P_X on all rows to be modified before attempting to acquire X locks on any of those rows. Since the preparatory P_X locks do not conflict with concurrent readers and their S locks, setting the P_X locks will likely succeed quickly. The transaction may wait when converting P_X locks to X locks, but while it is waiting for one row, no other transaction can acquire any new locks on any of the remaining rows.

In this specific example, there might not be much difference between a transaction acquiring a traditional U locks, i.e., $S+P_X$ in our notation, or merely a P_X lock. Modifying the example a little makes the difference more clear. Imagine that the updating transaction intends to lock not rows but entire pages or partitions in the clustered index. Other transactions may hold S, IS, or IX locks on those pages or partitions. None of these conflicts with a P_X lock, and P_X locks can be acquired on all needed pages or partitions without waiting. If, on the other hand, the updating transaction were forced to acquire X locks without preparatory P_X locks, it would likely wait for some of these pages or partitions. While the transaction is waiting for the first one, another transaction would be able to "sneak in" and acquire locks on one of the remaining ones.

By separating the upgrade lock mode from the original lock mode, any transaction attempting to acquire an exclusive lock may first acquire a P_X lock. The same considerations about lock compatibility, waiting, and deadlocks apply to P_X locks as to U locks. A transaction may acquire a P_X lock immediately even if other E, S, IS, or IX locks are already in place. The primary effect of the P_X lock is that no further E, S, IS, or IX locks will be granted. Thus, a transaction may be able to place multiple P_X locks without waiting, and then convert those into X locks in a second pass.

In summary, because there are multiple lock modes that can be converted to an exclusive lock, the traditional upgrade lock as an intermediate step between two lock modes might be replaced by a preparatory lock that is specific to the desired lock mode regardless of the existing lock mode.

3.8   INSERT AND DELETE

Our next subject is how new rows are created in materialized views, how new keys are inserted into indexes on materialized views, or how rows and keys are deleted in materialized views and their indexes. As an example, imagine a clustered index on the date columns in Figure 3.2, i.e., the grouping columns of the view form the search key in a B-tree that contains all columns of the table. The crucial difficulty is that record insertions and deletions require exclusive locks rather than escrow locks. If such locks are retained until end-of-transaction and thus potentially for a long time, lock contention might disrupt the flow of updates in an indexed view. Considering Figure 3.2, once order processing advances to a new day of shipping, i.e., once the first transaction creates a new summary row in the materialized view, many transactions need to increment counters and sums in that row. Thus, immediately after a new row in a materialized view or a new record in the view index is created, contention for the new row or record can be just as high as for prior rows and records, and holding an exclusive lock until the end of the shipping transaction might not be acceptable.

3.8.1 ESCROW LOCKS AND KEY RANGE LOCKING

Clearly, key value locks and key range locks are important for high concurrency in B-tree indexes. Key range locking has introduced some new lock modes, e.g., "IS-S" [Lomet, 1993], which have proven practical and efficient in some commercial implementations. These lock modes are combination locks of a special kind, combining two locks at different granularities in the locking hierarchy yet mapped to the same lockable resource, e.g., a single key value, in order to reduce the number of lock manager invocations. Each range between two existing keys (including ghost records) in an index is considered a lockable resource. The range must be locked if any component within is to be locked, specifically the one actual key within (and at the end) of the range. For example, "IS-S" means that the range between two keys is locked in "IS" mode and the key is locked in "S" mode. However, these lock modes must be understood as a performance optimization; they do not affect concurrency control theory or the locking protocol.

As a concrete example, assume a B-tree's only leaf contains valid records with keys 4 and 9 as well as a ghost record with the key value 6. Assume further that the interval associated with each key ranges from a lower key exclusively to the next higher key inclusively. Thus, the ranges that can be locked are (, 4], (4, 6], (6, 9], and (9,), which are represented in the lock manager by the actual key values 4, 6, and 9 as well as the artificial key value , respectively. Before locking and reading a key and its record, say key 9, a transaction first requires an intent-to-share (IS) lock on the range (6,9]. Before inserting a new key, e.g., 8, a range lock is required for the range that includes 8, because the insertion of a new key could reduce the value of a range lock already held, i.e., from (6,9] to (8,9]. Thus, a read-only query might hold an "IS-S" lock precisely to prevent insertion of phantoms [Lomet, 1993].

It helps to consider each combined lock mode as two separate locks when deciding how these lock modes interact with escrow locks and intent-to-escrow locks. Specifically, update transactions that need to increment or decrement a summary row must obtain an IE lock on the range followed by an E lock on the key or record. Using the same optimization, an "IE-E" lock mode must be provided for key range escrow locking. Note that, as shown in Figure 3.11 and its discussion, intention locks never conflict. Thus, other locks can obtain other intention locks on the range, although they can only obtain escrow locks on the specific key or record, because escrow locks are compatible only with other escrow locks.

The most interesting case are insertions of new keys into a B-tree index. For those, it is actually not required to lock the boundary of the gap into which a new key is inserted. Instead, only the gap itself is locked, and only briefly, because once the new key is inserted, it is a resource that can be locked in its own right. Insertions are the main topic of the next section.

3.8.2   RECORD CREATION BY SYSTEM TRANSACTIONS

Our solution for this problem relies on two concepts discussed earlier, namely system transactions and the unification of ghost bit and duplicate count into a delta count in each stored record. Recall that a query scanning an indexed view must ignore records with a delta count equal to zero, because this value is equivalent to the traditional ghost bit indicating an invalid record left behind by a prior deletion. Thus, when a deletion of a row in a database table decrements a delta count in an indexed view to zero, there is actually no need to delete this record—the record automatically is semantically equivalent to a deleted record. Leaving it behind may even speed up a future insertion in the table and increment of the count in the materialized view. If that does not happen, erasing the record and reclaiming the space can safely be left to an asynchronous clean-up utility or a future operation that reorganizes the page contents in order to insert a new record. Just as for traditional ghost records, the actual deletion should be performed by a system transaction, which must obtain a suitable lock on the ghost record in order to ensure that no other transaction still retains a lock on it, e.g., because the transaction that turned the record into a ghost has not committed yet or because another transaction has obtained an escrow lock on the record in order to increment its counts and sums.

Inserting a new summary row in the materialized view and thus a new record in each index on the view can work quite similarly, also using a system transaction. The main difference is that a system transaction is invoked to insert a record that, due to a delta count equal to zero, is semantically not there in the sense that no query will include it in its result. This system transaction is triggered when an update attempts to modify a row that does not exist. In other words, inserting a new key in an indexed view with delta count equal to zero (as well as all fields that represent sums that can be incremented and decremented) does not modify the contents of the database, and thus is a good candidate for the short system transaction that can quickly commit and release its locks that were needed for creating the record.

It might be helpful to compare this procedure with traditional key insertion based on key-range locking protocols, which acquire and release locks on the range between keys when inserting a new key into an existing index. Basically, the insert must first lock the range into which a new key is inserted such that no other concurrent transaction can insert precisely the same key. Once the new key is inserted, it represents a database resource that can be locked in its own right. After an exclusive lock is obtained on the new key and registered in the system's lock manager, the danger of another transaction inserting precisely the same key is averted, and the lock on the range between the two pre-existing neighboring keys can be released. Note that this lock is released with a transaction still progressing, even though releasing a lock prior to transaction commit is usually dangerous.

3.8.3   LOCKING AND LOGGING IN SYSTEM TRANSACTIONS

In the proposed design, it is a system transaction that inserts a new ghost record using key range locking; the user transaction merely modifies the ghost bit or its replacement, the delta count.

The user transaction locks only a specific row or index key and only in E mode, whereas the system transaction requires a key-range lock on the entire gap between the two pre-existing neighbors of the new key. Quite obviously, when the system transaction commits, it can release its locks, in particular the one on the key range. However, the user transaction that invoked the system transaction may acquire an E lock on the new record or key while the system transaction still holds an X lock on it, exploiting the lock compatibility between the two transactions. This E lock then permits the user transaction to increment the newly created record or row.

In the traditional locking protocol, a user transaction retains its IX lock on the materialized view or its index until it commits. Thus, if another transaction needs to increment many or most of the rows in the materialized view, it cannot obtain an E lock on the entire view or its index. In the proposed scheme, the IX lock is held only very briefly (for the duration of the system transaction), thus enabling higher concurrency among large and small update transactions. Note that a bulk insert transaction with an E lock on the entire index can still spawn a system transaction that inserts a new key for a new summary row using IX and X locks: while these locks ordinarily conflict, system transactions are lock-compatible with their invoking transaction.

Insertion and commit of ghost records might be objected to because a ghost record remains in the index if the user transaction rolls back. However, it must be considered that the ghost record only occupies space otherwise unused in its B-tree leaf. If the insertion of the ghost record triggers a leaf split, the traditional scheme would also require a leaf split. As discussed earlier, that page split would also be performed using a system transaction that is similarly not rolled back during rollback of the user transaction.

Moreover, it can be argued that the ghost of a summary row remaining in an indexed view can serve good purposes. First, since it represents a group in which there is at least some data and some update activity, the summary row might soon be needed in any case. This includes, of course, restarting the same insertion or update in the base table after the initial user transaction's successful rollback. Retaining the ghost record saves creating a ghost record during this second attempt. Second, since even a ghost record defines a range boundary in key range locking, it permits more fine-grained locks within the indexed view. In fact, one might consider even read-only transactions that insert ghost records into B-tree indexes (using system transactions) solely for the purpose of locking precisely the key range defined by the current query predicate. While maybe not a good idea in general, it can be a good idea when parallel threads create a new index, with each thread responsible for one or more key ranges in the new index.

3.9 ONLINE INDEX OPERATIONS

In addition to the ghost bit and the duplicate count, the delta count in each stored record within an indexed view also replaces the anti-matter bit, which is used in online index operations based on the "no side file" approach [Mohan and Narang, 1992]. A negative value in the delta count is equivalent to the anti-matter bit, which the index builder must weigh against the records obtained while scanning base tables and computing the view result. After the index builder has completed its insertions into the future indexed view, all anti-matter must be resolved, i.e., all stored delta counts must be non-negative, such that queries never encounter negative delta counts. As discussed earlier, queries ignore records with a delta count equal to zero, which is equivalent to a ghost bit.

The delta count contributes even more in an index on a materialized summary view, i.e., an index in which each record summarizes multiple base table rows. For example, consider a user transaction that deletes multiple rows in the base table (e.g., the Figure 3.1) all belonging to the same group in the view (e.g., the view in Figure 3.2). Similarly, multiple user transactions might delete multiple rows in the table that all affect the same group in the view. Assume that the index builder is still scanning and sorting rows, i.e., the future index on the view is still empty. In this case, the user transaction must mark not one but multiple deletions in a future summary record. A negative delta count readily supports this need. To extend the metaphor, the delta count also serves to track multiple quanta of anti-matter.

In fact, even if multiple concurrent transactions insert and delete multiple rows in the base table that all affect the same summary row, no special logic is required. Once a system transaction has created an appropriate summary record with a delta count equal to zero, all user transactions simply increment and decrement counts and sums, including in particular the delta count. Note that multiple uncommitted concurrent transactions may affect the same summary rows, because escrow locking applies even to indexes still being built. In this way, user transactions are not affected by the preliminary status of the future index or the records within it, and they require no special logic to turn an invalid record into a ghost record or vice versa, to turn a "multi-deletion" record into a "multi-insertion" record, etc. Thus, the delta count provides a valuable simplification of what otherwise could require fairly complex logic not only during the initial forward processing but also during transaction rollback.

What is assumed, however, is a sharp separation of the database updates prior to and during index creation. Updates concurrent to the index operation are propagated to the future index by their respective transactions; thus, the index builder must not include any of those updates. Fortunately, the index builder may satisfy this need by relying on the same mechanism employed for read transactions, namely multiversion concurrency control and a snapshot scan on the tables and indexes used by the index builder to compute the view's contents.

There is one special consideration that applies only while indexes are still being built, i.e., when records in the summary view reflect changes applied after the snapshot time of the index builder's scan. Consider, for example, a view that includes both a count of rows (the delta count) and a sum for a particular column, and assume that the view is still being materialized and that the index builder is still scanning and sorting data in the underlying tables. If a concurrent transaction modifies a value in that particular column for an existing row in an underlying table, and if the change affects a sum in a summary row in the view, the delta count in the view does not change, whereas the sum does. If the summary row does not exist in the materialized view yet, a system transaction creates a new record in the view's index, with delta count and sum equal to zero, and the user transaction may then update the sum. Note that the delta count is still zero, which usually indicates a ghost record that can be erased without change in the view's contents; however, this row must not be erased since its sum is non-zero. During online index creation, a summary row in a view and its indexes represents not a state but the delta since the snapshot time of the index builder's scan, and a record is truly a ghost record only if the delta count and all sums (if any) are equal to zero, i.e., if the record represents no actual delta in any of the aggregated columns. Fortunately, since queries never search or scan indexes still being built, queries can never encounter such records. Thus, they only need to test the delta count, which was discussed earlier and which matches today's test of ghost bits.

On the other hand, it is also very desirable to create indexes incrementally rather than in a single, large, expensive step, e.g., using "instant indexes" as proposed earlier [Graefe, 2003]. The basic idea of that proposal is to interpret an index as a materialized view defined with a range predicate on the key that determines the scanning order, e.g., the search key of the clustered index, and to extend incrementally the range over which the new index is fully operational, i.e., supports both queries and updates. As index construction proceeds, more and more sections of the new index become fully operational while others are still being built. Thus, full versioning semantics as discussed earlier must be provided for at least some sections. In that case, the simplest design might be to apply versioning for all records in the new index, even for those that cannot be queried yet, although more precise enablement of versioning is also possible with moderate additional complexity in the index maintenance code.

3.10 CORRECTNESS

The large design presented here in substantial detail combines existing techniques and novel extensions, e.g., multi-granularity escrow locks and non-serial but serializable commit processing. The design's correctness relies on the proven correctness of its components.

Specifically, IE locks and their compatibility with other locks are derived using sound methodology [Korth, 1983]. Deadlocks during concurrent commit processing are avoided using the proven method of acquiring locks in a prescribed order. These commit-time-only exclusive locks guarantee that commit processing is serializable; therefore, it is equivalent to serial commit processing. As serial commit processing guarantees a traditional linear history for each summary row and for the entire database, versioning and snapshot isolation are made compatible with escrow locking even if multiple transactions commit concurrently.

Contents-neutral keys and records in B-tree indexes do not affect the semantics of a database, and system transactions may create them just as they erase them in commercial systems today. Delta counts in summary rows can subsume the roles of ghost bits in pseudo-deleted records and of anti-matter bits during online index operations because they can represent more information than those two separate bits can.

Transaction, media, and system failures and their recovery rely on traditional logging in stable storage (not on virtual log records), and our design calls for traditional logging and X locks at the time when changes are actually applied to the database. Thus, changes can be replayed for media and system recovery, and any transaction can be rolled back at any time until the final commit record is logged. In other words, even a failure during commit processing can be rolled back or compensated based on the recovery log.

3.11 PERFORMANCE

The performance advantages of locking methods that permit multiple concurrent increment operations have been demonstrated in a prototype based on a commercial product [Luo et al., 2003], although that design supports neither concurrent read and update transactions (over the same data) nor concurrent execution and commit processing for small and large update transactions.

Further performance effects of the presented design must be considered for two different cases. First, assume a database system's only current user attempts to perform a large update of tables and of materialized views over those tables. In this case, any and all concurrency control is wasted effort, and performance will not improve in the present design and might even deteriorate due to additional overheads. Second, if high concurrency is required around the clock, and if both data analysis and database maintenance operations are required, our design creates entirely new opportunities not supported by prior work.

For the first case, consider the overhead of saving earlier versions in each update. Clearly, update processing will slow down due to creating and copying old versions of records. Alternatively, some versioning techniques do not retain prior versions during the update but recreate them on demand when needed by a query transaction; or creating and copying old record versions can be suppressed if no other transaction is active at the time of the update. Either one of these alternatives applies to any multi-version concurrency control scheme, and would also apply to and improve the design presented here. Successful commercial database management system products demonstrate that multi-version snapshot isolation can perform very well.

With respect to virtual log records, it is worthwhile to consider that IMS/FastPath performs very well using intention lists. Thus, with careful implementation and tuning effort, the cost difference should be quite moderate between the presented design and a traditional design based entirely on shared and exclusive locks.

For the second case, the presented design enables new scenarios, which must be considered both in terms of concurrency and in terms of availability of tables, views, and their indexes. In a traditional design, materialized views and their indexes are maintained either instantly within the user transaction or periodically in large batches. In the former case, contention for summary rows might render real-time information analysis and monitoring infeasible. In the latter case, large (table or index) locks are required during view maintenance, leading to periods during which the database is not available for queries or update. During those periods, traditional locking schemes would simply defer any incoming query or update transaction, whereas the presented design can process updates instantly with full use of all tables, views, and indexes; and it can be employed to support concurrent update transactions while a separate large batch transaction refreshes or re-creates the materialized view. Given the current interest in stream processing, continuous full availability is very desirable, whereas periods of high load and large locks are very undesirable. If the waiting time is considered part of a query or update transaction's performance, the presented design should compare extremely favorably to traditional designs.

3.12   SUMMARY AND CONCLUSIONS

In summary, the presented combination of snapshot isolation and escrow locking, the latter generalized to exploit and complement proven database implementation techniques, is a relatively simple yet robust and efficient solution for concurrency control and recovery of materialized summary views and their indexes. Combining these techniques, including some novel techniques to make their combination possible, achieves several goals not addressed in prior research. Foremost among those is contention-free concurrent high read traffic and high update traffic over the same summary data. Second is the ability to combine read and update traffic with large bulk operations, e.g., data import and even online index creation.

The novel techniques presented include multi-granularity (hierarchical) escrow locking and serializable (instead of serial) commit processing. The latter is desirable when deferred increment operations based on virtual log records increase commit processing time for large operations such as bulk data loading. It is achieved using commit-time-only exclusive locks, and deadlocks between concurrent commit activities are proactively avoided by sorting the keys for which commit-time-only locks are required. Such commit-timeonly locks generalize the serial commit processing employed in IBM's FastPath product, and can also serve as a template for installing validated updates in optimistic concurrency control methods.

Moreover, the presented design considers not only concurrency control but also logging and recovery. Slight modifications in the format of log records describing record updates and moderate extensions in the interpretation during *undo* processing extend the Aries recovery method for transaction rollback, media recovery, and system recovery. Transaction rollback to save points requires some additional consideration for virtual log records, akin to use of virtual log records in today's commercial systems for large operations such as dropping an index or a table. Checkpoints are not affected by multiple concurrent updates, new transactions can be accepted before restart recovery is complete, and checkpoints during all phases of restart recovery are possible. Virtual (logical *redo*) log records processed during transaction commit ensure a serial history for each record and thus enable versioning support even when multiple update transactions hold concurrent locks on the same data item.

Finally, the design unifies ghost bits, anti-matter bits, duplicate counts, reference counts, group size, and delta counts to enable increment and decrement operations by multiple concurrent uncommitted user transactions. Queries ignore records with counts equal to zero (similar to queries today ignoring records with a ghost bit), and contents-neutral system transactions create and erase records with counts equal to zero such that user update transactions indeed only increment and decrement values but never insert and delete records or keys in a materialized view or any of its indexes. By melting multiple concepts (including the anti-matter used in online index operations) into a single delta count, the presented design is the first to permit online creation of indexed views that require grouping or that might include duplicate rows.

In conclusion, the presented design is a novel combination of implementation techniques that are already proven in database transaction processing, and we hope that it will prove successful in supporting real-time business analysis. Having completed the high-level design, our next steps are to prototype, implement, tune, evaluate, document, release, and support these techniques in a commercial database management system.

3.13 REFERENCES

Arun, G. and Joshi, A. (1998). KODA—The architecture and interface of a data model independent kernel. *VLDB Conference*, pp. 671–674. 85

Berenson, H., Bernstein, P. A., Gray, J., Melton, J., O'Neil, E. J., and O'Neil, P. E. (1995). A critique of ANSI SQL isolation levels. *ACM SIGMOD Conference*, pp. 1–10. DOI: 10.1145/223784.223785. 84

Bernstein, P. A., Hadzilacos, V., and Goodman, N. (1987). *Concurrency Control and Recovery in Database Systems*, Addison-Wesley Longman Publishing Co., Inc., Boston, MA. 84

Blakeley, J. A., Coburn, N., and Larson, P. (1986). Updating derived relations: Detecting irrelevant and autonomously computable updates. *VLDB Conference*, pp. 457–466. DOI: 10.1145/68012.68015. 80, 94

Blakeley, J. A., Larson, P., and Tompa, F. W. (1986). Efficiently updating materialized views. *ACM SIGMOD Conference*, pp. 61–71. DOI: 10.1145/16856.16861. 94

Blasgen, M. (2003). Personal communication. 90

Bridge, W., Joshi, A., Keihl, M., Lahiri, T., Loaiza, J., MacNaughton, N. (1997). The oracle universal server buffer manager. *VLDB Conference*, pp. 590–594. 84

Chang, J.-W., Lee, Y.-K., and Whang, K.-Y. (2002). Global lock escalation in database management systems. *Information Processing Letters*, 82(4), pp. 179–186. DOI: 10.1016/s0020-0190(01)00261-7. 86

Chang, J.-W., Whang, K.-Y., Lee, Y.-K., Yang, J.-H., and Oh, Y.-C. (2005). A formal approach to lock escalation. *Information Systems*, 30(2), pp. 151–166. DOI: 10.1016/j.is.2003.10.009. 86

DeWitt, D. J., Katz, R. H., Olken, F., Shapiro, L. D., Stonebraker, M., and Wood, D. A. (1984). Implementation techniques for main memory database systems. *ACM SIGMOD Conference*, pp. 1–8. DOI: 10.1145/602260.602261. 89

Gärtner, A., Kemper, A., Kossmann, D., and Zeller, B. (2001). Efficient bulk deletes in relational databases. *IEEE ICDE*, pp. 183–192. DOI: 10.1109/icde.2001.914827. 103

Gawlick, D. (2003). Personal communication. 83

Gawlick, D. and Kinkade, D. (1985). Varieties of concurrency control in IMS/VS fast path. *IEEE Data Engineering Bulletin*, 8(2), pp. 3–10. 82, 89, 101

Gottemukkala, V. and Lehman, T. J. (1992). Locking and latching in a memory-resident database system. *VLDB Conference*, pp. 533–544. 86

Graefe, G. (2003). Sorting and indexing with partitioned B-tree. *Conference on Innovative Data Systems Research*, Asilomar, CA, January. http://www-db.cs.wisc.edu/cidr 121

Gray, J. and Reuter, A. (1993). *Transaction Processing: Concepts and Techniques*, Morgan Kaufmann, San Mateo, CA. 85, 90, 111, 115

Gupta, A. and Mumick, I. S. Eds. (1999). *Materialized Views: Techniques, Implementations, and Applications*, The MIT Press, Cambridge, MA. DOI: 10.7551/mitpress/4472.001.0001. 80

Halici, U. and Dogac, A. (1991). An optimistic locking technique for concurrency control in distributed databases. *IEEE Transactions on Software Engineering*, 17(7), pp. 712–724. DOI: 10.1109/32.83907. 110, 111

Härder, T. and Reuter, A. (1983). Principles of transaction-oriented database recovery. *ACM Computing Surveys*, 15(4), pp. 287–317. DOI: 10.1145/289.291. 89

Härder. T. (1984). Observations on optimistic concurrency control schemes. *Information Systems*, 9(2), pp. 111–120. DOI: 10.1016/0306-4379(84)90020-6. 112

Johnson, T. and Shasha, D. (1989). Utilization of B-trees with inserts, deletes and modifies. *PODS Conference*, pp. 235–246. DOI: 10.1145/73721.73745. 90

Joshi, A. M. (1991). Adaptive locking strategies in a multi-node data sharing environment. *VLDB Conference*, pp. 181–191. 86

Kawaguchi, A., Lieuwen, D. F., Mumick, I. S., Quass, D., and Ross, K. A. (1997). Concurrency control theory for deferred materialized views. *ICDT*, pp. 306–320. DOI: 10.1007/3-540-62222-5_53. 80

Kim, S. H., Jung, M. S., Park, J. H. and Park, Y. C. (1999). A design and implementation of savepoints and partial rollbacks considering transaction isolation levels of SQL2. *DASFAA Conference*, pp. 303–312. DOI: 10.1109/dasfaa.1999.765764. 87

Korth, H. F. (1983). Locking primitives in a database system. *JACM*, 30(1), pp. 55–79. DOI: 10.1145/322358.322363. 85, 112, 121

Kung, H. T. and Robinson, J. T. (1979). On optimistic methods for concurrency control. *VLDB Conference*, p. 351. DOI: 10.1145/319566.319567. 110

Kung, H. T. and Robinson, J. T. (1981). On optimistic methods for concurrency control. *ACM TODS*, 6(2), pp. 213–226. DOI: 10.1145/319566.319567. 110

Lausen, G. (1982). Concurrency control in database systems: A step towards the integration of optimistic methods and locking. *ACM Conference*, pp. 64–68. DOI: 10.1145/800174.809759. 111

Lehman, T. J. and Carey, M. J. (1989). A concurrency control algorithm for memory-resident database systems. *FODO*, pp. 490–504. DOI: 10.1007/3-540-51295-0_150. 86

Liskov, B. and Scheifler, R. (1982). Guardians and actions: Linguistic support for robust, distributed programs. *POPL Conference*, pp. 7–19. DOI: 10.1145/582153.582155. 82

Lomet, D. B. (1992). MLR: A recovery method for multi-level systems. *ACM SIGMOD Conference*, pp. 185–194. DOI: 10.1145/130283.130314. 81, 90

Lomet, D. B. (1993). Key range locking strategies for improved concurrency. *VLDB Conference*, pp. 655–664. 117

Luo, G., Naughton, J. F., Ellmann, C., and Watzke, M. (2003). Locking protocols for materialized aggregate join views. *VLDB Conference*, pp. 596–607. DOI: 10.1016/b978-012722442-8/50059-8. 80, 81, 122

Luo, G., Naughton, J. F., Ellmann, C. J., and Watzke, M. (2005). Locking protocols for materialized aggregate join views. *IEEE Transactions on Knowledge Data Engineering*, 17(6), pp. 796–807. DOI: 10.1109/tkde.2005.96. 80, 81

Mohan, C. (1990). ARIES/KVL: A key-value locking method for concurrency control of multiaction transactions operating on B-tree indexes. *VLDB Conference*, pp. 392–405. 90

Mohan, C. (1990). Commit_LSN: A novel and simple method for reducing locking and latching in transaction processing systems. *VLDB Conference*, pp. 406–418. 85, 90

Mohan, C. (1992). Less optimism about optimistic concurrency control. *RIDE-TQP*, pp. 199–204. DOI: 10.1109/ride.1992.227405. 112

Mohan, C., Haderle, D. J., Lindsay, B. G., Pirahesh, H., and Schwarz, P. M. (1992). ARIES: A transaction recovery method supporting fine-granularity locking and partial rollbacks using write-ahead logging. *ACM TODS*, 17(1), pp. 94–162. DOI: 10.1145/128765.128770. 81, 82, 108

Mohan, C. and Narang, I. (1992). Algorithms for creating indexes for very large tables without quiescing updates. *ACM SIGMOD Conference*, pp. 361–370. DOI: 10.1145/141484.130337. 91, 119

O'Neil, P. E. (1986). The escrow transactional method. *ACM TODS*, 11(4), pp. 405–430. DOI: 10.1145/7239.7265. 82, 100

Palpanas, T., Sidle, R., Cochrane, R., and Pirahesh, H. (2003). Incremental maintenance for non-distributive aggregate functions. *VLDB Conference*. DOI: 10.1016/b978-155860869-6/50076-7.

Quass, D. (1996). Maintenance expressions for views with aggregation. *Workshop on Materialized Views: Techniques and Applications (VIEW)*, pp. 110–118, Montreal, Canada, June 7. 94

Reuter, A. (1982). Concurrency on high-traffic data elements. *ACM PODS Conference*, pp. 83–92. DOI: 10.1145/588111.588126. 83

Samaras, G., Britton, K., Citron, A., and Mohan, C. (1993). Two-phase commit optimizations and tradeoffs in the commercial environment. *IEEE ICDE*, pp. 520–529. DOI: 10.1109/icde.1993.344028. 89, 109

Shasha, D. (1985). What good are concurrent search structure algorithms for databases anyway? *IEEE Database Engineering Bulletin*, 8(2), pp. 84–90. 82

Skeen, D. (1981). Nonblocking commit protocols. *ACM SIGMOD Conference*, pp. 133–142. DOI: 10.1145/582338.582339. 90

Transaction Processing Performance Council. `http://www.tpc.org/tpch` DOI: 10.1007/978-3-319-77525-8_100350. 76

Weikum, G., Hasse, C., Brössler, P., and Muth, P. (1990). Multi-level recovery. *ACM PODS Conference*, pp. 109–123. DOI: 10.1145/298514.298548. 81

Weikum, G. and Schek, H.-J. (1984). Architectural issues of transaction management in multi-layered systems. *VLDB Conference*, pp. 454–465. 81

CHAPTER 4

Controlled Lock Violation

Goetz Graefe, Mark Lillibridge, Harumi Kuno, Joseph Tucek, and Alistair Veitch, *Hewlett-Packard Laboratories*

ABSTRACT

In databases with a large buffer pool, a transaction may run in less time than it takes to log the transaction's commit record on stable storage. Such cases motivate a technique called early lock release: immediately after appending its commit record to the log buffer in memory, a transaction may release its locks. Thus, it cuts overall lock duration to a fraction and reduces lock contention accordingly.

Early lock release also has its problems. The initial mention of early lock release was incomplete, the first detailed description and implementation was incorrect with respect to read-only transactions, and the most recent design initially had errors and still does not cover unusual lock modes such as "increment" locks. Thus, we set out to achieve the same goals as early lock release but with a different, simpler, and more robust approach.

The resulting technique, controlled lock violation, requires no new theory, applies to any lock mode, promises less implementation effort and slightly less run-time effort, and also optimizes distributed transactions, e.g., in systems that rely on multiple replicas for high availability and high reliability. In essence, controlled lock violation retains locks until the transaction is durable but permits other transactions to violate its locks while flushing its commit log record to stable storage.

4.1 INTRODUCTION

A simple database transaction takes 20,000–100,000 instructions [Anon et al., 1985], depending on the transaction logic, on index structures, on the quality of the implementation, and on compiler optimizations. For example, assuming 40,000 instructions per transaction, 1 instruction per CPU cycle on average, a 4 GHz CPU clock, and no buffer faults, a modern processor core can execute the transaction logic in about 0.01 ms. Committing such a transaction, however, may take much longer. If "stable storage" for the recovery log is a pair of traditional disk drives, the time to commit might approach 10 ms. If stable storage for the recovery log is provided by flash storage, commit time might be faster by two orders of magnitude, i.e., 0.1 ms, but it is still an order of magnitude longer than transaction execution.

If a transaction acquires locks right at its start, e.g., key value locks in a B-tree index, and holds them until transaction commit is complete, it retains the locks for about 0.01 ms while the transaction logic proceeds and for another 0.1 ms (or even 10 ms) during commit processing, i.e., after the transaction logic is complete. Given these relationships, it is not surprising that researchers have sought to reduce lock contention during commit processing. Retaining locks for only 0.01 ms, not 0.11 ms (or even 10.01 ms), should appreciably reduce lock contention, in particular for "hot spot" locks such as appending index entries to an index on transaction time or on an attribute with high correlation to transaction time, e.g., order number or invoice number.

Figure 4.1 illustrates the relationship between transaction execution time and commit duration. The diagram shows a factor of 10. In the traditional sequence of actions during commit processing, each transaction holds its locks for the entire time shown by the blue line above the time line. In a transaction with early lock release, lock retention is as short as the green line below the time line. The same performance improvement is achieved by a new technique, controlled lock violation, even in its simple form.

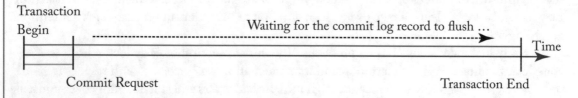

Figure 4.1: Lock retention times in traditional and optimized commit sequences.

Multiple prior research efforts have described early lock release, which lets a transaction release its locks immediately after space for a commit record is allocated in the log buffer in memory. In other words, the locks are released before the commit record is flushed to stable storage and thus before the transaction becomes durable. Soisalon-Soininen and Ylönen [1995] proved this technique correct, i.e., recoverable, but their proof does not address concurrency control and transaction isolation. Johnson et al. [2010] and Kimura et al. [2012] measured dramatic improvements in lock contention and in transaction throughput. Unfortunately, early lock release can also produce wrong results, including incorrect updates, because an implementation may fail to respect commit dependencies among participating transactions, as illustrated in Figure 4.2. In essence, one transaction must not publish or persist another transaction's update until the update is durable.

Recent work by Kimura et al. [2012] describes a new variant of early lock release that avoids these wrong results yet preserves performance and scalability. The principal idea is to remove the locks from the lock manager early but to retain "tags" to convey commit dependencies among transactions. In some cases, commit dependencies are respected that do not exist, i.e., the technique is too conservative. As importantly, the tags do not fully optimize distributed transactions, e.g., in modern database systems that maintain multiple replicas for high availabil-

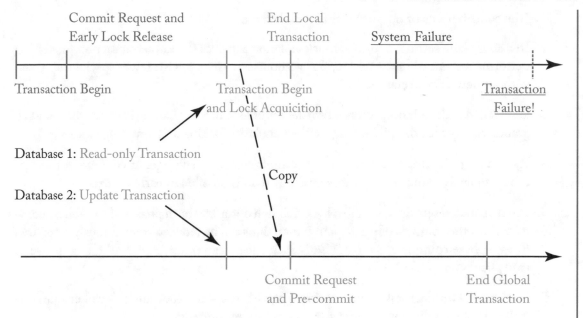

Figure 4.2: Bad database contents due to early lock release.

ity and high reliability. Nonetheless, lacking other correct implementations, we take this as the prototypical representative of early lock release.

Controlled lock violation is a new and superior alternative to early lock release. It eschews early lock release and the need for tags. Instead, each transaction retains its locks until its commit process is complete. With respect to concurrency, controlled lock violation matches early lock release as it permits subsequent transactions to violate or ignore lock conflicts, but only in very controlled situations. More specifically, a subsequent transaction may acquire a lock that violates an existing lock if the transaction holding the lock is already in its commit process, i.e., if it has allocated a commit record in the log buffer. Thus, controlled lock violation enables concurrency in all situations in which early lock release (corrected with tags) enables concurrency.

Moreover, controlled lock violation can improve the concurrency not only of centralized, single-site transactions but also of distributed transactions. Thus, controlled lock violation can increase concurrency during commit processing in modern system designs that rely on replicas. The same issue—multiple separate recovery logs and two-phase commit—equally applies to many partitioned databases. For example, in a large database partitioned such that individual partitions (and their individual recovery logs) can easily move in order to achieve elastic scaling, transactions over multiple partitions require two-phase commit even when all affected partitions currently reside on the same server. In contrast to early lock release, controlled lock violation optimizes commit processing and lock conflicts in all those settings.

The contributions of our new technique are these:

1. In a single-site setting, controlled lock violation achieves the same transaction processing performance as early lock release, but without new theory, with fewer special cases, and without new data structures.

2. Controlled lock violation covers a broader set of lock modes than early lock release and all granularities of locking, including multi-granularity locking and key-range locking.

3. By retaining the original locks during commit activities, subsequent conflicting transactions can analyze the conflict more precisely than is possible in early lock release.

4. In a distributed setting, controlled lock violation optimizes both phases of two-phase commit. Thus, the conflicts of participant transactions can be reduced tremendously compared to two-phase commit execution. (Early lock release can optimize only the final phase of two-phase commit.)

5. For "canned transactions" coded as stored procedures, static code analysis can enable controlled lock violation even before a transaction's commit request.

The following section reviews related prior work, in particular on early lock release and two-phase commit. Section 4.3 introduces controlled lock violation and contrasts it to early lock release. Section 4.4 extends controlled lock violation to two-phase commit and Section 4.5 applies it to canned transactions. Section 4.6 compares the performance of controlled lock violation with that of early lock release in those cases when early lock release applies. Section 4.7 compares controlled lock violation with further related techniques, e.g., speculative execution. The final section contains our summary and conclusions.

4.2   RELATED PRIOR WORK

DeWitt et al. [1984] described early lock release back in 1984, albeit without an implementation. Ailamaki and her research group have described a highly optimized implementation as well as the resulting speed-up in transaction processing [Johnson et al., 2009]. Kimura et al. describe an oversight in the earlier designs as well as a technique to avoid over-eager commit of read-only transactions [Kimura et al., 2012]. These efforts are discussed below, followed by a summary of other but unrelated cases of early lock release as well as some background information on distributed two-phase commit.

We assume concurrent and serializable transactions implemented by commonly used techniques, including write-ahead logging, log sequence numbers, record-level locking, logical "undo" by logged compensating updates rather than rigid physical "undo," an in-memory buffer pool for data and recovery log plus persistent block-access storage such as traditional disks, durability by forcing commit records to the recovery log on "stable storage," two-phase commit in distributed transactions, etc. The intention behind these assumptions is broad applicability of the work.

4.2.1   MAIN MEMORY DATABASES

An early paper [DeWitt et al., 1984] on implementation techniques for main memory database systems described early lock release as follows (original emphasis):

> "A scheme that amortizes the log I/O across several transactions is based on the notion of a pre-committed transaction. When a transaction is ready to complete, the transaction management system places its commit record in the log buffer. The transaction releases all locks *without waiting for the commit record to be written to disk*. The transaction is delayed from committing until its commit record actually appears on disk. The 'user' is not notified that the transactions has committed until this event has occurred.
>
> By releasing its locks before it commits, other transactions can read the pre-committed transaction's dirty data. Call these *dependent transactions*. Reading un-committed data in this way does not lead to an inconsistent state as long as the pre-committed transaction actually commits *before* its dependent transactions. A pre-committed transaction does not commit only if the system crashes, never because of a user or system induced abort. As long as records are sequentially added to the log, and the pages of the log buffer are written to disk in sequence, a pre-committed transaction will have its commit record on disk before dependent transactions."

In this design, locks are released early, without distinction by lock mode, e.g., shared or exclusive. It is well known that read locks can be released early, e.g., during the pre-commit phase of distributed transactions with two-phase commit. Write locks, on the other hand, re-quire longer retention in traditional transaction processing. Similarly, this design does not dis-tinguish between read-only and read-write transactions among the dependent transactions. It turns out that the next design repeats this erroneous omission. (Figure 4.2 shows an example error scenario.)

4.2.2   EARLY LOCK RELEASE IN SHORE-MT

Researchers at CMU and EPFL implemented early lock release as part of tuning Shore-MT [Johnson et al., 2009], specifically to remove logging from the critical path of transaction processing by avoiding all lock contention while a transaction becomes durable.

Johnson et al. demonstrate "speedup due to ELR [early lock release] when running the TPC-B benchmark and varying I/O latency and skew in data accesses" while logging on dif-ferent forms of stable storage, including logging to a slow traditional disk (10 ms for a write to stable storage) and logging to flash (write in 0.1 ms) [Johnson et al., 2010]. Running TPC-B (which produces many lock conflicts) against a traditional logging device, their work shows that early lock release can speed up system throughput 30-fold; for a fast logging device, system throughput improves 3-fold.

While the speed-ups are impressive, early lock release as originally described and implemented in Shore-MT can produce wrong results and even wrong database contents [Kimura et al., 2012]. For example, consider a transaction T_0 acquiring an exclusive lock to update a database record, then releasing the lock after formatting a commit record in the log buffer, whereupon transaction T_1 acquires a lock on the same database record. If both transactions T_0 and T_1 are update transactions, then the sequencing of commit records enforces the commit dependency between them. What happens, however, if the dependent transaction T_1 does not require a commit record because it is a read-only transaction? In this case, it may read and report a value written by transaction T_0 before the commit of transaction T_1 is complete. Transaction T_1 may terminate successfully and thus commit to the user a value that may never exist in the database if the commit record of transaction T_0 is never saved on stable storage, e.g., due to a system crash.

For an example resulting in bad database contents, consider a transaction T_0 that updates a record in the database D_0 from old value 10 to new value 11 and then begins its commit activities. After T_0 has formatted its commit record in the log buffer and released its locks, transaction T_1 reads the value 11, copies it into another database D_1, and then performs its own commit. This commit is a two-phase commit between databases D_0 and D_1. Assume that database D_1 provides commit coordination and logs global commit records. Since transaction T_1 is a read-only transaction in database D_0, the pre-commit phase is sufficient there, the second commit phase is not required, and no log record is written in database D_0 for transaction T_1. Moreover, assume that stable storage for database D_1 is fast (e.g., flash storage) whereas stable storage for database D_0 is slower (e.g., a traditional disk). In this case, it is quite possible that transaction T_1 commits, including saving its final global commit record on stable storage, before transaction T_0 can do the same and become durable. If database D_0 crashes in the meantime, database D_0 rolls the data record back to value 10, whereas database D_1 contains value 11. Clearly, this result of "copying" from database D_0 to database D_1 is not acceptable transactional behavior.

Figure 4.2 illustrates this example. There are two parallel timelines for the two databases. One transaction (blue) in Database 1 reaches its commit point but never achieves durability due to a system failure (red); thus, this transaction and all its updates are rolled back during system recovery. The distributed transaction (green) attempts a two-phase commit prior to the system failure; the local read-only sub-transaction in Database 1 immediately responds and does not participate in the second commit phase. The coordinator may commit the global transaction even after one of the participating sites fails, because the local sub-transaction on Database 1 terminated successfully. At the end, the value copied from Database 1 to Database 2 will remain in Database 2 but be rolled back in Database 1, such that Database 2 is no longer a faithful copy of Database 1.

4.2.3   EARLY LOCK RELEASE IN FOSTER B-TREES

As part of an effort to prototype and evaluate a new B-tree variant, early lock release was also implemented in the context of prototyping Foster B-trees [Graefe et al., 2012], although design and implementation of the locking subsystem are orthogonal to its usage in any specific data structure. This is the first implementation of early lock release to avoid the danger of wrong results and wrong database contents. The technique employed relies on tags in the lock manager's hash table [Kimura et al., 2012]. When an update transaction releases a lock as part of early lock release, it leaves a tag containing the log sequence number of its commit record. Any subsequent transaction acquiring a lock on the same object must not commit until the appropriate log page has been written to stable storage.

Figure 4.3 illustrates where tags are attached in the lock manager's hash table. The tag contains a high water mark, i.e., a log sequence number. Any transaction acquiring any lock on the same object cannot commit until this log record is on stable storage.

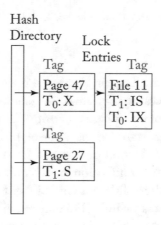

Figure 4.3: Hash table with tags.

Figure 4.4, copied from Kimura et al. [2012], shows performance improvements due to early lock release in Shore-MT [Johnson et al., 2009], including the version with Foster B-trees [Graefe et al., 2012] instead of the original Shore-MT indexes. The relative performance of Foster B-trees and the original Shore-MT B-tree implementation is not relevant here as it is partially due to differences in representation and compression of records in pages. A comparison of fully implemented early lock release (purple triangles) with the same code minus early lock release (blue stars) demonstrates performance advantages across almost the entire range from an insert-only workload (read ratio 0%) to read-only queries (read ratio 100%). The performance advantage reverses for a read-only workload "because ELR checks the transaction's lock requests twice at commit time" [Kimura et al., 2012]. This experiment logs on flash storage; the effects are similar or stronger with the recovery log on traditional disks.

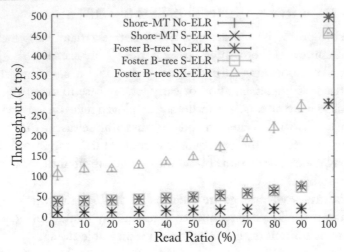

Figure 4.4: Performance effects of early lock release, © VLDB Endowment.

The performance of early lock release in Figure 4.4 is also indicative of the performance of controlled lock violation. This is because they are equivalent in their effect, at least in single-site cases (they are not in the context of two-phase commit). After all, one transaction releasing its locks is effectively the same as other transactions ignoring those same locks (in the same cases).

Unfortunately, after the introduction of tags had "repaired" early lock release, it needed yet another repair. Early lock release for intention locks requires tags just like absolute locks (i.e., nonintention locks), but they require a different kind of tag. For example, two transactions may both acquire intention locks on the same index but may touch different index entries. Thus, tags for intention locks should introduce commit dependencies only in conflicts with absolute locks but not with intention locks [Kimura et al., 2012].

Of course, one wonders how many additional kinds of tags might be required. For example, Microsoft SQL Server uses multiple special locks such as "insert" locks, "bulk insertion" locks, "schema stability" and "schema modify" locks, etc. In other words, what seems needed is either a theory for deriving appropriate tags from lock modes (as in Korth [1983]) or a mechanism (including an appropriate theory and policy) that avoids tags altogether.

One may also wonder how early lock release may optimize distributed transactions with two-phase commit. It turns out, unfortunately, that the optimizations of early lock release apply to the final commit phase only but not to the pre-commit phase. In other words, a participant transaction may release its read-only locks during the pre-commit phase (as is well known) but it must retain its update locks until the local participant transaction has appended its final commit record to the log buffer. Lock retention time is reduced only by the time to write the final commit record to stable storage but not by the time for writing the pre-commit record during the initial phase or for communication and coordination during a two-phase commit. This is discussed further in Section 4.4.

4.2.4   OTHER CASES OF EARLY LOCK RELEASE

In addition to the instances outlined above, other instances of early lock release have been mentioned in the literature or are used in real systems.

First, when a transaction employs "save points," e.g., between individual SQL statements, and if a transaction rolls back to an earlier save point, then it may release the locks it acquired after that save point. For example, if a transaction's first statement touched only index I_1 and the second statement touched index I_2, but the second statement failed and the transaction rolls back to the save point between the two statements, then all locks on index I_2 may be released during this partial rollback.

Second, when a transaction must abort, it may release all its read-only locks immediately. Only the write locks are required to protect the rollback actions. As the rollback logic proceeds, it may release locks as it completes the rollback ("undo," compensation) actions, i.e., in reverse order of lock acquisition.

Third, when the global coordinator in a two-phase commit requests that local participant transactions prepare for transaction commit, read-only participants may terminate immediately [Traiger et al., 1982]. This includes releasing all their locks; obviously, those are all read-only locks. In addition, a read-only participant has no need to participate in the second phase of the two-phase commit. This is perhaps the most well known example of early lock release.

Fourth, read-write participants in a two-phase commit may release their read-only locks immediately upon receiving the request to prepare for a transaction commit. In other words, early lock release in two-phase commit is not dependent on the overall behavior of the local participant but on the nature of the locks—a transaction may release its read-only locks immediately after the commit request.

Fifth, even in the absence of distribution and two-phase commit, a transaction may release its read-only locks as soon as it has allocated space for a commit record in the log buffer. This technique requires that each transaction scans its set of locks twice, once to find (and release) its read-only locks and once again (at the very end) to release the remaining locks. Early lock release requires only one such scan, which releases all locks and inserts tags into the lock manager's hash table. These tags will be cleared out by subsequent transactions finding tags that expired. Controlled lock violation requires only the final scan after all commit activities; it may, however, use an earlier scan over all its locks in order to identify all transactions already waiting for those locks and able to resume with controlled lock violation.

Sixth, existing locks may be modified in their lock modes in order to strip out the read-only aspects. For example, an SIX lock [Gray et al., 1975] may be reduced to a lock in IX mode. (An SIX lock combines a shared S lock and an intent-exclusive IX lock on the same object—the compatibility matrix for intention locks is shown in Figure 4.5.) Locks may also be reduced in their coverage or granularity of locking. For example, an exclusive X lock on an entire index may be reduced to an IX lock on the index combined with appropriate X locks on individual pages or index entries. Note that lock de-escalation can proceed without checking for lock conflicts and cannot create a deadlock. Thus, the X lock on the index is not released but instead it is much reduced in its strength or coverage.

	IS	IX	S	X	SIX
IS	✓	✓	✓	–	✓
IX	✓	✓	–	–	–
S	✓	–	✓	–	–
X	–	–	–	–	–
SIX	✓	–	–	–	–

Figure 4.5: Compatibility of hierarchical locks.

Finally, key range locking raises special cases for the last two points. Some key range locks guarantee the absence of possible future database contents, specifically locks on the open interval between two existing key values in an ordered index such as a B-tree. Such locks are required to prevent phantoms and to ensure true serializability [Gray et al., 1976]. As special forms of read-only locks, they can be released prior to the transaction's commit activities. Other key range locks combine read-only and update parts, with only the update aspect required during commit activities. For example, a XS lock ("key exclusive, gap shared") [Graefe, 2010] can be reduced to an XN lock ("key exclusive, gap free") as part of releasing all readonly locks. Figure 4.6 shows a B-tree node with a few key values as well as some of these lock modes and their scope.

```
      S       SN       NS
   [      )[ ]      (    )
   20     30     40     50
```

Figure 4.6: Lock scopes in key range locking.

4.2.5   DISTRIBUTED COMMIT

The traditional standard for committing a transaction over multiple nodes (or multiple recovery logs) has been two-phase commit, with all locks retained until all commit activities are complete. Thomson et al. [2012] observe that "The problem with holding locks during the agreement protocol is that two-phase commit requires multiple network round-trips between all participating machines, and therefore the time required to run the protocol can often be considerably greater than the time required to execute all local transaction logic. If a few popularly-accessed records are frequently involved in distributed transactions, the resulting extra time that locks are held on these records can have an extremely deleterious effect on overall transactional throughput." Therefore, their design sequences transactions deterministically in order to "eliminate distributed commit protocols, the largest scalability impediment of modern distributed systems." In contrast, controlled lock violation reduces the "contention footprint" [Thomson et al., 2012] of two-phase commit by judiciously violating locks held by committing transactions.

Kraska et al. [2012] similarly aim to reduce lock conflicts by reducing commit communication. They "describe a new optimistic commit protocol for the wide-area network. In contrast to pessimistic commit protocols such as two-phase commit, the protocol does not require a prepare phase and commits updates in a single message round-trip across data centers if no conflicts are detected" [Kraska et al., 2012]. An essential part of this protocol seems to be that each request for work includes a request to prepare for commit, quite comparable to the first phase of a traditional two-phase commit. In either case, a local transaction guarantees that it will abide by a subsequent global decision to commit or abort.

With this guarantee in place, a single message carrying the global decision can achieve the final commit, comparable to the second phase of a traditional two-phase commit. As each work request includes a request for commit preparation, each work step with local database updates requires a prepared-to-commit log record in each local recovery log. Moreover, a prepared local transaction is protected, i.e., it cannot be terminated, e.g., if it becomes part of a deadlock. Note that a local participant may subsequently receive additional work requests for the same transaction. If the additional work request includes database updates, it invalidates the prior commit preparation and requires a new one, including another suitable log record written to stable storage.

Kraska et al. measured round-trip response times between various regions on Amazon's EC2 cluster over a number of days [Kraska et al., 2012]. Even communication links with response times around 0.1–0.2 seconds most of the time can spike to about 1 second and even to about 4 minutes. Note that these are message delays, not failures. If such delays affect communication during two-phase commit, and if transactions retain locks during commit coordination, spikes in communication latency likely produce spikes in lock contention.

Kraska et al. [2012] propose to address the problem by imposing the cost to prepare a two-phase commit on every remote invocation within every transaction, whether or not network latency is currently spiking. In contrast, controlled lock violation addresses the problem by permitting subsequent transactions to violate locks and proceed while earlier transactions run their commit activities.

4.3   CONTROLLED LOCK VIOLATION

While early lock release removes locks from the lock manager before writing the commit record to stable storage, controlled lock violation retains the locks until transaction end. In order to match the concurrency and performance of early lock release, however, controlled lock violation permits new transactions to acquire conflicting locks in a controlled way. Specifically, in the simplest form of controlled lock violation, lock acquisition is permitted if the transaction holding the lock has appended its commit record to the log buffer. The advanced forms of controlled lock violation have more relaxed rules, e.g., for two-phase commit (Section 4.4) or for canned transactions (Section 4.5).

Figure 4.7 illustrates a sequence of three transactions that all require a lock on the same database object. The green horizontal lines represent the time needed to execute transaction logic; the red horizontal lines represent time spent waiting for locks or for log records to flush to stable storage. The top diagram shows subsequent transactions acquiring the contested lock only after each preceding transaction has finished all its commit activities. The bottom diagram shows how subsequent transactions may acquire the contested lock and run the transaction logic immediately after the preceding transaction has started its commit activities, specifically after adding its commit log record to the in-memory log buffer. Note that in the lower figure, the commit log records of transactions T_0 and T_1 happen to go to stable storage in the same I/O operation. Obviously, controlled lock violation enable transactions to follow each other in faster succession. The "price" for this performance gain is that multiple transactions require rollback during recovery in case of a system failure; recall that a transaction with a commit log record in the log buffer can fail only if the entire system crashes.

4.3.1 PRINCIPLES

It is well known that if a transaction T_1 reads an update by a preceding yet uncommitted transaction T_0, also known as a dirty read, then T_1 incurs a commit dependency on T_0. In other words, in a serializable transaction execution schedule, transaction T_1 may commit only after transaction T_0 commits. More generally, if a transaction T_1 ignores or violates a concurrency control conflict, e.g., conflicting locks, with another transaction T_0, a commit dependency results.

The only exception is a read-only lock held by the earlier transaction. In this case, a commit dependency is not required. On the other hand, a read-only lock acquired in conflict with an earlier lock causes a commit dependency. In fact, this is the case overlooked in early designs for early lock release.

Of course, should transaction T_0 subsequently read or update a data item after transaction T_1 has updated it, then a circular dependency results. In such cases, serializability becomes impossible and transaction T_1 must abort.

One can consider a rollback of transaction T_0 as such a case: modern recovery techniques essentially "update back" the changes of failed transactions rather than reverse byte for byte. Logical transaction compensation is required whenever the granularity of locking, e.g., key value locking, lets multiple concurrent transactions modify the same physical data structure, e.g., a B-tree node. If transaction T_0 fails and rolls back after transaction T_1 has updated a data item already updated by transaction T_0, then the "update back" action completes a circular dependency

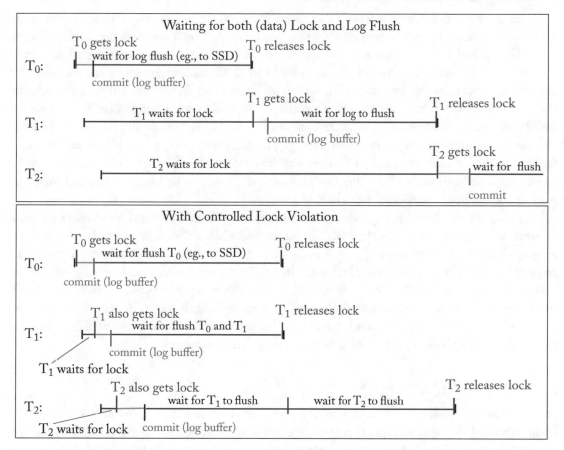

Figure 4.7: Sequences of three transactions (T_0, T_1, and T_2) without (top) and with (bottom) controlled lock violation.

that can be resolved only by aborting transaction T_1. Thus, thinking of rollback as "updating back" nicely explains the commit dependency mentioned above.

4.3.2 APPROACH

In a traditional database system without early lock release, imagine a transaction T_0 holding a lock and another transaction T_1 requesting a conflicting lock. In this case, T_1 might wait for T_0's commit (and the implied lock release) or T_1 might abort T_0 (and thus force immediate lock release). For a decision between these alternatives, it compares the priorities of T_0 and T_1. It also checks the state of T_0. If T_0 has already added a commit record to the log buffer, or if T_0 is part of a distributed transaction in pre-commit state, or if T_0 is already aborting and rolling back, then

T_0 is protected and T_1 cannot force T_0 to abort. Importantly, before transaction T_1 decides on a course of action, it must acquire information about transaction T_0 and its transactional state.

Controlled lock violation aims to achieve the performance advantages of early lock release (corrected with tags) but without releasing locks until all commit activities are complete. In controlled lock violation, transaction T_0 retains all its locks until its commit record indeed is on stable storage. However, if transaction T_1 comes along and looks at transaction T_0 (in order to decide its course of action, e.g., whether to abort T_0), and if T_0 already has a commit record in the log buffer (even if not yet on stable storage), then T_1 may proceed in spite of any locks T_0 still holds. Specifically, transaction T_1 may acquire its desired lock in spite of the conflict but it must take a commit dependency on T_0. Transaction T_0 retains its locks, so the lock manager may grant and hold conflicting locks in this case.

Actually, the commit dependency is required only if the lock held by transaction T_0 is an update lock, e.g., an exclusive lock, "intent exclusive" lock, "increment" lock, etc. In other words, violation of anything but a read-only lock creates a commit dependency. A write lock acquired in conflict with an earlier lock must be registered as a commit dependency, even if two update transactions and their commit records usually ensure a correct commit ordering. This is necessary because the write lock might be used only for reading: if the entire transaction remains a readonly transaction without any log records, then no commit record is required and the error case may occur unless the commit dependency is explicitly enforced.

4.3.3   IMPLEMENTATION TECHNIQUES

In the above examples, the crucial task missing from transaction T_0's commit is writing the commit record to stable storage; the other tasks are acknowledgement of the commit to the user (or application) and releasing locks and other resources such as threads and memory. As soon as the log write is complete and thus the transaction durable, the commit dependency is resolved.

Thus, the commit dependency is really equivalent to a high water mark in the recovery log. When the recovery log has been written to stable storage up to and including this high water mark, transaction T_1 is free to commit. In other words, when transaction T_1 acquires a lock that conflicts with a non-read-only lock held by transaction T_0, which is permitted because transaction T_0 has already written its commit record to the log buffer, then the LSN (log sequence number) of T_0's commit record is registered as the high water mark governing the commit of T_1. Transaction T_1 cannot commit until the recovery log has been written to stable storage up to and including this log record.

If transaction T_1 is an update transaction, then it will eventually append its own commit record to the log buffer and the log on stable storage. In this case, the sequencing of commit records in the recovery log will ensure correct enforcement of the commit dependency. In other words, the commit dependency is almost meaningless and enforced as a matter of course.

If, on the other hand, transaction T_1 is a read-only transaction without any log records and thus without a commit record, and if transaction T_1 has incurred a commit dependency by violating a lock of a committing transaction T_0, then T_1 must wait until the commit record of T_0 is saved on stable storage. This is precisely what the high water mark enforces. Thus, this technique delays a committing read-only transaction only if a lock violation has indeed occurred and only as much as absolutely necessary.

If transaction execution is faster than writing a commit record to stable storage, perhaps even orders of magnitude faster, then transactions may form long chains of commit dependencies. In the extreme example of 0.01 ms execution time and 10 ms commit time, a chain of 1,000 transactions seems possible. If only one of those transactions were to abort, all subsequent ones must abort, too. In other words, this seems to be a bad case of "abort amplification" or "cascading abort."

One must recognize, however, that a traditional transaction processing system would have let none of the subsequent transactions acquire conflicting locks; thus, transactions aborted in this design would never even have started or made progress past the conflicting lock request. More importantly, all transactions whose locks may be violated have reached their commit point and have appended a commit record to the log buffer; thus, practically the only cause for a transaction failure is a system failure, in which all subsequent transactions would fail even without the chain of commit dependencies.

4.3.4   COMPARISON WITH EARLY LOCK RELEASE

Controlled lock violation is similar to early lock release, at least in some aspects. First, a transaction T_1 can proceed as soon as an earlier, conflicting transaction T_0 has added its commit record to the log buffer in memory (or at least allocated space and an address for it). Second, most read-only transactions can commit instantly, except those that encounter a lock conflict and incur a commit dependency. (In this exception case, controlled lock violation is "slower" than early lock release because controlled lock violation behaves correctly whereas early lock release does not—see Figure 4.2 and the corresponding discussion.)

Controlled lock violation is also quite different from early lock release. First, transaction T_0 retains its locks in controlled lock violation as long as in traditional lock release, so it does not release any locks early. Second, locks can be violated while transaction T_0 commits, but only after T_0 has added its commit record to the log buffer. Third, hardly any new mechanism is required—for example, neither the allocation nor the clean up of tags are required. Fourth, if there is no conflict between committing and active transactions, controlled lock violation does not impose any restrictions or overheads, whereas early lock release forces committing transactions to install tags in the lock manager's hash table just in case a subsequent transaction might create a lock conflict. Finally, and perhaps most importantly, controlled lock violation requires very little if any new theory—violation of lock conflicts and resulting commit dependencies are already part of the traditional theory of concurrency control and recovery.

4.3.5   COMBINED LOCKS

Retaining the original locks during commit activities is more precise than early lock release. This is because controlled lock violation preserves all lock information during commit activities whereas early lock release reduces that information to a tag. The detailed information about locks is particularly useful in cases with combined lock modes such as SIX (see Figure 4.5).

A conflict involving a combined lock mode does not always induce a commit dependency, because a combined lock may include read-only and update parts. Thus, controlled lock violation is more precise than early lock release, because early lock release reduces the conflict analysis to tags whereas controlled lock violation retains the precise lock. Early lock release would introduce commit dependencies in all of the following examples.

Consider, for example, transaction T_0 holding a combination lock, e.g., an SIX lock on a file (to read the entire file and update selected pages). A commit dependency is required only if a lock acquired by a later transaction conflicts with the update part. For example, if transaction T_1 requests an IS lock (in preparation of locking individual pages in S mode), there is no conflict at all because lock modes SIX and IS are compatible. (There is no conflict over this lock for the entire file; there may be a conflict if T_0 and T_1 attempt to lock the same page.) Further, if transaction T_2 acquires an IX lock on the file (in preparation of acquiring X locks on individual pages), which conflicts only with the readonly S part of the SIX lock of transaction T_0, no commit dependency is required. On the other hand, if another transaction T_3 acquires an S lock on the file, which conflicts with the IX part of the SIX lock of transaction T_0, then T_3 incurs a commit dependency on T_0. (In this particular case, transaction T_3 also incurs a commit dependency on T_2 due to the conflict between IX and S locks.)

Another example is key range locking in B-tree indexes. Consider the specific case illustrated in Figure 4.8. Transaction T_0 has locked key value 30 in XS mode ("key exclusive, gap shared") [Graefe, 2010] and is in its commit phase with the commit record in the log buffer. If transaction T_1 acquires a violating NX lock ("key free, gap exclusive"—N stands for no lock), should that imply a commit dependency? The correct answer is "no." If trans-action T_2 acquires a violating SN lock ("key shared, gap free"), should that imply a commit dependency? The correct answer is "yes." With early lock release and a tag in the lock manager's hash table, it is impossible to derive these correct answers. Controlled lock violation makes the correct decision easy: as the NX lock of transaction T_1 conflicts only with the read-only part of the XS lock held by transaction T_0, no commit dependency is required. On the other hand, since the SN lock of transaction T_2 conflicts with the update part of the XS lock held by transaction T_0, T_2 incurs a commit dependency on T_0. (Locks of modes SN and NX do not conflict; therefore, T_2 does not incur a commit dependency on T_1.)

4.3.6   WEAK TRANSACTION ISOLATION LEVELS

Many databases and their applications run with a transaction isolation level weaker than serializability, e.g., "read committed." This isolation level permits releasing read-only locks immediately

20	30	40	50

$$[\quad) \text{ XS of } T_0$$
$$(\quad) \text{ NX of } T_1$$
$$[\ ]\quad \text{ SN of } T_2$$

Figure 4.8: Conflicts and dependencies in key range locking.

after use, e.g., when a scan advances to the next record. Write locks, on the other hand, are retained until the transaction ends.

If a transaction finds a desired data item locked, it waits. Only the "dirty read" transaction isolation level ignores existing locks (and consequently provides no meaningful transaction isolation). With controlled lock violation, this wait may not be required—a subsequent transaction may violate locks held by a transaction already in its commit activities. If a read-only lock of transaction T_1 violates a write lock of an earlier transaction T_0, it incurs a commit dependency. This is true even if the transaction T_1 releases this read-only lock soon thereafter, i.e., long before it attempts to commit.

A special case is an earlier transaction T_0 that deletes a record. Most implementations employ ghost records, also known as invalid records or pseudo-deleted records. These records still exist in the data structure but are marked as logically deleted. Their value is that a locked data item remains in the data structure until the transaction commits, thus avoiding special cases in the concurrency control code and simplifying rollback code. Any scan or query must ignore ghost records. If a transaction T_1 finds a locked ghost record, and if the lock-holding transaction T_0 is in its commit activities, then T_1 may violate the lock but it incurs a commit dependency. Transaction T_1 may commit only if transaction T_0 indeed commits the ghost record. If transaction T_0 fails and rolls back, transaction T_1 erroneously ignored a valid record and it therefore must abort as well.

4.3.7 SUMMARY

In summary, controlled lock violation matches early lock release in the principal goal: when and where early lock release applies, controlled lock violation permits the same concurrency. However, controlled lock violation is simpler, e.g., with respect to data structures, yet it is more general, e.g., with respect to lock modes, and more accurate, e.g., with respect to combined locks and key range locking.

Early lock release and controlled lock violation can complement each other, for example in the following way. Once a transaction has determined its commit LSN, it may release its read-only locks. All remaining locks remain active but subsequent lock requests may violate them.

The early lock release part of this hybrid design can also weaken combined locks by removing the read-only component, e.g., from SIX to IX in hierarchical locking or from XS to XN in key-range locking. Moreover, it may notify waiting threads and transactions of released or weakened locks. Weakening SIX to IX locks seems particularly valuable in systems that let threads retain intention lock (e.g., IX) from one transaction to another, a technique known as speculative lock inheritance [Johnson et al., 2009]. Incidentally, both early lock release and controlled lock violation can treat a U (upgrade [Korth, 1983]) lock as if it were an S lock.

Hybrid models are readily possible because in some sense, controlled lock violation differs from early lock release only in the information they retain: while tags in corrected early lock release retain a synopsis of the released lock, controlled lock violation retains the entire lock with all its detailed information. Retaining all lock information permits precision and functionality impossible with early lock release, unless each retained tag effectively replicates the released lock.

4.4 DISTRIBUTED TRANSACTIONS

As mentioned earlier, early lock release applies only to the final commit phase of two-phase commit, not to the pre-commit phase. In other words, early lock release cuts the lock retention time by the time for writing the final commit record but not by the time for communication during the two-phase commit and for writing the pre-commit record to stable storage.

Figure 4.9 illustrates a distributed transaction and its two commit phases. The execution time is short but each commit phase requires communication and at least one write to stable storage. Traditional lock release retains locks until all commit activities are complete, shown by a blue line above the time line. Early lock release retains locks throughout the first phase of a two-phase commit, shown by a green line below the time line. In contrast, controlled lock violation enforces locks only during transaction execution, shown by a short red line at the bottom left. Using the times for transaction execution and for flushing commit records to stable storage from the introduction, and assuming for simplicity negligible communication times, execution takes 0.01 ms and each commit phase takes 10 ms (logging on a pair of traditional disks) or 0.1 ms (logging on flash memory). Traditional commit processing holds all locks for 20.01 ms (log on disks) or 0.21 ms (log on flash); early lock release holds all locks for 10.01 ms or 0.11 ms; and controlled lock violation enforces locks for only 0.01 ms (independent of the log device). In other words, with the log on a pair of traditional disks, effective lock retention times are 2,000 times shorter than with traditional commit processing and 1,000 times shorter than with early lock release; with the log on flash memory, effective lock retention times are 20 or 10 times shorter, respectively.

Specifically, imagine an update transaction T_1 that is a local participant in a distributed transaction coordinated by remote transaction T_0, and another transaction T_2 that requests a lock conflicting with a lock held by T_1. With early lock release, T_2 must wait until T_1 has added its final commit record to the log buffer. With controlled lock violation, once the local transaction T_1 has received the request for the first commit phase, T_2 may acquire a conflicting

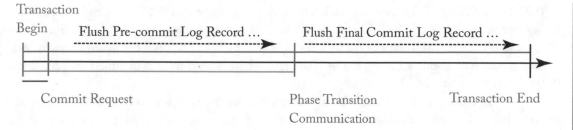

Figure 4.9: Lock retention times in two-phase commit.

lock. Of course, T_2 incurs a commit dependency on T_1 and thus on T_0. If those fail, T_2 must roll back as well.

4.4.1 IMPLEMENTATION OF COMMIT DEPENDENCIES

Implementation of commit dependencies in distributed settings are somewhat complex. Fortunately, the commit dependencies required here are always within a single site (node). Thus, fairly simple mechanisms suffice.

A recent detailed description of such mechanisms was published, for example, by Larson et al. [2011]. They call their design a "register-and-report approach" in which "T1 registers its dependency with T2 and T2 informs T1 when it has committed or aborted." Essential to the implementation is a counter (similar to a reference counter) and a set data structure capturing dependent transactions. They explain further:

> "To take a commit dependency on a transaction T2, T1 increments its Commit-DepCounter and adds its transaction ID to T2's CommitDepSet. When T2 has committed, it locates each transaction in its CommitDepSet and decrements their CommitDepCounter. If T2 aborted, it tells the dependent transactions to also abort by setting their AbortNow flags. If a dependent transaction is not found, this means that it has already aborted.

> Note that a transaction with commit dependencies may not have to wait at all the dependencies may have been resolved before it is ready to commit. Commit dependencies consolidate all waits into a single wait and postpone the wait to just before commit" [Larson et al., 2011].

4.4.2 PERFORMANCE EFFECTS

Perhaps a concrete example is best to illustrate the advantages of eliminating lock conflicts during both phases of a two-phase commit. If the transaction logic runs 0.01 ms (e.g., 40,000 instruction cycles on a core running at 4 GHz) and each commit phase runs 0.1 ms (to force a commit record to flash storage), then early lock release improves the contention footprint by almost a factor of

2 (0.21 ms ÷ 0.11 ms) whereas controlled lock violation improves the time with lock conflicts by more than a factor of 20 (0.21 ms ÷ 0.01 ms). If stable storage is realized with traditional disks, and if the time to force a log record to stable storage is 10 ms, then the factor for early lock release remains at about 2 (20.01 ms ÷ 10.01 ms) whereas the factor is about 2,000 (20.01 ms ÷ 0.01 ms) for controlled lock violation.

If locks can be violated immediately after a distributed transaction begins its commit sequence, lock contention during the two-phase commit sequence may cease to be a concern for performance and scalability. In other words, the major concern about or argument against two-phase commit loses weight and credibility. By removing lock conflicts during communication and coordination of two-phase commit, controlled lock violation may substantially contribute to increased use of two-phase commit with distributed transactions and thus to the consistency and reliability of distributed systems.

4.4.3   SUMMARY

Both early lock release and controlled lock violation reduce the effective lock retention times during two-phase commit. Neither improves the elapsed time, communication time, or logging effort during commit processing. However, since early lock release pertains only to the final phase of the two-phase commit, its improvement of effective lock retention times is very small in comparison to that of controlled lock violation.

4.5   CANNED TRANSACTIONS

In some cases, controlled lock violation may be advantageous even before the user (or application) requests a transaction commit for the transaction holding the lock. In general, such lock violation is a bad idea. For example, if transaction T_0 needs and acquires a lock, transaction T_1 violates this lock, and then T_0 performs another action that requires the same lock again, then transaction T_0 needs to violate the lock held by T_1 and transactions T_0 and T_1 have mutual, i.e., circular, commit dependencies on each other. Only aborting transaction T_1 can resolve this situation.

If, however, it is certain that transaction T_0 will not require again a specific lock that it holds, then another transaction T_1 may violate this lock. For example, a "canned" transaction T_0 may run a stored procedure, that stored procedure may consist of multiple statements, and each statement may touch its own set of tables, i.e., disjoint from the tables in other statements. All of these are not unreasonable assumptions as many stored procedures satisfy them. When they apply, then another transaction T_1 may violate any lock from an earlier statement. The precise condition is that locks may be violated if neither the current nor any future statement might need them.

Figure 4.10 shows source code for a very simple stored procedure. It moves money from one account to another and then inserts a record of it in a table of activities. After the first two statements, the table of accounts will not be touched again, except perhaps to roll back the updates in case of a transaction failure, e.g., due to a deadlock. Thus, while the third statement is still executing, a later transaction may violate the locks on the accounts table still held by an active transaction. Even in this simple example, controlled lock violation during one of three statements reduces the time with lock conflicts for the accounts table by one third (not including lock retention after the commit request). In other words, in addition to eliminating lock contention while a commit record is written to stable storage, controlled lock violation can reduce lock contention even further.

> Begin transaction
> Update accounts set balance += …
> Update accounts set balance -= …
> Insert activities values (…)
> Commit transaction

Figure 4.10: A canned transaction.

Note that controlled lock violation of read-only locks does not incur a commit dependency. In other words, controlled lock violation of a read-only lock has no negative effect at all. Thus, for tables touched only by a single statement of a stored procedure, controlled lock violation gives the semantics and consistency of full serializability but with the contention footprint and with the lock conflicts of "read committed" transaction isolation.

The tables involved in each statement can easily be extracted from the source code of the stored procedure. If disambiguation of table names requires a binding based on the user invoking the stored procedure, such static analysis might not be possible, in particular if tables and views may have multiple names or aliases. Cases requiring user-specific name resolution are discouraged in practice, because these cases also prevent pre-compilation, cached query execution plans, and compile-time query optimization. Therefore, static analysis is usually possible. It might focus on tables and materialized views (i.e., objects of the logical database design) or on indexes and partitions (i.e., objects of the physical database design). In the former case, it is sufficient to analyze the request syntax; in the latter case, query execution plans must also be considered.

Gawlick and Kinkade [1985] wrote: "Consider, for example, an ultra-hot spot: a counter updated by every transaction. To achieve a high transaction rate, we want a transaction to be able to access the counter without waiting for any other transaction. We also want to guarantee the integrity of the counter, consistency with other parts of the data base, etc." Their solution introduced a new "change" verb to the language, i.e., a restriction to increment and decrement operations instead of general read and write operations. Note that an "increment" lock is perfectly compatible with serializable transactions but it does not imply a read lock, i.e., it does not bestow the right to expect repeatable reads.

Wolfson [1986] described a static analysis of stored procedures and an algorithm to identify points when explicit early lock release may be permitted without the danger of deadlocks.

The analysis algorithm is, unfortunately, NP-complete and needs to run whenever the text of a stored procedure is altered. Moreover, the work is limited to single-site deployments and to shared and exclusive locks.

The present design offers an alternative to both prior approaches: a transaction may acquire a traditional write (exclusive) lock on the counter, increment its value, and then hold the lock until all commit activities are complete. Because such a transaction touches the counter only once, subsequent transactions may violate this lock immediately after the increment operation. In other words, controlled lock violation can offer practically the same concurrency but without the need for "increment" locks.

In summary, controlled lock violation can happen even before the commit request in some cases that may be expected common in practice. It might for many applications combine the advantages of "read committed" and serializable transaction isolation levels. In many cases, it also enables traditional exclusive locks with the concurrency of special "increment" locks.

4.6   PERFORMANCE EVALUATION

We implemented and measured controlled lock violation in the context of Shore-MT [Johnson et al., 2009], an experimental database system.

4.6.1   IMPLEMENTATION

We implemented controlled lock violation in Shore-MT by adding a binary flag to each transaction descriptor that indicates whether other transactions may violate the transaction's locks. Lock acquisition ignores conflicts with locks held by transactions with this flag set when determining if locks can be granted. The flag starts unset and is set at the same point early lock release would release locks, namely once the commit record has been allocated in the log buffer.

We also modified the lock acquisition code so that when a transaction violates another transaction's lock, the acquiring transaction advances its high-water mark to equal or exceed the holding transaction's commit LSN. A transaction's high water mark (part of the preexisting implementation of early lock release) is the highest LSN that must be flushed to stable storage before a read-only transaction is allowed to commit and return data to a client. The preexisting code to implement this delay takes less than 60 lines of C++ including comments and debugging code but not tests. Such delays affect only read-only transactions.

The present implementation omits many possible optimizations. For example, it maintains a transaction's high-water mark even when a lock acquisition violates a read-only lock and it fails to wake up waiting transactions when lock violation becomes possible. (We expect to have this remedied very soon.) We also have not yet implemented controlled lock violation in the context of two-phase commit or of canned transactions.

4.6.2   RESULTS

In the following, we report the performance of controlled lock violation versus two variants of early lock release (releasing S locks only and releasing both S and X locks) for the industry standard TPC-B benchmark, which models simple database transactions. To cover a range of logging delays, we logged to a RAM disk but added an extra delay ranging from 0.1 ms to 10 ms to simulate a range of stable storage devices. The database data itself was stored on disk and our experimental machine is a 4-socket Intel Xeon X7542 machine running at 2.7 GHz with 24 cores.

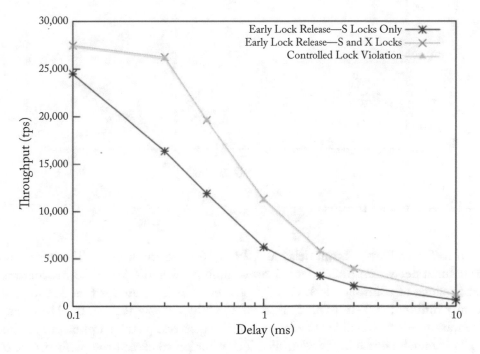

Figure 4.11: 24 cores, 24 threads.

Figures 4.11 and 4.12 show the transaction throughput (transactions per second) for competing commit processing techniques as the extra delay is varied. Figure 4.11 is for 24 threads (one per core) while Figure 4.12 is for 48 threads (two per core). Extra threads can perform useful work when other threads are blocked, waiting for locks or, more likely in the case of controlled lock violation, for their commit record to be flushed to stable storage.

Note that the relatively low performance for 48 cores at small delay is expected, since the threads block only for a very short time and hence the additional threads merely add overhead (e.g., due to true contention, context switching overhead, etc.).

As can be seen, both controlled lock violation and early lock release for S and X locks outperform the traditional approach of releasing read-only locks early by large factors for sizable

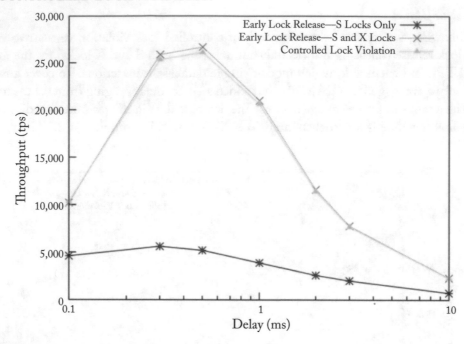

Figure 4.12: 24 cores, 48 threads.

delays: up to 5× at 1 ms commit delay and 2× at 10 ms commit delay. The improvement is smaller at small delays: up to 2.2× at 0.1 ms commit delay and 4.5× at 0.3 ms commit delay. The performance of controlled lock violation and early lock release for S and X locks are not significantly different; a T-test fails to reject the null hypothesis at p = 0.05. However, as our implementation of controlled lock violation is missing several possible optimizations (see Section 4.6.1) it may be possible for controlled lock violation to exceed the performance of early lock release.

Since controlled lock violation sometimes delays read-only transactions, we also experimented with a variant of TPC-B with 70% of the transactions made read-only by omitting their writes. The results, shown in Figure 4.13 for 48 threads, again show sizable improvements for controlled lock violation.

4.7   DISCUSSION

Both early lock release and controlled lock violation are specific forms of speculative execution. The speculation risk, however, is very small, as both techniques require that the earlier transaction reaches its commit point and formats a commit record in the log buffer before speculative execution begins. Nonetheless, with all other things equal, a system should schedule (process)

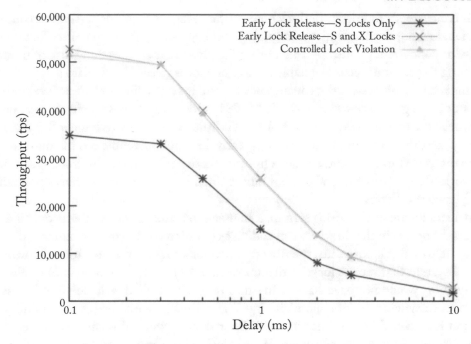

Figure 4.13: 24 cores, 48 threads, 70% read-only.

a transaction without commit dependency ahead of one with, or one with fewer commit dependencies ahead of one with more. In other words, a transaction with commit dependencies should progress only if there no is work pending that is less speculative, or when the processing resources would remain idle except for speculative work. This is particularly true in the advanced forms of controlled lock violation discussed in later sections.

Outside the research area of database management, Nightingale et al. [2008] investigated scenarios similar to ours. The issue was the same—guaranteeing durability yet hiding the latency until information had been written to disk. Their context was a file system and its "sync" operations. Their solution acknowledges the write operation immediately and lets the invoking process continue while preventing the process from communication. In other words, speculative execution of the process enabled further local progress but in the unlikely case that the sync operation failed, the process can be rolled back and the speculative execution is wasted. Thus, by relying on inexpensive checkpoints and speculative execution, their system achieved performance similar to asynchronous writes to disks but the semantics of synchronous writes. Early lock release and controlled lock violation similarly rely on speculative execution with an extremely low risk of failure and of wasted work.

Both early lock release and controlled lock violation also seem related to optimistic concurrency control, in the sense that new transactions may proceed ignoring existing transactions and their concurrency footprint. Both techniques, however, are forms of pessimistic concurrency control, i.e., locking. Both techniques employ traditional locking techniques for synchronization atomicity or concurrency control—only during the phase that ensures durability of transaction, i.e., flushing the commit record to stable storage, are locks released or violated.

This reliance on pessimistic concurrency control is very deliberate. Carey's extensive simulation studies (e.g., Carey and Stonebraker [1984] and multiple subsequent studies) point out that the mechanism of concurrency control matters little in systems with few conflicts. In systems with many conflicts, avoiding wasted work by early detection of conflicts is the most important determinant of performance (other than a fine granularity of locking). Controlled lock violation wastes work (due to "cascading aborts" or "abort amplification") only if a transaction fails after reaching its commit point.

In a single-site or single-log system, a transaction starts cascading aborts only if a system failure (crash) occurs in the time between adding a commit record to the log buffer and completing the write to stable storage, i.e., the time required for a single write operation. Moreover, in a traditional system that retains locks until a transaction is durable, the transactions failed due to cascading abort would not have started. In other words, controlled lock violation is pessimistic with respect to synchronization atomicity but it is optimistic with respect to durability once a transaction has started its commit activities. The risk and extent of wasted work are miniscule compared to the performance advantage of early lock release and controlled lock violation.

In a system with multiple logs and thus with two-phase commit, frequent failures during the first commit phase would suggest delaying controlled lock violation to the second phase. If, however, most transactions that start their commit activities also finish them successfully, the risk of cascading aborts is low. Similar considerations apply to controlled lock violation prior to the commit point of canned transactions—if failures are frequent, controlled lock violation should be restricted to the commit phase. Early lock release and controlled lock violation avoid multiversion concurrency control and its complexities by delaying any conflicting transaction until the lock-holding transaction has finished its updates. Thus, there is no need for multiple versions of the same record. However, should a rollback be required, e.g., because a distributed transaction fails in the second phase of its two-phase commit, it is possible that multiple transactions need to roll back, which could take a single record back in time through multiple states. Nonetheless, at any one time, there is only a single version of each record in the database.

4.8   SUMMARY AND CONCLUSIONS

In summary, the simple form of controlled lock violation is comparable to early lock release. Early lock release can boost the performance of transaction processing by a small factor or even an order of magnitude as shown in Figure 4.4. In those cases in which early lock release applies, controlled lock violation enables the same amount of additional concurrency compared to traditional commit processing. However, there are multiple reasons to prefer controlled lock violation over early lock release.

First, controlled lock violation is simpler and more robust because it has fewer special cases. It applies to all lock types—any lock may be violated and violation of any but a read-only lock induces a commit dependency. Even after multiple rounds of correction and improvement, early lock release still does not cover "increment" locks. The same is true for more specialized locks that are used in real database systems, e.g., "bulk insertion" or "schema stability" or "schema modify" locks in SQL Server, as well as the various special designs for key range locking and their lock modes. Controlled lock violation is a simple, consistent solution for all of these lock types, easy enough for implementation, quality assurance, and maintenance by most software engineers working on data management code.

Second, controlled lock violation is more precise than early lock release with tags. For key range locking, a precise separation of concurrency and conflict is required, in particular for hot spots known in many databases and their indexes. Controlled lock violation carries that precision to the commit dependency, whereas early lock release may introduce a commit dependency where none is required.

Third, controlled lock violation works well with two-phase commit. With early lock release, a transaction can avoid lock conflicts if an earlier transaction is in the final phase of the twophase commit. With controlled lock violation, a transaction can avoid lock conflicts during both phases, i.e., already during the initial phase. Thus, the opportunity for lock conflicts during twophase commit is much smaller with controlled lock violation than with early lock release. It could be argued that this reduction in lock conflicts takes most of the performance costs out of twophase commit. For example, it might enable immediate (as opposed to eventually consistent) maintenance of all copies in a system relying on replicas for high reliability and high availability. These effects and their implications require further research.

Fourth, controlled lock violation applies even before the user (or application) requests a commit. In a "canned" transaction with a fixed sequence of statements, locks can be violated prior to the commit request if neither the current nor any future statement might need the locks, and this can be based on static analysis of the stored procedure and its source code.

In conclusion, we believe that controlled lock violation matches the promise of early lock release but it is simpler, more accurate, and more general. In other words, we believe it is superior in multiple dimensions.

4.9 ACKNOWLEDGEMENTS

Hideaki Kimura implemented the tag-based design for early lock release with read-only transactions. Eric Anderson pointed out the possible relationship between controlled lock violation and optimistic concurrency control. Haris Volos helped with the performance evaluation. Martin Scholl alerted us to the recent work on MDCC. Gary Smith suggested some concerns regarding dispatching waiting transactions and transaction isolation levels weaker than serializability. Barb Peters suggested some improvements in style and grammar.

We thank all developers and researchers of the Shore-MT team at EPFL, CMU and UW-Madison for making the Shore-MT code-base available. We especially thank Anastassia Ailamaki and her students for their thoughtful work on early lock release.

4.10　REFERENCES

Anon et al. (1985). A measure of transaction processing power. *Datamation*, April 1. `http://research.microsoft.com/~gray/papers/AMeasureOfTransactionProcess ingPower.doc` 129

Carey, M. J. and Stonebraker, M. (1984). The performance of concurrency control algorithms for database management systems. *VLDB*, pp. 107–118. 154

DeWitt, D. J., Katz, R. H., Olken, F., Shapiro, L. D., Stonebraker, M., and Wood, D. A. (1984). Implementation techniques for main memory database systems. *ACM SIGMOD*, pp. 1–8. DOI: 10.1145/602260.602261. 132, 133

Gawlick, D. and Kinkade, D. (1985). Varieties of concurrency control in IMS/VS fast path. *IEEE Database Engineering Bulletin*, 8(2), pp. 3–10. 149

Graefe, G. (2010). A survey of B-tree locking techniques. *ACM TODS*, 35(3) (Chapter 1). DOI: 10.1145/1806907.1806908. 138, 144

Graefe, G., Kimura, H., and Kuno, H. (2012). Foster B-trees. *ACM TODS*, 37(3). DOI: 10.1145/2338626.2338630. 135

Gray, J., Lorie, R. A., Putzolu, G. R., and Traiger, I. L. (1975). Granularity of locks in a large shared data base. *VLDB*, pp. 428–451. DOI: 10.1145/1282480.1282513. 137

Gray, J., Lorie, R. A., Putzolu, G. R., and Traiger, I. L. (1976). Granularity of locks and degrees of consistency in a shared data base. *IFIP Working Conference on Modeling in Data Base Management Systems*, pp. 365–394. 138

Johnson, R., Pandis, I., Hardavellas, N., Ailamaki, A., and Falsafi, B. (2009). Shore-MT: A scalable storage manager for the multicore era. *EDBT*, pp. 24–35. DOI: 10.1145/1516360.1516365. 132, 133, 135, 150

Johnson, R., Pandis, I., and Ailamaki, A. (2009). Improving OLTP scalability using speculative lock inheritance. *PVLDB*, 2(1), pp. 479–489. DOI: 10.14778/1687627.1687682. 146

Johnson, R., Pandis, I., Stoica, R., Athanassoulis, M., and Ailamaki, A. (2010). Aether: A scalable approach to logging. *PVLDB*, 3(1), pp. 681–692. DOI: 10.14778/1920841.1920928. 130, 133

Kimura, H., Graefe, G., and Kuno, H. (2012). Efficient locking for databases on modern hardware. *ADMS Workshop*, Istanbul, August. 130, 132, 134, 135, 136

Korth, H. F. (1983). Locking primitives in a database system. *JACM*, 30(1), pp. 55–79. DOI: 10.1145/322358.322363. 136, 146

Kraska, T., Pang, G., Franklin, M. J., and Madden, S. (2012). MDCC: multi-data center consistency. Submitted for publication. `http://mdcc.cs.berkeley.edu` DOI: 10.1145/2465351.2465363. 139

Larson, P., Blanas, S., Diaconu, C., Freedman, C., Patel, J. M., and Zwilling, M. (2011). High-performance concurrency control mechanisms for main-memory databases. *PVLDB*, 5(4), pp. 298–309. DOI: 10.14778/2095686.2095689. 147

Nightingale, E. B., Veeraraghavan, K., Chen, P. M., and Flinn, J. (2008). Rethink the sync. *ACM TOCS*, 26(3). DOI: 10.1145/1394441.1394442. 153

Soisalon-Soininen, E. and Ylönen, T. (1995). Partial strictness in two-phase locking. *ICDT*, pp. 139–147. DOI: 10.1007/3-540-58907-4_12. 130

Thomson, A., Diamond, T., Weng, S.-C., Ren, K., Shao, P., and Abadi, D. J. (2012). Calvin: Fast distributed transactions for partitioned database systems. *ACM SIGMOD*, pp. 1–12. DOI: 10.1145/2213836.2213838. 138, 139

Traiger, I. L., Gray, J., Galtieri, C. A., and Lindsay, B. G. (1982). Transactions and consistency in distributed database systems. *ACM TODS*, 7(3), pp. 323–342. DOI: 10.1145/319732.319734. 137

Wolfson, O. (1986). An algorithm for early unlocking of entities in database transactions. *Journal of Algorithms*, 7(1), pp. 146–156. DOI: 10.1016/0196-6774(86)90043-x. 149

CHAPTER 5

Orthogonal Key-Value Locking

Precise concurrency control in ordered indexes such as B-trees

Goetz Graefe

ABSTRACT

B-trees have been ubiquitous for decades in databases, file systems, key-value stores, and information retrieval. Over the past 25 years, record-level locking has also become ubiquitous in database storage structures such as B-trees. There are multiple designs for fine-granularity locking in B-tree indexes, each a different tradeoff between (i) high concurrency and a fine granularity of locking during updates, (ii) efficient coarse locks for equality queries and range queries, (iii) run-time efficiency with the fewest possible invocations of the lock manager, and (iv) conceptual simplicity for efficient development, maintenance, and quality assurance as well as for users' ease of understanding and prediction of system behavior.

Unnecessarily coarse lock scopes have contributed to giving locking and serializability a reputation for poor concurrency, poor scalability, and poor system performance. The diagram below illustrates the extent of the problem and of the opportunity in ordered indexes such as B-trees, using as example phantom protection for non-existing key value "Harry" within an index on given names. Shading indicates the required lock scope and the actual lock scopes in a variety of locking techniques. There are similar big differences between traditional and novel techniques for a wide variety of queries and updates.

Index Entries and Gaps → ↓ Techniques	Entry (Gary, 1)	Gap			Entry (Jerry, 3)	Gap	Entry (Jerry, 6)	Gap	
		Gary, >1	>Gary, <Jerry	Jerry, <3				Jerry, >6	>Jerry
Traditional B-tree locking					S				
			S						
Orthogonal key-value locking			S						

Orthogonal key-value locking is simple and efficient yet supports both fine and coarse granularities of locking. A lock request may cover (i) a key value with its entire set (in a non-unique index) of (existing and possible) rows (in a primary index) or of row identifiers (in a secondary index), (ii) a distinct key value and a subset of its (existing and possible) rows or row identifiers, (iii) a gap (open interval) between two (existing) distinct key values, or (iv) a subset of (non-existing) key values within such a gap. In other words, each lock or each lock request covers some or all row identifiers associated with an existing key value plus some or all non-existing key values in a gap between adjacent existing key values.

Using specific examples such as insertions, deletions, equality queries, range queries, and phantom protection, case studies with diagrams like the one above compare the new design for locks in B-tree indexes with four prior ones. For queries, the new design dominates all prior ones including the designs in industrial use today. For updates, the new design is practically equal to the most recent prior design, which dominates all earlier ones. Experiments demonstrate that the new technique reduces the number of lock requests yet increases transactional concurrency, improving transaction throughput for both read-only queries and read-write transactions. Both the case studies and the experiments suggest that new B-tree implementations as well as existing ones ought to adopt the new techniques.

5.1   INTRODUCTION

Many data stores support indexes on multiple attributes of stored data items. In databases, for example, these are known as secondary indexes or as non-clustered indexes. Most database systems permit dozens or even hundreds of secondary indexes for each table in a database. In practice, each database table has a few secondary indexes, e.g., on all foreign keys and on non-key columns frequently searched by applications and users.

Key values in secondary indexes may or may not be unique. There may be many, even thousands, of rows in a database table with the same value in an indexed attribute. In those cases, compression is useful, e.g., a bitmap instead of a list of row identifiers. Such representation choices, however, are entirely independent of choices for transactional concurrency control, where further improvements are possible despite multiple existing techniques [Graefe, 2010] and decades with only moderate progress.

5.1.1   MOTIVATION

Transaction processing applications require record-level locking in their databases. Moreover, reliably correct applications require the simplest and most robust programming model with respect to concurrency and recovery, which only "serializable" transactions can guarantee. Thus, this work focuses on transactional isolation beyond "read committed" and "repeatable read" transaction isolation. Unfortunately, many systems developers disparage both serializability and locking due to their effects on concurrency, perceiving them as unreasonably limiting. Their remedies are often system designs and implementations that fail to preserve serializability among concurrent queries and updates, thus leaving substantial work to application developers and users to prevent or detect and repair cases in which insufficient transaction isolation leads to erroneous database output or even erroneous database updates. The present work aims to weaken arguments against serializability. Its new mechanisms for fine-granularity locking restrict concurrent transactions where truly required but otherwise enable maximal concurrency.

The present research offers a new design with a new tradeoff between

1. high concurrency and a fine granularity of locking during updates,

2. efficient coarse locks for equality and range queries,

3. run-time efficiency with the fewest possible invocations of the lock manager, and

4. conceptual simplicity for efficient development, maintenance, and testing.

Invocations of the lock manager imply substantial run-time costs beyond a mere function invocation. Each invocation searches the lock manager's hash table for pre-existing locks and for lock requests waiting for the same lockable resource. Beyond the cost of the search, a lock manager shared among many threads requires low-level concurrency control, which is relatively expensive in many-core processors and multi-socket servers.

Among all components of a database management system, lock managers most urgently need simplicity in design, implementation, maintenance, test design, and test execution. "Stress-testing into submission" is not an efficient or pleasant way of releasing new software versions. Instead, a good theory can be immensely practical (Kurt Lewin). Creative techniques outside of established theory, e.g., instant-duration locks and insertion locks, can play havoc with understanding, correctness, code maintenance, quality assurance, and release schedules.

In pursuit of a new tradeoff, the new design employs locks that may cover any combination of

1. a gap (open interval) between two (existing) distinct key values,

2. specific (non-existing) key values within such a gap,

3. a key value with its entire list of (existing and possible) row identifiers, and

4. specific pairs of distinct key value and row identifier.

Using specific examples such as insertions, deletions, equality queries, and phantom protection, case studies compare the new design for locks in B-tree indexes with four prior ones. Experiments demonstrate that the new technique reduces the number of lock requests yet increases transactional concurrency, improving transaction throughput for read-only queries, for read-write transactions, and for mixed workloads.

5.1.2 CONCURRENCY CONTROL AND LOCK SCOPES

In transactional concurrency control, pessimistic techniques (i.e., locking) may focus on rows in a table across all indexes (e.g., ARIES/IM [Mohan and Levine, 1992]) or on key values in an individual index (e.g., ARIES/KVL [Mohan, 1990]). When locking entries within a non-unique secondary index, the finest granularity of locking may be an individual index entry (representing one row and its value in the indexed attribute) or a distinct key value (such that a single lock covers all instances of the same value in the indexed attribute).

Locks on individual index entries are more desirable for insertions, updates, and deletions, because they permit concurrent transactions to modify different rows with the same value in an indexed column. The disadvantage of this approach is that queries may need to acquire a lock on each index entry, possibly thousands for a single key value. Many individual lock acquisitions not only incur overhead but also the danger of a lock acquisition failure (e.g., deadlock) late in the process. In such cases, the entire statement or transaction aborts and all earlier efforts are wasted.

Locks on distinct key values are more desirable for search and selection operations, because a query with an equality predicate needs to retrieve (and, for serializability, to lock) all items satisfying the predicate. The disadvantage of this approach is reduced concurrency when multiple concurrent transactions need to modify separate index entries. A single lock may cover thousands of index entries among which only one is needed.

The proposed design combines these benefits, i.e., high concurrency (by using a fine granularity of locking) and low overhead (by using a coarse granularity of locking). It is a variant of multi-granularity locking (hierarchical locking) [Gray et al., 1975, 1976], with a new technique that locks multiple levels of the hierarchy by a single invocation of the lock manager yet copes with a large or even infinite domain of values in the lower level of the hierarchy.

5.1.3 DESIGN GOALS

The primary design goal is correctness, e.g., two-phase locking and serializable transactions. The second design goal is simplicity for easier design, understanding, development, maintenance, and quality assurance. Accordingly, the proposed design is simpler than all prior ones, e.g., obviating "instant duration" locks, "insertion" lock modes, and similar ideas that are creative but outside the traditional concise theory for transactions and concurrency control.

The third design goal is high concurrency and therefore a fine granularity of locking, wanted for updates and in particular for insertions as well as for deletions and updates guided by searches in other indexes. Accordingly, the proposed design enables locks on individual index entries within lists associated with distinct key values as well as individual non-existing key values within a gap between two adjacent existing key values.

The final design goal is run-time efficiency and therefore a coarse granularity of locking, wanted in particular for large operations such as range queries and equality queries in non-unique indexes, including index search in nested loops join operations as well as the read-only search required to determine a set of rows to update or to delete. All transactions benefit from a minimal number of lock manager invocations as well as the fewest and earliest lock acquisition failures in cases of contention. Accordingly, the proposed design enables locks on distinct key values and their entire lists of index entries.

5.1.4 OUTLINE

The following section reviews prior techniques for record-level locking in B-tree indexes, i.e., key-value locking and key-range locking. Section 5.3 introduces the new design and Section 5.4 compares the techniques using practical example scenarios. Section 5.5 outlines some future opportunities. Section 5.6 sums up the techniques and the results.

5.2 PRIOR DESIGNS

For B-tree indexes in databases, we assume the current standard design that has data records or index entries with user contents only in the leaf nodes, also known as B+-trees. Therefore, this chapter focuses on key-value locking and key-range locking applied to key values in the leaf nodes only.

By default, locks are possible on all key values in an index, including those marked as ghost records, also known as invalid or pseudo-deleted records. Ghost records are usually marked by a bit in the record header. In a non-unique secondary indexes with a list of bookmarks for each distinct key value, a ghost record is a distinct key value with an empty list or one in which all remaining entries are themselves ghosts.

In this chapter, the term "bookmark" means a physical record identifier (device, page, and slot number) if the table's primary data structure is a heap. If the table's primary data structure is an index such as a B-tree, a bookmark is a unique search key in the primary index. Such primary indexes are known as a primary key index in Tandem's NonStop SQL, as a clustered index in Microsoft's SQL Server, and as an index-organized table in Oracle.

In most systems, an unsuccessful search within a serializable transaction locks a gap between adjacent existing key values, known as phantom protection. An alternative design inserts an additional key value (for precise phantom protection) either in the index or in some auxiliary data structure. For example, NonStop SQL includes such a key value within the lock manager but not in data pages. It seems that code stabilization for this design was difficult and tedious. All methods discussed below (except Section 5.4.3) lock a gap by locking an adjacent pre-existing key value.

5.2.1 HISTORY OF LOCKING IN B-TREES

Early work on locking in B-tree data structures focuses on protecting the physical data structure rather than the logical contents. Bayer and Schkolnick [1977] introduce a notion of safety that requires a unique path from the root to each leaf node; Lehman and Yao [1981] introduce temporary overflow nodes that violate the original B-tree design and its strictly uniform and logarithmic path length from root to any leaf node; and Foster B-trees [Graefe et al., 2012] bridge that divide by letting an overflowing node serve as temporary parent ("foster parent") for its overflow node, with no permanent pointers among nodes at the same B-tree level.

Recent designs for lock-free (non-blocking) B-trees optimistically avoid blocking: updates prepare alternative nodes and then attempt to install them using a single atomic compare-and-swap instruction applied to a child pointer. In times of low contention among updaters, this approach promises better performance; in cases or places of high contention among updates (also known as hot spots), this approach promises a lot of wasted work because concurrent updates prevent installation of prepared alternative nodes. For example, a sequence of ever-increasing insertions creates a hot spot at the right edge of a B-tree. Lock-free designs are not suitable for this access pattern. Another weakness of lock-free algorithms and data structures is the lack of a shared or read-only access mode.

A notable compromise between traditional pessimistic latching and lock-free data structures is partially optimistic, e.g., in the form of read-only shared latches [Cha et al., 2001]. They address the issue that a traditional shared latch counts the number of concurrent readers and thus twice updates the cache line containing the latch. In systems with multiple caches and CPU cores, exclusive access to a cache line incurs bus traffic, invalidations, etc. Read-only shared latches have each exclusive operation (writer) increment a version counter twice, i.e., before and after an update. When a shared operation (reader) starts, it can verify, without modifying the state of the latch, that the version counter is even and therefore no writer is active. When a shared operation ends, it can verify that the version counter is unchanged and therefore no writer has been active in the meantime. Read-only shared latches are particularly valuable for non-leaf index nodes, where updates are infrequent and can often be deferred, e.g., in Foster B-trees [Graefe et al., 2012].

Protection of the physical data structure is not the topic of this chapter, however. Instead, following Graefe [2010], the proposed design assumes a strict division of low- and high-level concurrency control. The former, also known as latching, coordinates threads in order to ensure the physical integrity of in-memory data structures, including those of lock manager, transaction manager, buffer pool, etc., as well as in-memory images of database pages. The latter, usually relying on locking, coordinates transactions in order to protect the logical contents of database tables and indexes. Figure 5.1, copied verbatim from Graefe [2010], summarizes most differences between locking and latching.

The proposed design assumes the need for a granularity of locking finer than pages or entire B-tree nodes. ARIES/KVL ("key-value locking") [Mohan, 1990] and ARIES/IM ("index management") [Mohan and Levine, 1992] are early designs that break through the preceding restriction to page-level locking. This restriction had been imposed on System R [Chamberlin et al., 1981], for example, by its recovery techniques [Gray et al., 1981] that rely on idempotent "redo" and "undo" actions applied to page images [Gray, 1978]. The alternative is "exactly once"

	Locks	Latches
Separate ...	User transactions	Threads
Protect ...	Database contents	In-memory data structures
During ...	Entire transactions	Critical sections
Modes ...	Shared, exclusive, update, intention, escrow, schema, etc.	Read, write, (perhaps) update
Deadlock ...	Detection & resolution	Avoidance
... by ...	Analysis of the waits-for graph, timeout, transaction abort, partial rollback, lock de-escalation	Coding discipline, "lock leveling"
Kept in ...	Lock manager's hash table	Protected data structure

Figure 5.1: Locks and latches.

application of log records, including rollback log records, based on page version information or PageLSN values [Mohan et al., 1992]. These log records are also known as "compensation" log records or "update back" log records.

Product developers and researchers at DEC [Lomet, 1993] and later Microsoft designed "key-range locking," which partially separates locking index entries from locking the ranges (gaps, open intervals) between index entries. A later design [Graefe, 2007] separates those lock scopes completely. This design exploits ghost records for logical deletion and insertion. These records are called "pseudo-deleted records" in ARIES and are used there only for deletion but not for insertion of new index entries. Asynchronous system transactions, akin to "top-level actions" in ARIES, clean up superfluous ghosts. Based on these separations of index entry versus gap, logical versus physical insertion and deletion, and user transaction versus system transaction, let us call this last design "orthogonal key-range locking."

The most recent developments apply the concepts of orthogonality and hierarchy to key-value locking. A distinct key value is locked orthogonally from a gap between existing distinct key values, and partitioning is applied to both the set of bookmarks associated with an existing key value and the set of non-existing key values in a gap. This design, called "orthogonal key-value locking," is the focus of a subsequent section.

Figure 5.2 summarizes the history of fine-granularity locking in ordered indexes such as B-trees. It ignores latching, i.e., coordination of threads to protect in-memory data structures, as well as snapshot isolation and multi-version concurrency control, which seem to be the next frontier [Bornea et al., 2011, Cahill et al., 2009, Lomet et al., 2012, Ports and Grittner, 2012]. Perhaps the ideal is a hybrid model [Bernstein et al., 1987] using snapshot isolation supported by multi-version storage for read-only transactions and two-phase locking for read-write transactions [Chan et al., 1982]. In this hybrid, the serialization order (commit point) of a read-only transaction is equivalent to the transaction's start time whereas the serialization order (commit point) of a read-write transaction is equivalent to the transaction's end time.

Design Name and Origin	Granularity of Locking	Comments
System R IBM 1981	Page	Due to recovery logic
ARIES/KVL IBM 1990	Distinct key value	All possible instances including gap to next lower "Instant duration" IX locks for insertions
ARIES/IM "data-only locking" IBM 1992	Logical row	Heap record + all index entries + gaps to next lower index entries
ARIES/IM "index-specific locking" IBM 1992	Index entry	Including gap to next lower index entry
Key-range locking DEC 1993	Existing index entry Half-open interval	Partial separation of index entry vs. gap Combined lock modes "Insert" lock mode
Orthogonal key-range locking Microsoft 2007	Existing index entry Open interval between existing index entries	Cartesian product—simple derivation of combined lock modes and their compatibility
Orthogonal key-value locking HP 2014	Distinct key value Partition of bookmarks Open interval between distinct key values	All possible instances Hierarchy of key value and partitions
Orthogonal key-value locking 2016	Added: partition of possible gap values	Hierarchy of gap and partitions

Figure 5.2: Historical summary.

As read-only transactions never block read-write transactions and read-write transactions never block read-only transactions, Chan et al. [1982] wrote about this hybrid: "Read-only (retrieval) transactions, on the other hand, do not set locks. Instead, each of these transactions can obtain a consistent (but not necessarily most up-to-date) view of the database by following the version chain for any given logical page, and by reading only the _first_ version encountered that has been created by an update transaction with a completion time _earlier_ than the time of its own initiation. Thus, read-only transactions do not cause synchronization delays on update transactions, and vice versa."

In the remainder of this chapter, we focus entirely on serializable read-write transactions, ignoring read-only transactions, snapshot isolation, and multi-version concurrency control.

5.2.2   ARIES/KVL "Key-Value Locking"

ARIES/KVL [Mohan, 1990] locks distinct key values, even in non-unique indexes. Each lock on a distinct key value in a secondary index covers all bookmarks associated with that key value as well as the gap (open interval) to the next lower distinct key value present in the index. A lock within a secondary index does not lock any data in the table's primary data structure or in any other secondary index.

Figure 5.3, copied verbatim from Mohan [1990], enumerates the cases and conditions required for a correct implementation of ARIES/KVL. At the same time, it illustrates the complexity of the scheme. Note that IX locks are used for insertions into an existing list of bookmarks, which permits other insertions (also with IX locks) but neither queries nor deletions. In other words, ARIES/KVL is asymmetric as it supports concurrent insertions into a list of bookmarks but not concurrent deletions. Note also the use of locks with instant duration, in violation of traditional two-phase locking. This exemplifies how, from the beginning of record-level locking in B-tree indexes, there has been some creative use of lock modes that ignores the traditional theory of concurrency control but enables higher concurrency without actually permitting wrong database contents or wrong query results. Nonetheless, it substantially expands the test matrix, i.e., cost, complexity, and duration of quality assurance.

Figure 5.3 provides guidance for insertions and deletions but not for updates. A value change in an index key must run as deletion and insertion, but an update of a non-key field in an index record may occur in place. Non-key updates were perhaps not considered at the time; in today's systems, non-key updates may apply to columns appended to each index record using, for example, a "create index" statement with an "include" clause, in order to "cover" more queries with "index-only retrieval." Moreover, in transaction processing databases, a table's primary storage structure may be a B-tree, e.g., as a "clustered index" or as "index-organized table." Most importantly, toggling a record's "ghost" flag (logical deletion and re-insertion of an index entry) is a non-key update. Clearly, re-insertion by toggling a previously deleted key value requires more than an IX lock; otherwise, multiple transactions, at the same time and without noticing their conflict, may try to turn the same ghost into a valid record.

		Next Key Value	Current Key Value
Fetch and fetch next			S for commit duration
Insert	Unique index	IX for instant duration	IX for commit duration if next key value *not* previously locked in S, X, or SIX mode X for commit duration if next key value previously locked in S, X, or SIX mode
	Non-unique index	IX for instant duration if *apparently* insert key value *doesn't* already exist No lock if insert key value already exists	IX for commit duration if (1) next key not locked during this call OR (2) next key locked now but next key *not* previously locked in S, X, or SIX mode X for commit duration if next key locked now and it had already been locked in S, X, or SIX mode
Delete	Unique index	X for commit duration	X for instant duration
	Non-unique index	X for commit duration if *apparently* delete key value will no longer exist No lock if value will definitely continue to exist	X for instant duration if delete key value will *not* definitely exist after the delete X for commit duration if delete key value *may* or will still exist after the delete

Figure 5.3: Summary of locking in ARIES/KVL.

5.2.3   ARIES/IM "Index Management"

ARIES/IM [Mohan and Levine, 1992] locks logical rows in a table, represented by records in the table's primary data structure, which the design assumes to be a heap file. With no locks in secondary indexes, its alternative name is "data-only locking." A single lock covers a record in a heap file and a corresponding entry in each secondary index, plus (in each index) the gap (open interval) to the next lower key value. Compared to ARIES/KVL, this design reduces the number of locks in update transactions. For example, deleting a row requires only a single lock, independent of the number of indexes for the table. The same applies when updating a single row, with some special cases if the update modifies an index key, i.e., the update requires deletion and insertion of index entries with different key values.

Figure 5.4, copied verbatim from Mohan and Levine [1992], compares in size and complexity rather favorably with Figure 5.3, because of much fewer cases, conditions, and locks. The conditions for index-specific locking apply to the table's primary data structure. In other words, insertion and deletion always require an instant-duration lock and a commit-duration lock on either the current or the next record.

	Next Key	Current Key
Fetch and fetch next		S for commit duration
Insert	X for instant duration	X for commit duration if index-specific locking is used
Delete	X for commit duration	X for instant duration if index-specific locking is used

Figure 5.4: Summary of locking in ARIES/IM.

These conditions apply to secondary indexes and their unique entries (made unique, if necessary, by including row identifiers) if ARIES/IM is applied to each individual index, i.e., if "data-only locking" is abandoned. The inventors claim that "ARIES/IM can be easily modified to perform index-specific locking also for slightly more concurrency compared to data-only locking, but with extra locking costs" [Mohan and Levine, 1992] but no such implementation seems to exist. SQL Server key-range locking comes very close.

ARIES/IM is far from optimal for queries run with end-of-transaction commit time, e.g., a query that is part of an update transaction. If an index covers the query and thus the query execution plan exploit index-only retrieval, serializable transaction isolation requires locks on the key range scanned in the index. With ARIES/IM, that means locking logical rows including their index entries in all indexes. If the query execution plan intersects scan results from two indexes, all rows satisfying either predicate clause must remain locked until end-of-transaction. Thus, ARIES/IM is suitable for transaction processing with small queries and updates, for query processing only in conjunction with snapshot isolation and multi-version storage, but not for mixed workloads with mixed transactions containing both queries and updates.

5.2.4 SQL SERVER KEY-RANGE LOCKING

Both ARIES/KVL and ARIES/IM reduce the number of lock manager invocations with locks covering multiple records in the database: a lock in ARIES/KVL covers an entire distinct key value and thus multiple index entries in a non-unique index; and a lock in ARIES/IM covers an entire logical row and thus multiple index entries in a table with multiple indexes. ARIES/IM with "index-specific locking" is mentioned in passing, where each lock covers a single index entry in a single index. The next design employs this granularity of locking and further introduces some distinction between an index entry and the gap to the adjacent index entry.

SQL Server implements Lomet's description of key-range locking [Lomet, 1993] quite faithfully. Locks pertain to a single index, either a table's clustered index (elsewhere known as primary index or index-organized table) or one of its non-clustered indexes (secondary indexes). Each lock covers one index entry (made unique, if necessary, by including the table's bookmark) plus the gap to the next lower index entry (phantom protection by next-key locking). There is no provision for locking a distinct key value and all its instances with a single lock request. Instead, page-level locking may be specified instead of key-range locking for any clustered and non-clustered index.

The set of lock modes follows [Lomet, 1993]. S, U, and X locks are shared, update, and exclusive locks covering a gap and an index entry; N stands for no lock. RSS, RSU, RXS, RXU, and RXX locks distinguish the lock mode for the gap between index entries (the mode prefixed by "R" for "Range") and for the index entry itself. RIN, RIS, RIU, and RIX are "insertion" locks, all held for instant duration only and used for insertions into gaps between existing index entries. The RI_ lock modes are outside the traditional theory of concurrency control. Both the design and the implementation lack RSN, RSX, RXN, and all possible RU_ modes.

SQL Server uses ghost records for deletion but not for insertion. It supports B-tree indexes on materialized views but not "increment" locks, not even in "group by" views with sums and counts.

5.2.5   ORTHOGONAL KEY-RANGE LOCKING

Orthogonal key-range locking is somewhat similar to key-range locking in SQL Server, but with completely orthogonal locks on index entry and gap. Prior-key locking (rather than next-key locking) is recommended such that a lock on an index entry may include a lock on the gap to the next higher index entry [Graefe, 2007, 2010].

Figure 5.5 illustrates combined lock modes covering index entry and gap derived from traditional lock modes. Concatenation of a lock mode for index entries and a lock mode for gaps defines the set of possible lock modes. Additional lock modes are easily possible, e.g., update or increment locks. The names of the locks mention key and gap; for example, the XN lock is pronounced "key exclusive, gap free."

If index entry and gap are locked in the same mode, Figure 5.5 uses a single lock mode for the combination of index entry and gap. In this way of thinking, all other (two-letter) lock modes imply an intention lock for the combination of index entry and gap, e.g., SX ("key shared, gap exclusive") implies an IX lock on the combination of index entry and gap. Alternatively, one can stay with separate (two-letter) lock modes and derive lock compatibility strictly component by component. There is no practical difference between these two ways of thinking, e.g., in the enabled concurrency or in the number of lock manager invocations.

Gap → ↓ Index Entry	No Lock: _N	Shared: _S	Exclusive: _X
No Lock: N_	N	NS	NX
Shared: S_	SN	S	SX
Exclusive: X_	XN	XS	X

Figure 5.5: Construction of lock modes.

Figure 5.6 shows the compatibility matrix for the lock modes of Figure 5.5. Two locks are compatible if the two leading parts are compatible and the two trailing parts are compatible. This rule just as easily applies to additional lock modes, e.g., update or increment locks. Some compatibilities may be surprising at first, because exclusive and shared locks show as compatible. For example, XN and NS (pronounced "key exclusive, gap free" and "key free, gap shared") are compatible, which means that one transaction may modify non-key attributes of an index entry while another transaction freezes a gap. Note that a ghost bit in a record header is a non-key attribute; thus, one transaction may mark an index entry invalid (logically deleting the index entry) while another transaction requires phantom protection for the gap (open interval) between two index entries.

Requested → ↓ Held	S	X	SN	NS	XN	NX	SX	XS
S	✓	–	✓	✓	–	–	–	–
X	–	–	–	–	–	–	–	–
SN	✓	–	✓	✓	–	✓	✓	–
NS	✓	–	✓	✓	✓	–	–	✓
XN	–	–	–	✓	–	✓	–	–
NX	–	–	✓	–	✓	–	–	–
SX	–	–	✓	–	–	–	–	–
XS	–	–	–	✓	–	–	–	–

Figure 5.6: Lock compatibility.

5.2.6 SUMMARY OF PRIOR DESIGNS

The present work assumes latches for low-level concurrency control, i.e., protecting in-memory data structures by coordinating threads, and focuses on locks for high-level concurrency control, i.e., protecting logical database contents by coordinating transactions. Moreover, it assumes earlier designs for hybrid concurrency control, i.e., snapshot isolation for read-only transactions and locking for all data accesses within read-write transactions. Thus, the remainder of this chapter focuses on shared and exclusive locks that coordinate read-write transactions.

All prior solutions imply hard choices for the finest granularity of locking in a database index: it may be a logical row with all its index entries (e.g., ARIES/IM), a distinct key value with all its index entries (e.g., ARIES/KVL), or an individual index entry (requiring many locks if a distinct key value has many occurrences and thus index entries, e.g., Microsoft SQL Server). Each prior solution suffers either from limited concurrency, i.e., a coarse granularity of locking, or from excessive overhead, i.e., too many lock manager invocations. In contrast, orthogonal key-value locking, introduced next in Section 5.3, offers multiple lock scopes focused on a distinct key value within an index. Section 5.4 expands upon these differences among the techniques including a finer semantics of gaps between key values. It also illustrates these differences in Figure 5.20–5.26.

5.3   ORTHOGONAL KEY-VALUE LOCKING

What seems needed is a design that permits covering a distinct key value and all its index entries with a single lock acquisition but also, at other times, permits high concurrency among update transactions. The proposed design combines principal elements of orthogonal key-range locking (complete separation of lock modes for key value and gap) and of ARIES key-value locking (a single lock for a distinct key value and all its instances). Therefore, its name is orthogonal key-value locking.

5.3.1   DESIGN GOALS

As stated earlier in Section 5.1.3, the overall design goals are correctness, simplicity, concurrency, and efficiency. More specifically, the goal is to combine the advantages of key-value locking and of orthogonal key-range locking:

- a single lock that covers a key value and all possible instances (e.g., a list of bookmarks);
- concurrent locks on individual instances (e.g., entries within a list of bookmarks); and
- independent locks for key values and for the gaps between them.

Orthogonal key-value locking satisfies two of these goals and comes very close to satisfying the remaining one. In addition, it introduces phantom protection with better precision than prior methods for database concurrency control.

5.3.2   ORTHOGONALITY

In orthogonal key-value locking, the focus of each lock, and in fact its identifying "name" in the lock manager, is one distinct key value within one index. For each lock request, there are at least two lock modes, one for the key value and one for an adjacent gap, i.e., the gap to the next higher key value. Thus, the technique permits orthogonal lock modes for data and gaps. In contrast to prior orthogonal locking techniques, the data here are a distinct key value. A lock for a key value covers all its instances, including both the present ones and all non-existing, possible instances.

Figure 5.7 illustrates how in orthogonal key-value locking a lock can cover a distinct key value (including all existing and non-existing row identifiers), a gap between distinct key values, or the combination of distinct key value plus succeeding gap. The case studies in Section 5.4 and in particular Figures 5.18 and 5.19 provide more detail on the underlying table and its index.

Index Entries and Gaps	Entry (Gary, 1)	Gap		Jerry, <3	Entry (Jerry, 3)	Gap	Entry (Jerry, 6)	Jerry >6	Gap	Mary <5	Entry (Mary, 5)
		Gary, >1	>Gary, <Jerry						>Jerry <Mary		
A key value											
A gap											
Their combination											

Figure 5.7: Orthogonal locks for key values and gaps.

5.3.3 PARTITIONED LISTS

The second innovation of the new design is most easily explained in the context of a non-unique secondary index. Although representation and concurrency control are orthogonal, it might help to imagine a list of bookmarks with each distinct key value, each bookmark pointing to an individual record in the table's primary data structure.

The proposed technique divides a set of bookmarks for a specific existing key value into a fixed number of partitions, say k partitions. Methods for lock acquisition specify not just one but multiple lock modes in a single lock manager invocation. Some designs for key-range locking, specifically Lomet's design implemented in Microsoft SQL Server and orthogonal key-range locking, provide a precedent: in those designs, a single lock identified by a key value in an index has two modes, one for the open interval between two existing key values and one for the record with the given key value. Using two lock modes, it is possible to lock the key value without locking the gap between key values and vice versa, with some restrictions in Lomet's design.

The proposed innovation extends this idea to k+1 lock modes for locking a distinct key value. One of the lock modes covers the gap to an adjacent distinct key value. The other k lock modes pertain to the k partitions of index entries. A lock acquisition may request the mode "no lock" for any partition or for the gap to the next key value.

Figure 5.8 illustrates an index record within a non-unique secondary index on an imagined employee table. Each index record contains a key value, a count of instances, and the set of instances as a sorted list of bookmarks (here, primary key values). This list is partitioned into k = 4 partitions, indicated by bold and italic font choices in Figure 5.8. In this example, the assignment from bookmark value to partition uses a simple "modulo 4" calculation. Index entries within the same partition (and for the same index key value) are always locked together; index entries in different partitions can be locked independently.

Gender	Count	List of EmpNo Values
"male"	173	2, **3**, *5*, **8**, 10, **12**, 13, *14*, **19**, 21, …

Figure 5.8: A partitioned list of bookmarks.

Figure 5.9 illustrates lock scopes possible due to partitioning within a list of bookmarks, using the format and index entries of Figure 5.7. Again using k = 4 partitions and a "modulo 4" calculation as a hash function, partitions 3 and 1 are shown.

Index Entries and Gaps	Entry (Gary, 1)	Gap			Entry (Jerry, 3)	Gap	Entry (Jerry, 6)	Gap			Entry (Mary, 5)
		Gary, >1	>Gary, <Jerry	Jerry, <3				Jerry, >6	>Jerry, <Mary	Mary, <5	
An entire key value											
Partitions thereof											

Figure 5.9: Partitions within a list of bookmarks.

It makes little difference whether the lock acquisition method lists 2 lock modes (as in existing designs for key-range locking) or k+1 lock modes (in the proposed design), and whether these lock modes are listed individually (e.g., in an array) or new lock modes are defined as combinations of primitive lock modes (as in Figure 5.5). For example, orthogonal key-range locking defines lock modes such as "XN" or "NS" (pronounced "key exclusive, gap free" and "key free, gap shared"). They are formed from exclusive ("X"), shared ("S"), and no-lock ("N") modes on key and gap. Additional primitive lock modes, e.g., update and increment locks, can readily be integrated into orthogonal key-range locking as well as orthogonal key-value locking.

Specifically, each lock request in orthogonal key-value locking lists k+1 modes. In order to lock only the gap between key values for an implementation with k = 4 partitions per list, phantom protection may need a lock in mode NNNNS, i.e., no lock on any of the partitions plus a shared lock on the gap to the next key value.

A request may lock any subset of these partitions, typically either one partition or all partitions. For example, a query with an equality predicate on the non-unique index key locks all partitions with a single method invocation, i.e., all existing and possible row identifiers, by requesting a lock in mode SSSSN for k = 4 partitions and no lock on the gap following the key value. An insertion or a deletion, on the other hand, locks only one partition for one key value in that index, e.g., NXNNN to lock partition 1 among k = 4 partitions. In this way, multiple transactions may proceed concurrently with their insertions and deletions for the same key value, each with its own partition locked, without conflict (occasional hash conflicts are possible, however). An unusual case is a lock request for two partitions, e.g., while moving a row and thus modifying its bookmark without modifying the indexed key value.

Individual entries within a list are assigned to specific partitions using a hash function applied to the unique identifier of the index entry, excluding the key value. In a non-unique secondary index, the bookmarks (pointing to records in a primary data structure) serve as the input into this hash function. Using locks on individual partitions, concurrent transactions may modify different entries at the same time, yet when a query requires the entire set of entries for a search key, it can lock it in a single lock manager call. For example, orthogonal key-value locking lets two concurrent transactions delete bookmarks 8 and 13 in Figure 5.8, which is not possible with traditional key-value locking, i.e., ARIES/KVL.

For k = 1, the new design is similar to the earlier design for orthogonal key-range locking. Recommended values are k = 1 for unique indexes (but also see Section 5.3.6 below) and 3-100 for non-unique indexes. The best value of k depends on the desired degree of concurrency, e.g., the number of hardware and software threads in the system.

5.3.4   PARTITIONED GAPS

A serializable transaction requires phantom protection for an unsuccessful query, i.e., a query with an empty result set. Without phantom protection, there is no guarantee for a repeatable count within the transaction.

Traditional locking techniques lock an entire gap. For example, ARIES/IM and key-range locking lock a gap between two existing index entries and ARIES/KVL locks the gap between two distinct key values. However, if the predicate in an unsuccessful query is an equality predicate, locking an entire gap freezes more than is truly required. In other words, locking an entire gap prevents insertions that do not truly conflict with the unsuccessful query.

For example, if key values 80 and 90 are adjacent entries in an ordered index, a search for key value 84 comes up empty. Ensuring "repeatable count" transaction isolation (serializability) means preventing insertion of an index entry with key value 84. However, insertions of key values 81, 82, 83, 85, 86, 87, 88, or 89 could proceed without an actual conflict with the required protection for key value 84.

For those cases, Tandem introduced special-case logic in which an unsuccessful query may introduce a new value into the database or only into the lock manager. Anecdotal evidence suggests that this design required many test cases, many test runs, and much debugging effort. For example, multiple transactions may query and insert many key values within the same gap, some transactions may use range predicates that may end within gaps and on key values, some transactions may roll back to a savepoint or abort altogether, etc.

In contrast, orthogonal key-value locking can partition not only the list of bookmarks associated with an existing key value but also the set of possible, non-existing key values in a gap between two existing distinct key values. A lock request specifies a lock mode for each individual partition of possible key values. Note that in Section 5.4 partitions and their lock modes pertain to existing and non-existing bookmarks associated with an existing key value, whereas here partitions and their lock modes pertain to non-existing key values. It is not required that the two counts of partitions be equal but the discussion below assumes so for simplicity.

Figure 5.10 illustrates the set of non-existent key values in the example, using italic and bold font choices to indicate k = 4 partitions with hash partitioning using a simple modulo calculation.

Possible key values
81, *82*, **83**, *84*, 85, *86*, **87**, **88**, 89

Figure 5.10: A partitioned set of non-existing key values.

Figure 5.11 illustrates lock scopes possible due to partitioning within a gap, using the format and index entries of Figure 5.7. In contrast to all prior methods of concurrency control in ordered indexes such as B-trees, phantom protection for a missing value, e.g., Larry, freezes less than a gap between adjacent index entries or key values.

Index Entries and Gaps	Entry (Gary, 1)	Gap			Entry (Jerry, 3)	Entry (Jerry, Gap	Entry (Jerry, 6)	Gap			Entry (Mary, 5)
		Gary, >1	>Gary, <Jerry	Jerry, <3				Jerry >6	>Jerry <Mary	Mary <5	
An entire gap											
A partition thereof											

Figure 5.11: Partitions within a gap.

Continuing the earlier example, if hash partitioning forms a few disjoint subsets of possible key values between 80 and 90, an unsuccessful query for key value 84 locks only one of the partitions while the other key values remain unlocked. Thus, insertions of values between 80 and 90 but different from 84 remain possible.

Ideally, a locked partition contains only a single value, e.g., 84 in the example. It is possible that it contains multiple values due to hash conflicts. For example, if the partitioning function is a modulo calculation for k = 4 partitions, then a lock to protect key value 84 implicitly but unnecessarily prevents insertion of key value 88. The desired degree of concurrency governs the number of partitions.

If another transaction indeed inserts a new distinct key value into a partition remaining unlocked in a phantom protection lock, the system needs to augment the lock held for phantom protection. Specifically, the system transaction creating a ghost record with the new distinct key value needs to create a lock on the new key value and assign it to the reader transaction. Thus, when the system transaction ends, the reader transaction has phantom protection on the two gaps below and above the new distinct key value. If there are multiple transactions with locks on partitions of this gap, all of them require additional locks in this way. If the system supports incremental lock release during rollback to a savepoint or during transaction abort, each new lock must be next to its original lock.

For example, if a user transaction holds a lock for phantom protection for key value 84 and another user transaction needs to insert key value 87, it first locks the partition of non-existing key value 87 for phantom protection and then invokes a system transaction to create a ghost with that key value. This system transaction duplicates locks such that the same partitions are locked for phantom protection in the gap between 80 and 87 and the gap between 87 and 90. Put differently, the system transaction copies all locks on the gap between 80 and 90 from the pre-existing key value 80 to the new key value 87. This is required because the original lock on the partition containing key value 84 does not indicate whether it is only for key value 84, only for key value 88, or for both (assuming a modulo 4 hash calculation). The inserting user transaction requires an exclusive lock on the ghost with key value 87 before changing it into a valid index entry.

Figure 5.12 illustrates the example with locks of the two transactions shown by different shading. Both transactions hold locks on key value 80 or, more precisely, on disjoint partitions within the gap between key values 80 and 90. Neither transaction requires a lock on key value 90 for this example.

Key	Gap				Key
80	84, 88	81, 85, 89	82, 86	83, 87	90

Figure 5.12: Shared locks on gap partitions before insertion of a new ghost.

Figure 5.13 illustrates locks in the near-final state of the example, just before the insertion transaction commits. Both user transactions hold locks on both key values 80 and 87. The read-only transaction locks the non-existing key value 84 and its hash collisions in both gaps, while the insertion transaction holds an exclusive lock on the new key value 87 and shared locks on its hash collisions in both gaps, even the empty partition shown next to key value 90.

Key	Gap		Key	Gap			Key
80	84	81, 85	82, 86	83	87	88	89		90

Figure 5.13: Locks after insertion of new key value 87.

An alternative execution sequence, i.e., an alternative design, first invokes a system transaction to insert a ghost with key value 87, which includes copying locks, and only then permits the user transaction to lock key value 87 for its insertion, i.e., turning the ghost into a valid index entry. In this design, the insertion transaction does not require any shared locks on partitions within the original gap between key values 80 and 90 or in the two final gaps below and above key value 87. Thus, this alternative permits more concurrency. For example, a third concurrent transaction could insert key value 83 without a lock conflict.

The complexity of copying locks in a system transaction inserting a ghost record (key values 83 and 87 in the example) is the price for the additional concurrency enabled by partitioning a gap between existing key values. All other serializable concurrency control techniques reject any attempt to insert key values 83 or 87 while another user transaction requires phantom protection for key value 84 within the gap between key values 80 and 90.

If the ghost insertion requires reorganization of the database page (e.g., ghost removal and free-space compaction) or even splitting an index leaf, locks on key values are not affected. Any such space management belongs into separate system transactions coded and invoked for these representation changes. The need for these system transactions is independent of orthogonal key-value locking, as are their design and implementation.

Insertion into a gap with a locked partition has no effect on the adjacent key values and on locks for these key values (as opposed to locks for gaps). In the example, it is not required to copy locks on the bookmarks of key value 80, and user transactions as well as the system transactions can ignore key value 90 and its locks.

In a query with a range predicate, all hash partitions between two adjacent key values must be locked with the same lock mode for all partitions. An alternative design dedicates one lock mode to the entire gap in a special application of hierarchical locking. With this dedicated lock mode covering all partitions, a query with an equality predicate may lock a single partition only together with an intention lock on the entire gap.

5.3.5   LOCK MANAGER IMPLEMENTATION

Lock requests specify k lock modes for partitions of bookmarks and another k lock modes for partitions of non-existing key values. Lock requests with 2k lock modes impose a little extra complexity on the lock manager. Specifically, each request for a lock on a key value in a B-tree index must be tested in each of the 2k partitions. On the other hand, in most implementations the costs of searching in a hash table and of concurrency control (latching) in the lock manager dominate the cost of manipulating locks. Locks are identified in the lock manager's hash table by the index identifier and a distinct key value, e.g., Gender in Figure 5.8, just as in ARIES/KVL.

The definition of lock compatibility follows the construction of Figure 5.6 from Figure 5.5: lock modes are compatible if they are compatible partition by partition. For example, multiple exclusive locks on the same key value but on different partitions are perfectly compatible. Finally, if the lock manager speeds up testing for compatibility by maintaining a "cumulative lock mode" summarizing all granted locks (for a specific index and key value), then this mode is computed and maintained partition by partition.

Releasing a lock usually requires re-computing the cumulative lock mode by scanning the list of all granted locks. The alternative is maintenance of multiple reference counts per lock. Releasing a lock on a single partition, however, might be simpler, because such a lock will often be an exclusive lock. In such cases, the cumulative lock mode may simply set the appropriate partition to "no lock."

While one transaction holds a shared lock for phantom protection on a partition of a gap, another transaction may acquire an exclusive lock on a different partition for insertion of a new key value. As part of the insertion, the query transaction needs to acquire an additional lock such that it achieves phantom protection on the same partition within the gaps on both sides of the new key value. In other words, both the insertion transaction and the query transaction hold locks on the new key value: the insertion on the key value and the query on the adjacent gap. A system transaction is the right implementation mechanism for creation of a new ghost record and for duplicating the existing lock. Should the user transaction and its insertion roll back, the deletion should be merely logical and retain the new key value as a ghost record. Eventually, another user transaction will turn the ghost into a valid record or a system transaction can remove the ghost record when it is unlocked.

This design follows the rule that user transactions inspect and modify logical database contents whereas system transactions modify its representation. Ghost removal, like all system transactions, requires no transactional locks. Instead, latches coordinate threads and protect data structures. For recovery, log records describe ghost removal because subsequent user transactions may log their actions with references to slot numbers within pages rather than key values. System transactions commit without log flush.

For small values of k, e.g., k = 3 or even k = 1 (e.g., for unique indexes), checking each partition is efficient. For large values of k, e.g., k = 31 or k = 127, and in particular if queries frequently lock all partitions at once, it may be more efficient to reserve one lock mode for the entire key value, i.e., all partitions of bookmarks, and another component for the entire gap, i.e., all partitions of non-existing key values. These additional entries in each lock request should also be reflected in the cumulative lock mode in the lock manager's internal state. In a sense, this change re-introduces a lock on the distinct key value and on the gap, combining aspects and advantages of both ARIES/KVL (locking all existing and possible instances of a key value with a single lock request and a uniform lock mode) and of orthogonal key-range locking (two separate lock modes for key value and gap).

With the additional lock on an entire distinct key value and on an entire gap, the number of components in the lock increases from 2k to 2k+2 lock modes for each key value in the index. Each of these two additional lock components permit absolute lock modes (e.g., S, X) as well as intention lock modes (e.g., IS, IX) and mixed modes (e.g., SIX). A lock request for an individual partition must include an intention lock on the entire key value or gap. A lock request for all partitions at once needs to lock merely the entire key value in an absolute mode, with no locks on individual partitions. A mixed mode combines these two aspects. For example, an SIX lock on a key value combines an S lock on all possible instances of that key value and the right to acquire X locks on individual partitions.

5.3.6   UNIQUE SECONDARY INDEXES

Another optimization pertains to unique indexes. A natural inclination might be to employ orthogonal key-value locking with k = 1, i.e., a single partition, at least for the list of bookmarks. An alternative specifically for multi-column unique keys locks some prefix of the key like the key in a non-unique index and the remaining columns (starting with the suffix of the unique key) like the bookmarks in the design for non-unique indexes.

Perhaps an example clarifies this case. Imagine two tables, e.g., "course" and "student," plus a many-to-many relationship in its own table, e.g., "enrollment." An index on enrollment may be unique on the combination of course number and student identifier, which suggests orthogonal key-value locking with a single partition (k = 1).

The alternative design locks index entries as in a non-unique index on the leading field, e.g., on course number. In that case, queries may lock the entire enrollment information of one course (a class roster) with a single lock (locking all partitions in the list of student identifiers), yet updates may lock subsets of student identifiers (by locking only a single partition within a roster). With an appropriate number of partitions, the concurrency among updates is practically the same as with locks on individual pairs of course number and student identifier.

Figure 5.14 illustrates the idea, even adding a further column into a secondary index. For each distinct key value, here the course number, there is a list of entries, each containing all remaining index columns. Note that the physical organization of the data structure and the techniques for concurrency control are independent of each other. The entries in the list are hash partitioned on the field that completes the unique index key, here the student identifier.

CourseNo	Count	List of (StudentId, Grade) pairs
CompSci 101	23	(**007**, A), (*13*, F), …

Figure 5.14: A partitioned list of index entries.

This pattern of queries is quite typical for many-to-many relationships: a precise retrieval in one of the entity types (e.g., a specific course), an index that facilitates efficient navigation to the other entity type (e.g., on enrollment, with course number as leading key), and retrieval of all instances related to the initial instance. The opposite example is similarly typical, i.e., listing a single student's enrollment information (a student transcript) using an enrollment index with student identifier as leading column. It must be equally well supported in a database system, its indexes, its repertoire of query execution plans, its concurrency control, etc. B-tree indexes cluster relevant index entries due to their sort order; the proposed use of orthogonal key-value locking supports these queries with the minimal number of locks and the minimal number of lock requests.

Splitting unique keys into prefix and suffix and applying orthogonal key-value locking to prefixes affect phantom protection. For example, in an index with course number as prefix and student identifier as suffix, phantom protection for a specific missing student identifier within an existing course must lock a partition of suffixes, i.e., similar to a partition of bookmarks, whereas phantom protection for a non-existing course must lock a partition of course numbers, i.e., similar to a partition of non-existing key values. A range predicate on student identifiers within an existing course number must lock the entire course number, i.e., similar to locking an entire key value with all its partitions of bookmarks. Perhaps these locking pattern for course number and student identifier, or for prefix and suffix within a unique index, reflect the behavior of applications more naturally than traditional locking techniques. The traditional real-world terms roster and transcript suggest that these access patterns are indeed common.

5.3.7   PRIMARY INDEXES

In many cases, a table's primary key is also the search key in the table's primary index. In other cases, in particular if the user-defined search key in the primary index is not unique, the table's bookmark adds a system generated value to the user-defined search key. This value can be unique by itself within the table or even the entire database. For example, some systems attach a unique, high-resolution time stamp to each row upon creation, often called "database key" or a similar name. In some systems, the system-generated value is unique only for a specific table and for a specific value of the user-defined search key. If a specific value of the user-defined search key happens to be unique, this system-generated "uniquifier" might be null or even entirely absent.

If the user-defined search key for a primary index is unique, orthogonal key-value locking in the primary index does not benefit from partitioning. In those cases, orthogonal key-value locking with k = 1 works like orthogonal key-range locking, except that gaps may still be partitioned. For primary indexes with non-unique keys, partitioning is appropriate for the system-generated key suffix. In other words, the user-defined key value is locked like a distinct key value in a non-unique secondary index and system-defined suffix values are partitioned like bookmarks.

With this design, when a unique bookmark value (including the suffix) is used to search the primary index, e.g., when fetching additional columns after searching a secondary index, a single partition is the appropriate granularity of locking in the primary index. When a specific value only for the user-defined search key is used to search the primary index, e.g., based on an equality predicate in a query, orthogonal key-value locking can, with a single invocation of the lock manager, lock all rows with that search key value.

When a search is not successful in a serializable transaction, phantom protection is needed in primary indexes just as much as in secondary indexes. Orthogonal key-value locking, using a lock on the gap between distinct key values or on partitions thereof, protects such a transaction against insertion of phantom records without blocking any operations on the adjacent key values. In other words, insertion and deletion of rows with one of the adjacent user-defined key values remain unrestricted by the lock required for phantom protection. With partitioning of the gap between distinct values of the user-defined key, phantom protection locks only a subset of possible future values.

5.3.8   MASTER-DETAIL CLUSTERING

Merged indexes [Graefe, 2011] are B-tree structures with entries obtained from multiple indexes, typically on multiple tables, with key values constructed in such a way that related data is co-located by the sort order in the B-tree. For example, in order to cluster information on orders and order details, all records and their sort keys start with an order number. The index identifier (and thus the indication of a record's internal format) is a minor sort key. As another example, two indexes on a table representing a many-to-many relationship (e.g., enrollment of students in courses) may be merged with indexes on two tables representing the connected entity types (e.g., students and courses).

Key-value locking in merged indexes enables a form of object locking. For example, if each lock covers all index entries with a given order number, it covers an order and its order details. This lock scope is often desirable as it satisfies a query's concurrency control needs with a single invocation of the lock manager. Similarly, a single key-value lock on a student identifier may cover a student record plus all index entries for the student's transcript.

Orthogonal key-value locking can satisfy these situations but also other ones. Specifically, by partitioning the records, it is possible to lock only a single order detail. In more complex object types and in merged indexes, a partition may cover a specific group. For example, within a customer object and an index on customer identifier, one partition might cover all orders or all invoices of a specific customer.

As pointed out earlier, the choices of data representation and of the granularity of locking are independent. In other words, the techniques outlined here also work in separate indexes. For example, if orders and order details are indexed in separate B-trees, locks on complex objects may still be used. A referential integrity constraint between order details and orders enables locking in one index without inspecting the other index.

Figure 5.15 illustrates a specific representation of a master record, e.g., order 4711, and its detail records, e.g., line items. This representation could guide a traditional assignment of index entries and gaps to locks, where each master record and each detail record are locked separately.

Gap	Key	Gap	Key	Gap	Key	Gap
	4711, ...		4711,1, ...		4711,2, ...	

Figure 5.15: Master and detail records as individual key values.

Figure 5.16 illustrates an alternative representation that would guide an alternative assignment to locks. The entire complex object including master and detail records can be locked as a unit or the individual records can be locked as partitions. If indeed many transactions access master and detail records together, then locking entire complex object seems advantageous. While these representations may suggest alternative lock assignments, representation and lock assignment are orthogonal and either lock assignment could be used with either representation. Taking this thought further, it seems possible to apply orthogonal key-value locking to multiple tables and indexes that are related, e.g., orders and their line items even if stored in multiple storage structures.

Gap	Key			Gap
	4711, ...	4711,1, ...	4711,2, ...	

Figure 5.16: Master and detail records as instances of a single key value.

5.3.9   SUMMARY OF ORTHOGONAL KEY-VALUE LOCKING

A new technique, to be called orthogonal key-value locking, combines all the advantages of locking a distinct key value and all its index entries in a single lock manager invocation, i.e., high efficiency and low overhead for locking, and most of the advantages of locking individual index entries, i.e., high concurrency and low lock contention. Moreover, for unsuccessful equality queries, partitioning within a gap enables phantom protection with much better precision and with less impact on concurrent updates and insertions than prior techniques for concurrency control in databases, their tables, and their indexes. Specific optimizations apply to unique secondary indexes, primary indexes with compound keys, and merged indexes for master-detail clustering.

Figure 5.17 summarizes the lock scopes that orthogonal key-value locking supports for key value Jerry, based on the database table shown in Figure 5.18 and its index entries shown in Figure 5.19. Note that locking a partition of bookmarks, e.g., for EmpNo 3 or 5, always includes partitions within the intervals at the ends of a key value, e.g., EmpNo < 3 and EmpNo > 6. Orthogonal key-value locking also supports any combination of lock scopes. For example, a serializable transaction searching the index with the predicate "FirstName in ('Harold', 'Harry')" may lock two partitions within the gap between Gary and Jerry. For another example, a search for "FirstName in ('Gerald', 'Jerry')" may lock all instances of existing key value Jerry plus one partition in a gap. For a final example, a range query can, with a single invocation of the lock manager, lock a key value and its adjacent gap. This lock covers all existing and non-existing instances of the locked key value as well as all non-existing key values in the adjacent gap. For comparison, the last line of Figure 5.17 shows the one and only lock scope possible in ARIES/KVL, i.e., a gap and an adjacent distinct key value with all instances.

Index Entries and Gaps	Entry (Gary, 1)	Gap			Entry (Jerry, 3)	Gap	Entry (Jerry, 6)	Jerry >6	Gap		Entry (Mary, 5)
		Gary, >1	>Gary <Jerry	Jerry, <3					>Jerry <Mary	Mary, <5	
An entire key value			█	█	█	█	█	█			
A partition thereof				█		█		█			
An entire gap									█	█	
A partition thereof								█	█		
Maximum combination			█	█	█	█	█	█	█	█	
ARIES/KVL		█	█	█							

Figure 5.17: Lock scopes in orthogonal key-value locking.

5.4   CASE STUDIES

In order to clarify and compare the specific behaviors of the various locking schemes, this section illustrates the required locks in each design for all principal types of index accesses. These comparisons are qualitative in nature but nonetheless serve to highlight the differences among the schemes. Quantitative differences in performance and scalability depend on the workload.

The comparisons rely on a specific (toy) example table with employee information. This table has a primary index on its primary key and a secondary index on one of the other columns. The primary key is, of course, unique and not null; the secondary index is non-unique in this case. The table could have additional secondary indexes.

Figure 5.18 shows index records in the primary index, which is also the table's primary key in this example. The figure shows the rows sorted and the reader should imagine them in a B-tree data structure. Note the skipped values in the sequence of EmpNo values and the duplicate values in the column FirstName. This toy example has only two duplicate instances but a key value in a real index may have hundreds or thousands of instances. Figure 5.19 shows index records in a non-unique secondary index on FirstName. This index format pairs each distinct key value with a list of bookmarks. Unique search keys in the primary index serve as bookmarks; they are also the table's primary key here.

5.4.1   EMPTY QUERIES–PHANTOM PROTECTION

The first comparison focuses on searches for non-existing key values. Assuming a serializable transaction, a lock is required for phantom protection until end-of-transaction. In other words, this first comparison focuses on techniques that lock the absence of key values. The example query is "Select... where FirstName = 'Harry' ", which searches the gap between key values Gary

EmpNo	FirstName	PostalCode	Phone	HireYear
1	Gary	10032	1122	2014
3	Jerry	46045	9999	2015
5	Mary	53704	5347	2015
6	Jerry	37745	5432	2015
9	Terry	60061	8642	2016

Figure 5.18: An example database table.

FirstName	Count	EmpNos
Gary	1	1
Jerry	2	3, 6
Mary	1	5
Terry	1	9

Figure 5.19: Records in an example non-unique secondary index.

and Jerry. Section 5.4.3 considers designs like Tandem's in which an empty query may introduce a new value into the database or the lock manager. The discussion here considers locks only on the pre-existing key values and index entries shown in Figure 5.19. Figure 5.20 illustrates the following discussion.

ARIES/KVL cannot lock the key value Harry so it locks the next higher key value, Jerry. This locks all occurrences of the distinct key value without regard to EmpNo values. Thus, no other transaction can insert a new row with FirstName Harry but in addition, no other transaction can modify, insert, or delete any row with FirstName Jerry. While the example shows only two instances of FirstName Jerry, there may be thousands in other examples. ARIES/KVL would lock all of them, giving an unsuccessful search a surprisingly large lock footprint.

ARIES/IM locks the next higher index entry, i.e., it locks the first occurrence of Jerry and thus the row with EmpNo 3. A single lock covers the row in the table and its entire representation, i.e., the index entry in the primary index, the index entry in the secondary index on FirstName, an index entry in each further secondary index, and (in each index) the gap between those index entries and the next lower index entry. While this lock is in place, no other transaction can insert a new row with FirstName Harry. In addition, no other transaction can insert new index entries (Gary, 7) or (Jerry, 2), for example, because these index entries also belong into the gap locked for phantom protection, whereas new index entries (Gary, 0) and (Jerry, 4) could proceed. Moreover, no other transaction can insert any row with EmpNo 2, because the lock includes in the primary index the gap below EmpNo 3. Finally, if the database table of

Figure 5.18 has another secondary index on PostalCode, the lock on EmpNo 3 also stops other transactions from inserting any PostalCode values between 37745 and 46045. These are rather surprising and counter-intuitive effects of a query with a predicate on FirstName.

Key-range locking in Microsoft SQL Server locks the first index entry following the unsuccessful search, i.e., the index entry (Jerry, 3). The unsuccessful search in the secondary index does not acquire any locks in the primary index. Insertion of a new row with FirstName Jerry is possible if the EmpNo is larger than 3, e.g., 7. Insertion of a new employee (Jerry, 2) or (Gary, 7) is not possible until the transaction searching for Harry releases its locks.

Orthogonal key-range locking locks the key preceding a gap, i.e., the index entry (Gary, 1), in NS mode (pronounced "key free, gap shared"). Insertion of new rows with FirstName Gary are prevented if the EmpNo value exceeds 1. On the other hand, non-key fields in the index entry (Gary, 1) remain unlocked and another transaction may modify those, because a lock in NS mode holds no lock on the index entry itself, only on the gap (open interval) between index entries. The restriction to updating non-key fields is less severe than it may seem: recall from Section 5.2.5 that an index entry's ghost bit is a non-key field, i.e., logical deletion and insertion by toggling a ghost bit are possible. Key-range locking in Microsoft SQL Server lacks a RangeS_N mode that would be equivalent to the NS mode in orthogonal key-range locking.

Finally, orthogonal key-value locking locks the preceding distinct key value, Gary, in a mode that protects the gap (open interval) between Gary and Jerry but imposes no restrictions on this key value or its lists of EmpNo values. For example, another transaction may insert a new row with FirstName Gary or Jerry and with any EmpNo value. Removal of rows with FirstName Jerry has no restrictions; deletion of rows with FirstName Gary and removal of their index entries requires that the key value Gary remain in the index, at least as a ghost record, until the need for phantom protection ends and the lock on key value Gary is released.

Figure 5.20 illustrates required and actual lock scopes for an example unsuccessful query, i.e., for phantom protection. The column headings indicate ranges in the domain of the index keys. Among the three sub-ranges of the gap between index entries (Gary, 1) and (Jerry, 3), a serializable query for Harry requires concurrency control only for one. An S in Figure 5.20 indicates that a serializable locking technique acquires a transaction-duration shared lock in order to prevent insertion of index value Harry. It is clear that ARIES/KVL locks the largest scope. ARIES/IM shows the same range as key-range locking only because Figure 5.20 does not show the lock scope in other indexes of the same table. Orthogonal key-range locking locks less than key-range locking due to separate lock modes for index entry and gap. Orthogonal key-value locking locks the smallest scope, even without the partitioning techniques of Section 5.3.4.

In this example with an equality predicate on the index key, partitioning within a gap as introduced in Section 5.3.4 can reduce the lock scope even further, i.e., to a fraction as illustrated in the last line of Figure 5.20. By hash partitioning the possible key values within the gap between existing key values, the footprint of the lock and thus of phantom protection is as narrow as

Index Entries and Gaps	Entry (Gary, 1)	Gap			Entry (Jerry, 3)	Gap	Entry (Jerry, 6)	Gap	
		Gary, >1	>Gary, <Jerry	Jerry, <3				Jerry >6	>Jerry
ARIES/KVL			S on "Jerry"						
ARIES/IM		S on "3"							
KRL		S on "(Jerry, 3)"							
Orth. krl		NS on "(Gary, 1)"							
Orth. kvl			S						
w/gap part'g									

Figure 5.20: Required and actual lock scopes in phantom protection for "Harry."

the single FirstName Harry and its hash collisions. People with first names such as Gerhard, Gottfried, and Hank will appreciate the increased concurrency.

In summary, while all techniques require only a single lock manager invocation, orthogonal key-value locking provides phantom protection with the least restrictive lock scope. All other techniques restrict concurrent operations not only on the non-existing key value "Harry" but also on pre-existing adjacent key values "Gary" and "Jerry."

5.4.2 SUCCESSFUL EQUALITY QUERIES

The second comparison focuses on successful index search for a single key value. This case occurs both in selection queries and in index nested loops joins. The example query predicate is "…where FirstName = 'Jerry'," chosen to focus on a key value with multiple instances in the indexed column. While the example shows only two instances, real cases may have thousands. Serializability requires that other transactions must not add or remove instances satisfying this search predicate. Figure 5.21 illustrates the following discussion, with subscripts indicating separate locks and thus multiple lock manager invocations.

ARIES/KVL requires a single lock for all instances of FirstName Jerry. This lock pertains to the secondary index only, with no effect on the primary index. It includes phantom protection, i.e., it prevents insertion of additional index entries with FirstName Jerry. The lock also covers the gap to the next lower key value, i.e., FirstName Gary. Thus, this lock also prevents insertion of a key value other than Jerry, e.g., FirstName Harry.

ARIES/IM locks three rows in the table, one more than the number of rows matching the query. These locks include the rows with FirstName Jerry (rows 3 and 6) and the next higher index entry, i.e., row 5 with FirstName Mary. The last lock is required to prevent other transactions from inserting additional instances, e.g., (Jerry, 7). These locks include the gap to the next lower key in each index, i.e., both the primary index and the secondary index. Thus, they

Index Entries and Gaps	Entry (Gary, 1)	Gap			Entry (Jerry, 3)	Gap	Entry (Jerry, 6)	Gap			Entry (Mary, 5)
		Gary, >1	>Gary, <Jerry	Jerry, <3				Jerry >6	>Jerry <Mary	Mary <5	
ARIES/KVL					S						
ARIES/IM			S_1				S_2			S_3		
KRL			S_1				S_2			S_3		
Orth. krl			S_1			S_2			S_3			
Orth. kvl					S							

Figure 5.21: Lock scopes in an equality query for "Jerry."

prevent insertion of new rows with FirstName Jerry and EmpNo 2 or 4 as well as rows with FirstName Larry and rows with FirstName Mary and EmpNo smaller than 5.

SQL Server locks each instance of the desired key value with its unique index entry, i.e., (Jerry, 3) and (Jerry, 6), plus the next higher existing index entry, i.e., (Mary, 5). The last lock prevents additional entries with FirstName Jerry and EmpNo values greater than 6, but it also prevents insertion of additional entries with FirstName Mary and EmpNo smaller than 5 as well as key values between Jerry and Mary, e.g., Larry.

Orthogonal key-range locking is similar to SQL Server locking except it locks the next lower key value from Jerry instead of the next higher key value, i.e., Gary instead of Mary, and it leaves the additional record itself unlocked. A lock in NS mode (pronounced "key free, gap shared") on index entry (Gary, 1) leaves the existing index entry unlocked but it prevents insertion of new index entries with FirstName Gary and EmpNo values higher than 1, with FirstName values between Gary and Jerry, e.g., Harry, and with FirstName Jerry and EmpNo value smaller than 3. Only the second group is truly required to protect the result of the example query. This problem is inherent in all locking schemes focused on index entries rather than distinct key values.

Finally, orthogonal key-value locking needs only one lock for all existing and possible index entries with FirstName Jerry. Both adjacent key values remain unlocked, i.e., Gary and Mary. Even the gaps below and above FirstName Jerry remain unlocked, i.e., other transaction can insert new index entries with FirstName Harry or Larry.

In summary, among all locking schemes for B-tree indexes, only orthogonal key-value locking allows repeatable successful equality queries with perfect precision and with a single lock, even if other methods employ multiple locks. Someone named James or Jim would appreciate the precise lock scope of orthogonal key-value locking.

5.4.3 PHANTOM PROTECTION WITH GHOST RECORDS

The discussion of locking in successful equality queries also helps understanding lock scopes in phantom protection with a ghost record left behind by a prior deletion. For example, consider the example of Section 5.4.1 and a pre-existing ghost with FirstName Harry. In this case, locks for an unsuccessful equality query are equal to the locks for a successful equality query for a key value with only a single instance or bookmark.

Figure 5.22 illustrates phantom protection for an unsuccessful selection query using a pre-existing ghost record. The header row indicates the required lock scope and, with the strikethrough font, the pre-existing ghost record. The two methods locking distinct key values require a single lock on FirstName Harry. Whereas orthogonal key-value locking locks only FirstName Harry, ARIES/KVL also locks the gap between Gary and Harry. The other three techniques require two locks in order to cover the ranges of EmpNo values below and above 47.

Figure 5.22 shows a case with a single ghost record. If there were multiple ghost records matching the query predicate, then Figure 5.22 would resemble Figure 5.21 even more closely.

Index Entries and Gaps	Entry (Gary, 1)	Gap		Harry, <47	Ghost (Harry, 47)	Harry >47	Gap		Entry (Jerry, 3)
		Gary, >1	>Gary, <Harry				>Harry <Jerry	Jerry <3	
ARIES/KVL			S	S	S				
ARIES/IM		S_1	S_1	S_1			S_2	S_2	
KRL		S_1	S_1	S_1			S_2	S_2	
Orth. krl		S_1	S_1		S_2	S_2	S_2		
Orth. kvl				S	S				

Figure 5.22: Phantom protection with a pre-existing ghost record.

If no ghost record exists that matches an unsuccessful selection query, a query could invoke a system transaction to insert a suitable ghost record. For the methods focused on index entries rather than distinct key values, a careful choice of the EmpNo value in the ghost record improves upon the locks shown in Figure 5.22. If the chosen EmpNo is $+\infty$, a single lock suffices in ARIES/IM and in key-range locking. Orthogonal key-range locking can use $-\infty$ in the same way. These values differ because the traditional methods use next-key locking in order to cover a gap whereas the orthogonal methods use prior-key locking. Instead of $-\infty$, orthogonal key-range locking can also simply use *null*, assuming it sorts lower than all non-*null* values.

Figures 5.23 and 5.24 show the locks and their scopes for phantom protection using a new ghost record with a carefully chosen index entry. ARIES/KVL and orthogonal key-value locking have the same lock counts (one) and lock scopes as in Figure 5.22. The other three methods require two locks in Figure 5.22 but only one in Figures 5.23 and 5.24. ARIES/IM and key-range locking no longer lock FirstName values above Harry and orthogonal key-range locking no longer locks FirstName values below Harry. Conceivably, two ghost entries with FirstName Harry and EmpNo values $-\infty$ and $+\infty$ could further reduce over-locking. In effect, such a pair of ghost entries permits locking a distinct key value using mechanisms focused on individual index entries.

Index Entries and Gaps	Entry (Gary, 1)	Gap		Ghost (Harry, $+\infty$)	Gap		Entry (Jerry, 3)
		Gary, >1	>Gary, <Harry	Harry, <+∞	>Harry <Jerry	Jerry <3	
ARIES/KVL			S				
ARIES/IM			S				
KRL			S				

Figure 5.23: Single-lock phantom protection with next-key locking.

Index Entries and Gaps	Entry (Gary, 1)	Gap		Ghost (Harry, *null*)	Harry, *>null*	Gap		Entry (Jerry, 3)
		Gary, >1	>Gary, <Harry			>Harry <Jerry	Jerry <3	
Orth. krl				S				
Orth. kvl				S				

Figure 5.24: Single-lock phantom protection with prior-key locking.

Locking the EmpNo value $+\infty$ in ARIES/IM has surprising consequences, however. In an ordered index on EmpNo, this value protects the high end of the key domain. If new EmpNo values, e.g., for newly hired employees, are chosen in an increasing sequence, unsuccessful selection queries with predicates on the FirstName column may prevent insertions of newly hired employees even with different FirstName values. Therefore, this optimization for phantom protection has surprising and thus undesirable consequences in systems and tables locked with ARIES/IM.

In summary, both with a pre-existing ghost record and with a new ghost record, none of the prior locking methods can match the perfect precision of orthogonal key-value locking.

5.4.4   RANGE QUERIES

The fourth comparison focuses on range queries. The example query predicate is "…where First-Name between 'Jerry' and 'Mary'." The query result includes all instances of Jerry and Mary. Locking for serializability must prevent insertion of additional instances of these key values and of key values in between. Figure 5.25 illustrates the following discussion.

ARIES/KVL needs two locks on key values Jerry and Mary. These locks cover the key values and the gaps between them. In addition, the first lock covers the gap below Jerry. This is required to prevent insertion of a new row with FirstName Jerry and EmpNo 2 but it also prevents new rows with FirstName Harry, Howard, Jack, etc.

ARIES/IM acquires four locks on rows with EmpNo 3, 6, 5, and 9. The lock on row with EmpNo 9 is required to stop other transactions from inserting new index entries with FirstName Mary and EmpNo values greater than 5, but it also prevents new rows with FirstName Mason, Taylor, etc. Moreover, these locks also lock index entries in further indexes as well as the gaps (open intervals) below each of those index entries.

Key-range locking in SQL Server requires four locks on index entries (Jerry, 3), (Jerry, 6), (Mary, 5), and (Terry, 9). As in ARIES/IM, the first lock includes the gap below (Jerry, 3) and the last lock protects the gap above (Mary, 5) from new entries with FirstName Mary and EmpNo values greater than 5.

Orthogonal key-range locking requires locks on (Jerry, 3) and (Jerry, 6) in S mode to cover the index entries and the gaps to the next higher key. Moreover, a lock on (Gary, 1) in NS ("key free, gap shared") prevents insertion of rows with FirstName Jerry and EmpNo less than 3 but also rows with FirstName Harry etc. Finally, a lock on (Mary, 5) must be in S mode in order to cover both the key value and the gap above. Locking the gap prevents new index entries with FirstName Mary and EmpNo values greater than 5, although it also prevents new entries with FirstName greater than Mary, e.g., FirstName Mason or Terrence. Thus, orthogonal key-range locking seems similar to key-range locking in SQL Server as both lock three index entries within the range of the query predicate and one index entry outside. Orthogonal key-range locking is slightly more precise than SQL Server as it locks the outside key value in a less restrictive mode not available in SQL Server's lock matrix.

Finally, orthogonal key-value locking requires locks on the two distinct key values within the range of the query predicate, i.e., FirstName Jerry and Mary. For these, it locks all existing and possible EmpNo values. A range query in a serializable transaction locks gaps between key values and all their partitions. For the highest key value within the range of the query predicate, i.e., FirstName Mary, the lock request leaves the gap to the next higher key value free (no lock). Thus, two locks protect precisely the key range of the query predicate, with other transactions free to insert index entries outside the predicate range.

Figure 5.25 illustrates lock scopes for the example range query. ARIES/KVL and orthogonal key-value locking require only two locks because they lock distinct key values, not individual index entries. The other techniques require four locks and thus four lock manager invocations. All prior methods lock more than required, whereas orthogonal key-value locking locks precisely the required part of the key domain. People with first names such as Irv, Mike, and Mohan will appreciate the improved concurrency and system performance.

Index Entries and Gaps	Entry (Gary, 1)	Gap Gary, >1	>Gary, <Jerry	Entry Jerry, <3	(Jerry, 3)	Gap	Entry (Jerry, 6)	Jerry, >6	Gap >Jerry, <Mary	Mary, <5	Entry (Mary, 5)	Mary, >5	Gap >Mary, <Terry	Terry, <9	Entry (Terry, 9)
ARIES/ KVL			S_1						S_2						
ARIES/IM		S_1			S_2			S_3			S_4				
KRL		S_1			S_2			S_3			S_4				
Orth. krl			S_1		S_2			S_3				S_4			
Orth. kvl						S_1			S_2						

Figure 5.25: Lock scopes in a range query.

In summary, orthogonal key-value locking requires the fewest locks yet it is the only technique that protects a key range with perfect precision. This also applies to key ranges that exclude one or both end points.

5.4.5 NON-KEY UPDATES

The fifth comparison focuses on updates that modify non-key columns. In the primary index of the running example, such an update modifies any column other than the primary key. The secondary index of the running example requires a small definition change for such an update to be possible, namely a column added to each index entry, e.g., using the "include" clause supported by some systems, which puts the included column behind the bookmark in each index record. It is therefore irrelevant for the sort order and the index organization. A non-key update of this extended secondary index modifies such an included column. In the list representation of non-unique secondary indexes, each element in the list carries an instance of the included columns. This is the case discussed below. Imagine the secondary index of Figure 5.19 extended by "include PostalCode" and an update "update… set PostalCode = … where EmpNo = 3."

ARIES/KVL acquires locks in each index; in the non-unique secondary index of the extended example, it locks all instances of FirstName Jerry as well as the gap between FirstName Gary and FirstName Jerry.

ARIES/IM locks the affected logical row including all its index entries and the gaps below those index entries. With only a single lock request required, this case seems to be the principal design point for ARIES/IM.

Key-range locking in SQL Server locks only the index entry (Jerry, 3) and the gap below it. All other index entries, including all other index entries with FirstName Jerry, remain unlocked.

Orthogonal key-range locking locks only the index entry (Jerry, 3) but leaves the gaps below and above it completely unlocked. This is possible with a lock in XN mode (pronounced "key exclusive, gap free").

Finally, orthogonal key-value locking locks the distinct key value Jerry but only a single partition within the list of instances. For k = 7 partitions, for example, this locks about 1 in 7 or 14% of those instances. For a short list as shown in Figure 5.19, this is usually a single instance. For a longer list, locking a partition may mean locking multiple instances even if only one instance needs locking. Larger choices of k may alleviate hash conflicts and false sharing. The gaps below and above FirstName Jerry remain unlocked.

Figure 5.26 illustrates required and actual lock scopes for a non-key update of a single index entry. ARIES/KVL locks all instances of a distinct key value and ARIES/IM locks an entry and a gap in each index of the table. Key-range locking locks a single entry plus a gap in a single index. Orthogonal key-range locking leaves the gap unlocked and thus locks precisely as much as needed for this update operation. Orthogonal key-value locking locks a partition of index entries, ideally a partition containing only one entry.

Figure 5.26 also illustrates the lock scopes of user transactions inserting and deleting index entries via ghost records, because toggling the ghost bit in a record header is a prototypical case of a non-key index update. Without ghost records, older techniques lock more, in particular also an adjacent key value or index entry as detailed in Figures 5.3 and 5.4. The following sections provide more details.

Index Entries and Gaps	Entry (Gary, 1)	Gap Gary, >1	>Gary, <Jerry	Jerry, <3	Entry (Jerry, 3)	Gap	Entry (Jerry, 6)	Jerry >6	Gap >Jerry
ARIES/KVL					X				
ARIES/IM			X						
KRL			X						
Orth. krl					X				
Orth. kvl					X				

Figure 5.26: Lock scopes in a non-key update.

In summary, all schemes support an individual non-key update with a single lock. Orthogonal key-range locking is most precise, with orthogonal key-value locking equally precise given an appropriate number of partitions.

5.4.6 DELETIONS

The sixth comparison focuses on deletion of rows in a table and of index entries in a B-tree. Within an index, any update of a key column usually requires a pair of deletion and insertion. Thus, the sixth and seventh comparisons also cover updates on key columns in indexes. An example here is "delete… where EmpNo = 3."

There are three cases to consider. With increasing complexity, these are (i) turning an existing, valid index entry into a ghost, (ii) deletion of a single index entry, with other index entries remaining for the same key value, and (iii) removal of a distinct key value as part of deleting its last remaining index entry.

Non-unique secondary indexes need one bit for each index entry to indicate the ghost status. A key value becomes a ghost when its list is empty or when all remaining entries are ghosts. Ghost removal happens outside of user transactions, i.e., in system transactions [Graefe, 2010] or ARIES top-level actions [Mohan et al., 1992].

Deletion via a ghost is a standard technique. Among other advantages, it ensures simple and reliable transaction rollback if a user transaction aborts or fails. Specifically, rollback of a user transaction never requires space allocation, e.g., splitting a B-tree node. Deletion via a ghost record, i.e., by toggling a ghost bit, requires the same locks as a non-key update, discussed in Section 5.4 and illustrated in Figure 5.26.

The remainder of this section pertains to deletion without ghosts, even if it is not the recommended implementation technique. If nothing else, it offers a level comparison with ARIES, e.g., Figure 5.4, where the commit-duration X lock on the next key indicates the assumption of immediate record removal, i.e., removal without ghost records. Given that the purpose of commit-duration locks after a deletion is to ensure conflict-free re-insertion in case of a transaction rollback, in most cases the locks equal those required for phantom protection.

ARIES/KVL distinguishes cases (ii) and (iii) above as well as unique and non-unique secondary indexes, as summarized in Figure 5.3. In all cases, one distinct key value remains locked in X mode until end-of-transaction in order to protect the transaction's ability to roll back. Even if the transaction removes only a single entry in a list of thousands, the entire list remains locked together with the key value and the gap to the next lower distinct key value. Worse yet, upon removal of a key value and its empty list, the next key remains locked, which also covers the gaps below and above the deleted key value in addition to the deleted key value itself.

ARIES/IM needs to lock the affected logical row as well as, in each unique secondary index, the row with the next higher index entry. The latter locks prevent concurrent insertion of other logical rows with conflicting unique index keys. A system using the ARIES/IM techniques definitely benefits from deletion via ghost records.

SQL Server deletes via ghost records, which system transactions eventually remove. In order to adapt SQL Server key-range locking to deletion without ghost records, locks on the deleted index entry as well as the next higher index entry are required. The lock manager might as well remove the lock on the deleted (and removed) index entry as soon as the entry disappears in the page image in the buffer pool, quite comparable to the instant locks of the ARIES techniques (see Figures 5.3 and 5.4).

The design of orthogonal key-range locking calls for ghost records during both insertion and deletion. If ghost records must be avoided for some reason, cases (ii) and (iii) above must lock the next lower index entry in the index in NX mode ("key free, gap exclusive") until end-of-transaction. The effect is quite similar to key-range locking in SQL Server, except that the next lower index entry itself remains unlocked.

Finally, orthogonal key-value locking also works best with ghost records during both insertion and deletion. When forced to operate without ghost records, case (ii) above requires a lock on one of the partitions within the newly created gap and case (iii) above requires a lock on one of the partitions within the set of bookmarks for the existing and remaining key value. In a unique index, there is only a single set of partitions.

In summary, for deletion via ghost status, which has long been the preferred implementation technique, locking follows the rules for non-key updates, where orthogonal key-range locking and orthogonal key-value locking are best. For deletion without ghosts, ARIES/KVL and ARIES/IM lock much more than truly required, orthogonal key-range locking is slightly better than SQL Server key-range locking, and orthogonal key-value locking benefits from partitioning bookmarks and gaps. ARIES/IM requires the fewest locks in tables with multiple non-unique indexes but has the largest cost in terms of concurrency control scope and excluded concurrent transactions.

5.4.7 INSERTIONS

The seventh comparison focuses on insertion of new rows into a table and thus new index entries in primary and secondary indexes. An example here is "insert… values (4, 'Jerry,' 54546, 4499)."

As insertion is the opposite of deletion, there are again three cases to consider. With increasing complexity, these are (i) insertion via ghost status, (ii) insertion of another instance of an existing key value, and (iii) insertion of an entirely new distinct key value. The ghost record may be a remnant of a prior deletion or the product of a deliberately invoked system transaction. When a user transaction turns a ghost record into a valid record, which is the recommended implementation at least for the orthogonal locking techniques, it acquires locks as discussed in Section 5.4 and illustrated in Figure 5.26. The remainder of this section focuses on traditional techniques that do not employ ghost records as preliminary states when inserting new entries into tables and indexes.

ARIES/KVL distinguishes cases as shown in Figure 5.3. In all cases, one of the distinct key values in the index remains locked in X mode until end-of-transaction, together with the gap to the next lower key value as well as possibly thousands of index entries.

ARIES/IM locks, with a single lock request, the new row in the table including all its new index entries as well as the gaps to the next lower key in each index. As in all techniques, a short test (called an instant-duration lock in ARIES) ensures that no other transaction holds a conflicting lock for phantom protection.

Key-range locking in SQL Server briefly locks the next index entry in RangeI_N mode (discussed as RI-N in Section 5.4 to test for conflicting phantom protection and then creates the new index entry, retaining a lock in X mode on the new index entry. The lack of a RangeN_X mode forces this X mode lock, i.e., other transactions cannot query or update the gap between the new index entry and the next lower index entry.

Orthogonal key-range locking works best with a system transaction ensuring that a suitable index entry exists as a ghost, whereupon the user transaction merely turns the ghost into a valid index entry as a non-key update. For insertion without a ghost, orthogonal key-range locking first tests that no other transaction ensures phantom protection by holding a lock on the gap above the next lower index entry and then locks the new index entry, not including the gaps around it.

Finally, orthogonal key-value locking also works best with a ghost left behind by a prior deletion or by a system transaction. Once the ghost is in place, orthogonal key-value locking locks the appropriate partition of bookmarks associated with the distinct key value, exactly as described earlier for updates on non-key attributes. If insertion via a ghost record is undesirable for some reason, insertion of a new distinct key value requires a lock on the gap above the next lower distinct key value. This lock is for phantom protection and may be held only briefly. Thereafter, a lock on the new distinct key value and the appropriate partition are required, with no lock on the other partitions or on the gaps above or below the new key value. If the insertion merely adds another instance of an existing key value, a lock on the appropriate partition of bookmarks suffices.

In summary, for insertion via ghost status, locking follows the rules for non-key updates, where orthogonal key-range locking and orthogonal key-value locking are best. For insertion without ghosts, ARIES/IM requires the fewest locks but holds the largest concurrency control scope, whereas orthogonal locking techniques merely hold a lock on the newly inserted index entry after testing for conflicting locks retained for phantom protection. Insertion via ghost status is the recommended implementation technique for the two orthogonal techniques but it also offers advantages for the traditional techniques.

5.4.8   KEY UPDATES

Modifying the key value of an index entry requires (in practically all cases) deletion of the old index entry and insertion of a new index entry at a location appropriate for the new key value. Both the deletion and the insertion benefit from ghost records as discussed above. If ghost records are used, both the deletion and the insertion require locks as discussed in Section 5.4 and illustrated in Figure 5.26. Thus, orthogonal key-range locking and orthogonal key-value locking provide the required concurrency control with better precision than all prior methods.

5.4.9   NON-UNIQUE PRIMARY INDEXES

The final case study assumes an alternative physical database design, namely a primary index on a non-unique attribute such as the HireYear column in the database table of Figure 5.18. (In a large and growing company with only weekly or monthly starting dates and orientation sessions for new employees, there may be hundreds of new employees on a specific day and thousands within a year.) In database tables with high insertion rates, a primary storage structure is desirable such that updates can be appended with high bandwidth; thus, a time-ordered primary storage structure is not uncommon. Data warehouse tables often benefit from a time-ordered storage structure because most queries focus on specific time periods.

If the primary storage structure has a non-unique search key such as HireYear, then index entries in secondary indexes refer to specific index entries in the primary storage structure using a search key plus an artificial additional value that uniquely identifies a row in the table. For example, in the database table of Figure 5.18, the database might silently append an integer value to the HireYear. Since this internal database value counts or numbers, in effect, the new employees within each calendar year, we will call it the HireNo below. A more generic but less pleasing name might be "uniquifier."

Locking in a non-unique primary storage structure may focus on individual rows, e.g., employees in Figure 5.18, or on distinct key values, e.g., years of hire. The access pattern of interest here is fetching rows from the primary index after a search in one or more secondary indexes. For example, index intersection in a data warehouse query may produce a set of pairs of HireYear and HireNo. The question then is the look footprint of each technique in the table's primary index upon a lookup with a pair of HireYear and HireNo. Let the example intersect index searches on "FirstName = 'Mary'" and "PostalCode = 53704" and then retrieve the row with HireYear 2015 and HireNo 2.

ARIES/KVL, which IBM never applied to primary indexes because primary storage structures in IBM's DB2 database systems are always heaps but not search structures such as B-trees, would lock an entire HireYear, i.e., all employees hired in 2015 plus the gap after 2014. In this particular example, the gap happens to be empty or non-existing because there is no year between 2014 and 2015 or because 2014 and 2015 are consecutive integer values. In a read-only data warehouse, locking all employees hired in 2015 seems perfectly acceptable, but in other environments (or during concurrent load operations in a data warehouse), locking an entire year's worth of employees when fetching column values for a single employee seems excessive.

ARIES/IM would not acquire any locks when accessing the primary storage structure; all required locks would have been acquired during the scans in the secondary indexes. Note, however, that index intersection typically eliminates most index entries found in the individual index scans. Retaining locks on all these logical rows, i.e., the union of two predicate clauses, seems excessive for freezing merely their intersection (even if the example query and database do not illustrate the difference between union and intersection). The obvious remedy releases locks on rows eliminated in an intersection operation, but this approach requires special logic for rows satisfying multiple individual clauses in queries with multiple clauses linked by both "and" and "or."

SQL Server locks individual index entries or rows in a non-unique primary storage structure such as a clustered index on HireYear. Thus, fetching a single row locks only the record identified by a pair of HireYear and HireNo plus a gap to the prior index entry or row. If the query returns multiple employees hired in the same year, each row requires its own lock and lock manager invocation, even if there are hundreds or thousands of them. Thus, key-range locking fails to take advantage of a time-ordered storage structure for time-focused data warehouse queries.

Orthogonal key-range locking locks substantially less—only the index entry or row but not an adjacent gap to the neighboring index entry or row. Note that this gap can be substantial and locking it can be surprising if a query fetches the first hire of a year, i.e., a row with HireNo 1, because it affects the preceding year. This example illustrates clearly the advantage of orthogonality and the difference between orthogonal key-range locking and traditional key-range locking.

Orthogonal key-value locking offers two relevant granularities of locking. First, it can lock a distinct key value and thus all employees hired in 2015—this might be suitable for queries fetching many rows or as a lock escalation option for queries with large result sets. Second, it can lock merely a partition among the employees hired in 2015—this seems more suitable for selective queries and as a starting policy that permits subsequent lock escalation when warranted. In fact, simply fetching multiple rows with the same distinct key value will automatically achieve the effect of lock escalation when all partitions become locked. The number of fetched rows required for this effect depends on the number of partitions selected for the instances of the key value.

Figure 5.27 illustrates the preceding discussion. Due to the dense sequence of calendar years and thus of HireYear values, the difference between ARIES/KVL and orthogonal key-value locking is not immediately apparent. The same is true for the differences between ARIES/IM, key-range locking, and orthogonal key-range locking. What is immediately apparent, however, is that orthogonal key-value locking offers two granularities of locking and thus the advantages both of ARIES/KVL, i.e., few locks and few lock manager invocations, and of key-range locking, i.e., precise locks and high concurrency.

Index Entries and Gaps	Entry (2014,1)	Gap 2014,>1	Entries (2015,1)	(2015,2)	(2015,3)	Gap 2015,>3	Entry (2016,1)
ARIES/KVL							
ARIES/IM							
KRL							
Orth. krl							
Orth. kvl							

Figure 5.27: Lock scopes when fetching from a non-unique primary index.

5.4.10 SUMMARY OF THE CASE STUDIES

The preceding cases cover all principal types of index accesses and compare their locking requirements. The comparison criteria include both lock scope, i.e., locked database contents beyond the truly required scope, and overhead, i.e., the number of locks and thus of lock manager invocations.

In all comparisons, orthogonal key-value locking fares very well. In queries, it is better than the prior techniques, including orthogonal key-range locking introduced only a few years earlier. The partitioning technique of Section 5.3.4 increases the advantage further. In updates including deletion and insertion via ghost status, orthogonal key-range locking is best and orthogonal key-value locking performs equally well except in the case of hash collisions due to an insufficient number of partitions.

While the case studies above focus on selection predicates, both empty queries and successful index searches also occur in join operations, in particular during index nested loops joins. Index nested loops join can be superior to merge join and hash join not only in terms of I/O and CPU effort but also in terms of concurrency control. Since each inner loop of an index nested loops join acquires locks as illustrated in Figures 5.20–5.24 (and in Figure 5.25 for the case of non-equality join predicates), join operations multiply the detrimental effects of excessive lock counts and of excessive lock scopes.

5.5   FUTURE OPPORTUNITIES

Possible future research might apply orthogonality and lock partitioning in other contexts. The following is an initial outline for some of these directions.

5.5.1 COLUMN-LEVEL LOCKING

The essence of orthogonal key-value locking is a single distinct key value with multiple locks and lock modes, plus partitioning bookmarks and gaps. Section 5.3.6 extended partitioning of bookmarks to horizontal partitioning of index entries associated with a distinct key prefix. An alternative design considers vertical partitioning, i.e., partitioning the set of columns in a table or an index. Note that there are two independent choices between vertical and horizontal partitioning, one for the representation or data structure and one for locks and concurrency control.

In this approach, each column in a table or index is assigned to one of the partitions and thus covered by one of the lock modes in a lock request. One of the lock modes may be reserved for the entire set of columns. Thus, a small number of partitions may be sufficient even for a table with tens or hundreds of columns.

Lock requests may be for individual index entries or for distinct key values. In the former case, each lock request covers columns in a single row or record. In the latter case, each lock request covers the same columns or fields in a set of index entries or records, namely those with the same distinct key value.

With a large set of choices, the application and its expected access patterns ought to guide the detailed design.

5.5.2 ORTHOGONAL ROW LOCKING

While SQL Server key-range locking locks individual index entries in individual indexes, both ARIES methods aim to reduce the number of locks required in a query or an update. ARIES/KVL optimizes queries, in particular retrieval from non-unique indexes, whereas ARIES/IM optimizes single-row updates. Both approaches have their merits. Orthogonal key-value locking is a refinement of ARIES/KVL and it seems worthwhile to consider an equivalent refinement of ARIES/IM.

Figure 5.28 summarizes locking techniques by their granularity of locking. The rows in Figure 5.28 indicate the granularity of locking. For example, in index-specific ARIES/IM, a lock covers a single row's representation in a single index. The granularity of locking also implies the search key in the lock manager's hash table. For example, in ARIES/IM, locks are identified by the record identifier in the table's primary storage structure. The columns in Figure 5.28 indicate the scope of each lock. For example, all ARIES techniques lock a gap between index entries together with an adjacent index entry, whereas key-range locking was the first to separate gap and key, albeit not fully and orthogonally.

Granularity of locking	Traditional locking: key and gap as unit	Some separation	Orthogonal locking
Individual index entries	Index-specific ARIES/IM	Key-range locking	Section 5.2.5
Distinct key values	ARIES/KVL		Section 5.5.3
Logical rows	ARIES/IM		Section 5.5.2

Figure 5.28: Locking techniques by granularity of locking.

The foundation of ARIES/IM is to lock logical rows of a table: by locking a bookmark, a transaction locks a record in the primary data structure, one index entry in each secondary index, plus a gap (to the next lower index entry) in each secondary index. While good for single-row updates, the design suffers from too many locks in non-unique secondary indexes (compared to ARIES/KVL, where each lock covers a distinct key value with all its instances) and from too much scope. For example, for phantom protection, one might want to lock a gap between two index entries in some secondary index, but the only lock scope available also locks the index entry above the gap as well as the logical row it pertains to, even including index entries in other indexes as well as gaps between index entries in other indexes.

Improvements in orthogonal key-value locking over ARIES/KVL include (i) the separation of key value and gap, (ii) partitioning within the list of bookmarks, (iii) partitioning of non-existing key values in a gap between existing distinct key values, and (iv) a hierarchy of an entire key value and its partitions of bookmarks and of non-existing key values, with lock modes that reduce the number of lock manager invocations. These ideas could also improve ARIES/IM, one improvement at a time, yielding what might be called "orthogonal row locking."

First, one could split a lock into two such that one lock applies only to the table's primary storage structure and the second one applies to any and all secondary indexes. This would allow one transaction to search an index or even multiple indexes while another transaction updates non-indexed columns in the table. For a table without any secondary indexes, this change alone achieves the same granularity of locking as orthogonal key-range locking, whether the user-defined index key is unique or not.

Second, one could separate the index entries from their adjacent gaps as well as the logical row from its adjacent gap. In other words, a lock on a logical row would have two modes, one for the row one for the adjacent gap, and the lock on all index entries also would also have two modes, one for the index entries and another one for the gaps in all the indexes. This would permit, for example, one transaction locking a row merely for phantom protection in one of the indexes while another transaction modifies the row including some of its index entries. This update may modify non-key fields including the ghost bits, thus logically deleting the row and all its index entries. Combined lock modes, constructed in the spirit of Figure 5.5 with lock compatibility derived as in Figure 5.6, reduce the number of lock manager invocations.

Third, one could apply partitioning to the index entries belonging to the same logical row, possibly including the record in the table's primary storage structure. For that, a lock for a logical row is augmented with a list of indexes in which index entries are to be locked. If the set of possible indexes is very large, one could limit the size of this list by partitioning the set of possible indexes such that locks cover a partition rather than a specific index. Thus, one transaction might update the row in the primary data structure as well as some affected indexes while another transaction searches other indexes of the same table, including index entries for the row being updated (in indexes not affected by the update).

Fourth, one could partition the indexes and in particular their gaps, i.e., a lock request for a logical row would specify the indexes in which gaps ought to be locked. This would permit, for example, phantom protection with a locked gap in a single index only. With hash collisions, it would lock gaps in multiple indexes.

Fifth, one could define a hierarchy of lock scopes—the finest granularity of locking would be the set of partitions, the coarsest granularity of locking would be the row and all its index entries and all gaps, i.e., all partitions. Combined lock modes, constructed in the spirit of Figure 5.5, enable lock acquisition with the scope and speed of the original ARIES/IM design as well as locks with much reduced scope with little additional overhead. For example, for phantom protection, a single lock request for a logical row can lock merely the gap between two index entries within a single index.

Figure 5.29 summarizes these ideas applying the techniques of orthogonal key-value locking to locking logical rows, i.e., to refining ARIES/IM in ways similar to orthogonal key-value locking refining ARIES/KVL. For each of the extensions listed above, Figure 5.29 indicates the number of lock modes required in each lock manager invocation.

Technique	Modes Per Lock
Split primary storage structure vs. secondary indexes	2
Split row vs. gap in each secondary index	3
Split index entry vs. gap in the primary storage structure	4
Partitioning the set of index entries	k
Partitioning the set of gaps	k
Hierarchical locking	~3+2k

Figure 5.29: Lock counts in orthogonal row locking.

Figure 5.30 illustrates possible lock scopes in alternative locking techniques applied to the database table of Figure 5.18 and its columns. Locking focuses on logical rows and row identifiers rather than individual indexes and their key values. ARIES/IM "data-only locking" has only a single granularity of locking. Index-specific ARIES/IM locks an entry and an adjacent gap one index at a time. Orthogonal row locking permits locking records without any gaps, whether in the primary index, a single secondary index, or multiple indexes; an open interval (gap only) or a half-open interval (index entry and gap) in just one index; any combination of the above; or all of the above thus mirroring the lock scope of ARIES/IM.

5.5.3 ORTHOGONAL LOCKING IN TABLES AND INDEXES

Systems with page-, row-, or key-locking typically employ hierarchical locking with an intention lock for each table or index followed by another lock request, e.g., for key-range locking or key-value locking. A new alternative using only table- or index-level locking reduces lock acquisitions per index by half, i.e., from two to one.

If the entire database or at least the working set fit in memory and if interactive transactions with multiple messages between database process and application process are rare, then there is little advantage in using more software threads than hardware threads (CPU cores). With only 10s of hardware threads, the number of partitions in a locking scheme and in each lock request may exceed the desired degree of concurrency. In such a case, it may be sufficient to lock only tables or indexes rather than pages, key values, or index entries.

Index Entries and Gaps	Primary Index on EmpNo	Gap in EmpNo	Secondary Indes on FirstName	Gap in FirstName	Secondary Index on PostalCode	Gap on PostalCode
ARIES/IM						
Index-specific ARIES/IM						
Orthogonal row locking						

Figure 5.30: Lock scopes in alternative row locking techniques.

For example, if the hardware in a system, e.g., a single node in a cluster, supports 16 hardware threads, then 32 software threads may be sufficient to keep all hardware busy all the time. A partitioning scheme with 128 partitions may be sufficient to avoid most false conflicts due to hash conflicts, independent of the number of rows in the table. Thus, table- or index-level locking may be sufficient, due to partitioning and a lock mode per partition.

Hash partitioning works well, but only for equality queries. If query predicates specify key ranges, the outlined design often requires locks on entire tables or indexes. Thus, a design based on hash partitioning is only of limited use and requires a complementary locking technique that is effective and efficient for key ranges.

This suggests a combination of hash partitioning and range partitioning. This combination employs m hash partitions and n range partitions for each file, table, or index. Each data access requires absolute locks (e.g., S or X) on one kind of partition and intention locks (e.g., IS or IX) on the other. For example, a range query may take absolute locks on the appropriate set of range partitions and intention locks on all hash partitions.

Figure 5.31 lists access patterns and their locking requirements. An equality query benefits from the precision of hash partitioning whereas a range query benefits from the efficiency of locking key ranges. A non-key update takes exclusive locks with the same scope as an equality query. Insertion and deletion via ghost records are non-key updates. A key update requires one deletion and one insertion, each with the appropriate locks. The last line of Figure 5.31 anticipates a consideration below.

	Hash Partitions	Range Partitions
Equality query	One S	One IS
Range query	All IS	Some S
Non-key update, Insertion,	One X	One IX
Deletion	One IX	One X
Key update	Two X	Two IX
Orthogonal key-value locking	Some IS or IX	Some IS or IX

Figure 5.31: Locking in combined hash and range partitions.

Relying on range partitioning might be sub-optimal if accesses are not balanced across key ranges. If the storage structure is an ordered hierarchical index such as a B-tree, the key range boundaries may be selected from the separator keys in a structure's root page. Updates of the root page should affect these key range boundaries only while it is entirely unlocked.

For even higher concurrency, a fine granularity of locking may be desired that cannot be achieved by hash and range partitioning with the table or index lock. For example, by acquiring IS locks on all hash partitions and all range partitions, a single range query plus a single equality query may prevent an update on even a single row.

Such applications and database accesses may require locking individual data items in the index leaves. As indicated in the last line of Figure 5.31, those index accesses must acquire intention locks on both kinds of partitions together with the intention lock on the table or index as a whole, whereupon they may use record-level locking within index leaves, e.g., orthogonal key-value locking. By doing so, they permit other applications and accesses to rely entirely on table or index locks with partitions. Actual conflicts, if and when they exist, can be found reliably and efficiently. This design adds to the theory of multi-granularity locking (beyond hierarchical locking) [Gray et al., 1975, 1976] multiple lock modes in a single lock manager invocation as well as hash and range partitioning.

Figure 5.32 illustrates this hierarchy of lock scopes. Index and key value are traditional granularities of locking. The intermediate lock scopes, i.e., hash partitions and range partitions, are the new level. Folding them into the index lock ensures in the worst case the same efficiency in lock acquisition and release as the traditional design, yet with the opportunity of reasonable concurrency with a single lock only on the index and its partitions.

5.5.4 ORTHOGONAL SCHEMA LOCKING

Another possible research direction applies combined lock modes (in the spirit of Figure 5.5) and partitioning to schemas and catalogs, yielding what might be called "orthogonal schema locking." Most database systems support an interpreted data definition language (DDL) and

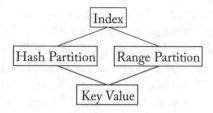

Figure 5.32: A hierarchy of lock scopes.

thus require type information stored as data in catalogs rather than compiled into all programs and scripts written in the system's data manipulation language (DML). Microsoft SQL Server, for example, has special lock modes for this schema information. The "schema stability" lock is used, among other times, during query optimization—without any locks on data such indexes, partitions, pages, records, or keys. The "schema modification" lock is used, for example, while dropping an index—ensuring exclusive use of both schema and all data structures. All other lock modes permissible for a table (e.g., S, X, IS, IX) imply a schema stability lock. They are implied by a schema modification lock and incompatible with another transaction's schema modification lock. Other database management products with dynamic schema modifications employ similar systems for concurrency control on metadata.

In order to simplify schema management and schema locking in databases, it seems possible and desirable to avoid these special lock modes, to map the concurrency control requirements to combined locks, and to avoid any increase in lock manager invocations. In fact, it seems possible and useful to divide either the schema or the data and to achieve a finer granularity of locking using combined locks.

In a design with combined lock modes, query optimization might hold an SN lock (pronounced "schema shared, data free" here), whereas dropping an index requires an XX lock (pronounced "schema exclusive, data exclusive" here). Intention lock modes must be supported, at least for the data (somewhat similarly to Section 5.4). Thus, achieving parity with the existing design seems quite possible.

A further optimization divides the data lock into individual data structures, e.g., a table's set of indexes. In other words, rather than locking a table and all its data structures, a single lock request (with a list of lock modes) may lock individual indexes. Typically, a table has only a few indexes, but it can have dozens. With only a few indexes, each index may have its own entry in a list of lock modes provided with each lock request for a table. With a multitude of indexes, the set of indexes might be partitioned using a hash function to map index identifiers to positions in the lock list. The most immediate benefit may be to reduce the number of lock requests: where a small transaction today may lock first a table in IX mode and then two indexes each in IX mode, in the future a transaction may lock the table in IX mode and, within the same lock manager request, acquire IX locks on two indexes (or actually, on two partitions within the set of indexes, with each partition probably containing only a single index).

Another optimization divides the schema lock into individual components of a schema, e.g., column set or individual columns, index set or individual indexes, integrity constraints, partitions (of table or indexes), histograms, etc. Sets of schema entries with individual locks may improve concurrency among changes in the data definition or, probably more importantly, concurrency of schema changes (DDL) with query and transaction processing (DML). For example, one transaction's query execution may join two secondary indexes while another transaction adds a new index. Thus, online index creation no longer requires a "schema modify" lock for the entire table when it first registers a new index and when it releases the completed index for unrestricted use. The ideal outcome of this research direction would improve the online behavior of DDL with minimal impact on active users and applications.

Without doubt, more research is required to validate these possible research directions, to work out details of alternative designs and their limitations, and to assess with a prototype whether simplicity, robustness, performance, scalability, concurrency, or online behavior can be improved in future database systems.

5.5.5   SUMMARY OF FUTURE OPPORTUNITIES

Multiple research directions, albeit outlined above only vaguely, may improve locking precision and locking overheads using a common technique. The ideas common to all are orthogonality and partitioning. Orthogonality separates locks, e.g., on existing and non-existing data. Partitioning maps possibly infinite sets, e.g., of index entries, to a fixed set of disjoint partitions. A single lock manager invocation can lock any subset of partitions by indicating a lock mode for each partition as well as for the entire set as a whole.

5.6   CONCLUSIONS

In summary, sharing structured data is the principal purpose of databases and of database management software. Effective sharing requires explicit schema information including integrity constraints, logical and physical data independence including automatic mapping (optimization) of queries and updates to execution plans, and atomic transactions including concurrency control and durability. Integrity constraints and concurrency control interact in ways very easy to overlook. For example, query optimization may remove a semi-join from a query expression if the schema contains an equivalent foreign key integrity constraint—but only in serializable transaction isolation, because weak transaction isolation may permit concurrent transactions with temporary integrity constraint violations. More specifically, one transaction may read a foreign key value that it cannot find as primary key value due to a deletion by another transaction. With weak transaction isolation, the same effect can occur during navigation from a table's secondary index to the same table's primary storage structure. These and other forms of havoc cannot occur in serializable transaction isolation. Thus, the focus of this research is on full transaction isolation and serializability.

A new technique, orthogonal key-value locking, combines design elements and advantages of (i) key-value locking in ARIES, i.e., a single lock for an equality query, (ii) key-range locking, i.e., locking individual index entries for highly concurrent updates, and (iii) orthogonal key-range locking, i.e., independent lock modes for gaps between key values. In addition, orthogonal key-value locking enables phantom protection with better precision than prior methods. The principal new techniques are (i) partitioning (only for the purpose of locking) each set of bookmarks within a non-unique secondary index, (ii) partitioning the set of possible key values in a gap between adjacent existing key values, and (iii) specifying a lock mode for each partition. With these new techniques, orthogonal key-value locking can lock none, some, or all of the row identifiers associated with an existing key value plus none, some, or all of the non-existing key values in a gap between adjacent existing key values.

Partitioning a set of bookmarks is superior to key-range locking (locking individual index entries) because key-value locking requires only a single lock request per distinct key value and because the principal lock scope matches that of query predicates, in particular equality predicates as well as end points of range predicates. Partitioning the set of non-existing key values in a gap cuts the concurrency control footprint of phantom protection to a fraction of the footprint of prior methods. Thus, orthogonal key-value locking promises truly serializable transaction isolation without the traditional high cost of false conflicts among transactions.

A detailed case study compares prior and new locking methods for ordered indexes, e.g., B-trees. For both successful and unsuccessful (empty) queries, the case study demonstrates that orthogonal key-value locking is superior to all prior techniques. For updates, it effectively equals orthogonal key-range locking, which is superior to all prior techniques. Orthogonal key-value locking is sub-optimal only if ghost records must not be used for some reason or if the number of partitions is chosen so small that hash collisions within a list of bookmarks lead to false sharing and thus to false lock conflicts.

A prototype validates the anticipated simplicity of an implementation in any database management system that already uses similar, traditional techniques, namely key-range locking or key-value locking. Like orthogonal key-range locking, and unlike prior techniques for B-tree indexes, orthogonal key-value locking permits automatic derivation of combined lock modes (e.g., for entire key value and gap) and automatic derivation of the compatibility matrix. It seems possible to automate even the derivation of test cases including expected test outcomes.

An experimental evaluation validates the insights gained from the case study: in situations with high contention, orthogonal key-value locking combines the principal advantages of key-value locking and of (orthogonal) key-range locking. A read-only experiment shows an increase in retrieval throughput by 4.8 times and a mixed read-write workload shows a transaction throughput 1.7–2.1 times better than with prior locking techniques. Thus, the experiments confirm our expectations from the case studies. We expect to find the new techniques in new implementations of B-trees and hope that they will replace the locking schemes in existing implementations. We hope that this study will affect design and implementation of databases, key-value stores, information retrieval systems, and (modern, B-tree-based) file systems alike.

Even if research into B-tree locking may seem no more than a quaint relict of bygone decades (or of a bygone millennium!), there continue to exist good reasons to pursue it. B-trees and their variants have been ubiquitous for a long time and seem hard to displace, in particular if carefully constructed keys enable partitioning within an index (and thus read- and write-optimized operations), versioning (e.g., for multi-version concurrency control), master-detail clustering (for application objects and for graph data), spatial indexes (including moving objects), and more [Graefe, 2011]. Designs and implementations of locking must ensure optimal lock modes, e.g., including update locks and increment locks [Graefe and Zwilling, 2004], minimal lock duration, e.g., by early lock release or controlled lock violation [Graefe et al., 2013], and the optimal granularity of locking, e.g., by orthogonal key-value locking.

5.7 REFERENCES

Bayer, R. and Schkolnick, M. (1977). Concurrency of operations on B-trees. *Acta Information*, 9, pp. 1–21. DOI: 10.1007/bf00263762. 163

Bernstein, P. A., Hadzilacos, V., and Goodman, N. (1987). *Concurrency Control and Recovery in Database Systems*, Addison-Wesley. DOI: 10.1145/356842.356846. 165

Bornea, M. A., Hodson, O., Elnikety, S., and Fekete, A. (2011). One-copy serializability with snapshot isolation under the hood. *ICDE*, pp. 625–636. DOI: 10.1109/icde.2011.5767897. 165

Cahill, M. J., Röhm, U., and Fekete, A. D. (2009). Serializable isolation for snapshot databases. *ACM TODS*, 34(4). DOI: 10.1145/1620585.1620587. 165

Cha, S. K., Hwang, S., Kim, K., and Kwon, K. (2001). Cache-conscious concurrency control of main-memory indexes on shared-memory multiprocessor systems. *VLDB*, pp. 181–190. 164

Chamberlin, D. D., Astrahan, M. M., Blasgen, M. W., Gray, J., King III, W. F., Lindsay, B. G., Lorie, R. A., Mehl, J. W., Price, T. G., Putzolu, G. R., Selinger, P. G., Schkolnick, M., Slutz, D. R., Traiger, I. L., Wade, B. W., and Yost, R. A. (1981). A history and evaluation of System R. *Communications of the ACM*, 24(10), pp. 632–646. DOI: 10.1145/358769.358784. 164

Chan, A., Fox, Lin, W.-T. K., Nori, A., and Ries, D. R. (1982). The implementation of an integrated concurrency control and recovery scheme. *ACM SIGMOD*, pp. 184–191. DOI: 10.1145/582383.582386. 166

Graefe, G. (2007). Hierarchical locking in B-tree indexes. *BTW*, pp. 18–42 (Chapter 2). 165, 170

Graefe, G. (2010). A survey of B-tree locking techniques. *ACM TODS*, 35(3) (Chapter 1). DOI: 10.1145/1806907.1806908. 160, 164, 170, 194

Graefe, G. (2011). Modern B-tree techniques. *Foundations and Trends in Databases*, 3(4), pp. 203–402. DOI: 10.1561/1900000028. 182, 208

Graefe, G., Kimura, H., and Kuno, H. (2012). Foster B-trees. *ACM TODS*, 37(3). DOI: 10.1145/2338626.2338630. 164

Graefe, G., Lillibridge, M., Kuno, H. A., Tucek, J., and Veitch, A. C. (2013). Controlled lock violation. *ACM SIGMOD*, pp. 85–96 (Chapter 4). DOI: 10.1145/2463676.2465325. 208

Graefe, G., Volos, H., Kimura, H., Kuno, H., Tucek, J., Lillibridge, M., and Veitch, A. (2014). In-memory performance for big data. *PVLDB*, 8(1), pp. 37–48. DOI: 10.14778/2735461.2735465.

Graefe, G. and Zwilling, M. J. (2004). Transaction support for indexed views. *ACM SIGMOD*, pp. 323–334 (Chapter 3). DOI: 10.1145/1007568.1007606. 208

Gray, J. (1978). Notes on data base operating systems. *Advanced Course: Operating Systems*, pp. 393–481, Springer. DOI: 10.1007/3-540-08755-9_9. 164

Gray, J., Lorie, R. A., Putzolu, G. R., and Traiger, I. L. (1975). Granularity of locks in a large shared data base. *VLDB*, pp. 428–451. DOI: 10.1145/1282480.1282513. 162, 204

Gray, J., Lorie, R. A., Putzolu, G. R., and Traiger, I. L. (1976). Granularity of locks and degrees of consistency in a shared data base. *IFIP Working Conference on Modelling in Data Base MGMT Systems*, pp. 365–394. 162, 204

Gray, J., McJones, P. R., Blasgen, M. W., Lindsay, B. G., Lorie, R. A., Price, T. G., Putzolu, G. R., and Traiger, I. L. (1981). The recovery manager of the System R database manager. *ACM Computer Survey*, 13(2), pp. 223–243. DOI: 10.1145/356842.356847. 164

Johnson, R., Pandis, I., Hardavellas, N., Ailamaki, A., and Falsafi, B. (2009). Shore-MT: A scalable storage manager for the multicore era. *EDBT*, pp. 24–35. DOI: 10.1145/1516360.1516365.

Johnson, R., Pandis, I., Stoica, R., Athanassoulis, M., and Ailamaki, A. (2010). Aether: A scalable approach to logging. *PVLDB*, 3(1), pp. 681–692. DOI: 10.14778/1920841.1920928.

Jung, H., Han, H., Fekete, A. D., Heiser, G., and Yeom, H. Y. (2013). A scalable lock manager for multicores. *ACM SIGMOD*, pp. 73–84. DOI: 10.1145/2463676.2465271.

Jung, H., Han, H., Fekete, A. D., Heiser, G., and Yeom, H. Y. (2014). A scalable lock manager for multicores. *ACM TODS*, pp. 29:1–29:29. DOI: 10.1145/2691190.2691192.

Kimura, H., Graefe, G., and Kuno, H. A. (2012). Efficient locking techniques for databases on modern hardware. *ADMS@VLDB*, pp. 1–12.

Lehman, P. L. and Yao, S. B. (1981). Efficient locking for concurrent operations on B-trees. *ACM TODS*, 6(4), pp. 650–670. DOI: 10.1145/319628.319663. 163

Lomet, D. B. (1993). Key range locking strategies for improved concurrency. *VLDB*, pp. 655–664. 165, 170

Lomet, D. B., Fekete, A., Wang, R., and Ward, P. (2012). Multi-version concurrency via timestamp range conflict management. *ICDE*, pp. 714–725. DOI: 10.1109/icde.2012.10. 165

Mohan, C. (1990). ARIES/KVL: A key-value locking method for concurrency control of multiaction transactions operating on B-tree indexes. *VLDB*, pp. 392–405. 162, 164, 167

Mohan, C., Haderle, D. J., Lindsay, B. G., Pirahesh, H., and Schwarz, P. M. (1992). ARIES: A transaction recovery method supporting fine-granularity locking and partial rollbacks using write-ahead logging. *ACM TODS*, 17(1), pp. 94–162. DOI: 10.1145/128765.128770. 165, 194

Mohan, C. and Levine, F. E. (1992). ARIES/IM: An efficient and high concurrency index management method using write-ahead logging. *ACM SIGMOD*, pp. 371–380. DOI: 10.1145/130283.130338. 162, 164, 168, 169

Ports, D. R. K. and Grittner, K. (2012). Serializable snapshot isolation in PostgreSQL. *PVLDB*, 5(12), pp. 1850–1861. DOI: 10.14778/2367502.2367523. 165

Ren, K., Thomson, A., and Abadi, D. J. (2012). Lightweight locking for main memory database systems. *PVLDB*, 6(2), pp. 145–156. DOI: 10.14778/2535568.2448947.

http://www.tpc.org/tpcc/results/tpcc_perf_results.asp

PART II

Optimistic Concurrency Control

CHAPTER 6

Orthogonal Key-Value Validation

Fine-grained, efficient, and serializable optimistic concurrency control

Goetz Graefe

ABSTRACT

In pessimistic concurrency control (i.e., locking), "repeatable count" transaction isolation (i.e., serializability) can be enforced efficiently and at a fine granularity. For example, orthogonal key-value locking in ordered indexes such as B-trees protects distinct key values with all their index entries, partitions of index entries, gaps between distinct key values, or partitions of key values within gaps. The diagram below summarizes the lock scopes that orthogonal key-value locking supports for key value Jerry in a non-unique secondary index containing first names and row identifiers. In contrast to fine-grained locking techniques, the standard approaches in optimistic concurrency control have been to ignore serializability or to enforce it at the granularity of database pages, e.g., by tracking PageLSN values of index leaf nodes.

Index Entries and Gaps	Entry (Gary, 1)	Gary, >1	>Gary, <Jerry	Jerry, <3	Entry (Jerry, 3)	Gap	Entry (Jerry, 6)	Jerry, >6	>Jerry, <Mary	Mary, <5	Entry (Mary, 5)
An entire key value											
A partition thereof											
An entire gap											
A partition thereof											
Maximal combination											

This chapter adapts the fine-grained techniques of orthogonal key-value locking to optimistic concurrency control. Essential techniques include a focus on distinct key values, orthogonality of concurrency control for key values and for gaps, partitioning the set of row identifiers associated with an existing key value, and partitioning the set of non-existing key values in the gap between adjacent existing key values. Techniques not previously employed in the context of optimistic concurrency control include ghost records and system transactions.

With the new techniques, optimistic concurrency control can provide serializability as efficiently and as precisely as pessimistic concurrency control, i.e., orthogonal key-value locking. Numerous case studies with all access patterns common in database indexes illustrate this comparison and demonstrate precision, efficiency, and effective phantom protection.

6.1   INTRODUCTION

Recent advances in locking for ordered indexes such as B-trees have introduced novel granularities of locking. The scope of locks in orthogonal key-value locking matches more precisely than all prior techniques the scopes of equality queries, range queries, and updates including insertions and deletions. Moreover, precise locking of gaps between distinct key values in ordered indexes as well as partitioning of such gaps enables precise locking for phantom protection. Thus, recent advances in database locking have changed the tradeoffs between correct transaction semantics (serializability), performance, scalability, and simplicity of explanation, implementation, and quality assurance.

With that, optimistic concurrency control has become a trailing technology: most implementations of optimistic concurrency control require multiple, even hundreds, of items in a transaction's read set after an equality query in a non-unique index. More importantly, they either fail to guarantee full transaction isolation (serializability) or they do so by tracking and validating index leaf pages, e.g., their version numbers or their PageLSN values (i.e., per-page log sequence numbers [Mohan et al., 1992]). On the other hand, optimistic concurrency control has become the concurrency control technique of choice in many recent systems, particularly in NoSQL and key-value stores. Thus, the goal here is to assemble, adopt, and adapt techniques that together permit optimistic concurrency control to guarantee full transaction isolation with the same granularity of concurrency control as orthogonal key-value locking.

Some system designers have resigned themselves to providing less than full transaction isolation, handing the burden of deciding and ensuring the required isolation between application threads and their database accesses to application developers and testers. While this approach has enjoyed considerable commercial success, it falls short of the ideal and the principal premise of databases. Successful information sharing among users and applications with the required ease-of-use and predictability demands not only agreed-upon schemas and physical data independence but also isolation of user activities that happen to run concurrently. Development, maintenance, and quality assurance of a database application is difficult and tedious enough without having to worry about transaction isolation due to weak concurrency control. In contrast, our approach has been to eliminate the performance bottlenecks that might cause a database user to accept less than full transaction isolation and correctness.

For those application and transaction processing requirements, this research contributes the first design with

1. multiple granularities in optimistic concurrency control;

2. ghost records and system transactions in the context of optimistic concurrency control;

3. augmentation or repair of read and write sets;

4. key ranges (not just key values or index entries) in transactions' read and write sets;

5. optimistic concurrency control for distinct key values, gaps, and partitions of both;

6. optimistic concurrency control with fine-granularity phantom protection; and therefore

7. serializability enforced with precision, efficiency, scalability, and simplicity.

The next section reviews related prior work, in particular optimistic concurrency control, two-phase locking, and orthogonal key-value locking. Section 6.3 proposes orthogonal key-value validation, an adaptation of orthogonal key-value locking to optimistic concurrency control. Section 6.4 compares techniques using case studies. Section 6.5 briefly surveys alternative approaches and the final section summarizes and concludes.

6.2   RELATED PRIOR WORK

Since the proposed design builds on multiple proven prior techniques, this section briefly reviews these. Knowledgeable readers may choose to skip ahead.

The traditional B-tree is the assumed ubiquitous storage structure, with user-defined data records in the leaf nodes and branch keys (aka separator keys or guide keys) in the branch nodes. Branch keys may be computed rather than found in the data collection, e.g., by suffix truncation [Bayer and Unterauer, 1977].

6.2.1   TWO-PHASE LOCKING

Database concurrency control occurs at two levels [Weikum, 1991, Weikum and Vossen, 2002]: high-level concurrency control protects database contents by coordinating transactions whereas low-level concurrency control protects in-memory data structures by coordinating threads. Each level uses two-phase locking in many traditional implementations but optimistic techniques seem currently preferred. Low-level concurrency control is not covered in this chapter. All threads are assumed to employ appropriate techniques [Graefe, 2010] with suitable optimizations.

Two-phase locking requires that each data item be locked before accessed and that all lock acquisitions precede all lock releases. There may be many lock modes [Korth, 1983]—beyond the standard shared (S) and exclusive (X) locks, there may be update or upgrade (U) locks as well as increment (E) locks. Multi-granularity locking or hierarchical locking also employs intention locks (IS, IX).

While optimistic concurrency control resolves concurrency conflicts by transaction roll-back, two-phase locking also (in addition to transaction aborts) lets a transaction wait for a lock, preferably with limited wait depth [Thomasian, 1998] and with timeout, after which deadlock is assumed and some transaction must abort. If all lock requests have a timeout, and if the cause of a timeout is assumed to be a deadlock, then no further deadlock detection is required.

The basic lock manager data structures [Gray and Reuter, 1993] are a hash table plus doubly linked lists per transaction and per hash bucket. The hash table enables efficient search for a given database item, the linked list per transaction enables, for example, efficient lock release at end-of-transaction. Multiple transactions locking the same item at the same time require separation of database item (within the lock manager) and lock granted or requested.

Figure 6.1, copied from Gray and Reuter [1993], illustrates a traditional lock manager. Some details are omitted, e.g., lock modes. Each active transaction in the transaction manager (left) has a list of locks. These locks are searchable in the lock manager's hash table (top), e.g., by index identifier and key value or by their combined hash value. Each locked database item has a queue of waiting lock requests. Granted lock requests, waiting upgrade requests, and waiting acquisition requests can all be in a single queue or there can be separate lists and queues. Note that database items are identified in a lock header, whereas transactions are identified in each request. Similarly, the hash table and its linked lists enable searching for headers whereas the transaction manager and its linked lists enable searching for lock requests. All data structures

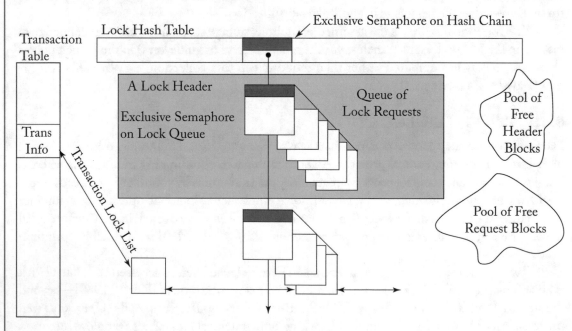

Figure 6.1: Basic lock manager data structure.

in the transaction manager and in the lock manager have fine-grained low-level concurrency control using semaphores or other forms of latching.

6.2.2   TRANSACTION ISOLATION LEVELS

The purpose of concurrency control is to maximize concurrency among of transactions but to present to each transaction, i.e., to its user or application developer, the fiction that it is the only activity. This is not always true with respect to load and performance but it is true with respect to database contents, at least if delays and transaction failures are permitted.

This "single user" fiction is formalized as serializability—a guarantee that all database reads and writes, executed by interleaved transactions, are equivalent to some serial execution of the same transactions, one after the other. Both the "single user" fiction and serializability require not only "repeatable read," i.e., preserving database contents once found, but also "phantom protection," i.e., preserving absence of database contents once sought and found missing or absent.

With traditional concurrency control, often enforced at the granularity of pages [Gray et al., 1975, Kung and Robinson, 1981], preserving both presence and absence often reduced performance and concurrency more than deemed acceptable. This is the origin and justification of weak transaction isolation levels. With precise lock scopes, e.g., in orthogonal key-value locking [Graefe and Kimura, 2015], situation-specific lock modes, e.g., "increment" locks [Graefe and Zwilling, 2004, Korth, 1983] and "reserved"/"pending" locks [SQLite, 2004], and short effective lock durations, e.g., in deferred lock enforcement [Graefe, 2019] and controlled lock violation [Graefe et al., 2013], one must wonder whether weak transaction isolation, e.g., "dirty read" and "read committed," is still a good tradeoff between database performance and application simplicity.

For read-only transactions, snapshot isolation is the ideal transaction isolation level, in particular if supported by multi-version storage. With read-only transactions in snapshot isolation and read-write transactions using locks, read-only transactions never block read-write transactions and read-write transactions never block read-only transactions. Chan et al. [1982] wrote about their implementation of this design: "Read-only (retrieval) transactions, on the other hand, do not set locks. Instead, each of these transactions can obtain a consistent (but not necessarily most up-to-date) view of the database by following the version chain for any given logical page, and by reading only the first version encountered that has been created by an update transaction with a completion time earlier than the time of its own initiation. Thus, read-only transactions do not cause synchronization delays on update transactions, and vice versa."

With multi-version storage, read-only transactions can run in snapshot isolation without any need for concurrency control, e.g., locks or end-of-transaction timestamp validation. Only read-write transactions truly require concurrency control. Therefore, the remainder of this chapter focuses on read-write transactions, ignoring read-only transactions.

Figure 6.2 summarizes transaction isolation levels commonly used in database management systems. Their definitions may focus on shared (read) locks, on anomalies, or on the points in time at which reads and writes appear to occur.

Transaction Isolation Levels	Read Locks	Anomalies
Serializable	Transaction-duration S locks for presence and absence	None—same as truly serial execution
Repeatable read	… only for presence	Phantoms
Read committed	"Instant-duration" S locks or conflict checks only	Changing values, inconsistent indexes[1]
Dirty read	No read locks	Any and all
"Split" snapshot isolation	Reads as of start-of-transaction, writes as of end-of-transaction	Write inconsistent data
Serializable snapshot isolation	Reads and writes both as of end-of-transaction	None—same as truly serial execution

[1] If S locks are held only for an instant or only checked but not held, and if a query execution plan accesses multiple indexes of the same table (e.g., searching a secondary index and then fetching full rows from the table's primary storage structure), and if there is a delay between (e.g., due to sorting or intersecting lists of row identifiers), and if separate locks pertain to different indexes (e.g., in ARIES/KVL [M 90] and in key-range locking [L 93], then the query may read inconsistent key values and assemble to rows that never existed. Therefore, some systems retain read locks for the duration of a single query execution plan, even of the encompassing transaction runs under read committed.

Figure 6.2: Transaction isolation levels.

6.2.3   GHOST RECORDS

Ghost records are logically invalid records physical present. In B-trees, ghost records include a key value and must obey the B-tree sort order. The earliest purpose of ghost records was to guarantee rollback of a deletion without allocations and thus the danger of allocation failures—thus the alternative names pseudo-deleted record or delete stub. They are equally useful for insertions, however, delegating all allocation actions to system transactions (see below) and limiting user transactions to non-key updates, in particular toggling the ghost bit in the record header. In addition to ghost records, database system designs may also include ghost keys, ghost entries in lists of row identifiers, ghost space within records, etc.

Ghosts participate in concurrency control, i.e., a deletion transaction may hold a lock on a ghost after logical deletion by toggling a valid record's ghost bit. System transactions (see below) perform asynchronous ghost removal but never of a ghost record locked by a user transaction.

Figure 6.3 shows distinct valid key values 40 and 60 as well as a ghost key value 50, indicated by strikethrough text. It further shows how two transactions might accomplish phantom protection for key values 45 and 50 using the ARIES/KVL method: both transactions lock the pseudo-deleted (ghost) entry 50 in shared mode, which includes the gap from the preceding key value.

	Gap	40	Gap	~~50~~	Gap	60	Gap
Transaction T_1			S				
Transaction T_2			S				

Figure 6.3: Phantom protection by locking a ghost.

Some B-tree logic, e.g., finding an index entry or key value to lock for phantom protection, is simpler if all B-tree nodes retain copies of branch keys as local fence keys [Graefe, 2004]. In each node, one fence key is always a ghost (see below) and one may be a valid record. Like all ghosts, fence keys participate in concurrency control. In contrast, traditional locking techniques sometimes must access a sibling node in a B-tree in order to determine the key to lock for phantom protection. With fence keys, the key to lock is always available within the same leaf node found in the initial root-to-leaf B-tree search. Fence keys also enable efficient offline consistency checks as well as comprehensive online consistency checks.

In general, fence keys are small due to suffix truncation (suffix compression) after splitting near (instead of precisely at) a leaf's midpoint [Bayer and Unterauer, 1977]. Splitting a B-tree leaf may insert a new ghost (fence key) into a locked gap between keys. In those cases, lock duplication is required such that the transaction holding a lock on the original gap holds an equivalent lock on the new fence key as well as the gaps on both sides.

6.2.4   SYSTEM TRANSACTIONS

System transactions are an implementation aid. Users cannot invoke system transactions, only code executing user transactions or other system transactions can do so. System transactions implement contents-neutral optimizations of storage structures, e.g., free-space compaction on a page, B-tree node splits and merges, load balancing among sibling nodes. This includes all allocation actions, e.g., creation and removal of ghosts.

System transactions are cheap and efficient. They run in the same software thread as the invoking transaction, i.e., their invocation does not acquire a new execution thread as user transactions typically do. For concurrency control, they only require latching. They never acquire locks but they may check on the state of locks, e.g., to prevent removal of a locked ghost record. Logging a system transaction usually requires only a single log record, including transaction begin and commit. The commit does not force the tail of the recovery log to stable storage because no user depends on completion and recovery of a system transaction. If recovery of a committed user transaction requires "redo" of a system transaction, then the commit of the user transaction also forced the log record of the system transaction to stable storage.

Figure 6.4, copied from Graefe [2012], summarizes the differences between user transactions and system transactions. Perhaps an alternative summary is: user transactions modify logical database contents but not representation and allocations whereas system transactions modify representation and allocations but not logical database contents.

	User Transactions	System Transactions
Invocation source	User requests	System-internal logic
Database effects	Logical database contents	Physical data structures
Data location	Database or buffer pool	In-memory page images
Parallelism	Multiple threads possible	Single thread
Invocation overhead	New thread	Same thread
Locks	Acquire and retain	Test for conflicting locks
Commit overhead	Force log to stable storage	No forcing
Logging	Full "redo" and "undo"	Omit "undo" in many cases
Recovery	Backward	Forward and backward

Figure 6.4: User transactions and system transactions.

6.2.5   ORTHOGONAL KEY-VALUE LOCKING

Orthogonal key-value locking [Graefe and Kimura, 2015] aims to remedy some of the shortcomings of ARIES key-value locking [Mohan, 1990]. While both techniques focus on existing distinct key values in indexes, there are three significant differences between the designs.

First, the gap (open interval) between two distinct key values has a lock mode separate from (and entirely orthogonal to) the concurrency control for the key value and its set of instances. Thus, phantom protection does not need to lock any existing index entries. Instead, it merely requires that a locked key value continue to exist in the index. While one transaction uses a key value for phantom protection, another transaction may lock the key value itself and turn it into a ghost entry. Subsequent transactions may use the ghost for phantom protection and may turn the ghost into a valid index entry again.

Second, the set of all possible instances of a key value (e.g., the domain of row identifiers) is hash-partitioned and each partition can have its own lock mode. The concurrency desired in a system determines the recommended number of partitions. An equality query may lock all partitions at once but an insertion, update, or deletion may lock just one partition such that other insertions, updates, and deletions may concurrently modify other rows with the same key value but a different row identifier. More precisely, a concurrent transaction may update or delete a row with a different hash value and thus belonging to a different partition. Each individual row identifier has its own ghost bit such that two deletions may indeed proceed concurrently and commit (or roll back) independently.

Third, the set of all possible key values in a gap is hash-partitioned and each partition can have its own lock mode. An equality query with an empty result locks merely a single partition within a gap, thus achieving "repeatable count" transaction isolation (serializability) yet permitting other transactions to insert into the same gap. Range queries may lock all partitions within a gap. With this recent refinement not included in earlier descriptions [Graefe and Kimura, 2015], orthogonal key-value locking can lock none, some, or all row identifiers associated with an existing key value plus none, some, or all non-existing key values in a gap between neighboring existing key values.

Figure 6.5 illustrates the lock scopes possible with orthogonal key-value locking for distinct key value "Jerry" in a non-unique secondary index on first names. The column headings indicate points and ranges in the domain of index keys. For comparison, the last line of Figure 6.5 shows the one and only lock scope possible in ARIES/KVL, i.e., a gap and an adjacent distinct key value with all instances. In addition to the lock scopes shown, orthogonal key-value locking also supports any combination. For example, a range query can, with a single invocation of the lock manager, lock a key value and its adjacent gap. This lock covers all existing and non-existing instances of the locked key value as well as all partitions of non-existing key values in the adjacent gap.

Index Entries and Gaps	Entry (Gary, 1)	Gary, >1	>Gary, <Jerry	Jerry, <3	Entry (Jerry, 3)	Gap	Entry (Jerry, 6)	Jerry, >6	>Jerry, <Mary	Mary, <5	Entry (Mary, 5)
An entire key value											
A partition thereof											
An entire gap											
A partition thereof											
ARIES/KVL											

Figure 6.5: Lock scopes in orthogonal key-value locking and in ARIES/KVL.

If another transaction indeed inserts a new distinct key value into a partition remaining unlocked in a phantom protection lock, the system needs to augment the lock held for phantom protection. Specifically, the system transaction creating a ghost record with the new distinct key value needs to create a lock on the new key value and assign it to the reader transaction. Thus, when the system transaction ends, the reader transaction has phantom protection on the two gaps below and above the new distinct key value. If there are multiple transactions with locks on partitions of this gap, all of them require additional locks in this way. If the system supports incremental lock release during rollback to a savepoint or during transaction abort, each new lock must be next to its original lock.

The additional complexity in the system transaction inserting a ghost record is the price for the additional concurrency permitted by partitioning each gap between key values in an index. Other serializable locking techniques simply reject any attempt to insert a new key value into a gap while another transaction requires phantom protection for a non-existing key value in the same gap.

6.2.6   A BRIEF COMPARISON OF LOCKING TECHNIQUES

The following diagrams compare ARIES/KVL, ARIES/IM, KRL, orthogonal key-range locking, and orthogonal key-value locking. Specifically, they compare the lock scope for phantom protection, for an equality query with multiple result rows, and for a single-row update. With insertion and deletion via ghost records, the lock footprint of non-key updates is equal to that of insertion and deletion.

ARIES/KVL (key-value locking) [Mohan, 1990] locks a distinct key value in a secondary indexes, including all existing and non-existing instances of the key value plus the gap to the next-lower existing key value. ARIES/IM ("index management") [Mohan and Levine, 1992] locks a logical rows including all its index entries and, in each index, the gap to the next-lower index entry. Key-range locking in Microsoft SQL Server [Lomet, 1993] locks one index entry in one index plus its preceding gap, with some separation between the lock mode for the index entry and lock mode for the gap. Orthogonal key-range locking permits two lock modes with each lock request, one for a index entry and one for the gap to the next-higher index entry.

Figure 6.6 illustrates required and actual locking scopes for the example of an unsuccessful query, i.e., for phantom protection. The column headings indicate ranges in the domain of the index keys. Among the three sub-ranges of the gap between index entries (Gary, 1) and (Jerry, 3), a serializable query for Harry requires concurrency control for only one. An S in Figure 6.6 indicates that a locking technique acquires a transaction-duration shared lock in order to prevent insertion of index value Harry. It is clear that ARIES/KVL locks the largest scope. ARIES/IM appears equal to key-range locking only because Figure 6.6 does not show the locking scope in the other indexes of this table. Orthogonal key-range locking locks less due to separate lock modes on index entry and gap. Orthogonal key-value locking locks the smallest scope. Without partitioning within the gap, its lock footprint matches precisely what is required as indicated in the header. With partitioning within the gap, which is possible due to the equality predicate for Harry, the lock footprint is cut to a fraction.

Partitioning the gap between key values is possible with this example query and reduces the lock scope even further, i.e., to a fraction of what is shown in Figure 6.6. By partitioning the possible non-existing key values within the gap between existing key values, the footprint of the lock and thus phantom protection is as narrow as the FirstName Harry and its hash

Index Entries and Gaps	Entry (Gary, 1)	Gary, >1	>Gary, <Jerry	Jerry, <3	Entry (Jerry, 3)	Gap	Entry (Jerry, 6)	Jerry, >6	>Jerry
ARIES/KVL					S				
ARIES/IM			S						
KRL			S						
Orth. krl			S						
Orth. kvl			S						

Figure 6.6: Required and actual locking scopes in phantom protection for "Harry."

collisions. People with first names Gerhard, Gottfried, Hank, Henry, and James will appreciate the increased concurrency.

Figure 6.7 shows lock scopes for an equality query with multiple result rows. Key-value locking requires only a single lock whereas the other techniques require multiple locks. In fact, due to their focus on index entries rather than distinct key values, they require more locks than there are matching instances. Due to separation of gap and key value, orthogonal key-value locking can lock the instance without locking the gap. Thus, it is the most precise technique (matching the query) and the most efficient technique (requiring only a single lock).

Index Entries and Gaps	Entry (Gary, 1)	Gary, >1	>Gary, <Jerry	Jerry, <3	Jerry, 3	Gap	Jerry, 6	Jerry >6	>Jerry, <Mary	Mary, <5	Entry (Mary, 5)
ARIES/KVL						S					
ARIES/IM			S_1				S_2		S_3		
KRL			S_1				S_2		S_3		
Orth. krl			S_1			S_2		S_3			
Orth. kvl						S					

Figure 6.7: Locking scopes in an equality query.

Figure 6.8 illustrates required and actual locking scopes for a non-key update of a single index entry. ARIES/KVL locks all instances of a distinct key value and ARIES/IM locks an entry and a gap in each index of the table. Key-range locking locks a single entry plus a gap in a single index. Orthogonal key-range locking leaves the gap unlocked and thus locks precisely as much as needed for this update operation. Orthogonal key-value locking locks a partition of index entries, ideally a partition containing only one entry.

Index Entries and Gaps	Entry (Gary, 1)	Gap			Entry (Jerry, 3)	Gap	Entry (Jerry, 6)	Gap	
		Gary, >1	>Gary, <Jerry	Jerry, <3				Jerry, >6	>Jerry
ARIES/KVL					X				
ARIES/IM			X						
KRL			X						
Orth. krl					X				
Orth. kvl					X				

Figure 6.8: Locking scopes in a non-key update.

Figure 6.8 also illustrates the locking patterns of user transactions inserting and deleting index entries via ghost records, because toggling the ghost bit in a record header is a prototypical case of a non-key index update. Without ghost records, older techniques lock more, in particular also an adjacent key value or index entry.

6.2.7 OPTIMISTIC CONCURRENCY CONTROL

The essence of optimistic concurrency control is that all conflict detection occurs at end-of-transaction. Until then, a transaction executes optimistically assuming that no conflict exists. When a transaction attempts to commit, it intersects its read set and its write set with those of other transactions. A transaction without conflicts may indeed commit whereas a conflict forces rollback and abort. Caching database updates in transaction-private update buffers simplifies transaction rollback but requires a separate propagation or write phase after validation.

Optimistic concurrency control can employ backward validation or forward valida-tion [Härder, 1984]. In backward validation, each committing transaction intersects its read and write sets with those of transactions already committed, i.e., a commit looks backward in time to preceding transaction commits. Each transaction gathers its read and write sets in a private data structure. Read and write sets of each committed transaction T must persist in a global data structure until no transactions remains active that overlapped with transaction T. In forward validation, each committing transaction intersects its read and write sets with those of active transactions, i.e., a commit looks forward in time to transactions presumably committing in the future. Each active transaction publishes new items of its read and write sets immedi-ately such that committing transactions can correctly intersect their read and write sets with all active transactions. There is no need to retain read and write sets of committed (completed) transactions.

Figure 6.9 illustrates backward and forward validation. When transaction T_2 attempts to commit, backward validation intersects its read and write sets with those of transaction T_1 and other committed transactions. The commit logic of transaction T_3 will find all conflicts between transactions T_2 and T_3. In contrast, with forward validation, transaction T_2 intersects its read and write sets with those of transaction T_3 and other active transactions. By the time transaction T_2 attempts to commit, the commit logic of transaction T_1 already found all conflicts between transactions T_1 and T_2.

Figure 6.9: Backward and forward validation.

Figure 6.9 also illustrates a rarely appreciated difference between backward and forward validation. In backward validation, the commit logic of transaction T_2 intersects the entire read and write sets of transactions T_1 and T_2. In forward validation, the commit logic of transaction T_2 intersects its entire read and write sets with the read and write sets of transaction T_3 inasmuch as they exist at that point in time. If transaction T_3 is only halfway through its application logic and has gathered only half of its final read and write sets, then the probability of a conflict in forward validation is only half that in backward validation. Incidentally, pessimistic concurrency control (locking) in more similar to forward validation than to backward validation in this regard.

The initial design of optimistic concurrency control specified validating one transaction at a time [Kung and Robinson, 1981]. In many-core systems, concurrent validation of multiple transactions seems desirable. requires that each transaction intersect its read and write sets not only with committed transactions (in backward validation) or with active transactions (in forward validation) but also with other committing transactions. The required data structure shared among all committing transactions, including its behavior and required protections with respect to concurrency, is quite similar to the hash table in a traditional lock manager.

While backward validation is the original design [Kung and Robinson, 1981] and seems to be more popular, forward validation seems to have a few advantages. First, backward validation compares pairs of complete transactions whereas forward validation compares a complete transaction with, on average, half-complete transactions. In other words, those transactions probably have acquired only half of their read and write sets. Thus, forward validation promises about half as many conflicts as backward validation. Put differently, about half of all conflicts found in backward validation are false conflicts. Second, if indeed two transactions conflict, earlier knowledge about the conflict reduces wasted effort on doomed transactions. Third, once a conflict has been found, backward validation permits only one remedy, to abort the transaction attempting to commit, whereas forward validation permits two possible remedies, to abort either one of the conflicting transactions. Finally, as mentioned above, in forward validation, each transaction's read and write sets become obsolete when the transaction commits; whereas in backward validation, the longest concurrent transaction determines the retention time of all concurrent transaction's read and write sets. A long-running transaction can force that read and write sets of very many transactions be retained for a long time.

Ever since the introduction of optimistic concurrency control broke the monopoly of locking on concurrency control in databases, it has held a steady fascination disregarding the critiques by experts [Härder, 1984, Mohan, 1994] as well as early performance simulations [Carey and Stonebraker, 1984]. These early simulations indicate that in workloads with few conflicts, all techniques for concurrency control perform well, and that in workloads with many conflicts, effort wasted on doomed transactions (those bound to fail validation) limits overall system throughput. It may be added that the granularity of concurrency control also plays a major role in the number of conflicts, particularly in false conflicts.

Many implementations, even some called serializable, indeed provide transaction isolation equivalent only to repeatable read, not repeatable count (full serializability). There are multiple approaches to achieving full serializability in optimistic concurrency control. A recent effort [Neumann et al., 2015] implements precision locks [Jordan et al., 1981] by adding a set of scan predicates to each transaction—items in other transactions' write sets that satisfy such a scan predicate indicate a conflict. A more common approach tracks scanned database pages and verifies, e.g., using on-page PageLSN values (log sequence numbers), that relevant parts of the database remain unchanged at end-of-transaction. This is a special form of optimistic concurrency control by end-of-transaction timestamp validation.

6.2.8 SUMMARY OF RELATED PRIOR WORK

To summarize related prior work, a variety of techniques developed over decades have improved pessimistic concurrency control, including precise and efficient phantom protection for serializable transaction isolation. On the other hand, optimistic concurrency control promises efficient, highly concurrent transaction execution without some of the limitations of locking, but usually with compromises or omission of phantom protection. What seems needed is optimistic transaction execution but precise and efficient phantom protection.

6.3 ORTHOGONAL KEY-VALUE VALIDATION

In the design proposed here, the principal granularity of concurrency control in an ordered index is a distinct key value including the gap to the next-lower existing distinct key value, with partitions within the set of row identifiers and the set of non-existing key values in the gap. This mirrors the granularity of locking of orthogonal key-value locking. For optimistic concurrency control, read and write sets contain key values plus partition identifiers within the set of row identifiers and the set of non-existing key values within a gap.

6.3.1   READ- AND WRITE-SETS

Each user transaction tracks its reads and its writes. There is no need that user transactions track creation or removal of database items due to the use of ghost records and system transactions as described below. The design can be augmented with sets of scan predicates or, if desired, with "increment sets" to match the concurrency of increment locks [Korth, 1983].

Instead of multiple sets for each transaction, e.g., read and write sets, there can be a single set of database accesses. Each element in this set, i.e., each access descriptor, identifies the access database item and names the access mode, e.g., read or write. A single set of access descriptors seems much more practical in some ways than multiple sets. Subsections below introduce more modes than just reading and writing, e.g., equivalent to intention locks in hierarchical and multi-granularity locking (Section 6.3.7).

For efficient checks whether active transactions have accessed a given database items, the global data structure for access descriptors is similar to a traditional lock manager, including the hash table for efficient search. In fact, for concurrent validation, it very much functions like a lock manager, including low-level concurrency control using latches. (Serial one-transaction-at-a-time validation uses a single latch for the entire data structure.) Thus, we will call it a lock manager. The main difference is that a traditional lock manager has queues for waiting lock acquisitions and lock upgrades, e.g., from shared to exclusive.

Each item is linked into a hash bucket for efficient search and into its transaction for efficient removal at end-of-transaction. Each item includes an index identifier, a key value, and an access mode. The access mode includes not only read and write access but also more detailed information to mirror the capabilities and lock scopes of orthogonal key-value locking. More specifically, modes capture accesses to partitions within sets of row identifiers or within gaps between key values.

Figure 6.10 shows two access descriptors for a key value in a database index. The top box identifies a granule of concurrency control, i.e., a distinct key value and its adjacent gap. The other two boxes represent items within transactions' read and write sets, i.e., two access descriptors. If necessary, end-of-transaction validation detects and resolves conflicts. The vertical arrows represent a hash bucket in the lock manager's hash table, i.e., the central data structure enabling search for conflicts and thus end-of-transaction validation. The horizontal arrows indicate linked lists that represent a transaction's read and write set, i.e., its set of access descriptors. The diagonal arrows represent the set of access descriptors attached to a single index and key value. These data structures are reminiscent of a traditional lock manager for pessimistic concurrency control. They are simpler in optimistic concurrency control than in pessimistic concurrency control because there is no wait queue. On the other hand, it has the same complexity as a lock manager that represents the sets of granted locks, of upgrade requests, and of acquisition requests in a single linked list, like the one shown in Figure 6.1.

For end-of-transaction validation, each transaction traverses its list of items in the lock manager and checks for conflicts. For forward validation, it checks against all active transac-

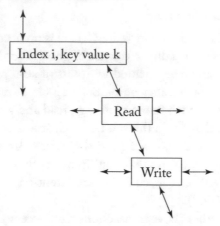

Figure 6.10: An access descriptor with read and write modes.

tions. After validation and propagation of updates from the transaction-private update buffer to the database or its buffer pool, the transaction can erase its items from the lock manager. For backward validation, it checks against all committed transactions with overlapping execution times. After update propagation from the transaction-private update buffer to the shared database buffer pool, the transaction's data structures in the transaction manager and in the lock manager should remain until the last overlapping transaction has completed.

The compatibility test is the same as in orthogonal key-value locking. Thus, the precision of conflict detection is the same in orthogonal key-value validation as in orthogonal key-value locking.

6.3.2 GHOST RECORDS AND SYSTEM TRANSACTIONS

As user transactions only read and modify allocated space, all allocation actions are delegated to system transactions. System transactions run immediately when invoked, e.g., inserting a ghost record, and also commit immediately. No concurrency control is required except low-level concurrency control, i.e., latching in-memory data structures such as the lock manager and database pages in the buffer pool.

Ghost records participate in high-level concurrency control, i.e., they are included in a user transaction's read and write sets. Concurrency conflicts over ghosts can force transaction rollback. Range queries must include ghost records including fence keys (of B-tree leaf nodes) in their read and write sets.

System transactions not only modify index structures, e.g., splitting B-tree nodes, but also create and remove ghost records. In lock-based systems, ghost removal must wait until the ghost is unlocked. In optimistic concurrency control, ghost removal requires absence of contradicting entries in any of the active transactions' read and write sets. Thus, even for backward validation that does not require sharing each transaction's read and write sets until the transaction commits, it is best to track transactions' read and write sets in the globally visible lock manager instead of transaction-private data structures. While an active transaction's read or write set includes ghost record, the ghost should remain in place.

Ghost insertion is simple in most cases. The exception is insertion of a ghost into a gap with concurrent phantom protection, i.e., into a gap included in an active transaction's read set. There are two cases: a leaf split with a new separator key, e.g., due to suffix truncation, and a new key value supplied by a user transaction, permissible due to partitioning of the gap. The first case is analogous to the duplication of locks as described in Section 6.2.3. The second case resembles lock-based systems duplicating locks as described in Section 6.2.5. In optimistic concurrency control, a system transaction inserting a new key value into a gap with concurrent phantom protection must duplicate entries in transactions' read and write sets. Section 6.3.4 provides further details in Figure 6.17 and Figure 6.18.

6.3.3   USER TRANSACTIONS

User transactions read and modify pre-allocated space in response to user requests, gathering read and write sets in the process. While transactions with backward validation usually gather their read and write sets in transaction-private space, here they must publish it immediately as in forward validation. Otherwise, after a user transaction invalidates a data item and turns it into a ghost, a system transaction may remove a data prematurely, i.e., while the invalidating transaction is still undecided and might need to roll back.

Logical insertion and deletion are mapped into non-key updates turning ghosts into valid index entries or vice versa. A logical insertion validates a pre-existing ghost into a valid record, if necessary after invoking a synchronous system transaction to create the required ghost. A deletion relies on an asynchronous system transaction to clean up the ghost at a time when no active user transaction has it in its read or write sets. In addition to protecting ghosts from premature removal, immediate publication of a transaction's read and write set also enables correct insertion of new ghosts.

Figure 6.11 summarizes the access modes that user transactions under orthogonal key-value validation can employ within ordered indexes. The field marked "not useful" assumes that only system transactions create and remove ghosts. Further access modes may be useful for other database objects, e.g., table schemas and index schemas. Section 6.3.7 introduces another specific example.

Figure 6.12 shows specific access modes for each transaction. Here, one transaction requires phantom protection for partition 3 within the gap between two existing key values and another transaction is modifying an index entry within partition 2. Read and write access modes are renamed shared and exclusive; in fact, these terms are used interchangeably from now. Otherwise, the diagram is similar to Figure 6.3.

↓ Scope Mode →	Shared	Exclusive	...
A distinct key value			
... a partition thereof			
A gap between key values		Not Useful	
... a partition thereof			

Figure 6.11: Access modes in orthogonal key-value validation.

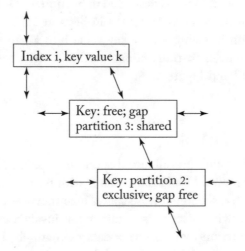

Figure 6.12: Access modes of user transactions.

Thus, orthogonal key-value validation plays to the strength of optimistic concurrency control, which traditionally provides excellent support and concurrency for reads and writes but often weak support for creation and removal of objects, rows, records, index entries, etc. With user transactions focused on reading and modifying pre-allocated data, the proposed design simplifies user transactions' concurrency control because most of the difficulties, e.g., phantom protection and the required data structures, are delegated to ghosts and system transactions.

6.3.4   PHANTOM PROTECTION

With ghost records, system transactions for all allocation actions, and user transactions limited to reading and modifying allocated data structures, phantom protection becomes fairly straightforward.

User transactions' read sets must include gaps between existing distinct key values or hash partitions of such gaps. This applies to both unsuccessful searches (empty query results) and to range queries. When a system transaction inserts a ghost record into a gap protected in this way, it augments the read sets of affected user transactions to include the ghost record, i.e., its key value, and the adjacent gaps on both sides. A user transaction turning the ghost record into a valid record includes the record in its write set. If a conflict occurs, it is visible as a standard conflict between one transaction's read set and another transaction's write set. This is the result of employing ghost records and system transactions, of separating the physical insertion of a ghost record from the logical insertion by a user transaction, and of augmenting a user transaction's read and write sets when a ghost record is inserted into a gap with phantom protection.

More concretely, since creating a ghost does not modify the logical contents of a database, only its representation, one or multiple ghosts can be inserted into any gap at any time. In pessimistic concurrency control, if a user transaction holds a lock on the gap where a new ghost is inserted, then the user transaction also must hold a lock on the new ghost. In other words, the system transaction creating the new ghost must also create a new lock and enter it into the lock manager on behalf of the user transaction. If, however, a user transaction using orthogonal key-value locking holds a lock on only one partition of a gap, and the ghost does not belong to that partition, then the ghost record and its key value may remain unlocked, even if the system transaction must create a new lock such that the user transaction holds locks on one partition each within the gaps below and above the new key value.

Optimistic concurrency control with orthogonal key-value validation works similarly. When a user transaction has a gap between two distinct key values in its read set and a system transaction creates a new ghost within this gap, the system transaction must augment the user transaction's read set. If the user transaction had the entire gap in its read set or if the user transaction had only one partition and the new ghost falls into this partition, the ghost itself becomes part of the user transaction's read set. In any case, the gap and the same partition below and above the new key value must become part of the user transaction's read set.

For example, in an ordered index on a numeric column, a system transaction may create a new ghost with key value 80 in the gap between key values 70 and 90. (It does not matter for this example whether the key values 70 and 90 are ghosts or valid records.) At the same time, transaction T1 requires phantom protection for key value 71 and transaction T2 requires phantom protection for key value 82. Both transactions hold key value 70 in their read sets in modes that leave key value 70 unprotected yet protect key values 71 and 82, respectively. Let's assume that key value 80 falls into a different partition than 71 but into the same one as 82. Neither user transaction prevents creation of the new ghost with key value 80 but the read sets of both user transactions require repair. The read set of transaction T1 retains key value 70 in a mode protecting one partition between 70 and 80; the repair adds to transaction T1's read set an entry for key value 80 in a mode protecting the same partition between 80 and 90. The read set of transaction T2 also retains its entry for key value 70 with one partition within the adjacent gap; the repair adds key value 80 to transaction T2's read set in a mode that protects the same partition between 80 and 90 plus the key value 80 itself.

Figure 6.13 illustrates the situation in the example above before the system transaction creates ghost key value 80. The two transactions have different gap partitions associated with key value 70 in their read sets, thus achieving phantom protection for missing key values 71 and 82. Figure 6.13 shows only two partitions in each gap although a somewhat larger number would be more realistic, in particular in many-core machines with many concurrent database threads.

	70	Gap	90
T_1			
T_2			

Figure 6.13: Read set entries before ghost creation.

Figure 6.14 illustrates the situation in the example above after a system transaction creates ghost key value 80. Each user transaction's read set includes the same partition in each gap. The system transaction does not have read or write set. If transaction T1 invoked the system transaction and turns the ghost into a valid index entry, it will fail validation due to a conflict with transaction T2. If transaction T2 invoked the system transaction and turns the ghost into a valid index entry, it will include key value 80 in its write set and both transactions T1 and T2 can commit. If another user transaction T3 invoked the system transaction and turns the ghost into a valid index entry, it will conflict with transaction T2 and either T2 or T3 will need to abort.

	70	Gap	80	Gap	90
T_1					
T_2					
System			n/a		

Figure 6.14: Read set entries after ghost creation.

Repairs of transactions' read sets require efficient access to all entries in read sets that pertain to a specific database page. Thus, it seems necessary that even in optimistic concurrency control with backward validation, all transactions publish their read sets immediately during their read phase, not after their validation phase. It is immaterial whether read and write sets are directly attached to each database page in the buffer pool or whether such access goes through an indexed in-memory data structure, presumably a hash table organized by database object identifiers such as index identifiers plus key values.

The complexity of repairing transactions' read sets is the price for achieving both maximal isolation (serializability) and maximal concurrency. Other forms of serializable optimistic concurrency control would not permit transaction T2 to insert a new key value into this gap. More precisely, they would permit the initial insertion but eventually one of the user transactions would fail validation and roll back. Most forms of pessimistic concurrency control would not permit this concurrency either, except orthogonal key-value locking. Note that other situations already require lock duplication, e.g., splitting a B-tree leaf or inserting an artificial branch key due to suffix truncation.

6.3.5   INTEGRITY CONSTRAINTS

Integrity constraints are as important to successful data sharing as concurrency control. Unfortunately, there are some curious interactions between the two concerns. For example, as mentioned earlier, query optimization may remove a semi-join from a query expression if the schema contains an equivalent foreign key integrity constraint—but only in serializable transaction isolation. As another example, without full transaction isolation, an insertion (e.g., of an order line item) may proceed after checking a foreign key integrity constraint that another transaction's deletion (e.g., of an order) invalidates before the insertion commits.

Enforcement of integrity constraints is commonly ignored in designs using optimistic concurrency control. Enforcement of "check" constraints including "not null" constraints does not raise any concern specific to optimistic concurrency control because the required tests are constrained to the same single database row being updated. For "unique" constraints, the best traditional technique is to verify during commit, i.e., the validation phase. Instead, a transaction's write set may include entire distinct key values, not individual index entries. If a second transaction modifies the same distinct key value, there is either a conflict (over the same instance) or a constraint violation (due to multiple instances).

Primary keys are a combination of "not null" integrity constraints and uniqueness. Enforcement of foreign key integrity constraints reads another table and includes the relevant rows or index entries in the transaction's read set. Thus, the rows relevant to the foreign key appear in a transaction's read set and end-of-transaction transaction validation naturally detects conflicting updates. Taken together, enforcement of traditional integrity constraints in relational databases can be supported in optimistic concurrency control.

The relationship between secondary and primary indexes as well as the relationship between materialized views and their base tables can be modeled as special, system-internal forms of foreign key integrity constraints. Thus, optimistic concurrency control can enable consistent transactional maintenance for those, too, which in turn ensures unchanged query results whether or not a query execution plan searches secondary indexes or materialized views.

6.3.6   TRANSACTION ISOLATION LEVELS

Orthogonal key-value validation enables all standard transaction isolation levels [Berenson et al., 1995, Gray et al., 1976].

With single-version storage, "dirty read" transactions run entirely without read sets, "read committed" transactions validate each read immediately as if it were an entire transaction, the read sets of "repeatable read" transactions contain key values, and the "serializable" transactions contain key ranges including gaps. Alternatively, the read sets of serializable transactions may contain predicates, e.g., in the form of compiled code for predicate evaluation [Neumann et al., 2015].

With multi-version storage, "industry-standard snapshot isolation" omits read sets whereas "serializable snapshot isolation" validates read and write sets at end-of-transaction against the current database state.

Figure 6.15 summarizes transaction isolation levels in a way similar to Figure 6.3 but with a focus on optimistic concurrency control rather than locking behaviors. Both the transaction isolation levels and the anomalies are copied directly from Figure 6.3. The validation behavior protecting read operations within read-write transactions depends on the isolation level.

Transaction Isolation Levels	Validation for Reads	Anomalies
Serializable	Key values and gaps in transactions' read sets	None—same as truly serial execution
Repeatable read	Only key values in transactions' read sets	Phantoms
Read committed	Individual reads validated immediately	Changing values, inconsistent indexes
Dirty read	Empty read sets	Any and all
"Split" snapshot isolation	Versioned reads, empty read sets	Write inconsistent data
Serializable snapshot isolation	Key values and gaps in transactions' read sets	None—same as truly serial execution

Figure 6.15: Transaction isolation levels under optimistic concurrency control.

6.3.7 HIERARCHICAL AND MULTI-GRANULARITY CONCURRENCY CONTROL

Orthogonal key-value validation enables hierarchical and multi-granularity concurrency control, quite similar to hierarchical and multi-granularity locking [Gray et al., 1975].

Hierarchical optimistic concurrency control requires additional access modes similar to intention locks. Transactions desiring a coarse granularity of concurrency control access large database items (e.g., entire tables or indexes) in standard read and write modes, whereas transactions desiring a fine granularity of concurrency control access large database items with intention modes and small database items (e.g., pages, key values, or index entries) in standard read and write modes.

These additional modes may lead to additional sets associated with each transaction, beyond the standard read and write sets. Alternatively, each transaction may have only a single set of data accesses with modes such as read, write, intention-to-read, and intention-to-write.

During end-of-transaction validation of a transaction's data accesses, their compatibility is quite similar to hierarchical and multi-granularity locking.

Figure 6.16 shows the compatibility matrix of data accesses including intentions. Intentions are always compatible, as shown in the bottom-right quadrant, because a finer granularity of concurrency control can detect any actual conflict. The top-left quadrant shows the standard compatibility of read and write accesses. The remaining two quadrants are copies the top-left quadrant. Combined modes such as read-with-intent-to-write are possible, too.

	R	W	IR	IW
Read (R)	✓	–	✓	–
Write (W)	–	–	–	–
Intent-to-read (IR)	✓	–		
Intent to write (IW)	–	–		✓

Figure 6.16: Compatibility of data accesses.

6.3.8   BEYOND B-TREE INDEXES

Orthogonal key-value validation works not only in ordered indexes and storage structures such as B-trees but also in unordered storage structures, e.g., heap files, hash tables, and multi-dimensional indexes. Note that bitmap indexes are just another form of compression; that run-length encoding in bitmaps is quite similar to representing a sorted list of row identifiers by their differences rather than their values; and that data representation in a storage structure is orthogonal to the method of transactional concurrency control and to the granularity of concurrency control.

In unordered storage structures, key values and their instances are similar to key values in ordered storage structures. Even valid records versus ghosts can work the same way. The problem is the definition of gaps between existing key values and phantom protection. The most promising solution is the same as for pessimistic concurrency control: a user transaction needing phantom protection invokes a system transaction to insert a ghost matching the predicate, includes the ghost in the user transaction's read set, and relies on standard end-of-transaction validation to detect actual conflicts. This approach works equally well in hash indexes limited to equality predicates for queries and phantom protection and in multi-dimensional indexes supporting bounding boxes for data items, key values, queries, and phantom protection.

The orthogonality of distinct key value versus gap breaks down in unordered indexes but the separations of ghost versus valid record, system transaction versus user transaction, and list versus list entry remain.

6.3.9   SUMMARY OF THE DESIGN

Traditionally, optimistic concurrency control focuses on read and write sets, mostly ignoring creation or removal of data items. The separation of creation and removal into system transactions limits user transactions to queries and non-key updates, justifying the traditional focus. User transactions merely read and write allocated records and traditional optimistic concurrency control applies.

Implementations of optimistic concurrency control have traditionally realized phantom protection by end-of-transaction validation of page versions, e.g., PageLSN values. This is, of course, page-level concurrency control, not record-level concurrency control. For fine-grained phantom protection, gaps between key values must be represented in read and write sets and must be considered in end-of-transaction validation.

Orthogonal key-value validation mirrors the granularity of concurrency control of orthogonal key-value locking. It merges a transaction's read and write sets but labels each access with a mode, e.g., read versus write or shared versus exclusive. Furthermore, it introduces access modes beyond read and write for a finer granularity of concurrency control. These modes implement the hierarchical understanding of distinct key values in an ordered index, both the separation of key value versus gap and partitioning of lists and of gaps. The result is efficient, fine-granularity optimistic concurrency control with full phantom protection.

6.4   CASE STUDIES

This section considers principal database access patterns and compares optimistic and pessimistic concurrency control including their granularity of conflicts and of coordination. This section does not consider or compare the duration of locks or of read and write sets, because other research has focused on that. Here, the comparisons focus on the scope or size of individual locks and of entries in read and write sets for end-of-transaction validation. Following the comparisons of Section 6.2.6, the baseline in the following comparisons is orthogonal key-value locking but ARIES key-value locking is included in some comparisons, too.

The comparisons rely on a specific (toy) example table with employee information. This table has a primary index on its primary key and a secondary index on one of the other columns. The primary key is, of course, unique and not null; the secondary index is non-unique in this example. The table could have additional secondary indexes.

Figure 6.17 shows index records in the primary index, which is also the table's primary key in this example. The figure shows the rows sorted and the reader should imagine them in a B-tree data structure. Note the skipped values in the sequence of EmpNo values and the duplicate values in the column FirstName. This toy example has only two duplicate instances but a key value in a real index may have hundreds or thousands of instances. Figure 6.18 shows index records in a non-unique secondary index on FirstName. This index format pairs each distinct key value with a list of row identifiers. Unique search keys in the primary index serve as row identifiers; they are also the table's primary key here. In addition to the index entries shown in Figure 6.18, the case studies below assume that the secondary index on FirstName also includes ghost entries for former rows, i.e., a ghost entry for FirstName "Harry" and one for "Larry."

EmpNo	FirstName	PostalCode	Phone	HireYear
1	Gary	10032	1122	2014
3	Jerry	46045	9999	2015
5	Mary	53704	5347	2015
6	Jerry	37745	5432	2015
9	Terry	60061	8642	2016

Figure 6.17: An example database table.

FirstName	Count	EmpNos
Gary	1	1
Jerry	2	3, 6
Mary	1	5
Terry	1	9

Figure 6.18: Records in an example non-unique secondary index.

6.4.1 QUERIES WITH EMPTY RESULTS–PHANTOM PROTECTION

The first comparison focuses on searches for non-existing key values. In other words, this first comparison focuses on techniques that ensure the continued absence of key values. After all, phantom protection and thus concurrency control for absent key values is the purpose and a principal innovation of orthogonal key-value validation.

The example query is "Select... where FirstName in ('Harold,' 'Harry')," which finds a ghost entry but serializability requires phantom protection for all possible instances of key value Harry. Figure 6.19 illustrates the following discussion.

ARIES/KVL locks the distinct key value Harry and with it the gap to the next-lower distinct key value, i.e., the gap between Gary and Harry. Thus, no separate lock is required for key value Harold. Had there been a further key value between Harold and Harry, e.g., Harpo,

Index Entries and Gaps → ↓Techniques	Entry (Gary, 1)	Gap			Ghost (Harry, 8)	Harry, >8	Gap		Entry (Jerry, 3)	Gap	Entry (Jerry, 6)
		Gary, >1	>Gary, <Harry	Harry, <8			>Harry, <Jerry	Jerry, <3			
ARIES/KVL											
Orth KVL											
Orth KVV											

Figure 6.19: Concurrency control for phantom protection.

whether valid or a ghost, then ARIES/KVL would have to lock two distinct key values, e.g., Harry as well as Harpo, the latter for the purpose of locking the gap between Gary and Harpo.

Orthogonal key-value locking locks the distinct key value Harry but, by virtue of orthogonal lock modes for key value and gap, neither gap below or above. Moreover, it locks a partition of the gap between Gary and Harry using a lock on distinct key value Gary. Thus, while requiring two locks and thus two lock manager invocations, it locks precisely all (existing and non-existing) instances of Harry as well as key value Harold plus its hash collisions. Unless Harpo falls into the same hash partition as Harold, one transaction can have phantom protection for Harry and Harold while another transaction can insert a new key value Harpo.

Orthogonal key-value validation retains in the transaction's read set two entries: the first one for distinct key value Harry with a mode indicating all instances of the key value, the second one for distinct key value Gary with a mode for just one partition within the gap following Gary. Note that a concurrent transaction and its insertion of new key value Harpo would not conflict with the reader transaction—both transaction would successfully validate and commit.

Figure 6.19 illustrates this discussion. Shading in the header row indicates the concurrency control requirements. Shading in the other rows indicates the actual scope of concurrency control mechanisms. Orthogonal key-value locking is more precise than traditional methods yet it is matched by orthogonal key-value validation. Other optimistic methods for serializable concurrency control may include the entire leaf page in the transaction's read set, thus conflicting with any update anywhere in the index leaf node.

Figure 6.20 illustrates phantom protection for key value Harold, i.e., a key value genuinely absent from the index. ARIES/KVL locks the next-higher present key value including all instances and its preceding gap. Orthogonal key-value locking locks only the gap between existing key values, more specifically only one partition within this gap. Orthogonal key-value validation similarly protects only one partition within the gap between existing key values.

Index Entries and Gaps → ↓Techniques	Entry (Gary, 1)	Gap			Ghost (Harry, 8)	Gap			Entry (Jerry, 3)	Gap	Entry (Jerry, 6)
		Gary, >1	>Gary, <Harry	Harry, <8		Harry, >8	>Harry, <Jerry	Jerry, <3			
ARIES/KVL											
Orth KVL											
Orth KVV											

Figure 6.20: Concurrency control for phantom protection.

6.4.2 SUCCESSFUL EQUALITY QUERIES

The second comparison focuses on equality queries, in particular with non-unique key values. The example query is "Select… where FirstName = 'Jerry'." Figure 6.21 illustrates the following discussion.

Index Entries and Gaps → ↓Techniques	Ghost (Harry, 8)	Gap			Entry (Jerry, 3)	Gap	Entry (Jerry, 6)	Jerry, >6	Gap		Entry (Mary, 5)
		Harry, >8	>Harry, <Jerry	Jerry, <3					>Jerry, <Mary	Mary, <5	
ARIES/KVL											
Orth KVL											
Orth KVV											

Figure 6.21: Concurrency control for an equality query.

ARIES/KVL locks the distinct key value Jerry including, due to its one and only lock scope, the gap between Harry and Jerry. No concurrent transaction can, for example, insert a new index entry and key value into this gap, e.g., Jane.

Orthogonal key-value locking locks the distinct key value only, leaving the gaps to Harry and to Mary unlocked such that other transactions can insert new key values such as Ingrid and Johanna. This lock on Jerry protects both valid records and ghost entries. For example, if Terry had been formerly misspelled as Jerry and if the ghost (Jerry, 8) remained in the storage structure, the lock would cover the ghost as well.

Orthogonal key-value validation retains a single entry in the transaction's read set, namely the distinct key value Jerry with a mode indicating all instances (and partitions) of the key value but no key values (nor partitions) in the gap between Jerry and Mary. Concurrent insertions of Ingrid and Johanna, for example, would not lead to validation failures and transaction rollback.

Figure 6.21 illustrates the discussion above. Orthogonal key-value validation is as precise as orthogonal key-value locking and more precise than ARIES/KVL. Note that other optimistic methods for serializable concurrency control may include the two entries matching the query predicate, but for guaranteed absence of other (new) entries with key value Jeffy, their must include the entire leaf page in the transaction's read set, thus conflicting with any update anywhere in the index leaf node.

6.4.3   RANGE QUERIES

The third comparison focuses on range queries. The example query is "Select… where FirstName between 'Jerry' and 'Larry." Let us assume an additional ghost left behind by a former deletion of FirstName Larry. Figure 6.22 illustrates the following discussion.

Index Entries	Gap			Entry		Entry		Gap		Ghost		Gap	
and Gaps →	Harry,	>Harry,	Jerry,	(Jerry,	Gap	(Jerry,	Jerry,	>Jerry,	Larry,	(Larry,	Larry,	>Larry,
↓Techniques	>8	<Jerry	<3	3)		6)	>6	<Larry	<7	7)	>7	<Mary
ARIES/KVL												
Orth KVL												
Orth KVV												

Figure 6.22: Concurrency control for a range query.

ARIES/KVL locks all distinct key values in the predicate range, including ghost records (known as pseudo-deleted records in ARIES), and a gap with each distinct key value. If the index does not hold a key value equal to the high end of the predicate range, ARIES/KVL locks a key value beyond the range.

Orthogonal key-value locking also locks all distinct key values in the range. At both ends of the predicate range, if there is a key value equal to the key value defining the predicate range, there is no need to lock a gap outside the predicate range. Ghosts are treated like valid index entries with respect to concurrency control.

Orthogonal key-value validation retains in the transaction's read set entries for the distinct key values locked in orthogonal key-value locking. The modes of distinct key values within the predicate range include key value and gap; the modes of distinct key values at the two ends of the predicate range include a gap if there is no distinct key value in the index equal to the key value defining the predicate range.

Figure 6.22 illustrates the discussion above. Differences in shading indicate multiple locks and thus lock manager invocations. Focused on distinct key values, all three methods divide the range into two sub-ranges, one for each distinct key value including the ghost. ARIES/KVL over-locks by one gap but otherwise the three method are equally or similarly precise. In other words, orthogonal key-value validation as a special form of optimistic concurrency control provides phantom protection and serializability with the same precision as orthogonal key-value locking and even better than traditional locking.

6.4.4 NON-KEY UPDATES

The fourth comparison focuses on non-key updates. For this comparison, assume that the secondary index on FirstName includes not only its own key column and the key column of the primary index but also some other columns. Many products support such secondary indexes, e.g., using an "include" clause during index creation. The key columns make index entries unique; therefore, additional columns do not affect the sort and their update does not move an index entry.

In this comparison, the example is "Update… where EmpNo = 6." In the secondary index, this request modifies one of the two entries with FirstName Jerry. Figure 6.23 illustrates the following discussion.

Index Entries and Gaps → ↓Techniques	Gap			Entry		Entry	Gap		
	Harry, >8	>Harry, <Jerry	Jerry, <3	(Jerry, 3)	Gap	(Jerry, 6)	Jerry, >6	>Jerry, <Larry	Larry, <7
ARIES/KVL									
Orth KVL									
Orth KVV									

Figure 6.23: Concurrency control for a non-key update.

ARIES/KVL locks a distinct key value with all its instances and with the gap to the preceding distinct key value. Thus, it locks substantially more than required for this update.

Orthogonal key-value locking leaves the gap unlocked and locks only a single partition of instances of FirstName Jerry. Ideally, the partition contains only a single existing instance. It always includes a fraction of the half-open ranges below the first instance and above the last instance.

Orthogonal key-value validation includes the affected distinct key value in the transaction's read set. The mode attached to this item in the transaction's read set reflects exactly one partition of instances, which includes the affected instance plus a fraction of the half-open ranges below the first instance and above the last instance.

Figure 6.23 illustrates the discussion above. While ARIES/KVL over-locks for a single-row update in a non-unique index, orthogonal key-range locking and orthogonal key-value validation protect just one partition of instances, i.e., precisely the required instance plus its hash collisions.

6.4.5 DELETIONS

The fifth comparison focuses on deletions of rows in the table and of index entries in the secondary index. The example is "Delete… where EmpNo = 3." In the secondary index, this affects one of the two entries with FirstName Jerry.

If deletion is implemented by toggling the ghost bit in an index entry, a logical deletion is implemented as a non-key update. In this case, ARIES/KVL locks a distinct key value with all its instances plus a gap; orthogonal key-value locking locks just one partition among all instances; and orthogonal key-value validation enters into the transaction's read just one partition of instances. In other words, all three methods behave exactly as described in Section 6.4.4 and illustrated in Figure 6.23.

Eventually, the ghost record left behind must be removed and its space reclaimed. In pessimistic concurrency control methods, e.g., ARIES/KVL and orthogonal key-value locking, the system transaction for ghost removal first verifies that no user transaction holds a lock on the ghost entry and then removes it. This check and the actual removal are a single critical section protected by a latch. No lock is needed for ghost removal. The check for locks held by user transactions has been called an "instant duration lock" in the past [Lomet, 1993, Mohan, 1990, Mohan and Levine, 1992].

Ghost removal is more challenging in the context of optimistic concurrency control. More specifically, under optimistic concurrency control with forward validation, each transaction registers its read and write set immediately in a global in-memory data structure. Thus, a system transaction invoked by one user transaction can verify that no other user transaction currently holds a ghost record in its read or write sets before removing such a ghost record. In a way, optimistic concurrency control with forward validation behaves like traditional locking but with lock compatibility checks delayed until end-of-transaction validation.

Under optimistic concurrency control with backward validation, transactions may retain their read and write sets in transaction-private data structures. Transactions "publish" their read and write sets only after a successful validation. For ghosts and system transactions to work correctly, a change is required. Transactions must publish their read and write sets immediately when they access data, i.e., there can be no transaction-private read and write sets. This change does not affect the logic of end-of-transaction backward validation, i.e., set intersection with read and write sets of committed transactions and retention of read and write sets until the last concurrent transaction is complete.

With these changes, optimistic concurrency control can process deletions as efficiently as pessimistic concurrency control, with precise concurrency control using ghost records, with system transactions removing ghost records precisely when and as required, and with no more concurrency control than a latch or equivalent implementation of a critical section.

6.4.6   INSERTIONS

Insertion is the opposite of deletion. Therefore, reversing an efficient deletions process is a promising candidate for efficient insertions. Specifically, system transactions can insert appropriate ghosts, e.g., in an ordered index such as a B-tree, and user transactions can turn these ghosts into valid index entries by toggling the ghost bit and modifying other fields as appropriate. With toggling a ghost bit implemented as a non-key update, the concurrency control footprint of turning a ghost into a valid index entry is the same as described in Section 6.4.4 and illustrated in Figure 6.23.

Therefore, ghost insertion is the crucial step. The specific example here is "Insert… values (4, 'Howard,' 54546, 2925, 2003)."

A system transaction inserting a ghost (or multiple ghosts) does not acquire locks in pessimistic concurrency control and does not have read and write sets in optimistic concurrency control. Instead, it merely inspects transactions' locks or their read and write sets. In pessimistic methods, the system transaction searches for locks user transactions hold for phantom protection, e.g., locks on gaps between index entries or key values. In optimistic methods, the system transaction searches for relevant entries in user transactions' read sets. This requires searching read sets across all user transactions, easily enabled by attaching items in read and write sets to database pages in the buffer pool or by organizing them in a hash table shared across all threads and transactions.

It is always permissible to insert a ghost record, even in a key range under phantom protection. The important aspect is that the transaction with phantom protection does not lose its guarantees. In other words, an optimistic transaction's read set must be repaired. If turning the ghost into a valid record would violate phantom protection, repairing the read set means including the new ghost and its key value, to be released when the user transaction releases its entire read set and thus its entire concurrency control protection.

Assuming a concurrent user transaction requiring phantom protection for FirstName Jane, ARIES/KVL holds a lock on key value Jerry including the preceding gap. If a ghost is inserted, this user transaction's lock set is repaired to include a lock on the ghost with key value Jane. Thus, the ghost insertion does not help the user transaction attempting to insert the new index entry for Howard.

In orthogonal key-value locking, the user transaction holds a lock on key value Harry in a mode protecting only one partition in the gap between Harry and Jerry. If Howard belongs to a different partition, the new ghost remains unlocked and the insertion transaction may turn it into a valid index entry. If Howard belongs to the same partition as Jane, the system transaction may insert the new ghost but the insertion transaction cannot lock it.

In orthogonal key-value validation, a system transaction may insert a new ghost with FirstName Howard. If Howard and Jane belong to the same partition, the system transaction must augment the user transaction's read set to include the new ghost in the read set. Thus, the insertion transaction will conflict with the user transaction requiring phantom protection during end-of-transaction validation. If Howard and Jane belong to different partitions, then both the user transaction requiring phantom protection and the insertion transaction can pass validation and commit.

With these extensions, orthogonal key-value validation is equal in precision to orthogonal key-value locking, both with full use of ghosts and system transactions.

6.4.7   KEY UPDATES

Key updates in a secondary index map to deletion and insertion of index entries, possibly of key values. Thus, all methods for concurrency control behave as discussed above.

6.4.8   SUMMARY OF THE CASE STUDIES

To summarize the case studies, the granularity of concurrency control and of phantom protection can be equal in optimistic concurrency control and in locking when separation of key and gap as well as partitioning of list and gap are transferred from orthogonal key-value locking to optimistic concurrency control. Orthogonal key-value validation is not superior to orthogonal key-value locking, but equal. It is therefore vastly superior to phantom protection in prior designs for optimistic concurrency control, where phantom protection required database pages in a transaction's read set or end-of-transaction validation of timestamps for database pages, e.g., PageLSN values. In other words, phantom protection in optimistic concurrency control used to be (at best) equivalent to page-level locking, whereas orthogonal key-value validation is equivalent to the most recent design for record-level locking.

The principal differences between optimistic and pessimistic concurrency control are not in the definition of concurrency control conflicts but in the timing of their discovery and in the options for conflict resolution at the time of conflict discovery. Locking detects conflicts prior to the second data access, i.e., before conflicting data accesses occur. At that time, waiting for lock release is a possible option for conflict resolution. Of course, even in pessimistic concurrency control, transaction abort upon conflict is an option, but is employed preferably only after a lock timeout. In contrast, optimistic concurrency control detects conflicts only during end-of-transaction validation. At that time, one of the conflicting transactions must abort. If one of the conflicting transactions is already committed, only the other, validating transaction can abort in order to resolve the concurrency control conflict.

Complementing this research into the granularity of concurrency control, there are separate investigations into lock modes and lock durations.

6.5   ALTERNATIVE APPROACHES

A number of locking techniques transfer to optimistic concurrency control. In fact, it seems that most or all of techniques mentioned in Section 6.2 could permit end-of-transaction validation instead of immediate conflict detection. The techniques differ in the scope assigned to each lock. For example, ARIES/IM focuses on logical rows, ARIES/KVL focuses on distinct key values within an index, and KRL focuses on individual index entries.

The adaptations require that each entry in a transaction's read and write sets cover not only the access to an index entry but also to the gap. (In the traditional techniques, it is the gap to the next-lower index entry or adjacent key value.) If one transaction requires phantom protection within a certain gap in an index, it maintains its read set as if it had read the next-higher index entry. If a transaction inserts a new index entry into a gap, it maintains its write set as if it had modified the next-higher index entry. This ensures that two transactions conflict if one needs phantom protection and the other one violates it.

Putting an adjacent index entry into a transaction's read or write set creates the same kinds of problems as over-locking. For example, if read and write sets contain distinct key values, phantom protection by adding an adjacent existing key value into a transaction's read set is just as bad as the over-locking of ARIES/KVL illustrated in Figure 6.6.

Further adaptations copy the principal idea of orthogonal key-value locking, i.e., separating concurrency control for an index entry and a gap. An immediate problem is that one transaction's phantom protection may permit updates but must prevent deletion of an adjacent index entry. Thus, in order to complete the separation, optimistic concurrency control requires ghost records such that deletion in a user transaction is actually a non-key update. System transactions are required for asynchronous ghost removal. Ghost insertion by a system transaction can reduce the write set of the invoking system transaction, very similar to the advantage of ghost insertion by system transactions in systems using locking.

The differences between key-range locking and key-value locking are treatment of duplicate key values and the boundaries of locking scopes. For example, as illustrated in Figure 6.6, key-range locking for FirstName Harry also locks some possible index entries for FirstName Gary and FirstName Jerry, whereas key-value locking matches query predicates more precisely. Finally, orthogonal key-value locking introduces partitioning for each set of row identifiers and for the non-existing key values in a gap, making it the best starting point for fine-grained, serializable optimistic concurrency control.

Multi-version storage structures may or may not be regarded as an alternative approach to concurrency control. The value of multi-version storage structures for read-only transactions is well known and very beneficial. They also work well for "industry-standard snapshot isolation," which runs all database reads as if part of a read-only transaction in snapshot isolation and all database writes as if part of a separate read-write transaction with end-of-transaction commit point. In truly serializable read-write transactions over multi-version storage structures, readers lock the latest committed version or protect it in their read sets, writers lock a new uncommitted version or protect it in their write sets, and transactions may commit when none of their writes has a concurrent reader.

An alternative to end-of-transaction validation of read and write sets is end-of-transaction validation of timestamps attached to database pages and records, for example. For page-level optimistic concurrency control, the PageLSN values using in ARIES, for example, can serve as timestamps. Other work examines fine-grained and serializable optimistic concurrency control using end-of-transaction timestamp validation.

6.6   CONCLUSIONS

In summary, ghost records and system transactions permit restricting user transactions to reading and writing allocated space, the traditional focus on optimistic concurrency control. In orthogonal key-value validation, user transactions track their read and write sets in terms of distinct key values, with partitioning of sets of row identifiers for additional precision. Including gaps between key values in the read sets, with partitioning of gaps when appropriate, adds fine-grained phantom protection to optimistic concurrency control. Case studies illustrate precision and efficiency of orthogonal key-value validation for database concurrency control including phantom protection.

Härder [1984] described phantom protection in optimistic concurrency control decades ago: "Token streams based on records do not handle the case where records are missing during read operations, later inserted by another transaction, and then re-read by the original transaction. Since the records were originally missing, there are no tokens to validate, and therefore no way to catch that a logical conflict has occurred. This problem can be alleviated to some degree, if page-level tokens are chosen and the insertion of a 'missing' record can be detected via the access path structures which it belongs to." Härder immediately anticipated the solution: "In locking schemes, […] preventive measures for missing records can be introduced at the record (entry) level. They include, for example, locking of key ranges in index structures […] Of course, such tricks could also be introduced into an optimistic CC scheme. For example, a successor or predecessor token of a missing record has to be inserted into the read set of the requesting transaction. A writer has to keep, in addition to the token for the newly inserted record, a token of the successor/predecessor in its write set. In order to validate these tokens, special interpretation rules have to be observed." Considering orthogonal key-value validation, one may disagree, however, with Härder's conclusion at the time: "Page-level CC seems to be the only choice for optimistic CC in a complex DB environment." Härder's last sentence [Härder, 1984] is about phantom protection: "Locking seems to be better suited to handle non-existence problems of records." Perhaps this verdict no longer holds.

In conclusion, a few innovations enable orthogonal key-value validation and thus fine-grained and serializable optimistic concurrency control. The 1st principal innovation is that read and write sets track distinct key values they query or modify. Key values are a logical concept in contrast to physical concepts such as records or pages tracked in traditional optimistic concurrency control designs. The 2nd principal innovation is the inclusion of key ranges in read sets, i.e., gaps between index entries or key values. This is not quite a powerful as predicates but simpler to implement and proven in pessimistic concurrency control. The 3rd principal innovation is the adaptation of ghost records and of system transactions for creation and removal of ghost records. System transactions commit immediately and ensure that user transactions only need to modify existing committed records. The 4th principal innovation is optimistic concurrency control using a global data structure similar to a lock manager to track read and write sets and to enable validations across transactions. This data structure is searched by a hash table, i.e., individual look-up operations replace the traditional intersection of operations of optimistic concurrency control. While the data structure is globally shared among all threads, it is accessed either from the transaction state in the transaction manager or from individual data pages in the database buffer pool. The 5th principal innovation is a variety of access modes that capture not only read or write access but also distinct key values, gaps, and partitions thereof. With these innovations, optimistic concurrency control can be as precise, efficient, and effective for phantom protection as the most recent locking techniques.

6.7   REFERENCES

Bayer, R. and Unterauer, K. (1977). Prefix B-trees. *ACM TODS*, 2(1): pp. 11–26. DOI: 10.1145/320521.320530. 215, 219

Berenson, H., Bernstein, P. A., Gray, J., Melton, J., O'Neil, E. J., and O'Neil, P. E. (1995). A critique of ANSI SQL isolation levels. *ACM SIGMOD*, pp. 1–10. DOI: 10.1145/223784.223785. 233

Carey, M. J. and Stonebraker, M. (1984). The performance of concurrency control algorithms for database management systems. *VLDB*, pp. 107–118. 226

Chan, A., Fox, S., Lin, W. T. K., Nori, A., and Ries, D. R. (1982). The implementation of an integrated concurrency control and recovery scheme. *ACM SIGMOD*, pp. 184–191. DOI: 10.1145/582383.582386. 217

Graefe, G. (2004). Write-optimized B-trees. *VLDB*, pp. 672–683. DOI: 10.1016/b978-012088469-8/50060-7. 219

Graefe, G. (2010). A survey of B-tree locking techniques. *ACM TODS*, 35(3), pp. 16:1–16:26 (Chapter 1). DOI: 10.1145/1806907.1806908. 215

Graefe, G. (2012). A survey of B-tree logging and recovery techniques. *ACM TODS*, 37(1), pp. 1:1–1:35. DOI: 10.1145/2109196.2109197. 220

Graefe, G. (2019). Deferred lock enforcement (Chapter 11). 217

Graefe, G., Lillibridge, M., Kuno, H. A., Tucek, J., and Veitch, A. C. (2013). Controlled lock violation. *ACM SIGMOD*, pp. 85–96 (Chapter 4). DOI: 10.1145/2463676.2465325. 217

Graefe, G. and Kimura, H. (2015). Orthogonal key-value locking. *BTW*, pp. 237–256 (Chapter 5). 217, 220, 221

Graefe, G. and Zwilling, M. J. (2004). Transaction support for indexed views. *ACM SIGMOD*, pp. 323–334 (Chapter 3). DOI: 10.1145/1007568.1007606. 217

Gray, J., Lorie, R. A., Putzolu, G. R., and Traiger, I. L. (1975). Granularity of locks in a large shared data base. *VLDB*, pp. 428–451. DOI: 10.1145/1282480.1282513. 217, 234

Gray, J., Lorie, R. A., Putzolu, G. R., and Traiger, I. L. (1976). Granularity of locks and degrees of consistency in a shared data base. *IFIP Working Conference on Modeling in Data Base Management Systems*, pp. 365–394. 233

Gray, J. and Reuter, A. (1993). *Transaction Processing: Concepts and Techniques*, Morgan Kaufmann. 216

Härder, T. (1984). Observations on optimistic concurrency control schemes. *Information Systems*, 9(2), pp. 111–120. DOI: 10.1016/0306-4379(84)90020-6. 224, 226, 246

Jordan, J. R., Banerjee, J., and Batman, R. B. (1981). Precision locks. *ACM SIGMOD*, pp. 143–147. DOI: 10.1145/582338.582340. 226

Korth, H. F. (1983). Locking primitives in a database system. *Journal of the ACM*, 30(1), pp. 55–79. DOI: 10.1145/322358.322363. 215, 217, 227

Kung, H. T. and Robinson, J. T. (1981). On optimistic methods for concurrency control. *ACM TODS*, 6(2), pp. 213–226. DOI: 10.1145/319566.319567. 217, 225

Lomet, D. B. (1993). Key range locking strategies for improved concurrency. *VLDB*, pp. 655–664. 222, 242

Mohan, C. (1990). ARIES/KVL: A key-value locking method for concurrency control of multiaction transactions operating on B-tree indexes. *VLDB*, pp. 392–405. 220, 222, 242

Mohan, C. (1994). Less optimism about optimistic concurrency control. *RIDE-TQP*, pp. 199–204. DOI: 10.1109/ride.1992.227405. 226

Mohan, C., Haderle, D. J., Lindsay, B. G., Pirahesh, H., and Schwarz, P. M. (1992). ARIES: A transaction recovery method supporting fine-granularity locking and partial rollbacks using write-ahead logging. *ACM TODS*, 17(1), pp. 94–162. DOI: 10.1145/128765.128770. 214

Mohan, C. and Levine, F. E. (1992). ARIES/IM: An efficient and high concurrency index management method using write-ahead logging. *ACM SIGMOD*, pp. 371–380. DOI: 10.1145/130283.130338. 222, 242

Neumann, T., Mühlbauer, T., and Kemper, A. (2015). Fast serializable multi-version concurrency control for main-memory database systems. *ACM SIGMOD*, pp. 677–689. DOI: 10.1145/2723372.2749436. 226, 234

SQLite: File locking and concurrency in SQLite version 3. http://sqlite.org/lockingv3.html 217

Thomasian, A. (1998). Performance analysis of locking methods with limited wait depth. *Performance Evaluation*, 34(2), pp. 69–89. DOI: 10.1016/s0166-5316(98)00025-x. 216

Weikum, G. (1991). Principles and realization strategies of multilevel transaction management. *ACM TODS*, 16(1), pp. 132–180. DOI: 10.1145/103140.103145. 215

Weikum, G. and Vossen, G. (2002). *Transactional Information Systems: Theory, Algorithms, and the Practice of Concurrency Control and Recovery*, Morgan Kaufmann. 215

CHAPTER 7

Serializable Timestamp Validation

Fine-grained phantom protection in optimistic concurrency control

Goetz Graefe

ABSTRACT

Optimistic concurrency control and its end-of-transaction validation logic may compare concurrent transactions' read and write sets or it may focus on timestamps attached to database objects. The former technique intersects sets of database items read and written; the latter technique compares database timestamps at the time of data access and at the time of transaction commit. Both techniques have been used in practice. However, full guarantees for serializable transaction isolation and of phantom protection have been either absent or enforced at a coarse level, e.g., at the granularity of database pages rather than of distinct key values or of individual records.

This chapter introduces new designs for optimistic concurrency control with end-of-transaction timestamp validation. Each technique guarantees serializable transaction isolation including phantom protection. The designs differ in the granularity of concurrency control, e.g., at the levels of individual index entries or of distinct key values.

This chapter further introduces new techniques for managing timestamps for data in the persistent database and its in-memory buffer pool. The result is fine-granularity timestamp validation without inflating the database size with lots of timestamp values.

7.1 INTRODUCTION

Optimistic concurrency control relies on end-of-transaction validation [Kung and Robinson, 1981]. There are two forms of validation, either comparing multiple transactions' read and write sets or validating timestamps. Timestamps are usually attached to data items, e.g., database pages, rows in a table (i.e., the table's primary storage structure), or entries in an index (i.e., even in secondary indexes). Alternatively, timestamps could be attached to tables, indexes, or distinct key values in an index. In today's designs, no timestamps are attached to gaps or to non-existing data items, e.g., non-existing index keys. In the best case, which is unusual, records may form a parent-child relationship such that a parent and its timestamp can provide phantom protection for the gaps between its children—but that does not provide phantom protection for the gaps between parents. Thus, there is no concurrency control for gaps, which means there is no phantom protection and no guaranteed equivalence to serial execution. In traditional database terms, timestamp techniques ensure "repeatable read" transaction isolation but not serializability.

Figure 7.1 summarizes standard transaction isolation levels for read-write transactions. In addition, read-only transactions may run in snapshot isolation, ideally paired with multi-version storage. In all transaction isolation levels, read-write transactions retain write locks until end-of-transaction in order to ensure conflict-free rollback in case of transaction abort. Serializable locking differs from the next weaker level in *what* each transaction locks in shared mode, whereas the other levels differ in *how long* each transaction holds its shared locks. The present chapter is about the difference between the two shaded fields in Figure 7.1, specifically *what* in a database requires concurrency control and thus timestamps.

Transaction Isolation Level	Locking (pessimistic Concurrency control)	Timestamps (optimistic concurrency control)
Dirty read	No shared locks	
Read committed	Instant lock duration	
Repeatable read	End-of-transaction read locks on data	
Serializable	End-of-transaction read locks on keys and on gaps	

Figure 7.1: Transaction isolation levels.

Phantom protection is about preventing harmful insertions and thus about absence. For example, in ordered indexes, it is about the gaps between existing key values. For phantom protection, pessimistic concurrency control techniques lock a gap as part of an adjacent index entry, and such a lock prevents insertion into a gap. Section 7.2 surveys related prior techniques for database concurrency control including alternative designs for key-range locking and key-value locking.

In order to provide serializability with phantom protection, optimistic concurrency control must verify at end-of-transaction that a gap has remained unchanged. Thus, gaps must participate in end-of-transaction validation. In optimistic concurrency control using timestamp validation, each gap must be assigned to a timestamp in the database. An insertion into a gap updates that timestamp such that a reader can test for phantom protection. Many alternative designs are possible for mapping gaps to timestamps. Many of these add new timestamps to databases. These alternatives offer various tradeoffs between simplicity, overhead, and concurrency. Section 7.3 introduces such techniques and their tradeoffs.

High concurrency demands a fine granularity of concurrency control and thus many timestamps. Adding many new timestamps to a database, e.g., to each database row, record, index entry, or key value, substantially increases the database size. Instead of adding these timestamps to the database, however, some or all of them can be retained in memory. In fact, the extreme solution is a technique for end-of-transaction timestamp validation with no timestamps at all within the persistent database. Section 7.4 describes multiple new techniques up to and including this extreme design.

In pessimistic concurrency control, high concurrency depends on suitable lock modes, optimized lock durations, as well as the scope or granularity of each lock. A fine granularity of locking implies many locks; thus the invention and ubiquitous use of hierarchical locking. Optimistic concurrency control lacks hierarchical methods as well as an equivalent to intention locks. Moreover, a fine granularity of concurrency control in a world of timestamps requires many distinct timestamps. In an extreme design, the size of all timestamps in a database might approach the size of the user-defined data. Thus, Section 7.5 introduces end-of-transaction timestamp validation combining coarse and fine granularities.

Finally, Section 7.6 summarizes all new techniques and the contributions of this research.

7.2   RELATED PRIOR WORK

This section sketches techniques from optimistic and pessimistic concurrency control that can be useful in timestamp validation and phantom protection.

7.2.1   GHOST RECORDS AND SYSTEM TRANSACTIONS

Ghost records and system transactions are implementation techniques with no role or mention in a logical data model, e.g., in relational theory or in a database schema. Most software systems fail to employ and exploit ghost records and system transactions to their full potential.

Ghost records are physically present but logically invalid. For example, queries skip over ghost records. Nonetheless, ghost records occupy space and they participate in concurrency control, e.g., key-range locking and orthogonal key-value locking.

Ghost records, also known as "pseudo-deleted" records or "delete stubs," simplify transaction rollback after a deletion: rollback without allocation cannot suffer allocation failures. Ghosts are also useful for insertions, because a user transaction that merely turns a ghost into a valid record has no need for a transaction-duration lock on a neighboring key.

System transactions modify the physical database representation but never the logical database contents. Prototypical examples include ghost removal and node splits in B-trees. Other examples include ghost creation and page compaction. System transactions require latches for low-level concurrency control, i.e., coordinating threads in order to protect in-memory data structures, but system transactions never require locks, i.e., coordinating user transactions in order to protect database contents. If necessary, system transactions may check the state of the lock manager, e.g., in order to prevent ghost removal while the ghost is locked.

Ghost records may also serve as fence keys in self-testing and self-repairing B-trees, in lieu of replacement of neighbor pointers. Ghost records, including those serving as fence keys, should participate in concurrency control, e.g., when locking gaps between index entries or key values in an index.

7.2.2 MULTI-VERSION STORAGE AND SNAPSHOT ISOLATION

Snapshot isolation is a transaction isolation level typically used with multi-version storage. Each update transaction creates a new version of each modified page, record, or index entry, depending on the granularity of versioning. Read accesses always choose a committed version. Therefore, reads do not require locks and cannot block writes, and vice versa. This is the attractive quality of snapshot isolation; the undesirable quality is that snapshot isolation fails to ensure serializability and thus fails to completely isolate concurrent transactions.

An alternative focuses on entire transactions rather than individual database accesses. Thus, read-only transactions choose databases contents already committed at start-of-transaction and read-write transactions read and modify up-to-date database contents.

This design is not new. Chan et al. [1982] wrote "that update transactions perform two-phase locking. That is, only a single update transaction can be granted the exclusive privilege of creating a new version for any data object at any point in time, and the update transaction must also base its updates on the latest consistent version of the database. ... Read-only (retrieval) transactions, on the other hand, do not set locks. ...by reading only the first [i.e., newest] version encountered that has been created by an update transaction with a completion time earlier than the time of its own initiation. Thus, read-only transactions do not cause synchronization delays on update transactions, and vice versa." With read-only transactions in snapshot isolation and thus removed from locking, serializable read-write transactions can build on two-phase locking with minimal concurrency conflicts.

7.2.3 TRADITIONAL LOCKING

With concurrency control preceding data accesses, two-phase locking is simple and reliable, with provable properties and proven in practice. For database indexes, the numerous variants and their individual characteristics may not be widely known or appreciated, e.g., with respect to phantom protection, i.e., ensuring continued absence by locking gaps between index entries or key values.

Figure 7.2 illustrates the most basic lock matrix with S (shared) and X (exclusive) locks. It is often extended with a U (upgrade) lock mode, which is a shared lock with a scheduling component, i.e., only one transaction can hold a U lock and thus have precedence for upgrading to an X lock.

Hierarchical locking permits combining the advantages of efficient coarse locks and concurrent fine locks. Like U locks, the required intention locks rely on a coherent theory and proven industrial practice [Gray and Reuter, 1993, Korth, 1983].

Requested → ↓ Held	S	X
S	✓	–
X	–	–

Figure 7.2: Basic lock matrix.

Figure 7.3 illustrates a traditional lock compatibility matrix including shared, exclusive, and intention locks. A transaction acquires an intention lock at a coarse granularity, e.g., a table or index, if it intends to acquire a traditional, "absolute" lock at a fine granularity, e.g., a row or page. An SIX lock combines an S lock, e.g., for scanning an entire index, with an IX lock, e.g., for updating individual index pages. Intention locks are always mutually compatible, shown by a single large block in Figure 7.3. The blocks above and left thereof mirror the compatibility of S and X locks.

Requested → ↓ Held	S	X	IS	IX	SIX
S	✓	–	✓	–	–
X	–	–	–	–	–
IS	✓	–	✓		✓
IX	–	–		✓	–
SIX	–	–	✓	–	–

Figure 7.3: Hierarchical or intention locks.

7.2.4 ORTHOGONAL KEY-VALUE LOCKING

Orthogonal key-value locking [Graefe and Kimura, 2015] aims to remedy some of the shortcomings of ARIES key-value locking [Mohan, 1990]. While both techniques focus on existing distinct key values in indexes, there are three significant differences between the designs.

First, the gap (open interval) between two distinct key values has a lock mode separate from (and thus orthogonal to) the concurrency control for the key value and its set of instances. Thus, phantom protection does not need to lock any existing index entries. Instead, it merely requires that a locked key value continue to exist in the index. While one transaction uses a key value for phantom protection, another transaction may lock the key value itself and turn it into a ghost entry. Subsequent transactions may use the ghost for phantom protection and may turn the ghost into a valid index entry again.

Second, the set of all possible instances of a key value (e.g., the domain of row identifiers) is hash-partitioned and each partition can have its own lock mode. The concurrency desired in a system determines the recommended number of partitions. An equality query may lock all partitions at once but an insertion, update, or deletion may lock just one partition such that other insertions, updates, and deletions may concurrently modify other rows with the same key value but a different row identifier. More precisely, a concurrent transaction may update or delete a row with a different hash value and thus belonging to a different partition. Each individual row identifier has its own ghost bit such that two deletions may indeed proceed concurrently and commit (or roll back) independently.

Third, the set of all possible key values in a gap is hash-partitioned and each partition can have its own lock mode. An equality query with an empty result locks merely a single partition within a gap, thus achieving "repeatable count" transaction isolation (serializability) yet permitting other transactions to insert into the same gap. Range queries may lock all partitions within a gap. With this recent refinement not included in earlier descriptions [Graefe and Kimura, 2015], orthogonal key-value locking can lock none, some, or all row identifiers associated with an existing key value plus none, some, or all non-existing key values in a gap between neighboring existing key values.

Figure 7.4 illustrates the lock scopes possible with orthogonal key-value locking for distinct key value "Jerry" in a non-unique secondary index on first names. The column headings indicate points and ranges in the domain of index keys. For comparison, the last line of Figure 7.4 shows the one and only lock scope possible in ARIES/KVL, i.e., a gap and an adjacent distinct key value with all instances. In addition to the lock scopes shown, orthogonal key-value locking also supports any combination. For example, a range query can, with a single invocation of the lock manager, lock a key value and its adjacent gap. This lock covers all existing and non-existing instances of the locked key value as well as all partitions of non-existing key values in the adjacent gap.

Ancillary differences include use of system transactions and of ghost records for insertion of new key values as well as system transactions creating and removing ghost space within records. Thus, system transactions perform all allocation and de-allocation operations in short critical sections with inexpensive transaction commits (no log flush on commit). User transactions merely modify pre-allocated space, including the ghost bits in each index entry. This greatly simplifies logging and rollback of user transactions as well as space management.

Incidentally, ghost records permit a specific optimization for a specific but frequent access pattern. In fact, this access pattern is found in some SQL dialects, e.g., as "upsert" command. This command or access pattern first checks the existence of a key value and, after finding no instance, inserts a new row with the same key value. In the default method for concurrency control, the initial check locks the key value's absence by locking an entire gap. Instead, the check can insert a ghost instance of the key value and then only lock that single key value, which the subsequent insertion will turn into a valid record. In this case, neither the check nor the

Index Entries and Gaps	Entry (Gary, 1)	Gap			Entry (Jerry, 3)	Gap	Entry (Jerry, 6)	Gap			Entry (Mary, 5)
		Gary, >1	>Gary, <Jerry	Jerry, <3				Jerry, >6	>Jerry, <Mary	Mary, <5	
An entire key value											
A partition thereof											
An entire gap											
A partition thereof											
ARIES/KVL											

Figure 7.4: Lock scopes in orthogonal key-value locking.

insertion need to lock a gap between existing key values, not even a partition within such a gap. Insertion of new ghost records for phantom protection is a bad idea in most other cases, in particular for queries with range predicates.

7.2.5   A QUICK COMPARISON

The following diagrams compare traditional and recent locking techniques for queries and update in ordered indexes, e.g., B-trees.

Figure 7.5 illustrates required and actual locking scopes for an unsuccessful query, i.e., for phantom protection. Among the three sub-ranges of the gap between index entries (Gary, 1) and (Jerry, 3), a serializable query for Harry requires concurrency control for only one. An S in Figure 7.5 indicates that a locking technique acquires a transaction-duration shared lock in order to prevent insertion of index value Harry. It is clear that ARIES/KVL [Mohan, 1990] locks the largest scope. In contrast, orthogonal key-value locking locks the smallest scope. With partitioning of non-existing key values within the gap, its scope is even less. ARIES/IM [Mohan and Levine,, 1992] appears equal to key-range locking [Lomet, 1993] only because Figure 7.5 does not show the locking scope in other indexes of this table. Orthogonal key-range locking [Graefe, 2010] locks less due to separate lock modes on index entry and gap.

Figure 7.6 illustrates required and actual locking scopes for a successful equality query for key value "Jerry." Shading and subscripts indicate separate locks and thus multiple lock manager invocations. Whereas the key-range locking methods require multiple locks, the key-value locking methods match the query predicate with a single lock; and whereas the traditional locking methods commingle key values or index entries with the gaps between them, the orthogonal locking methods do not.

Index Entries and Gaps	Entry (Gary, 1)	Gap			Entry (Jerry, 3)	Gap	Entry (Jerry, 6)	Gap	
		Gary, >1	>Gary, <Jerry	Jerry, <3				Jerry, >6	> Jerry
ARIES/KVL					S				
ARIES/IM			S						
KRL			S						
Orth.krl			S						
Orth.kvl			S						
w/gap part'g									

Figure 7.5: Required and actual locking scopes in phantom protection for "Harry."

Index Entries and Gaps	Entry (Gary, 1)	Gap			Entry (Jerry, 3)	Gap	Entry (Jerry, 6)	Gap			Entry (Mary, 5)
		Gary, >1	>Gary, <Jerry	Jerry, <3				Jerry, >6	>Jerry, <Mary	Mary, <5	
ARIES/KVL					S						
ARIES/IM			S_1				S_2			S_3		
KRL			S_1				S_2			S_3		
Orth.krl		S_1				S_2				S_3		
Orth.kvl				S								

Figure 7.6: Locking scopes in a successful equality query for "Jerry."

With techniques focused on index entries rather than distinct key values, an equality or range query with N result records requires N+1 locks in order to protect N−1 gaps between the N result records plus the ranges below the first and above the last index entry. Phantom protection (0 result records) requires 1 lock, an index entry with a unique key value (1 result record) requires locks on 2 index entries, etc. In contrast, techniques focused on distinct key values require only 1 lock per distinct key value, which protects both present and absent instances of this key value, including those with bookmarks below and above all existing bookmarks for the given key value.

Figure 7.7 illustrates required and actual locking scopes for a non-key update of a single index entry, i.e., an update that does not affect the sort order within an index. ARIES/KVL locks all instances of a distinct key value and ARIES/IM locks an entry and a gap in each index of the table. Key-range locking locks a single entry plus a gap in a single index. Orthogonal key-range locking leaves the gap unlocked and thus locks precisely as much as needed for this update operation. Orthogonal key-value locking locks only a single partition of index entries attached to the same key value, ideally a partition containing only one entry.

Index Entries and Gaps	Entry (Gary, 1)	Gap			Entry (Jerry, 3)	Gap	Entry (Jerry, 6)	Gap	
		Gary, >1	>Gary, <Jerry	Jerry, <3				Jerry, >6	>Jerry
ARIES/KVL					X				
ARIES/IM			X						
KRL			X						
Orth.krl					X				
Orth.kvl					X				

Figure 7.7: Locking scopes in a non-key update of row "3."

Figure 7.7 also illustrates the locking patterns of user transactions inserting and deleting index entries via ghost records, because toggling the ghost bit in a record header or in an index entry is a prototypical case of a non-key index update. Without ghost records, all older techniques lock more, e.g., a neighboring key value or index entry.

While one transaction locks a gap for phantom protection, another transaction may attempt to delete all instances of the relevant key value. Instead of physical removal, the other transaction may merely turn valid key values and index entries into ghosts. Actual removal of the ghosts is possible once all transactions release their locks on the ghosts. In other words, only with ghosts can orthogonal key-value locking realize its full potential and enable its maximal concurrency.

7.2.6   OPTIMISTIC CONCURRENCY CONTROL

In the original design of optimistic concurrency control [Kung and Robinson, 1981], each transaction has a read phase, a validation phase, and a write phase. The read phase executes the application logic and gathers a read set and a write set, the latter in a transaction-private update buffer. The validation phase intersects these sets with those of other transactions. The write phase propagates updates from the transaction-private update buffer to the shared, persistent database or at least the shared buffer pool. Once updates are in the shared buffer pool, i.e., even before they are written to the persistent database, no further concurrency control is required. In pessimistic concurrency control, early lock release and controlled lock violation [Graefe et al., 2013] are the most closely related techniques.

Validation and write phases (together!) must be atomic with respect to other transactions. Validation and write of one transaction at a time is the simplest implementation. Committing multiple transactions concurrently requires a shared data structure similar to a traditional lock manager. Serial validation is equivalent to a single lock on the entire database, held during the atomic validation-and-write phase.

In the original design of optimistic concurrency control, indexed databases "naturally choose the objects of the read and write sets to be the pages of the B-tree" [Kung and Robinson, 1981]. Note that read and write sets of physical containers such as pages, including catalog pages and branch nodes in B-tree indexes, implicitly provide phantom protection and serializability. Modified pages can be managed by the shared buffer pool if only one transaction at a time can have uncommitted changes in each page.

For higher concurrency, read and write sets may contain key values or perhaps even individual index entries rather than database pages or B-tree nodes. System transactions can handle node splits, posting new branch keys in parent nodes, etc., i.e., outside of user transactions. Section 7.3 introduces the first optimistic timestamp technique that provides phantom protection with a granularity smaller than a database page.

7.2.7   TIMESTAMP VALIDATION

In optimistic concurrency control with timestamp validation, each transaction has the same read, validation, and write phases. The principal difference to traditional optimistic concurrency control is the validation logic. Instead of relying on server state, i.e., the read and write sets of concurrent transactions, a transaction's validation logic relies on database state, i.e., timestamps embedded in the database. Implied differences are that validation does not consider other transactions and that even a transaction without concurrent transactions must execute its validation logic.

Timestamps are attached to database objects, either physical containers such as database pages or to logical database contents such as index entries. The PageLSN values (LSN = log sequence number) required to ensure exactly-once application of log records [Mohan et al., 1992] are suitable timestamps in database pages. For logical rows and their index entries, timestamps are artificially added fields and thus introduce a space overhead. The value of the timestamp can be real-world time or some system-generated increasing value.

While executing the transaction's application logic, the read phase gathers the timestamps of objects read or written (with writes buffered in a transaction-private update buffer). A transaction's validation fails if another transaction has changed some timestamp between data access and commit processing.

As in the original optimistic concurrency control, validation and write phases together must be atomic. Serial execution, i.e., one transaction at a time, is a possible but restrictive implementation. Concurrent validation and update propagation by multiple transactions requires shared server information similar in function and contents, if not in data structure, to a traditional lock manager.

When timestamp validation focuses on rows or index entries, phantom protection and serializability are either omitted or delegated to database pages. Many applications and transactions run without phantom protection and thus lacking serializable transaction isolation; those that require or desire phantom protection and serializability enforce it by checking page versions (e.g., PageLSN values) during end-of-transaction validation. For completeness, those systems ought to include ancestor nodes in hierarchical indexes as well as catalog pages in their validation logic.

Some systems employ mirrors for high availability rather than write-ahead logging. Without a recovery log, there are neither log sequence numbers nor PageLSN fields. Page version counters in page headers can serve the same function. Nonetheless, using pages for phantom protection permits concurrency as good as (or as poor as) page-level locking, replaced decades ago by record-level locking, key-range locking, key-value locking, etc. (also see Figure 7.13). Section 7.3 introduces new optimistic techniques that support phantom protection and serializability without resorting to page-level concurrency control.

7.2.8   SUMMARY OF RELATED PRIOR WORK

In summary of related prior work, database concurrency control has come a long way since the pioneering work by Gray et al. [1975], Kung and Robinson [1981], and Mohan et al. [1992]. Optimistic concurrency control and end-of-transaction validation nowadays focus on timestamps embedded in the database rather than transactions' read and write sets. Pessimistic concurrency control and locking have gained efficient and precise techniques for phantom protection and serializability. What is missing is an efficient and precise technique for phantom protection and serializability in the context of end-of-transaction timestamp validation.

7.3   PHANTOM PROTECTION WITH TIMESTAMP VALIDATION

In order to include absence in concurrency control by end-of-transaction timestamp validation, the basic principle must be that each gap in an ordered index is mapped to some timestamp. An insertion updates the appropriate timestamp and a transaction in need of phantom protection validates the timestamp at commit time.

Variations are all about the granularity of concurrency control, i.e., the number of timestamps in a database and their scope of protection—this is the topic of the present section. Another area of innovation is efficient management and maintenance of timestamps—this is the topic of Section 7.4.

It might be suggested to implement phantom protection by inserting a ghost record with the missing key value and applying end-of-transaction timestamp validation on this ghost record. This suggestion is impractical for two reasons. First, it seems wasteful to modify the persistent database for each unsuccessful query. If nothing else, it turns a read into a write, or a query into an update. It can produce surprising consequences; for example, a read-only workload triggering a database backup seems rather strange. Second, if an unsuccessful query (with empty result set) has a range predicate rather than an equality predicate, an infinite number of temporary or permanent ghost records would be required, even if a work-around using the start-

and end-keys of the query predicate plus a range lock might be complex but possible. Worse yet, even a successful range query almost always includes empty key ranges and thus would similarly require an infinite number of ghost records.

7.3.1   BASIC DESIGNS

The most basic design for fine-granularity or row-level concurrency control attaches all concurrency control logic to a logical row. Concurrency control for a logical row covers the row's index entries in all secondary indexes as well as a gap adjacent to each index entry. Let's define that to be the gap to the next-higher index entry in the index sort order.

This scope is similar to locks in IBM's ARIES/IM. When a timestamp covers a gap, an insertion into the gap must update the relevant timestamp, whereas an empty query or a range query must include the gap and its assigned index entry or row in the transaction's read set.

Figure 7.8 illustrates the scope of a single lock in ARIES/IM and of a single timestamp in the basic design for serializable timestamp validation, using an example table with employment information. If there is a B-tree index on EmpNo, a lock on row 3 in ARIES/IM includes the gap to EmpNo 5. In other words, while one transaction modifies some non-key column for row 3, its lock prevents any other transaction from insertion of a new row with EmpNo 4.

EmpNo	FirstName	PostalCode	Phone	HireYear
1	Gary	10032	1122	2014
3	Jerry	46045	9999	2015
5	Mary	53704	5347	2015
6	Jerry	37745	5432	2015
9	Terry	60061	8642	2016

Figure 7.8: Lock scope in ARIES/IM and basic timestamp scope.

Insertion of a single logical row into a table with multiple secondary indexes requires an insertion into each secondary index. The gaps into which the new index entries go are covered by their adjacent index entries, which in the various secondary indexes probably belong to different logical rows. Thus, insertion of a single row modifies multiple gaps (one in each secondary index) and must therefore modify the timestamps of multiple logical rows. In a table with K indexes (the primary index counts here), a single-row insertion requires locks or timestamps covering K^2 gaps, because each index needs a gap protected and each such protection actually protects a gap in K indexes. For example, insertion of a single row into a table with a primary index and two secondary indexes freezes K = 1+2 logical rows and $(1+2)^2 = 9$ gaps across all indexes such that a concurrent query in any of these gaps causes validation failure.

Queries, i.e., their scans and index searches, retain timestamps even for gaps and empty ranges. In fact, index searches in non-unique indexes must always protect one more index entries than they retrieve. For example, a successful equality query in a non-unique index might find only a single matching index entry but it requires phantom protection for the two gaps adjacent to that index entry. Thus, at end-of-transaction, this query must validate the timestamps not only for the retrieved row but also for one additional row.

Figure 7.9 illustrates this issue in a small example. Consider a query that counts employees in PostalCode 46045, of which there is one, with EmpNo 3. Phantom protection for this query requires prevention of any insertion with the same PostalCode. The lock on EmpNo 3 assures this for EmpNo values higher than 3 but not for lower ones; thus, full phantom protection requires another lock on EmpNo 6 even if that freezes PostalCode 37745 and the gap to 46045. Moreover, in another secondary index, e.g., on FirstName, locks on EmpNo values 3 and 6 lock entries and gaps entirely unrelated to the query and to the transaction requiring phantom protection. Any further secondary indexes have their own key ranges frozen by locks on EmpNo values 3 and 6. As can be seen from this example, end-of-transaction timestamp validation focusing on logical rows has problems similar to those of ARIES/IM.

Index Entries and Gaps	Entry (37745, 6)	Gap		Entry (46045, 3)	Gap		Entry (53704, 5)
		37745, >6	>37745, <46045	46045, <3		46045, >6	>46045, <53704	53704, <5	
ARIES/IM		S on "6"			S on "3"			
Basic timestamps								

Index Entries and Gaps	Entry (Gary, 1)	Gap		Entry (Jerry, 3)	Entry	Entry (Jerry, 6)	Gap	
		Gary, >1	>Gary, <Jerry	Jerry, <3		Gap		Jerry, >6	>Jerry
ARIES/IM					S on "3"			S on "6"	
Basic timestamps									

Figure 7.9: Protecting gaps below and above an existing index entry.

Join and aggregation queries as well as nested queries lose or suppress detail records, e.g., rows without match in a join or rows aggregated into summary rows. In serializable transactions (other than read-only transactions in snapshot isolation), timestamps of such detail records must be validated at end-of-transaction just as pessimistic concurrency control must retain locks on records that fail predicates. The identifiers of such records and their timestamps must be preserved in some system data structure or passed back and forth with the client if there is no transaction manager in the server.

An ordered index with N index entries has N−1 gaps between them but concurrency control must also cover the 2 gaps at the ends of the key domain. Thus, phantom protection requires one extra record with a key value at the end of the key domain, i.e., a key value $-\infty$ or *null*. While pessimistic concurrency control merely requires a special entry in the lock manager, i.e., in server state in memory, timestamp validation requires an entry in the database. This entry must not be a valid record, i.e., it must be a ghost. Ghost records and system transactions are very useful in the context of pessimistic concurrency control but also in the context of optimistic concurrency control. An alternative attaches the N+1st timestamp to a higher-level object, e.g., the table, index, partition, or file. Yet another alternative attaches the N+1st gap to the lowest or highest existing key value. In other words, one key value covers not only the usual adjacent gap but also its other adjacent gap. For example, in prior-key locking, where each key value also covers the gap to the next-higher key value, the lowest existing key value may also cover the gap to $-\infty$ or *null*.

In summary of the basic design, a timestamp per logical row covering entries and gaps in all secondary indexes will work correctly but not provide genuine fine-granularity concurrency control.

7.3.2 TECHNOLOGY TRANSFERS FROM TRADITIONAL LOCKING TECHNIQUES

Just as there are alternative locking techniques with a granularity of locking finer than ARIES/IM, there can be timestamp validation methods with a granularity of concurrency control finer than the basic design above. Traditional alternatives to ARIES/IM include "index-specific ARIES/IM," key-range locking, and ARIES/KVL. The purpose here is to transfer their advantages over ARIES/IM to concurrency control by timestamp validation.

The difference between ARIES/IM and index-specific ARIES/IM is locking logical rows (including an index entry in each secondary index) versus locking individual index entries. Thus, in index-specific ARIES/IM, the scope of each lock is contained within a single storage structure or index.

In timestamp validation, this granularity of concurrency control implies separate timestamps for entries in a table's primary storage structure and in its secondary indexes. For a single-row insertion into a table with K indexes, this reduces the number of gaps covered by locks or timestamps from K^2 to K—at the expense of K times more timestamps in the database as well as some increase in timestamps in queries and updates. An equality or range query with N results still requires N+1 timestamps, however; or twice that if index-to-index navigation is required, i.e., from a secondary index to a primary storage structure.

Key-range locking differs from index-specific ARIES/IM by the separation of lock modes for an index entry itself and for the adjacent gap also protected by the index entry. In other words, each lock request carries two lock modes, one for the index entry and one for the gap. Locks by two transactions on the same index entry are compatible if they are compatible in their modes for the index entry and in their modes for the gap. For example, one transaction may require phantom protection in the gap (leaving the index entry unlocked) while the other transaction modifies the index entry (leaving the gap unchanged and unlocked). While the original design for key-range locking lacks orthogonal lock modes for index entry and gap, orthogonal key-range locking uses two separate locks; two timestamps for index entry and gap enable the same concurrency as orthogonal key-range locking.

In timestamp validation, this granularity of concurrency control requires two timestamps for each entry in each index, one for the index entry itself and one for its adjacent gap. Phantom protection validates the timestamp on the gap and an insertion into the gap modifies it.

Figure 7.10 illustrates locks and timestamps for a query with the predicate "FirstName = 'Jerry'." Different shading indicates separate locks or timestamps. Instead of two lock modes per index entry (as in key-range locking), each index entry includes two timestamps, one for the index entry itself and one for the adjacent gap to the next index entry. While key-range locking permits locking an index entry and its adjacent gap in a single lock and single invocation of the lock manager, orthogonal key-range timestamp validation requires two separate timestamp values.

Index Entries and Gaps	Entry (Gary, 1)	Gap			Entry (Jerry, 3)	Gap	Entry (Jerry, 6)	Gap	
		Gary, >1	>Gary, <Jerry	Jerry, <3				Jerry, >6	>Jerry
Index-specific ARIES/IM									
KRL									
KR TSs									

Figure 7.10: Two timestamps per index entry.

ARIES/KVL differs from index-specific ARIES/IM by locking groups of index entries with the same key value, not just individual index entries. This difference is irrelevant in unique indexes but can reduce the lock count in non-unique indexes. Moreover, a key-value lock protects both present and absent instances. Nonetheless, a key-value lock requires at least one instance to be present, even if only as a ghost. A lock in ARIES/KVL also covers the gap to the next-higher distinct key value in the index.

In timestamp validation, this granularity of concurrency control is possible and relatively easy to implement if there is a data structure representing a distinct key value and its set of instances. In other words, if a non-unique index represents a set of instances by a single copy of the distinct key value plus a list of bookmarks, a timestamp attached to the distinct key value can serve for end-of-transaction timestamp validation with granularity equal to that of ARIES/KVL. Note that an insertion of a new key value, i.e., into a gap, must modify the timestamp of the distinct key value covering the gap; and that a query and transaction in need of phantom protection can rely on that timestamp.

Figure 7.11 illustrates timestamps for a granularity of concurrency control equal to that of ARIES/KVL for a query with the predicate "FirstName = 'Jerry'." Notice that both the lock and the timestamp cover all instances of the key value, including both existing and non-existing ones, as well as the gap to the next-higher distinct key value. Compared to index-specific ARIES/IM and to key-range timestamp validation, this results in significantly fewer locks or timestamps. Moreover, the scope of the lock or timestamp is only slightly wider than the query predicate, less so than the locks and timestamps in Figure 7.10. Put differently, concurrency control focusing on distinct key values match query predicates more precisely the predicates available in query languages.

Index Entries and Gaps	Entry (Gary, 1)	Gap			Entry (Jerry, 3)	Gap	Entry (Jerry, 6)	Gap			Entry (Mary, 5)
		Gary, >1	>Gary, <Jerry	Jerry, <3				Jerry, >6	>Jerry, <Mary	Mary, <5	
ARIES/KVL											
KV TSs											

Figure 7.11: A timestamp per distinct key value.

The disadvantage of the designs is apparent in insertions and deletions: an update modifying a single logical row requires locks or timestamps in each index but those protect much more than is required. For example, insertion of a new instance of key value Jerry locks or protects all instances of Jerry; it is not possible that two transactions insert two entirely different new instances of key value Jerry at the same time. For another example, insertion of a new key value such as Harry into the gap between Jerry and Mary uses the lock or timestamp for Jerry; thus, the transaction inserting Harry prevents all queries or updates for all instances of key value Jerry.

7.3.3 ORTHOGONAL KEY-VALUE TIMESTAMP VALIDATION

Orthogonal key-value locking differs from ARIES/KVL in three important ways. First, there are separate lock modes for the key value and the gap to the next key value. Thus, it is possible to lock a key value without the adjacent gap and vice versa. Second, the set of bookmarks (rows, pointers) associated with a distinct key value, including both present and absent bookmarks, is hash-partitioned into a fixed number of partitions and a lock request can specific separate lock modes for the partitions. Thus, it is possible to lock individual index entries (plus their hash collisions). Third, the set of possible, absent key values within a gap is also hash-partitioned. Thus, a query with an equality predicate can enforce phantom protection without locking an entire gap between existing key values. Figure 7.4 in Section 7.2.4 illustrates these differences.

Orthogonal key-value timestamp validation is a new technique designed to transfer these ideas to timestamp validation. It requires several changes from basic timestamp validation. First, timestamps must exist in each index, i.e., not only in a table's primary data structure but also in secondary indexes, and attached not to an individual index entry or record but to a distinct key value independent of its count of instances. Second, there must be a timestamp for each key value itself and another timestamp for one of the two adjacent gaps. Third, there may be multiple timestamps for each key value (a fixed number); existing and possible bookmarks are hash partitioned to one of these timestamps. Fourth, there may be multiple timestamps for each gap and all possible key values within the gap are hash partitioned to these timestamps.

Figure 7.12 illustrates a distinct key value ("20") in a leaf page of a secondary index, together with a list of 3 bookmarks (bmk) as well as a set of timestamps (ts) for the fixed-size set of bookmarks and another fixed-size set of timestamps for the adjacent gap. Each partition of bookmarks has its own timestamp, as does each partition of key values in the gap. Section 7.4 introduces new techniques to manage such a multitude of timestamps.

$$\boxed{\text{20 ts... 3 bmk bmk bmk ts...}}$$

Figure 7.12: A distinct key value in an index.

Figure 7.13 illustrates, in the style of Figure 7.11, possible lock scopes in orthogonal key-value locking as well as the scopes of individual timestamps in orthogonal key-value timestamps. In this example, hash partitioning of bookmarks uses four buckets, whereas hash partitioning of key values in gaps uses only three buckets. The number of buckets is chosen based on the desired multi-programming level. For example, in an in-memory database or any database with the application's working set in the buffer pool, the number of software threads should match the number of hardware threads. In a database that "hides" I/O delays by many concurrent transactions, many more partitions may be required to avoid false concurrency control conflicts.

7.3.4   SUMMARY OF TIMESTAMP VALIDATION WITH PHANTOM PROTECTION

There are a number of pessimistic concurrency control techniques that primarily differ in their granularity of locking. Practically the same granularities of concurrency control differentiate the various optimistic timestamp techniques introduced above.

Figure 7.14 summarizes optimistic and pessimistic concurrency control techniques for various granularities of concurrency control. By including gaps in lock scopes and in timestamp validation, all techniques in Figure 7.14 ensure serializability including phantom protection. Therefore, many existing designs and systems using optimistic concurrency control or timestamp validation do not have a place in Figure 7.14.

A timestamp per key value is not too complex if there is a storage structure that corresponds to a key value, e.g., a list of bookmarks. Note that this data structure can stretch over multiple pages. If each index entry is a separate record, there is also some implementation com-

Index Entries and Gaps	Entry (Gary, 1)	Gap			Entry (Jerry, 3)	Gap	Entry (Jerry, 6)	Gap			Entry (Mary, 5)	Gap	
		Gary, >1	>Gary, <Jerry	Jerry, <3				Jerry, <6	>Jerry, <Mary	Mary, <5		Mary, >5	>Mary
ARIES/KVL													
KV TSs													
Orth. KVL													
… key value only													
… key value partition													
… gap only													
… gap partition													
Orth. KV TSs													
… key value only													
… key value partition													
… gap only													
… gap partition													

Figure 7.13: Orthogonal key-value timestamps.

plexity, but only because there needs to be a single place where all transactions find the timestamp, not because there is any ambiguity which timestamp is needed.

Timestamps for non-existing data, e.g., gaps in an index, is a new concept. Timestamps attached to distinct key values are a new granularity in optimistic concurrency control. Separation of timestamps for instances equal to the key value and for instances in the gap between existing key values justifies the name orthogonal. Partitioning is also a new concept in timestamp-based database concurrency control.

7.4   MANAGEMENT OF TIMESTAMPS

The prior section assumes that timestamps can be stored and managed efficiently, both the timestamps of the database objects and the timestamps held by transactions for end-of-transaction validation. In addition to compression, a possible avenue toward efficient management of timestamps focuses on in-memory data structures rather than embedding of timestamps in databases and their storage and index structures.

Granularity of Concurrency Control	Locking Technique	Timestamp Technique	Count of Timestamps
Database table	Table locking	Schema version	1 per table
Database page	Page locking	PageLSN validation	1 per page
Logical row (incl. index entries and gaps)	ARIES/IM	Row validation	1 per logical row
Index entry (incl. gap)	Index-specific ARIES/IM	Key-range validation	1 per index entry
Index entry or gap	Orthogonal key-range locking	Orthogonal key-range validation	2 per index entry
Key value (incl. gap)	ARIES/KVL	Key-value timestamp validation	1 per key value
Key value or gap	Orthogonal key-value locking	Orthogonal key-value timestamp validation	2 per key value
Key value or gap or partition	… w/partitioning	… w/partitioning	2k + 2 per key value

Figure 7.14: Granularities of concurrency control.

7.4.1   COMPRESSING TIMESTAMPS

Orthogonal key-value validation partitions the instances of each distinct key value as well as the possible key values in each gap between adjacent existing key values. A timestamp for each partition may lead to many timestamps and thus have a detrimental effect on database size, scan performance, buffer pool hit and fault rates, backup performance, etc. Thus, it seems natural to consider compression of timestamp values.

An obvious approach is to reduce the precision of old timestamp values, e.g., to full seconds, minutes, hours, or days. Another obvious approach is to store only one timestamp value in its entirety, e.g., the oldest one, and to represent all other timestamp values attached to the same key value as interval, i.e., the numerical difference among the timestamp.

Figure 7.15 shows a few compression techniques applicable to timestamp values within a database page. Run-length encoding applies to equal values; dictionaries applies to few distinct values. Both of these methods usually apply to actual values but can also be applied to sets or lists with multiple values but few distinct differences between values. Rounding of timestamp values, e.g., from μs precision to seconds, where such lossy compression is semantically correct, not only shortens values but also may enable the other compression techniques.

Method	Use Cases	Space Savings
Run-length encoding	Equal timestamp values	Factors
	Equal differences between timestamp values	
Dictionary encoding	Few distinct timestamp values	Factors
	Few distinct differences between timestamp values	
Rounding	Excessive precision	Percentages

Figure 7.15: Forms of timestamp compression.

Many of the timestamps attached to a data item (e.g., a distinct key value) may have the same value. Even if not, they may have the same value for purposes of concurrency control. For example, all values older than the oldest active transaction have the same effect in all future transaction validations. There is no need to enumerate their precise values; instead, a value indicating "as old as or older than all active transactions" suffices. The persistent database may store that indicator until the data object, gap, or partition is modified again. In fact, a subsequent reader of some data object may discover additional timestamps may be compressed in this way. Finally, there is no need to store the same value multiple times, suggesting a compression techniques akin to run-length encoding for values with a difference of zero to the oldest timestamp value.

7.4.2   CACHING TIMESTAMPS

The essence of timestamp validation is the comparison of two timestamps (for each database object): the timestamp observed during transaction execution and another, up-to-date timestamp during transaction commit. In the past, the up-to-date timestamp has always been attached to a database object and stored with that object in the database. In designs with many timestamps, e.g., orthogonal key-value validation as introduced in Section 7.3.3 above, attaching all timestamps to database objects and storing all timestamps in the database may not be attractive.

While a database object is not in the active working set, i.e., not in the buffer pool, it might have only a single timestamp. For example, a distinct key value in an index may have a single timestamp that indicates the last update to any instance of the key value. When the key value and its database page is fetched into the buffer pool, individual timestamps are assigned to partitions of instances as well as partitions of the adjacent gap. As these timestamps may not all fit within the database page, they are kept or cached elsewhere in the server's working memory. When the buffer pool evicts the distinct key value and its database page, the maximum value of all these timestamps is assigned to the key value in persistent storage.

Figure 7.16 illustrates a buffer frame in a buffer pool holding an image of a database page. Inside the page is its timestamp in the form of a PageLSN value. Outside the buffer pool frame is a set of timestamps for individual records within the page.

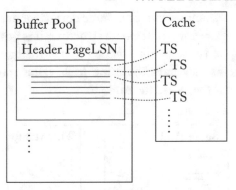

Figure 7.16: Detail timestamps attached to a buffer pool frame.

The data structure holding these timestamps can be distributed, i.e., pieces attached to individual database pages in the buffer pool, or it can be a central data structure, perhaps organized and indexed as a hash table. The preferred design depends on the greatest efficiency during transaction validation. If transaction validation can avoid re-accessing database objects and employ a data structure independent of the buffer pool, contention for the buffer pool and its data structures (e.g., its hash table) may diminish. Note that re-accessing database objects may include re-searching database indexes, because database objects may move during physical restructuring such as a node split in a B-tree. Note also that the data structure for such transient timestamps, indexed by database object identifiers, bears strong resemblance to the data structures of a traditional lock manager.

7.4.3 TIMESTAMP VALIDATION IN DATABASES WITHOUT TIMESTAMPS

An extreme form of caching timestamps removes all timestamps from the persistent database and keeps all required timestamps in memory. Thus, size and count of timestamps do not affect the size of the persistent database.

Each item not in the buffer pool has automatic (implicit) timestamps older than the oldest active transaction. When the buffer pool loads a database page and the objects it contains, it allocates the appropriate timestamps and initializes them with a value older than the oldest active transaction. The buffer pool must not evict objects and pages that participate in active transactions. An alternative design decouples the timestamp cache from the buffer pool such that the timestamp cache can retain timestamps as required by active transactions even if the buffer pool must evict the relevant database pages. With today's memory sizes, this alternative design does not seem required or advantageous in most server environments.

Figure 7.17 shows the same buffer pool frame and database page as Figure 7.16. Here, the timestamps are kept separate from the buffer pool and its page frames. A central in-memory data structure for all such timestamps seems one viable design for databases without timestamps. Depending on the precise organization of the data structure, it is possible that multiple database items in the buffer pool map to the same timestamp. This is analogous to a situation in locking, where multiple database items may have the same hash value and thus their locks and lock conflicts may be managed as if they were the same item.

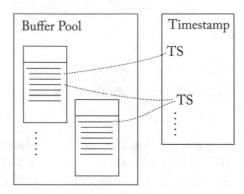

Figure 7.17: Timestamps separated from their database items.

Removing all timestamps from the persistent data structures easily solves a problem with no elegant solution otherwise. In an ordered index, N key values (or individual index entries, if that is the granularity of concurrency control) define N−1 gaps between them and N+1 gaps including the two ends. Thus, phantom protection using gaps and timestamps requires N+1 timestamps. N timestamps can be attached to the N key values (or individual index entries). The placement of the N+1st timestamp within a database, table, or index has no easy, elegant solution. If, however, there are no timestamps in the database and all timestamps are in server memory, an artificial key value (to be thought of as *null*, $-\infty$ or $+\infty$) readily solves the problem. This is the solution usually employed in key-range locking and key-value locking—thus, adopting this solution for timestamps renders the in-memory data structure ever more similar to that of a traditional lock manager.

7.4.4   CLIENT-SERVER DATABASE STORAGE

In some client-server systems, it is desirable that a server does not track a client's transactions. Instead, the server provides data augmented with a timestamp, the client manages transaction state including timestamps, and the client requests a server transaction only when it needs to commit its own transactions by updating the shared database on the server. In other words, server transactions are always short, just long enough to commit changes prepared on the client. In some ways, the client implements the transaction-private update buffer well known in the implementation of optimistic concurrency control with end-of-transaction validation.

In order to support this design of client-server transaction processing with end-of-transaction timestamp validation, the server provides timestamps with the initial request for data, the client submits its copy of the timestamps with its commit request, and the server verifies timestamps before applying updates to its database shared with many clients. Note that the server requires locks during timestamp validation and updates, either in the form equivalent to a database lock (serial validation) or as locks on individual database objects (for concurrent validation).

When serving the initial request for data, the server may find the required timestamps in the database or it may "make them up" as described in the preceding subsection. In the latter case, the server must not evict the relevant timestamps from its memory, which may imply that it must not evict the relevant database pages from its buffer pool, while a client transaction is active and might need to validate its copy of those timestamps during commit processing.

Figure 7.18 shows two buffer pools, one in the client and one in the server. A database page may be cached in both places, at times in different versions. Both places manage timestamps for the page, possibly with different schemes. When the client returns a modified page, the server verifies that no other client has submitted the page with conflicting changes, using timestamps attached to the page and its contents. The client submits not only the modified page but also the transaction's read set, i.e., the database contents underlying the database transaction, and a timestamp for each item in the read set.

If the commit logic validates not only timestamps of modified database objects but also of objects read, the memory and buffer pool requirements on the server might be substantial. Note that validation of objects read is essential for serializable transactions, comparable to holding read locks until end-of-transaction commit. For phantom protection, this includes timestamps covering absent data and key values, e.g., gaps between key values or entries in ordered indexes such as B-trees.

7.4.5   SUMMARY OF TIMESTAMP MANAGEMENT

In summary, end-of-transaction timestamp validation is one of two forms of optimistic concurrency control—the other one is the original design for optimistic concurrency control that compares read and write sets of concurrent transactions. Timestamp validation is popular because it seems simple, efficient, and scalable.

Timestamp validation with phantom protection as well as with concurrency as high as that enabled by orthogonal key-value locking requires multiple timestamps per data object, e.g., per distinct key value in a database index. Fortunately, compression can reduce the space overhead in a database. Moreover, the space overhead can move from the database to server state. In the process, timestamp management is also limited to active database objects. In the extreme case, a database may contain no timestamps at all and timestamps in server memory are required only for objects in active transactions.

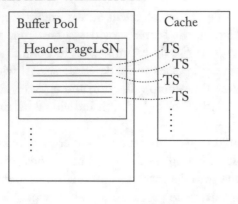

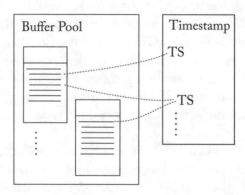

Figure 7.18: Buffer pools in client and server, plus timestamp data structures.

7.5   HIERARCHICAL TIMESTAMPS

There is a wide variety of techniques for database concurrency control and perhaps none fits all situations: all databases, tables, and indexes; all transactions and access patterns; all work-loads and all levels of contention. Thus, it is desirable to explore hybrids of multiple techniques. For example, one such promising hybrid relies on snapshot isolation exploiting multi-version snapshot isolation for read-only transactions and some other technique, e.g., key-value locking or timestamp validation, for serializable read-write transactions including their read operations. This hybrid design guarantees not only phantom protection and serializability but also that read-only transactions never block read-write transactions and read-write transactions never block read-only transactions [Chan et al., 1982].

In traditional pessimistic concurrency control, hierarchical locking [Gray et al., 1975] is an old and proven hybrid of coarse and fine granularities of locking. In timestamp concurrency control, hierarchies of database objects have been overlooked. Nonetheless, Sections 7.3.3 and 7.3.4 hint at hierarchical timestamps—trading off efficiency and overhead (coarse granularity of concurrency control) versus precision and concurrency (fine granularity of concurrency control). It turns out that hierarchical timestamps also offer another approach to timestamp compression in the database.

For example, when the buffer pool loads a root object, it also allocates additional memory for all other timestamps in the hierarchy and initializes them with the value of the stored timestamp. While the object remains in the buffer pool, transactions maintain and inspect timestamps across the entire hierarchy. When the buffer pool evicts the database object, it writes only the maximal timestamp value, already attached to the root object based on the rules above for hierarchical timestamps.

Figure 7.19 is derived from Figure 7.3 by removal first of column and row for X locks and then, due to lack of remaining conflicts, of column and row for IS locks. The correct interpretation of this compatibility matrix is that all transactions always and automatically hold an IS lock; therefore, other transactions cannot acquire X locks at this granularity of concurrency control. Timestamps can achieve the same transaction concurrency and coordination as locking using lock modes and compatibility shown in Figure 7.19.

Requested → ↓ Held	S	IX	SIX
S	✓	–	–
IX	–	✓	–
SIX	–	–	–

Figure 7.19: Limited hierarchical or intention locks.

For example, in orthogonal key-value validation, a timestamp is required for an entire key value and further timestamps are for instances of the key value (or partitions of instances). Each update must set not only the timestamp for the modified instance (or its partition) but also the timestamp for the entire key value. In other words, the timestamp of the entire key value is always the maximum of all timestamps for instances (or partitions). With these timestamps and updates, a read-only transaction may validate either the entire key value or an individual instance (or partition). If the timestamp of the entire key value is sufficiently old, validation of the read-only transaction is complete. If not, the read-only transaction can attempt to validate with the timestamps of instances (or partitions). Of course, this only works for a read-only transaction that has read fewer than all instances (or partitions).

In the above scheme, a reader transaction can skip over the timestamp for the key value and directly (and only) inspect the timestamp of the individual instance (or partition). In order to achieve the concurrency control equivalent to Figure 7.3 rather than Figure 7.15, readers must validate against timestamps at both granularities, i.e., the entire key value and the instance (or partition). Writers may modify just the overall timestamp for the entire key value and omit updating the individual timestamps.

Hierarchical timestamp validation works not only for key values and their instances but also for other hierarchies of database objects. Other examples include a key value and its adjacent gap either as a combined unit or as two objects with individual timestamps, a gap (between key values) as a whole or partitioned, etc. As may be obvious from this example, even hierarchies with more than two levels are possible, just as in orthogonal key-value locking.

This regimen of hierarchical timestamp validation suggests another compression technique for timestamps, specifically for items with low concurrency contention. For those, it is sufficient to keep only a single transaction for an entire key value; the timestamps for individual instances (or partitions) may be omitted. Even a dynamic scheme is thinkable that attempts to get by with a single timestamp but adds the individual timestamps if contention arises.

In summary, hierarchical timestamp scopes are just as useful as hierarchical locking schemes. They enable coarse granules and efficient concurrency control for large database operations as well as fine-granularity concurrency control and highly concurrent execution of many small database operations.

7.6   CONCLUSIONS

In summary, the essence to providing phantom protection with timestamps is to provide concurrency control for each gap between key values in indexes. This requires that each gap or piece of a gap must be mapped to some timestamp. An insertion into a gap updates the appropriate timestamp and phantom protection validates the timestamp.

There can be many or few timestamps in a database. They may be attached to the database, to each table, to each index or partition thereof, or to individual data items including index entries. For a table, index, or key value, the individual instances may be partitioned, with a timestamp for each partition. Moreover, a gap can be partitioned with an individual timestamp per partition. Attaching a fixed number of timestamps to each distinct key value, partitioning the instances of the key value, and partitioning each gap between key values provides transaction isolation and concurrency very similar to orthogonal key-value locking.

This chapter introduces multiple innovations to database concurrency control: timestamps for gaps, timestamps for distinct key values, orthogonal timestamps for key values and gaps, timestamps for partitions of bookmarks, timestamps for partitions within gaps, hierarchical timestamp scopes, compression of timestamps, caching timestamps in volatile memory, more granular timestamps in memory than in the database, and optimistic end-of-transaction timestamp validation in databases without timestamps. Each of these techniques contributes to efficient, effective, serializable, fine-granularity concurrency control based on end-of-transaction timestamp validation.

ACKNOWLEDGEMENTS

Alok Kumar and Ian Rae reviewed a very early version of this chapter; their questions and suggestions were greatly appreciated.

7.7   REFERENCES

Chan, A., Fox, S., Lin, W.-T. K., Nori, A., and Ries, D. R. (1982). The implementation of an integrated concurrency control and recovery scheme. *ACM SIGMOD Conference*, pp. 184–191. DOI: 10.1145/582383.582386. 254, 274

Graefe, G. (2010). A survey of B-tree locking techniques. *ACM TODS*, 35(3) (Chapter 1). DOI: 10.1145/1806907.1806908. 257

Graefe, G., Lillibridge, M., Kuno, H. A., Tucek, J., and Veitch, A. C. (2013). Controlled lock violation. *ACM SIGMOD Conference*, pp. 85–96 (Chapter 4). DOI: 10.1145/2463676.2465325. 259

Graefe, G. and Kimura, H. (2015). Orthogonal key-value locking. *BTW Conference*, pp. 237–256 (Chapter 5). 255, 256

Gray, J., Lorie, R. A., Putzolu, G. R., and Traiger, I. L. (1975). Granularity of locks in a large shared data base. *VLDB Conference*, pp. 428–451. DOI: 10.1145/1282480.1282513. 261, 274

Gray, J. and Reuter, A. (1993). *Transaction Processing Concepts and Techniques*, Morgan Kaufmann. 254

Härder, T. and Reuter, A. (1983). Principles of transaction-oriented database recovery. *ACM Computing Surveys*, 15(4), pp. 287–317. DOI: 10.1145/289.291.

Korth, H. F. (1983). Locking primitives in a database system. *Journal of the ACM*, 30(1), pp. 55–79. DOI: 10.1145/322358.322363. 254

Kung, H. T. and Robinson, J. T. (1981). On optimistic methods for concurrency control. *ACM TODS*, 6(2), pp. 213–226. DOI: 10.1145/319566.319567. 251, 259, 260, 261

Lomet, D. B. (1993). Key-range locking strategies for improved concurrency. *VLDB*, pp. 655–664. 257

Mohan, C. (1990). ARIES/KVL: A key-value locking method for concurrency control of multi-action transactions operating on B-tree indexes. *VLDB Conference*, pp. 392–405. 255, 257

Mohan, C., Haderle, D. J., Lindsay, B. G., Pirahesh, H., and Schwarz, P. M. (1992). ARIES: A transaction recovery method supporting fine-granularity locking and partial rollbacks using write-ahead logging. *ACM TODS*, 17(1), pp. 94–162. DOI: 10.1145/128765.128770. 260, 261

Mohan, C. and Levine, F. E. (1992). ARIES/IM: An efficient and high-concurrency index management method using write-ahead logging. *ACM SIGMOD Conference*, pp. 371–380. DOI: 10.1145/130283.130338. 257

CHAPTER 8

Repairing Optimistic Concurrency Control

Concurrent validation, premature publication, and distributed commit

Goetz Graefe

ABSTRACT

Optimistic concurrency control means end-of-transaction validation of read- and write-sets or of timestamps attached to database items. Optimistic concurrency control suffers from multiple problems the present chapter attempts to remedy. First, concurrent validation of multiple transactions requires communication among them in order to detect conflicting database accesses. Second, two-phase commit requires that all local participants prepare themselves to abide by the global coordinator's commit decisions, which means that other transactions must not read or write database items in conflict with a local participant of a committing distributed transaction. Third, the danger of premature publication of updates committed but not yet durable requires that the atomic phase at the end of each optimistic transaction must include not only validation and propagation of updates from the transaction-private update buffer to the shared buffer pool but also forcing the transaction's commit log record to stable storage.

The remedies proposed for the problems above are perhaps radical but definitely simple. They employ locks and a lock manager for commit processing in optimistic concurrency control. The remedy for the last problem relies on controlled lock violation, which prior research has introduced and considered only for pessimistic concurrency control.

8.1 INTRODUCTION

Optimistic concurrency control is defined by end-of-transaction validation. In contrast, pessimistic concurrency control detects conflicts during lock acquisition. The original design for optimistic concurrency control focuses on transactions' read- and write-sets. At the time, database pages seemed like the best granularity of concurrency control [Härder, 1984, Kung and Robinson, 1981].

Today, optimistic concurrency control focuses on end-of-transaction timestamp validation and on key values in unique indexes. Serializability requires phantom protection, i.e., guaranteed absence of rows satisfying a predicate of a query earlier within a transaction—if phantom protection is enforced at all, it is commonly enforced at page granularity, e.g., using PageLSN values (timestamps) of index leaf pages.

End-of-transaction commit processing includes a validation step and a write step. The former checks for concurrency control conflicts, whereupon the latter propagates a committing transaction's updates from its transaction-private update buffer to the persistent database or at least its shared buffer pool. Kung and Robinson [1981] stress that validation and write phase together must be atomic, i.e., either serial (one transaction at a time) or concurrent with coordination and information exchange among committing transactions.

Figure 8.1 illustrates the phases of a transaction in optimistic concurrency control. The "read" phase reads data values in the database, computes updates, and saves new values (including insertions and deletions) in a transaction-private update buffer. The "validation" phase checks for concurrency conflicts with other transactions. The "write" phase drains the transaction-private update buffer and applies its entries to the persistent database or the shared buffer pool. As argued below, perpetuating the transaction's updates should be part of write phase, i.e., the transaction is not complete until its commit log record is in the recovery log on stable storage. Flushing dirty database pages from the buffer pool to persistent storage is not part of the transaction. In optimistic concurrency control with backward validation, each transaction's read- and write-sets must be retained as long as any concurrent transaction might still need them for its own validation logic, i.e., as long as any concurrent transaction is still active. It may or may not be a longer period than required for the buffer pool flush.

Read Phase	Validation Phase	Write Phase		Buffer	Read- and
= transaction application logic	= conflict detention	= update propagation	+ log hardening	pool flush	write-set retention
No concurrency control	Critical section			After transaction end	

Figure 8.1: Transaction phases in optimistic concurrency control.

In the context of write-ahead logging, the write phase must include writing a commit log record to stable storage, typically on external storage devices. Transactional durability by mirroring uses the redundant copies as stable storage and the write phase must include synchronous replication. In these contexts, serial commit processing seems untenable in a shared database server. Thus, concurrent validation seems a ubiquitous requirement. Section 8.3 below suggests a radical and simple design for concurrent commit processing in optimistic concurrency control.

A serializable transaction schedule is equivalent to some serial schedule executing one transaction at a time. In a concurrent transaction schedule, once a transaction has a place in the equivalent serial schedule, its needs for concurrency control seem to end. The exception is the danger of premature publication of new database updates before they are durable. In an unfortunate case, a database query may find and produce database contents that never reaches the recovery log and thus never achieves durability. In a similarly bad case, a distributed transaction may apply a database update based on such contents. Traditional optimistic concurrency control has no defense against this danger. Section 8.4 introduces a simple and safe technique that reliably prevents premature publication in the context of optimistic concurrency control, yet minimizes the impact on concurrency and system performance.

Modern database servers often run on clusters with sharded or partitioned database contents and local recovery logs, with end-of-transaction commit coordination using two-phase commit (or Paxos or Raft). Designs for non-blocking three-phase commit purchase their advantages with additional communication, logging, and delays. Section 8.5 below adapts an existing technique for high-concurrency commit processing to three-phase commit, effectively removing the concurrency control exclusions that have prevented adoption of these classic non-blocking commit protocols.

The remainder of this chapter proceeds as follows. The next section reviews related work including traditional optimistic concurrency control, timestamp validation, locking, lock managers, two-phase commit, and controlled lock violation. Section 8.3 focuses on concurrent validation of multiple optimistic transactions—both its necessity and appropriate techniques. Section 8.4 focuses on premature publication of database updates not yet durable, a subtle oversight in early lock release repaired by controlled lock violation. Section 8.5 extends old and new techniques to distributed transaction. The final section summarizes and concludes.

8.2   RELATED PRIOR WORK

This section supplies background knowledge about prior technologies relevant to subsequent sections. Knowledgeable readers may choose to skip ahead.

8.2.1   TRADITIONAL OPTIMISTIC CONCURRENCY CONTROL

The defining behavior of optimistic concurrency control is end-of-transaction conflict detection. Each optimistic transaction runs in three phases. The "read" phase reads in the database and executes the transaction's application logic; the "validation" phase checks for concurrency conflicts with other transactions; and the "write" phase propagates the transaction's updates including insertions and deletions from the transaction-private update buffer in the shared database or its buffer pool [Kung and Robinson, 1981].

Figure 8.2 illustrates a particularly flawed way of implementing optimistic concurrency control. The critical section covers only the validation phase, i.e., conflict detection, but not the write phase. Moreover, the write phase does not include hardening a transaction by flushing its commit log record to the recovery log on stable storage or, equivalently, writing modified database pages to one or two remote mirrors.

There are three forms of end-of-transaction validation. In backward validation, the original design, a committing transaction intersects its read- and write-sets with concurrent trans-

Read Phase	Validation Phase	Write Phase	Log hardening	Buffer pool flush	Read- and write-set retention
= transaction application logic	= conflict detention	= update propagation			
No concurrency control	Critical section	No concurrency control		After transaction end	

Figure 8.2: Transaction phases incorrectly implemented.

actions already committed. This design requires that transactions' read- and write-sets are retained beyond transaction commit until all concurrent transactions have finished their validation phases. In forward validation, Härder's alternative [Härder, 1984], a committing transaction intersects its read- and write-sets with active transactions. This design requires that transactions publish their read- and write-sets incrementally as they progress through their read phase. In end-of-transaction timestamp validation, a transaction in its read phase reads the timestamp attached to each database object before accessing the object itself, and in its validation phase, compares the current timestamp value with the one cached during the read phase. Updates including insertions and deletions modify timestamps attached to database contents; reads do not.

There is some similarity between forward validation and locking in the way concurrent transactions share information about their data accesses; their main difference is the timing of conflict detection. They differ further in the options available upon detection of a concurrency conflict.

8.2.2   LOCKING TECHNIQUES

The defining behavior of pessimistic concurrency control are that each transaction, while executing its application logic, inserts a lock in a shared lock manager before accessing a database object, and that lock acquisition implies conflict detection. Beyond shared locks for reads and exclusive locks for writes, there are lock modes for commutative updates (e.g., Increment locks [Korth, 1983]) and for pairs of objects (e.g., an index key and a gap to the next index key [Graefe, 2007, Lomet, 1993]) as well as derived modes for hierarchical and multi-granularity locking (i.e., intention locks [Gray et al., 1976, Korth, 1983]) and lock modes with a scheduling component (e.g., Update [Korth, 1983], Reserved and Pending [SQLite, 2004]). Locks can further differ in their scopes (e.g., database, table, page, index, or index key value) and in their durations (e.g., in early lock release [DeWitt et al., 1984], controlled lock violation [Graefe et al., 2013], deferred lock acquisition, and deferred lock enforcement [Graefe, 2019a]). Finally, there are opportunities to optimize the lock acquisition sequence [Graefe, 2019b].

A lock manager is a service or data structure shared among all concurrent transactions, e.g., within a node of a cluster. It tracks the many-to-many relationship between transactions and database objects (lock scopes). For efficient search by database object during lock acquisition, there is a hash table on object identifiers, e.g., a combination of index identifier and key value. If multiple database objects share a hash value, they may be treated as a single object (permitting false conflicts) or there may be a set of objects per hash value, e.g., a linked list per hash bucket. If multiple transactions read the same database object at the same time, there must be multiple instances (data structures) of this many-to-many relationship between transactions and database objects. For efficient lock release after transaction commit, there may also be a linked list per transaction.

Figure 8.3 illustrates the principal data structures of a typical database lock manager. At the bottom is an array of transaction descriptors; many of those are inactive here. On the left is a hash table showing here only a single hash bucket along the top. Each element in that linked list represents an item in the database. Each item has one or more lock requests attached. Lock requests by the same transaction form a linked list for efficient lock release at end-of-transaction.

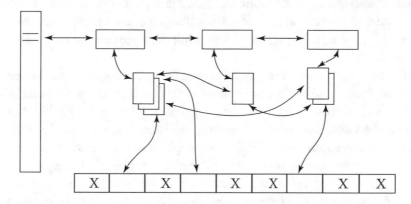

Figure 8.3: Principal data structures of a database lock manager.

Figure 8.3 shows a centralized data structure separate from other server data structures and modules, in particular from the buffer pool. An alternative design distributes the locks and attaches them to database pages in the buffer pool. If commit processing needs to finalize modifications on database pages, e.g., mark new version records with the log sequence number of the transaction's commit log record, then locks attached to buffer pool frames permit a single loop releasing a lock after each final update.

Equally important in the implementation of a lock manager are memory management (allocation and release of lock data structures) and low-level concurrency control (latching). For example, Jung et al. [2014] describe how "a lock manager with reduced latching... generally improves performance. ...Locks are preallocated in bulk... simple list manipulation operations during the acquire and release phases of a transaction," and all these improvements remove "latch contention in the lock manager as the bottleneck."

When a lock request cannot be granted immediately, the requesting transaction can wait or abort, or the transaction(s) holding the conflicting lock(s) can abort. Limited wait depth [Thomasian, 1998] and timeouts can prevent unlimited waiting and deadlocks. A request waiting for a lock acquisition or for a lock upgrade, e.g., from an update lock to an exclusive lock, is entered into the lock manager's data structure. The requesting transaction must wait, poll, or receive an asynchronous notification. If a transaction abort is chosen in response to a lock conflict or a timeout, a policy based on transaction priority, start time, size (e.g., count of log records), etc. may choose the transaction(s) to abort.

8.2.3   TWO-PHASE COMMIT

In a cluster with multiple nodes (e.g., multiple operating system instances) and in a distributed system, the standard design calls for local lock management until a transaction's commit request. Read-only transactions in snapshot isolation coordinate at start-of-transaction, read-write transactions coordinate and commit at end-of-transaction, most commonly using two-phase commit. More precisely, commit log records in multiple logs require commit coordination, e.g., two-phase commit.

In most commit protocols, the central commit decision requires guaranteed cooperation by all participants; the first phase in a two-phase commit solicits these promises of cooperation and the second phase distributes the commit decision. Each participant that votes to commit must implement the coordinator's global commit decision, i.e., each participant must remain able to commit but also to roll back. Failure to comply is not an option after a participant has voted to commit and promised to implement the central commit decision.

Figure 8.4 shows the communication pattern of a successful two-phase commit with 2 participants. From the work phase to the pre-commit phase and from the pre-commit phase to the committed state, each phase or state transition requires a round-trip of messages between the coordinator and all transaction participants. In addition, each participant tracks its transitions, which requires a log record and a log flush in each read-write participant.

If the commit coordinator fails or if communication is unreliable, some participant nodes may be blocked with their guarantee given but no commit decision. This is the case addressed by non-blocking commit protocols, e.g., three-phase commit and its variants [Skeen, 1981]. There are many other variants and optimizations of distributed commits. One of them is known for transactions with only a single participant in addition to the coordinator—in this case, the coordinator can act like a participant, delegate the global commit decision to the other node, and the entire commit process requires only one round-trip of messages. Another optimization is specific to read-only participants [Mohan et al., 1986], but it might require refinement from its original design [Graefe, 2019c].

Figure 8.5 shows the communication pattern of an optimized two-phase commit. First, the coordinator delegates the final global commit decision to one of the participants. Second, the read-only participant elects to skip the second phase of the two-phase commit. Thus, instead of 8 messages in a traditional two-phase commit with 2 participants, the entire commit process

Coordinator	First Participant	Second Participant
Receive user's commit request		
Send request for vote to each participant		
	Log pre-commit	Log pre-commit
	Send vote	Send vote
Make and log global commit decision		
Send commit decision to each participant		
	Log final commit	Log final commit
	Send completion	Send completion
Close transaction	Release locks	Release locks

Figure 8.4: Communication in two-phase commit.

requires only 4 messages. With these optimizations, three-phase commit requires 6 messages instead 12 messages without them.

8.2.4 CONTROLLED LOCK VIOLATION

With today's processors and I/O devices, hardening a transaction may take much longer than executing a small transaction over an in-memory database, as is common now in online transaction processing. Write-ahead logging on non-volatile memory may eventually reverse this imbalance.

Figure 8.6, copied from Graefe et al. [2013], illustrates the relative time required to execute a simple transaction and to harden its commit log record in a recovery log on stable storage. For example, the application logic of a simple transaction may require 50,000 instruction cycles or about 20 μs on a CPU running at 2.5 GHz, whereas writing to a flash device may take 200 μs (assuming the block had been erased earlier). The blue line represents the duration of locks in traditional locking; the green line represents the time during which controlled lock violation enforces locks in the traditional strong way.

Concurrency control and serializability must ensure that many interleaved transactions are equivalent to some serial execution. Once a transaction has a commit log record with an LSN (log sequence number) in the log buffer in memory, the transaction's position in the equivalent serial execution is final. The need for further concurrency control seems to end at this point. This is the central insight behind early lock release. Variants of early lock release relinquish either only the read-only locks or all locks at this point.

Coordinator	Read-Write Participant	Read-Only Participant
Receive user's commit request		
Log pre-commit and commit delegation to first participant		
Send request to decide to first participant, including pre-commit		
Send request for vote to second participant, including vote destination		
		Send pre-commit to first participant, marked read-only
	Make and log global commit decision	Release locks
	Send commit decision to original coordinator	
Log final commit	Release locks	
Close transaction		

Figure 8.5: Communication in two-phase commit with optimizations.

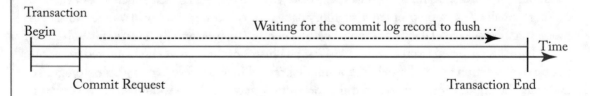

Figure 8.6: Durations of application logic and of hardening.

Controlled lock violation is similar to early lock release but also considers durability and write-ahead logging. It ensures that subsequent transactions cannot publish recent database updates before the relevant update transactions are durably committed and logged on stable storage. It retains all locks until a commit log record is on stable storage but locks are weak during hardening. Other transactions may acquire conflicting locks, and query or modify data, but cannot complete until the first transaction is durable. If the second transaction is a read-write transaction and must write a commit log record in the same recovery log as the first transaction, then this dependency is necessarily satisfied.

Put differently, when a transaction T2 requests a lock that conflicts with a weak exclusive lock held by a committing transaction T1, controlled lock violation grants the request but with a commit dependency. Thus, T2 cannot commit until T1 is completely durable. If T2 is a read-write transaction, this has little practical effect, since T2 will eventually write its own commit log record. If T1 is a local read-only participant in a global read-write transaction, then this commit dependency will cause a delay.

Figure 8.7 contrasts controlled lock violation and two forms of early lock release. Controlled lock violation achieves practically the same performance and scalability as early lock release of both S and X locks but without the danger of premature publication of not-yet-durable updates. Controlled lock violation and early lock release of only S locks are correct but with large differences in performance and scalability.

	Early Lock Release		Controlled Lock Violation
	S Only	S and X	
Trigger	LSN for commit log record		
Performance	Good	Best	Almost best
Consequence of a write-read conflict	Waiting	Premature publication	Commit dependency

Figure 8.7: Early lock release vs. controlled lock violation.

Controlled lock violation requires management of commit dependencies. Hekaton has proven that this is possible with high performance and scalability [Diaconu et al., 2013]. Hekaton also maintains a read set, a write set, and a scan set (key range) for each transaction. A read barrier holds back result sets in the server until all commit dependencies have cleared. In the published description, it remains unclear whether transaction hardening, i.e., writing a commit log record to the SQL Server recovery log, is considered such a commit dependency.

In distributed transactions coordinated with two-phase commit, controlled lock violation as described above applies to the second phase, i.e., after a local transaction's final commit log record has a log sequence number and a place in the log buffer. Controlled lock violation also applies to the first phase, i.e., before the global commit decision is made. In that case, a lock acquisition in violation of a write-read conflict imposes a commit dependency. If the distributed transaction aborts even after the local participant voted to commit, then the violating transaction must abort as well.

8.2.5   SUMMARY OF RELATED PRIOR WORK

In summary of related prior work, the proposals introduced below are all founded on traditional and proven techniques, including traditional optimistic concurrency control, pessimistic concurrency control (locking), and two-phase commit.

8.3   CONCURRENT VALIDATION

A modern processor runs hundreds of software threads on dozens of hardware threads using many cores and multiple threads in each core. Thus, data management systems often run hundreds of concurrent user transactions. With optimistic concurrency control, end-of-transaction validation (conflict detection) is a substantial component of a transaction's CPU activity. Thus, serial validation (one transaction at a time) creates a severe bottleneck.

Even the original introduction of optimistic concurrency control [Kung and Robinson, 1981] presented a motivation and a design for concurrent validation. The argument is now even stronger than it was then due to many-core processors and large memories, i.e., transactions without I/O delays.

This section first presents this argument in more detail and then proposes a design for simple, efficient, correct concurrent validation of optimistic transactions. The techniques of this section apply to validation based on intersecting read- and write-sets as well as validation based on timestamps attached to database objects.

8.3.1   THE NEED FOR CONCURRENT VALIDATION

The argument for concurrent validation is amplified by the fact that the atomic part of an optimistic transaction includes not only the actual validation phase, i.e., conflict detection, but also the write phase, i.e., update propagation. Until a transaction is sure to commit, its updates including insertions and deletions remain in a transaction-private update buffer. The write phase applies these updates to the shared database or to database pages in the buffer pool shared with other transactions. A transaction's need for concurrency control ends only after the transaction's updates are in the shared database or its buffer pool. Serial validation plus update propagation requires that the next transaction can start validation only after the last transaction finished applying its updates in the buffer pool, and therefore serial validation represents an unacceptable bottleneck.

Actually, the longest transaction phase is neither the read phase, i.e., execution of the transaction's application logic, nor the critical section combining validation and write phases, i.e., the traditional focus of optimistic concurrency control, but the hardening phase, i.e., writing the transaction's commit log record to the recovery log on stable storage. As argued in Section 8.4, correct failure atomicity and durability require that the write phase include hardening. Holding an exclusive lock on the entire database, which is the equivalent to serial validation, during the latter phase would be completely unacceptable.

Ignoring this last argument for now, an application's working set often fits in the database buffer pool nowadays. If parent-to-child pointers in indexes are swizzled within the buffer pool [Graefe et al., 2014], transactions can run just as fast as with an in-memory database. Another optimization can further speed up the write phase, e.g., for maintenance of a B-tree index. Whereas the read phase has to search an index, typically with binary search, the write phase can merely verify the earlier search and do its own search only if this verification fails. More specifically, consider an index nested loops join with its outer input sorted on its join key, also known as poor man's merge join. A B-tree index supporting these successive look-ups may start each search at the point of its last search, i.e., in a leaf rather than the B-tree root. For efficient progress to subsequent leaf nodes and larger sub-trees within the B-tree, this requires retaining an entire root-to-leaf path, e.g., retaining the slot number of the relevant key-pointer pair in each branch node on that path. The same mechanism may also be used in optimistic concurrency control. If the read phase retains information about root-to-leaf paths, the write phase can use it to speed up draining the transaction-private update buffer.

Nonetheless, even if the atomic validation and write logic phases were ten times shorter than a transaction's read phase, a fully utilized processor with ten hardware threads would always have one transaction in the atomic critical section; and a processor with more than ten threads would never be fully utilized by optimistic concurrency control with serial validation. Dedicating one of the hardware threads to validation and perhaps even another one to update propagation would not really help: a shared service thread processing all validation logic is tantamount to serial validation. A modern processor with many dozen hardware threads would suffer even worse from serial validation or from a single-threaded validation service.

Assuming a definite need for concurrent validation, and assuming the desire for robust implementations of it, the next step is a radically simple, rather obvious, and perhaps controversial design.

8.3.2   SIMPLE AND EFFICIENT CONCURRENT VALIDATION

The proposed design for concurrent validation in optimistic concurrency control is rather simple. It relies on a data structure shared among concurrently validating transactions. This data structure captures the many-to-many relationship between transactions and database objects. For efficient search by database object, there is a hash table on object identifiers, e.g., a combination of index identifier and key value. If multiple database objects share a hash value, they may be treated as a single object (permitting false conflicts) or there may be a set of objects per hash value, e.g., a linked list per hash bucket. If multiple transactions validate accesses to the same database object at the same time, e.g., in concurrent read accesses, there must be multiple instances (data structures) of this many-to-many relationship between transactions and database objects. For efficient removal of an entire transaction when validation finishes, including the transaction's accesses (read- and write-sets), there may also be a linked list per transaction. Finally, in order to enable multiple transactions validating concurrently, this data structure must be protected by low-level concurrency control, i.e., latches.

In other words, concurrent validation in optimistic concurrency control has precisely the same requirements as lock management in pessimistic concurrency control. A lock manager employs a hash table on database contents and it enables search and access by database object (for lock acquisition and conflict detection) and by transaction (for lock release and transaction commit). The same requirements suggest the same solution, namely a traditional lock manager as an implementation mechanism for concurrent validation in optimistic concurrency control. Items in a transaction's read-set create shared locks, items in a transaction's write-set create exclusive locks. There is no danger of deadlock because in optimistic concurrency control, detected conflicts lead to immediate transaction abort.

In the parlance of lock management, optimistic concurrency control is a form of deferred lock acquisition, with deferred lock acquisition applied to both shared and exclusive locks. In contrast, a dedicated paper [Graefe, 2019a] recommends deferred lock acquisition or better yet deferred lock enforcement only for exclusive locks.

In the same parlance, optimistic concurrency control with serial validation is equivalent to a single lock for the entire database. For concurrent validation, the details differ between backward validation, forward validation, and timestamp validation.

In optimistic concurrency control with the traditional backward validation, end-of-transaction validation acquires locks. Lock acquisition includes conflict detection. Locks must be retained until the later of two events, as already mentioned in the context of Figure 8.1. First, locks must remain in place until the transaction finishes all its phases including hardening by flushing its commit log record to the recovery log on stable storage. Second, locks of transaction T_0 must remain in place until all other transaction T_j have completed their end-of-transaction validation where the read and validation phases of T_0 overlapped with the read and validation phases of T_j. In other words, transaction T_0 must retain its locks until all transactions T_j finish that were active when T_0 finished its end-of-transaction validation step.

In optimistic concurrency control with forward validation, a transaction inserts its locks into the lock manager before each access, i.e., the timing of lock acquisition is similar to traditional locking. In contrast to pessimistic concurrency control, there is no conflict check at this time. Therefore, there is no waiting and no danger of deadlock during execution of a transaction's application logic. For example, two optimistic transactions may insert conflicting exclusive locks and write conflicting updates to their transaction-private update buffers. Conflict checks are delayed until end-of-transaction validation and detected conflicts imply immediate abort of one of the transactions involved. Locks must be retained only until a transaction is complete, i.e., until its commit log record is in the recovery log on stable storage.

In optimistic concurrency control by end-of-transaction timestamp validation, there are two possible designs. They differ in the location where pre-access timestamps are saved until end-of-transaction validation. In the first design, each transaction has a transaction-private collection of timestamps, i.e., effectively a read- and write-set augmented with timestamps. Only successful timestamp comparisons result in locks in the lock manager. In the second design, a transaction inserts its pre-access timestamp into the lock manager. In other words, each instance of a lock requires an additional field for a timestamp. Acquisition of these locks does not include conflict checks, similar to forward validation. During end-of-transaction timestamp validation, each of these locks is upgraded after appropriate timestamp comparisons to a real lock with traditional conflict behavior. Locks must be retained as in pessimistic concurrency control and in optimistic concurrency control with forward validation of read- and write-sets.

Figure 8.8 summarizes these differences. The traditional backward validation of read- and write-sets as well as one form of end-of-transaction timestamp validation run a transaction's read phase without any activity in the shared data structure, i.e., the lock manager. Forward validation and the other form of end-of-transaction timestamp validation post locks but without conflict checking. Only the traditional backward validation of read- and write-sets requires that locks remain in place beyond the transaction for subsequent validation attempts.

End-of-Transaction Validation	Read Phase = transaction application logic	Validation Phase = conflict detection	Write Phase = update propagation	+ log hardening	Buffer pool flush	Concurrent transactions
Backward	No concurrency control	Lock acquisition				Locks retained
Forward	Locks posted	Lock verification				Locks released
Timestamps		Lock acquisition				Locks released
Timestamps	Locks posted with timestamps	Timestamp verification				Locks released

Figure 8.8: Lock acquisition and retention in optimistic concurrency control.

8.3.3 SUMMARY OF CONCURRENT VALIDATION

In summary of concurrent validation, systems with optimistic concurrency control require concurrent validation today more than ever before. Transactions checking for conflicts require access to read- and write-sets both of completed (committed) transactions and of other transactions validating concurrently. Sharing read- and write-set information among transactions validating concurrently requires a shared data structure. This data structure requires efficient set intersection and low-level concurrency control, i.e., latching. Set intersection is most efficient with an index or hash table, familiar to database implementers in the forms of index nested loops join and hash join.

A traditional database lock manager with a hash table for search and latches for thread safety is precisely the data structure needed for concurrent validation. This design is radical in the sense that it employs pessimistic concurrency control as an implementation mechanism for optimistic concurrency control. It thus deviates from many people's understanding or implementation of optimistic concurrency control. Nonetheless, it is a pragmatic implementation choice and it enables other improvements in performance and scalability of transaction commit processing.

8.4   PREMATURE PUBLICATION

In traditional descriptions of optimistic concurrency control, transaction isolation ends with update propagation from the transaction-private update buffer to the shared database or its buffer pool. For completely correct ACID transaction properties, however, concurrency control must also cover the hardening phase, i.e., writing a transaction's commit log record to the recovery log on stable storage. In optimistic concurrency control with backward validation, this might occur accidentally, because locks are retained for transactions validating and committing later; this is probably the reason why the issue is not prominent. In optimistic concurrency control with forward validation or with timestamp validation, premature publication during hardening is a small but real danger. The discussion below contains examples.

The danger of premature publication not only enforces the need for concurrent validation but also strengthens the suggestion of using a lock manager during commit processing. Fortunately, using a lock manager as an implementation mechanism also permits transferring a locking optimization to optimistic concurrency control. Controlled lock violation reliably prevents premature publication but restricts concurrency only when truly required.

8.4.1   THE DANGER OF PREMATURE PUBLICATION

Users reasonably and rightfully expect that rows and column values in a query result are indeed present in a database. In some circumstances, usually unpredictable for users, this might not be the case. For example, if one transaction modifies a value and then the database software crashes before the update transaction can truly commit its updates, then the restart logic will restore the value prior to the update. If, however, another transaction retrieves this value just before the crash and presents it to a user, then the user sees a value never truly in the database.

If that case is not bad enough, consider a user who stores the retrieved value in another database. Alternatively, consider a single transaction that copies a value from one database to another. Surely a user may expect that after such a transaction commits successfully, the values in the two databases are the same. It turns out that transaction execution optimized with early lock release cannot guarantee this expectation.

Figure 8.9, copied from Graefe et al. [2013], illustrates a scenario in which early lock release permits premature publication of a transaction's update and thereupon incorrect database contents. The two horizontal arrows represent two nodes in a cluster and their actions over time. In database 1, the blue transaction updates a database item and then applies early lock release. Meanwhile, database 2 coordinates a distributed transaction that copies a value from database 1 to database 2. The read-only participant transaction on database 1 can read the recent update due to early lock release, whereupon database 2 writes the value into database 2 and then starts commit processing. Database 1 votes to commit and, as a read-only participant, elects to opt out of the second phase of the two-phase commit [Mohan et al., 1986]. When database 1 suffers a software crash, the commit log record of the blue update transaction is lost. Nonetheless, the distributed transaction commits on database 2. When database 1 restarts and runs its recovery logic, the blue transaction, lacking a commit log record in the persistent recovery log, rolls back. Database 2 now contains a value that does not exist in database 1, so it certainly is not a correct copy. In contrast to early lock release, controlled lock violation delays the vote to commit the distributed transaction until the blue transaction is durable with its commit log record on stable storage.

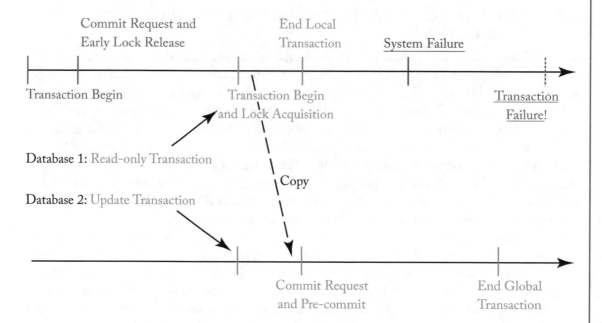

Figure 8.9: Incorrect database contents due to early lock release.

Figure 8.10 illustrates an implementation of optimistic concurrency control halfway between the solid design shown in Figure 8.1 and the incorrect design of Figure 8.2. Unfortunately, even this design permits premature publication, just like early lock release. Note, however, that the safe and correct design of Figure 8.1 permits commit processing of only one transaction at a time; the next transaction cannot start its commit logic until the prior one has hardened its commit log record in the recovery log on stable storage. What is needed is optimistic concurrency control as correct as the design of Figure 8.1 yet with concurrent validation as well as read and write access to new updates during a transaction's hardening phase.

Read Phase	Validation Phase	Write Phase	Log hardening	Buffer pool flush	Read- and write-set retention
= transaction application logic	= conflict detention	= update propagation			
No concurrency control	Critical section		No concurrency control	After transaction end	

Figure 8.10: Transaction phases in a seemingly good implementation.

8.4.2 OPTIMISTIC TRANSACTIONS WITHOUT PREMATURE PUBLICATION

If a traditional lock manager serves as implementation mechanism for concurrent end-of-transaction validation in optimistic concurrency control, an extension can eliminate the danger of premature publication. The most obvious design simply retains all locks at least until a transaction's commit log record is in the recovery log on stable storage. In fact, this is the traditional lock retention policy in pessimistic concurrency control. In contrast, in most implementations of optimistic transactions, concurrency control ends either after validation or after update propagation from the transaction-private update buffer to the shared database buffer pool. In fact, it is quite possible that much of the perceived advantage in performance and concurrency of optimistic over pessimistic concurrency control is due to this difference: longer lock retention means more concurrency conflicts and thus lower transaction throughput.

Nonetheless, this most obvious design is safe and the benchmark for correctness. It does, however, retain and enforce locks more rigorously than truly required. For pessimistic concurrency control, two related designs are early lock release [DeWitt et al., 1984] and controlled lock violation [Graefe et al., 2013]. Early lock release can suffer from premature publication, whereas controlled lock violation reliably prevents it. The difference is that early lock release, like traditional optimistic concurrency control, terminates concurrency control as soon as a transaction's commit log record has a place (a log sequence number) within the recovery log, i.e., long before the commit log record is on stable storage; whereas controlled lock violation retains all locks until a transaction's commit log record is on stable storage, but it permits concurrent and subsequent transactions to violate these locks. Upon violation of such a lock, the violating transaction must not commit until the violated lock is indeed released, i.e., its transaction completely logged and durable. If the violating transaction is a read-write transaction, this requirement is satisfied due to the violating transaction's own commit log record. If the violating transaction is a read-only transaction, e.g., a read-only participant in a distributed read-write transaction (see Figure 8.9), the commit logic might indeed need to wait. The waiting period takes no longer than writing the violated transaction's commit log record to stable storage.

Figure 8.11 illustrates how to combine concurrent end-of-transaction validation using a lock manager (as recommended in Section 8.3) with reliable prevention of premature publication (using controlled lock violation). This combination of techniques applies to all three forms of end-of-transaction validation. Transactions using timestamp validation or using forward validation of read- and write-sets release their locks after the commit log record is in the recovery log on stable storage. In contrast, transactions using backward validation retain their locks (representing each transaction's read- and write-sets) until all concurrent transactions have completed their own validation phase.

Read Phase	Validation Phase	Write Phase		Buffer pool flush	Read- and write-set retention
= transaction application logic	= conflict detention	= update propagation	Log hardening		
No concurrency control	Lock acquisition		Controlled lock violation	After transaction end	

Figure 8.11: Safe and concurrent end-of-transaction validation.

It might be unclear how controlled lock violation interacts with backward validation and its requirement to retain all locks (or all read- and write-sets) until the last concurrent transaction has finished validation. The answer is pretty simple: only those transactions may violate a lock that started their read phase after the lock-holding transaction has finished its validation phase. A violating transaction that started its read phase earlier will fail its validation in any case so there is no advantage to granting a violating lock. If the proportions of Figure 8.6 are approximately right, however, there can be many transactions that can take advantage of controlled lock violation. Of course, once the committing transaction has its commit log record safe on stable storage, controlled lock violation no longer plays any role, because there no longer is any danger of premature publication.

8.4.3   SUMMARY OF PREMATURE PUBLICATION

In summary, premature publication is a danger in optimistic concurrency control just as much as in pessimistic concurrency control. Once a commit log record has been placed in the recovery log within the log buffer, transaction isolation no longer requires concurrency control, but the danger of premature publication persists until the commit log record is safe on stable storage. With today's in-memory transaction execution exploiting in-memory databases or very large buffer pools, most transactions require more time for hardening than for execution of the application logic. Thus, the danger of premature publication has grown over time.

If a shared data structure similar to a lock manager's hash table is used for concurrent validation, as suggested in Section 8.3, then it is a small step to include the protection against premature publication invented for pessimistic concurrency control, namely controlled lock violation. Commit processing continues and locks remain in the lock manager until a transaction is completely hardened, but the transaction state indicates that other transactions may read and even overwrite uncommitted updates in the buffer pool but incur a commit dependency. If the violating transaction needs to write a local commit log record, the commit dependency is necessarily satisfied. Only if the violating transaction is a read-only transaction (not in snapshot isolation), the commit dependency may impose a small delay on that transaction's commit. This delay is no longer than the commit delay that a read-write transaction incurs for writing its commit log records to the recovery on stable storage. With recovery logging on non-volatile memory, this imposed delay is very small indeed, yet premature publication is reliably prevented in all cases.

8.5 DISTRIBUTED TRANSACTIONS

In most database systems, each distributed transaction runs as a set of local participant transactions whose commit decision is centralized in a coordinator. The coordinator is often the same thread that executes the transaction's scripting logic and communicates with the application outside the database system.

Until commit processing, local participant transactions may run in optimistic concurrency control. During the commit protocol, however, they must provide the same guarantees as local participants using pessimistic concurrency control. In other words, they must either vote to abort or, if they vote to commit, they must reliably promise to implement the centralized commit decision.

8.5.1 TWO-PHASE COMMIT

This promise is impossible with pure optimistic concurrency control. Instead, it requires lock acquisition before voting, i.e., during the first phase of a two-phase commit. Once a local participant transaction has acquired shared and exclusive locks equivalent to the transaction's read- and write-sets or to its set of timestamps, the local participant transaction no longer is an optimistic transaction; instead, it has become indistinguishable from a local participant transaction with traditional pessimistic lock acquisition during the transaction's read phase. For example, it does not matter whether the transaction's updates are in a transaction-private update buffer or in the database, as long as there are appropriate "redo" or "undo" log records that permit the local participant transaction to abort or to commit.

Importantly, even a local participant transaction that started as optimistic transaction can benefit from controlled lock violation. The traditional design requires that such a transaction retain its locks until two-phase commit is complete including hardening of the final commit log record on stable storage. Controlled lock violation does not modify the retention period of locks but it enables other transactions to read and even to overwrite database items in the optimistic transaction's read- and write-sets [Graefe et al., 2013].

Figure 8.12, copied from Graefe et al. [2013], illustrates the two levels of controlled lock violation. Traditional locking retains all locks until the transaction is complete, shown with the blue line. Controlled lock violation only during the second phase of a two-phase commit is shown with the green line. The line indicates the period of traditional strong enforcement of locks; lock retention is unchanged from the blue line. Controlled lock violation immediately after the commit request is shown with the red line. Another transaction may violate this transaction's locks during the first phase already but it incurs a commit dependency. In other words, if the distributed transaction aborts (e.g., due to another participants failure), then the violating transaction must also abort. If another transaction violates this transaction's locks during the second phase, it merely incurs a completion dependency. In other words, the other transaction must not commit until the distributed transaction is durable with its final commit log record in the recovery log on stable storage.

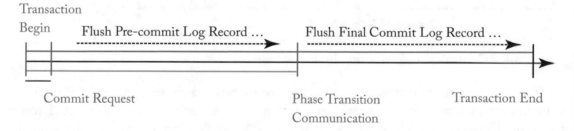

Figure 8.12: Controlled lock violation during two-phase commit.

8.5.2 THREE-PHASE COMMIT AND CONTROLLED LOCK VIOLATION

While the original introduction of controlled lock violation [Graefe et al., 2013] covered distributed transactions and two-phase commit, it did not cover non-blocking three-phase commit protocols. Fortunately, the essence of three-phase commit is an additional state and an additional round of communication between coordinator and local participant transactions. During this additional delay, other transactions can benefit from controlled lock violation. They incur completion dependencies for read-write conflicts and commit dependencies for write-read conflicts. This mirrors controlled violation of locks held by single-site transactions and by distributed transactions coordinated with two-phase commit. Write-write conflicts imply write-read conflicts, just as an exclusive lock implies permission to read the initial or modified value of the locked database object.

Figure 8.13 illustrates the effect of controlled lock violation in the context of a non-blocking three-phase commit. While the traditional lock retention and enforcement policy suffers from the additional round of communication and logging compared to two-phase commit, controlled lock violation permits other transactions to violate a committing transaction's lock immediately after the commit request from user or application. In other words, locks are enforced in the traditional strict way only until the commit request; immediately thereafter, other transactions can read and even update new database contents. Their only penalty for lock violation is a commit dependency: if the distributed transaction and its updates fail to commit, the violating transaction must also abort; moreover, the violating transaction cannot commit until the final commit decision for the distributed transaction is known. Note that the final commit decision is known after two rounds of logging and communication, just as in the traditional two-phase commit.

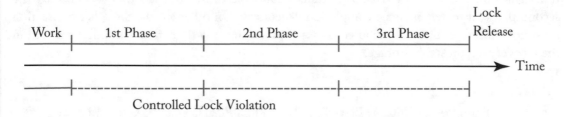

Figure 8.13: Controlled lock violation in three-phase commit.

In the past, three-phase commit has been considered expensive in multiple ways: more communication, more logging, more latency, and more concurrency control "footprint." Recent hardware advances, e.g., RDMA networking and non-volatile memory, may remedy communication, logging, and the user-visible latency they imply. Controlled lock violation used in the same way as in the context of two-phase commit may remedy the concerns about the concurrency control footprint of three-phase commit. This remedy applies equally whether the local participant transaction initially runs with optimistic or pessimistic concurrency control, and whether the local optimistic concurrency control compares read- and write-sets or timestamps.

8.5.3   SUMMARY OF DISTRIBUTED TRANSACTIONS

In summary of distributed transactions, communication for commit coordination and logging a local transaction's state transitions imply delays. During these delays, all local participant transactions must guarantee that they can implement the coordinator's global commit decision, i.e., they will be able to commit or to abort as directed. Even if a local participant transaction executes its local participant transaction in optimistic concurrency control, ensuring this guarantee requires reserved resources, i.e., locks on database contents affected by the global commit decision. Traditional database locks in a traditional lock manager are ideal to enable these guarantees. Controlled lock violation removes most of the ill effects of local participant transactions retaining their locks while waiting for a commit decision, not only during a traditional two-phase commit but also during a non-blocking three-phase commit.

8.6   CONCLUSIONS

In summary of the three preceding sections, traditional optimistic concurrency control can be improved by using a lock manager as an implementation mechanism for commit processing. This applies both to single-site transactions and to distributed transactions using two- and three-phase commit. In fact, lock acquisition during end-of-transaction validation permits transferring recent advances from pessimistic to optimistic concurrency control, in particular controlled lock violation. As in pessimistic concurrency control, controlled lock violation in optimistic concurrency control guarantees correct transaction completion and transaction isolation but also enables maximal concurrency during transaction hardening and during distributed commit coordination.

In conclusion, optimistic concurrency control and pessimistic concurrency control are in many ways more similar than different. Reliably correct implementation of ACID transaction semantics and maximal concurrency can be achieved by transferring ideas and techniques from one to the other. For example, deferred lock acquisition [Graefe, 2019a] transfers the advantages of transaction-private update buffers from optimistic to pessimistic concurrency control and in that way complements the present work.

8.7   REFERENCES

DeWitt, D. J., Katz, R. H., Olken, F., Shapiro, L. D., Stonebraker, M., and Wood, D. A. (1984). Implementation techniques for main memory database systems. *ACM SIGMOD*, pages 1–8. DOI: 10.1145/602260.602261. 282, 294

Diaconu, C., Freedman, C., Ismert, E., Larson, P., Mittal, P., Stonecipher, R., Verma, N., and Zwilling, M. (2013). Hekaton: SQL Server's memory-optimized OLTP engine. *ACM SIGMOD*, pages 1243–1254. DOI: 10.1145/2463676.2463710. 287

Graefe, G. (2007). Hierarchical locking in B-tree indexes. *BTW Conference*, pages 18–42 (Chapter 1). 282

Graefe, G. (2019a). Deferred lock enforcement (Chapter 11). 282, 290, 299

Graefe, G. (2019b). Avoiding index-navigation deadlocks (Chapter 9). 282

Graefe, G. (2019c). A problem in two-phase commit (Chapter 10). 284

Graefe, G., Lillibridge, M., Kuno, H. A., Tucek, J., and Veitch, A. C. (2013). Controlled lock violation. *ACM SIGMOD*, pages 85–96 (Chapter 4). DOI: 10.1145/2463676.2465325. 282, 285, 293, 294, 297

Graefe, G., Volos, H., Kimura, H., Kuno, H. A., Tucek, J., Lillibridge, M., and Veitch, A. C. (2014). In-memory performance for big data. *PVLDB*, 8(1), pages 37–48. DOI: 10.14778/2735461.2735465. 289

Gray, J., Lorie, R. A., Putzolu, G. R., and Traiger, I. L. (1976). Granularity of locks and degrees of consistency in a shared data base. *IFIP Working Conference on Modelling in Data Base Management Systems*, pages 365–394. 282

Härder, T. (1984). Observations on optimistic concurrency control schemes. *Information Systems*, 9(2), pages 111–120. DOI: 10.1016/0306-4379(84)90020-6. 279, 282

Jung, H., Han, H., Fekete, A. D., Heiser, G., and Yeom, H. Y. (2014). A scalable lock manager for multicores. *ACM TODS*, pages 29:1–29:29. DOI: 10.1145/2691190.2691192. 283

Korth, H. F. (1983). Locking primitives in a database system. *Journal of the ACM*, 30(1), pages 55–79. DOI: 10.1145/322358.322363. 282

Kung, H. T. and Robinson, J. T. (1981). On optimistic methods for concurrency control. *ACM TODS*, 6(2), pages 221–226. DOI: 10.1145/319566.319567. 279, 280, 281, 288

Lomet, D. B. (1993). Key range locking strategies for improved concurrency. *VLDB*, pages 655–664. 282

Mohan, C., Lindsay, B. G., and Obermarck, R. (1986). Transaction management in the R* distributed database management system. *ACM TODS*, 11(4), pages 378–396. DOI: 10.1145/7239.7266. 284, 293

Skeen, D. (1981). Nonblocking commit protocols. *ACM SIGMOD*, pages 133–142. DOI: 10.1145/582338.582339. 284

SQLite. (2004). File locking and concurrency in SQLite version 3. `http://sqlite.org/loc kingv3.html` 282

Thomasian, A. (1998). Performance analysis of locking methods with limited wait depth. *Performance Evaluation*, 34(2), pages 69–89. DOI: 10.1016/s0166-5316(98)00025-x. 284

PART III

Locking

CHAPTER 9

Avoiding Index-Navigation Deadlocks

Lock acquisition sequences in queries and updates

Goetz Graefe

ABSTRACT

Query execution plans in relational databases often search a secondary index and then fetch data from a table's primary storage structure. In contrast, database updates usually modify first a table's primary storage structure and then all affected secondary indexes. Deadlocks are likely if queries acquire locks first in the secondary index and then in the primary storage structure while updates acquire locks first in the primary storage structure and then in secondary indexes. In fact, some test teams use this scenario as a reliable means to create deadlocks in order to test deadlock resolution code. Some development teams have known of the problem for over 20 years but so far have failed to solve it, instead recommending that customers and application developers accept a weaker transaction isolation level and thus weaker correctness guarantees. A new technique uses the traditional, opposing navigation directions in queries and updates but the same locking sequence in both queries and updates. This design retains the efficiency of both queries and updates but avoids deadlocks caused by the traditional, opposing locking sequences.

9.1 INTRODUCTION

Even if only few deadlocks occur in most database applications, they lower system throughput and, perhaps more importantly, they reduce predictability of transaction durations and thus robustness of performance. If a traditional rule-of-thumb holds that only 1% of all transactions roll back, most of those due to deadlocks, this can still exceed 1,000 deadlocks and rollbacks per second in a high-performance server. Avoiding many or even most of these deadlocks and rollbacks seems a worthwhile goal if moderate effort and complexity can accomplish it.

Many deadlocks occur due to opposite navigation sequences in queries and updates. Queries usually search secondary indexes first and then fetch additional columns in a table's primary storage structure. Updates, on the other hand, usually modify a table's primary storage structure first and then adjust all affected secondary indexes. Updates here include insertions and deletions.

Updates retain their exclusive locks until end-of-transaction in order to enable transaction rollback without cascading aborts. Queries and searches retain their shared locks depending on the transaction isolation level. In "repeatable read" and "repeatable count" (serializable) transaction isolation, transactions retain their read locks until end-of-transaction. In "read committed" transaction isolation, scans release read locks when moving to the next record. This can have numerous surprising effects. For example, a query might retrieve a row identifier from a secondary index but fail to fetch the row because another transaction has deleted it in the meantime. For another example, a row may no longer satisfy the query predicate when fetched due to an update by another transaction.

These problems are particularly likely in sophisticated query execution plans. For example, intersecting multiple secondary indexes of the same table introduces a delay between index retrieval and final fetch operation, thus increasing the probability of an intervening update. One remedy runs each individual query execution plan in repeatable-read or serializable isolation, i.e., with shared locks held until end-of-statement, even if the overall transaction runs in weaker transaction isolation. Holding a shared lock until end-of-statement is sufficiently long, however, to participate in a deadlock.

If updates navigate from primary storage structure to secondary indexes and acquire locks in this sequence, and if queries navigate from secondary indexes to the primary storage structure and acquire locks in this opposite sequence, then deadlocks can occur whenever queries and updates access the same rows in a database table. In fact, this is one of the few cases when deadlocks occur predictably and, among all deadlocks, relatively frequently. Thus, it seems worthwhile to address this case with a specific and reliable solution. One product team's suggestion, which essentially recommends accepting a lower transaction isolation level and thus a weakened correctness criterion for concurrent transactions, seems like an escape from the problem rather than a solution.

A locking technique that avoids this problem altogether is ARIES/IM [Mohan and Levine, 1992]. While ARIES/KVL (key-value locking) [Mohan, 1990] and key-range locking [Lomet, 1993] acquire locks in each index or B-tree, ARIES/IM ("index management") locks logical rows of a table. A single lock covers a record in the table's primary storage structure, an entry in each secondary index, and (for phantom protection and thus serializability) the gap to the preceding index entry (in each index). ARIES/IM can have surprising effects on concurrency, however. For example, a search in an index on column A locks an entire logical row and thus a seemingly random key range (an index entry and an adjacent gap between index entries) in the index on column B and in the index on column C. This is true even if the search on column A actually produces an empty result. Perhaps less surprising than this behavior, these interactions have contributed to giving both locking and serializability a reputation for low concurrency.

What seems needed is a locking regimen with more precision. In orthogonal key-value locking [Graefe and Kimura, 2015], a lock pertains to a distinct key value within a single index. A lock may cover a distinct key value (including all actual and possible instances), a hash partition of all such instances, a gap between actual distinct key values, a hash partition of possible values within such a gap, or any combination thereof. These lock granularities match accurately the requirements of updates including insertions and deletions via ghost records (pseudo-deleted records in ARIES) as well as the requirements of equality and range queries with and without results. Lock modes include shared and exclusive locks but may also include increment locks (for materialized "group by" views and their indexes) or intention locks (for hierarchical locking).

Even if orthogonal key-value locking solves the problem of excessive lock scopes, it does not solve the problem of opposite lock acquisition sequences in updates and queries and thus the problem of deadlocks. This is the issue addressed here using a simple but novel scheme for deadlock avoidance. The new solution is easy to understand and to implement but it has not been proposed in the past, despite being desirable for decades. The likely reason is that traditional locking methods and their published descriptions require locks not only on affected index entries or key values but also on their neighbors.

Traditional concurrency control locks not only index entries or keys affected by updates but also their neighboring index entries or keys. Locking neighbors forestalls the new solution. Thus, a solution to the problem has been desirable but missing for over 20 years. The crucial enablers of the new solution are ghost records used not only for deletions but also for insertions, as recommended for orthogonal key-value locking. If ghost records are used consistently with the traditional locking methods, then the new solution works in those contexts, too.

The new technique for deadlock avoidance specifically addresses the opposing navigation and lock acquisition sequences in queries and updates. It does not address all deadlocks in a database system and thus cannot replace deadlock detection or an approximation by timeouts on lock requests. Nonetheless, if it avoids a common source of deadlocks, it not only increases system performance but also the robustness of system performance. System performance can often be improved by more, newer, or better hardware, but robustness of performance requires software techniques such as those introduced here.

The remainder of this chapter proceeds as follows. The next section reviews related work. The following section introduces the new lock acquisition sequence for insertions, updates, and deletions. The final section concludes with a summary and an outlook on future work.

9.2   RELATED PRIOR WORK

For B-tree indexes in databases, we assume the standard design with user contents only in the leaf nodes. Therefore, all designs for key-value locking and key-range locking apply to key values in the leaf nodes only.

In this chapter, the term "bookmark" means row identifier or record identifier in a table's primary storage structure. For example, if the table's primary data structure is a heap file, a bookmark may be a triple of device, page, and slot numbers. If the table's primary storage structure is an index such as B-tree, a bookmark may be a unique search key in the primary index. Such primary B-tree indexes are known as a primary index in Tandem's (eventually HP's) NonStop SQL, as a clustered index in Microsoft's SQL Server, and as an index-organized table in Oracle.

9.2.1   GHOST RECORDS AND SYSTEM TRANSACTIONS

By default, locks are possible on all key values in an index, including those marked as ghost records, also known as invalid or pseudo-deleted records. Ghost records are usually marked by a bit in the record header. For non-unique secondary indexes with a list of bookmarks attached to each distinct key value, a ghost record is a distinct key value with an empty list or one in which all remaining entries are themselves ghosts.

The initial purpose and application of ghost records was guaranteed rollback of deletions. After a user transaction erases a record from a page, e.g., a B-tree leaf, another transaction may insert a new record; but when the deletion transaction attempts to roll back, it might force a leaf split or other allocation action that might fail. Failing a transaction rollback is, of course, an anathema to reliable transactional database management. The commonly adopted solution splits a deletion in two: the user transaction merely marks a record logically deleted such that rollback merely needs to mark it valid again, and if the user transaction commits, an asynchronous clean-up operation erases the record. For example, any subsequent insertion may invoke removal of any unlocked ghost record.

Record removal is a transaction in its own right, called a system transaction, also known as a top-level action in ARIES. System transactions are very inexpensive because they run in the same thread as the invoking user transaction, a single log record can describe the entire transaction, transaction commit does not require forcing log records to stable storage, and system transactions never acquire locks since they do not modify logical contents. System transactions may, however, inspect the lock manager, e.g., to avoid erasing a ghost record locked by a user transaction.

System transactions may affect physical database representation but not logical database contents. Thus, node splits and other structural modifications in B-trees can run as system transactions that commit ahead of the invoking user transaction. In fact, all space management tasks should be delegated to system transactions: allocation of a new record in preparation of a user transaction's logical insertion, growing a record in preparation of a user transaction's update of a variable-size column to a larger value, shrinking a record after a user transaction's update to a smaller value, free space compaction within a page, and all other clean-up tasks. For example, insertion transactions and reorganization utilities invoke system transactions for space reclamation.

9.2.2   ARIES/KVL "Key-Value Locking"

ARIES/KVL [Mohan, 1990] locks distinct key values, even in non-unique indexes. A lock in a secondary index covers all bookmarks associated with a key value as well as the gap (open interval) to the next lower distinct key value present in the index. A lock within a secondary index does not protect any data in another storage structure.

Figure 9.1, copied verbatim from Mohan [1990], enumerates the cases and conditions required for a correct implementation of ARIES/KVL. At the same time, it illustrates the complexity of the scheme. Note that IX locks are used for insertions into an existing list of bookmarks, which permits other insertions (also with IX locks) but neither queries nor deletions. In other words, ARIES/KVL is asymmetric as it supports concurrent insertions into a list of bookmarks but not concurrent deletions. Note also the use of locks with instant duration, in violation of traditional two-phase locking. This exemplifies how, from the beginning of record-level locking in B-tree indexes, there has been some creative use of lock modes that ignores the traditional theory of concurrency control but enables higher concurrency without actually permitting wrong database contents or wrong query results. Nonetheless, it substantially expands cost, complexity, and duration of quality assurance and thus of each software release.

Figure 9.1 gives guidance for insertions and deletions but not for updates. A value change in an index key must run as deletion and insertion, which Figure 9.1 cover, but an update of a non-key field in an index record may occur in place. Non-key updates were perhaps not considered at the time; in today's systems, non-key updates may apply to columns appended to each index record using, for example, a "create index" statement with an "include" clause, in order to "cover" more queries with "index-only retrieval." More importantly, toggling a record's "ghost" flag is a non-key update, i.e., logical deletion and re-insertion of an index entry.

Clearly, re-insertion by toggling a previously deleted key value requires more than an IX lock; otherwise, multiple transactions, at the same time and without noticing their conflict, may turn a ghost into a valid record. Thus, we conclude that the 1990 design of ARIES/KVL did not yet employ or exploit ghost records or system transactions (called pseudo-deleted records and top-level actions in later ARIES publications).

Due to locking separately in each index, ARIES/KVL suffers opposite locking sequences in queries and updates. Moreover, it prevents a pragmatic solution by requiring locks on the modified key's neighbor.

9.2.3   ARIES/IM "Index Management"

ARIES/IM [Mohan and Levine, 1992] locks logical rows in a table, represented by records in the table's primary storage structure, typically a heap file. With no locks in secondary indexes, its alternative name is "data-only locking." A single lock covers a record in a heap file and a corresponding entry in each secondary index, plus (in each index) the gap (open interval) to the next lower index entry. Compared to ARIES/KVL, this design reduces the number of locks in update transactions. For example, deleting a row in a table requires only a single lock, indepen-

Fetch and Fetch Next		Next Key Value	Current Key Value
			S for Commit Duration
Insert	Unique index	IX for instant duration	IX for commit duration if next key value *not* previously locked in S, X, or SIX mode X for commit duration if next key value previously locked in S, X, or SIX mode
Insert	Non-unique index	IX for instant duration if *apparently* insert key value *doesn't* already exist No lock if insert key value already exists	IX for commit duration if (1) next key not locked during this call OR (2) next key locked now but next key *not* previously locked in S, X, or SIX mode X for commit duration if next key locked now and it had already been locked in S, X, or SIX mode
Delete	Unique index	X for commit duration	X for instant duration
Delete	Non-unique index	X for commit duration if *apparently* delete key value will no longer exist No lock if value will definitely continue to exist	X for instant duration if delete key value will *not* definitely exist after the delete X for commit duration if delete key value *may* or will still exist after the delete

Figure 9.1: Summary of locking in ARIES/KVL.

dent of the number of indexes for the table.[1] The same applies when updating a single row, with some special cases if the update modifies an index key, i.e., the update requires deletion and insertion of index entries with different key values.

Figure 9.2, copied verbatim from Mohan and Levine [1992], compares favorably in size and complexity with Figure 9.1, due to fewer cases, conditions, and locks. The rules for index-specific locking apply to the table's primary data structure. Insertion and deletion always require an instant-duration lock and a commit-duration lock on the current or next record.

---

[1]This is true only if ghost records are employed. Figure 9.2 shows the original design of ARIES/IM without ghost records, i.e., immediate removal of each record and index entry, which requires a commit-duration exclusive lock on a neighboring index entry.

	Next Key	Current Key
Fetch and Fetch Next		**S for Commit Duration**
Insert	X for instant duration	X for commit duration if index-specific locking is used
Delete	X for commit duration	X for instant duration if index-specific locking is used

Figure 9.2: Summary of locking in ARIES/IM.

ARIES/IM, by virtue of locking logical rows including all index entries, does not exhibit the problem of opposite locking sequences in queries and updates. It does, however, exhibit another severe problem in transactions with serializable isolation. When providing phantom protection by locking a gap between index entries in one secondary index, ARIES/IM locks the index entry at the high end of that gap by locking the logical row to which the index entry belongs. This lock freezes not only the gap but also the index entry itself as well as an index entry in each further secondary index on the same table plus a gap in each index. For example, a query predicate on column A with no satisfying rows needs to lock a gap in the index on A but also locks gaps and index entries in indexes on column B, on column C, etc. This certainly is a surprising and counter-intuitive effect of a query with a predicate on A. Index-specific ARIES/IM eliminates this surprise but it suffers from more locks and lock manager invocations and from the problem of opposite locking sequences in queries and updates. Finally, both forms of ARIES/IM prevent a pragmatic solution by requiring locks not only on the current key but also on a neighboring key, as indicated in Figure 9.2.

9.2.4 ORTHOGONAL KEY-VALUE LOCKING

Orthogonal key-value locking [Graefe and Kimura, 2015] aims to remedy some of the shortcomings of ARIES key-value locking. While both techniques focus on existing distinct key values, there are significant differences between the designs.

First, the gap (open interval) between two distinct key values has a lock mode separate from (and entirely orthogonal to) the concurrency control for the key value and its set of instances. Thus, phantom protection does not need to lock any existing index entries. Instead, it merely requires that a locked key value continue to exist in the index. While one transaction uses a key value for phantom protection, another transaction may lock the key value itself and turn it into a ghost entry. Subsequent transactions may use the ghost for phantom protection and may turn the ghost into a valid index entry again.

Second, the set of all possible instances of a key value (e.g., the domain of bookmarks) is hash-partitioned and each partition can have its own lock mode. The concurrency desired in a system determines the recommended number of partitions. An equality query may lock all partitions at once but an insertion, update, or deletion may lock just one partition such that other insertions, updates, and deletions may concurrently modify other rows with the same key value but a different bookmark. More precisely, a concurrent transaction may update or delete a row with a different hash value and thus belonging to a different partition. Each individual bookmark has its own ghost bit such that two deletions may indeed proceed concurrently and commit (or roll back) independently.

Third, the set of all possible key values in a gap is hash-partitioned and each partition can have its own lock mode. An equality query with an empty result locks merely a single partition within a gap, thus achieving "repeatable count" transaction isolation (serializability) yet permitting other transactions to insert into the same gap. Range queries may lock all partitions within a gap. With this recent refinement not included in earlier descriptions [Graefe and Kimura, 2015], orthogonal key-value locking can lock none, some, or all bookmarks associated with an existing key value plus none, some, or all non-existing key values in a gap between neighboring existing key values.

Figure 9.3 summarizes the lock scopes that orthogonal key-value locking supports for key value Jerry in a non-unique secondary index sorted on first names and on bookmarks. Orthogonal key-value locking also supports any combination of lock scopes. For example, a serializable transaction with predicate "FirstName in ('Harry,' 'Harold')" may lock two partitions within the same gap between Gary and Jerry. For another example, a range query can, with a single invocation of the lock manager, lock a distinct key value and its adjacent gap. In ARIES/KVL, this is the only available granularity of locking, as shown in the last line of Figure 9.3.

Index Entries and Gaps	Entry (Gary, 1)	Gap			Entry (Jerry, 3)	Gap	Entry (Jerry, 6)	Gap			Entry (Mary, 5)
		Gary, >1	>Gary, <Jerry	Jerry, <3				(Jerry, >6)	>Jerry, <Mary	(Mary, <5)	
An entire key value				█	█	█	█	█			
A partition thereof					█						
						█					
An entire gap										█	
A partition thereof		‖	‖	‖						█	
Maximal combination				█	█	█	█	█	█	█	
ARIES/KVL			█	█	█	█	█	█			

Figure 9.3: Lock scopes supported in orthogonal key-value locking.

Further differences include system transactions inserting new key values as ghost records as well as system transactions creating and removing ghost space within records. System transactions perform all allocation and de-allocation operations in short critical sections with inexpensive transaction invocation (no separate software thread), inexpensive logging (a single log record for the entire transaction), and inexpensive transaction commit (no log flush on commit). User transactions merely modify pre-allocated space, including the ghost space and the ghost bit within an index entry. This greatly simplifies logging and rollback of user transactions as well as free space management within each database page.

9.2.5   A BRIEF COMPARISON OF LOCKING TECHNIQUES

The following diagrams compare ARIES/KVL, ARIES/IM, KRL, orthogonal key-range locking, and orthogonal key-value locking. Specifically, they compare the lock scopes for phantom protection, for an equality query with multiple result rows, and for a single-row update. Assuming insertion and deletion via ghost records, the lock scope of an insertion or a deletion equals that of a non-key update.

ARIES/KVL [Mohan, 1990] locks an existing distinct key value in a secondary index, including all existing and non-existing instances of the key value plus the gap to the next-lower existing key value. ARIES/IM [Mohan and Levine, 1992] locks a logical row including all its index entries and, in each index, the gap to the next-lower index entry. Key-range locking in Microsoft SQL Server [Lomet, 1993] locks one index entry in one index plus its preceding gap, with some separation between the lock mode for the index entry and lock mode for the gap. Orthogonal key-range locking permits two lock modes with each lock request, one for an index entry and one for the gap to the next-higher index entry. Lock scopes of orthogonal key-value locking are summarized in Figure 9.3.

Figure 9.4 illustrates required and actual lock scopes for the example of a query for a non-existing FirstName value, i.e., lock scopes for phantom protection. The column headings indicate ranges in the domain of the index keys. An S in Figure 9.4 indicates a transaction-duration shared lock to prevent insertion of index value Harry. It is clear that ARIES/KVL locks the largest scope. ARIES/IM appears equal to key-range locking only because Figure 9.4 does not show the lock scope in the other indexes of this table. Orthogonal key-range locking locks less due to separate lock modes on index entry and gap. Orthogonal key-value locking locks the smallest scope. Without partitioning within the gap, its lock scope matches precisely the locking requirement indicated in the header. Partitioning each gap between distinct key values is useful with this example query and further reduces the lock scope. By partitioning the non-existing key values within the gap between existing key values, the lock scope of phantom protection is as narrow as the FirstName Harry and its hash collisions.

Figure 9.5 shows lock scopes for an equality query with multiple result rows. Key-value locking requires only a single lock whereas the other techniques require multiple locks (one more than matching instances). Due to separation of gap and key value, orthogonal key-value locking

Index Entries and Gaps	Entry (Gary, 1)	Gap			Entry Jerry, 3	Gap	Entry Jerry, 6	Gap	
		(Gary, >1)	(>Gary, <Jerry)	(Jerry, <3)				(Jerry, >6)	(>Jerry)
ARIES/KVL					S				
ARIES/IM			S						
KRL			S						
Orth.krl			S						
Orth.kvl			S						

Figure 9.4: Required and actual lock scopes in phantom protection for "Harry."

Index Entries and Gaps	Entry (Gary, 1)	Gap			Entry (Jerry, 3)	Gap	Entry (Jerry, 6)	(Jerry, >6)	Gap		Entry (Mary, 5)
		Gary, >1	>Gary, <Jerry	Jerry, <3					>Jerry, <Mary	(Mary, >5)	
ARIES/KVL					S						
ARIES/IM			S_1					S_2		S_3		
KRL			S_1					S_2		S_3		
Orth.krl			S_1			S_2				S_3		
Orth.kvl					S						

Figure 9.5: Lock scopes in an equality query for "Jerry."

can lock the instance without locking any adjacent gap. Thus, it is the most precise technique (matching the query) and the most efficient technique (with a single lock manager call).

Figure 9.6 illustrates required and actual lock scopes for a non-key update of a single index entry. ARIES/KVL locks all instances of a distinct key value and ARIES/IM locks an entry and a gap in each index of the table. Key-range locking locks a single entry plus a gap in a single index. Orthogonal key-range locking leaves the gap unlocked and thus locks precisely as much as needed for this update operation. Orthogonal key-value locking locks a partition of index entries, ideally a partition containing only one entry.

Figure 9.6 also illustrates the locking patterns of user transactions inserting and deleting index entries via ghost records. Toggling the ghost bit in a record header is a prototypical non-key index update. Without ghost records, older techniques lock more, in particular an adjacent key value or index entry as shown in Figures 9.1 and 9.2.

Index Entries and Gaps	Entry (Gary, 1)	Gap			Entry Jerry, 3	Gap	Entry Jerry, 6	Gap	
		(Gary, >1)	(>Gary, <Jerry)	(Jerry, <3)				(Jerry, >6)	(>Jerry)
ARIES/KVL					X				
ARIES/IM			X						
KRL			X						
Orth.krl					X				
Orth.kvl					X				

Figure 9.6: Lock scopes in a non-key update for row "3."

9.2.6   SUMMARY OF RELATED PRIOR WORK

In summary, there has been plenty of prior work on locking in database indexes. On the other hand, none of it has specifically addressed the problem of deadlocks among queries and updates due to index-to-index navigation in opposite directions. The only method that reliably prevents the problem of opposite lock acquisition sequences in queries and updates, ARIES/IM, has its own problems, namely counter-intuitive and excessive lock scopes in serializable transaction isolation. Both ARIES/IM and ARIES/KVL prevent a pragmatic solution by requiring locks not only on the current key but also on a neighboring key.

9.3   RECOMMENDED LOCKING SEQUENCES

The way to avoid deadlocks when queries and updates acquire their locks in primary storage structures and in secondary indexes is to let them acquire their locks in the same sequence. Thus, either queries must acquire locks in a table's primary storage structures before locks in secondary indexes or updates must acquire locks in secondary indexes before locks in a table's primary storage structure.

9.3.1   NEW TECHNIQUES

Queries access secondary indexes and primary storage structures in many ways, e.g., using index intersection or index joins. (An index join is a form of index-only retrieval: it combines two or more secondary indexes of the same table by joining them on their common bookmark field—if the columns in the indexes cover the query and its need for column values, scanning two indexes and their short records plus the join can be faster than scanning the primary storage structure with its large records [Graefe et al., 1998].) Given the wide variety of possible query execution plans, it seems unreasonable to modify all of them to invert their sequence of lock acquisitions. Moreover, in the case of intersections or joins of multiple indexes on the same table, no single index scan can reliably determine the set of rows that will require locks in the table's primary storage structure.

Therefore, the proposed new lock acquisition sequence pertains to updates and to index maintenance plans. Before modifying a table's primary storage structure, in fact before lock acquisition within the table's primary storage structure, the new lock acquisition sequence acquires all required locks in all affected secondary indexes, with orthogonal key-value locking recommended. In this design, the update and maintenance operations that actually modify the secondary indexes do not acquire any further locks, e.g., key-range locks or key-value locks.

The sequence of database accesses and of database updates remains unchanged—only the lock acquisition sequence changes. Thus, buffer pool management, log record creation, etc. all remain unchanged. Even lock release remains unchanged: early lock release [DeWitt et al., 1984] or controlled lock violation [Graefe et al., 2013] remain possible and, in fact, recommended.

Key-range locking and key-value locking must not acquire locks on index keys that do not exist. Thus, in most implementations, a thread retains a latch on an index leaf page while requesting a lock on a key value. (Waiting and queuing require special logic for latch release.) In the new regimen, it is not possible to hold a latch on an index page during lock acquisition for index keys. Thus, it might appear at first as if the new technique could attempt to lock non-existing key values. Fortunately, this is not the case. It is sufficient to hold a latch on the appropriate data page in the table's primary storage structure during acquisition of locks in secondary indexes. This latch guarantees that key values in secondary indexes remain valid during lock acquisition.

Deletions present hardly a problem—the deletion logic while accessing the table's primary storage structure can readily obtain all column values required for the secondary indexes and request the correct locks. This includes a bookmark if it is part of a unique entry in a secondary index and thus part of a lock identifier.

The original descriptions of ARIES locking assumed immediate removal of index entries, which required locks on a neighboring key in addition to the key being deleted [Mohan, 1990, Mohan and Levine, 1992]—see Figures 9.1 and 9.2. The update of a table's primary storage structure cannot anticipate neighboring key values in all affected secondary indexes. Thus, their deletion logic does not permit lock acquisition while modifying the table's primary storage structure, i.e., before accessing the appropriate leaf page in all secondary indexes. Later ARIES work recommends logical deletion, i.e., turning a valid record into a pseudo-deleted record and relying on subsequent asynchronous clean-up, e.g., as part of a later insertion attempt. Toggling the ghost (pseudo-deleted) bit in an index entry requires a lock only on the index entry or its key value but not its neighbor. Thus, deletion via ghost status, now the standard way of implementing deletion in database systems, enables the change in the sequence of lock acquisitions.

Insertions present a different problem: the required key values might not exist yet in the affected secondary indexes. In general, locks on non-existing key values seem like a bad idea. For example, Tandem's solution to phantom protection inserts a key value into the lock manager but not the index leaf; anecdotal evidence suggests long and onerous testing and debugging. Here, however, the locked key value will soon exist in the secondary index, created by the insertion transaction acquiring the lock. As soon as a system transaction creates the required new ghost index entry, invoked by the insertion for the secondary index, the system reaches a standard state and the user transaction can turn the locked ghost into a valid index entry.

Updates of non-key index fields, i.e., those that do not affect the placement of the entry within the index, permit the new timing of lock acquisition in secondary indexes. There is no issue with non-existing key values. Updates of key fields require deletion and insertion operations and should be locked as described above.

9.3.2 EXAMPLES

The following examples illustrate some query and update operations.

Figure 9.7 illustrates a query execution plan searching two secondary indexes of the same table, intersecting the obtained sets of bookmarks, and then fetching a few rows from the table's primary index. The primary index here is sorted or keyed on column A, the secondary indexes on columns B and C. Neither scan in a secondary index can reliably predict which records or key values in the primary index need locking. Thus, the recommended lock acquisition sequence is the same as the processing sequence: locks in each secondary index followed by locks in the primary index, but only on those index entries accessed by the query execution plan.

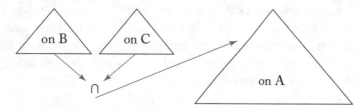

Figure 9.7: Query execution.

Figure 9.8 illustrates an update to an indexed column other than a bookmark column. In the row with primary key 9, column B is modified from 47 to 11. In the table's primary index, this is a non-key update. In the secondary index on column C, no changes and no locks are required. In the secondary index on column B, this update modifies a search key, which requires a deletion and an insertion. If the insertion merely turns an existing ghost record into a valid record, even if a system transaction just created that ghost record on behalf of the user transaction, then the user transaction can predict reliably and precisely all required locks. The traditional lock acquisition sequence follows the update logic from the primary index to the secondary index. The recommended sequence first acquires a latch on the affected page in the primary index, then predicts all required locks in all indexes, acquires locks in the secondary indexes (i.e., for insertion and deletion in the index on B), only then acquires a lock in the primary index, applies updates in the primary index, releases the latch, and finally proceeds to the secondary index.

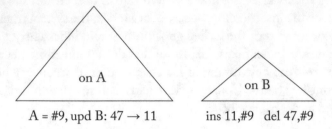

on A

A = #9, upd B: 47 → 11

on B

ins 11,#9   del 47,#9

Figure 9.8: Ordinary update.

Figure 9.9 illustrates an update of a bookmark column A (from value #9 to value #3), which requires a deletion and an insertion in the table's primary index. A change in a row's bookmark requires an update in each secondary index. If a user-defined key for a secondary index is unique, a change in a bookmark is a non-key update in this secondary index. Otherwise, the bookmark is part of the sort key in the index and a change in a bookmark requires a deletion and an insertion in that secondary index. (In the example, there might be another index entry with C = Joe and A between #3 and #9.) Figure 9.9 shows both the unique index on column B and the non-unique index on column C. In all cases, the user transaction can request all required locks before applying its deletions, updates, and insertions in the index storage structures. This is similar to the example of Figure 9.8 but with some differences. The principal difference is that there are two modification actions in the table's primary storage structure, one deletion and one insertion. Among several possible designs, one is to attach all lock acquisitions for deletions to the deletion in the primary index, and similarly for all insertions.

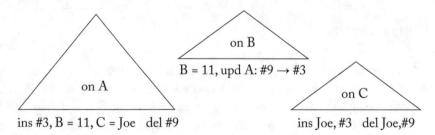

on B

B = 11, upd A: #9 → #3

on A

ins #3, B = 11, C = Joe   del #9

on C

ins Joe, #3   del Joe,#9

Figure 9.9: Bookmark update.

9.3.3   EFFECTS

The principal effect of making updates acquire locks in the same sequence as queries is, of course, that it avoids deadlocks due to opposing lock acquisition sequences. The new technique cannot eliminate all deadlocks, only those due to opposing lock acquisition sequences in queries and updates. Thus, deadlock detection, perhaps by timeouts of lock requests, is still required. With fewer deadlocks, however, a transaction processing system will roll back fewer transactions and achieve more consistent transaction durations.

A negative effect is slightly earlier lock acquisition in secondary indexes and thus slightly longer lock retention. Note, however, that this additional lock retention time is always concurrent to locks on the record or key value in the table's primary storage structure. Thus, the actual reduction of concurrency should be minimal.

With respect to the number of locks and of lock manager invocations, the new method is neutral—it neither adds nor removes any. The same is true for the size or scope of locks. For example, if a traditional update locks an index entry but no adjacent gap, then the new update logic does the same.

9.4   CONCLUSIONS

In summary, deadlocks may affect only 1% of database transactions but that can still mean thousands of deadlocks per second. A common cause of deadlocks is the fact that updates and queries navigate indexes in opposite directions and thus traditionally acquire their locks in opposite sequences. Locking logical rows (as in ARIES/IM) avoids this problem but forces large lock scopes and surprising concurrency limitations. In contrast, locking within each index, e.g., orthogonal key-value locking, permits lock scopes that accurately match successful and empty equality and range queries as well as updates including insertions and deletions via ghost records.

Opposite lock acquisition sequences in queries and updates have caused deadlocks for decades. A solution to the problem has been badly wanted for just as long. Recommending weak transaction isolation levels seems more of an escape than a solution. Traditional techniques that lock neighboring index entries or key values (as indicated in Figures 9.1 and 9.2) cannot lead to a solution because those values are not known until the update execution plan processes the appropriate index leaf pages. The introductions of the two orthogonal locking methods recommend ghost records not only for deletions but also for insertions. With ghost records, a user transaction only locks the index entries or key values affected, never the neighbors, which finally enables a solution.

In the past, the danger of deadlocks between queries and updates has been an argument in favor of index-only retrieval, often enabled by adding non-key columns to secondary indexes. On the other hand, adding non-key columns to secondary indexes undermines database compression. In-memory databases and non-volatile memory render index-only retrieval less relevant with respect to access latency and query performance; the present work renders it less relevant with respect to concurrency control and deadlocks.

The newly introduced simple change in the update logic reliably avoids deadlocks due to opposite lock acquisition sequences. It works for deletions (with guaranteed index entries in all secondary indexes), insertions (with new key values in secondary indexes), and updates (non-key updates as well as updates of index keys). It does not modify the number of locks required in a query or an update; it only modifies the lock acquisition sequence in index maintenance plans. It also does not modify lock retention or enforcement times, e.g., in controlled lock violation. In other words, it promises to avoid deadlocks without any detrimental change in transaction processing efficiency.

Our current work pursues two directions. First, can a further refinement alleviate the slightly longer lock retention times in the new lock acquisition scheme? Second, with orthogonal key-range locking refining the original design for key-range locking and with orthogonal key-value locking refining ARIES/KVL, can orthogonal locking also refine row-level locking, i.e., ARIES/IM? We expect positive answers for both questions.

ACKNOWLEDGEMENTS

Steve Lindell, Mike Zwilling, and Srikumar Rangarajan confirmed the described locking behavior in Microsoft SQL Server including the deadlocks addressed here. Caetano Sauer and Wey Guy helped clarify the problem and its solution. Thanh Do helped tighten the presentation and shorten the chapter.

9.5 REFERENCES

Carey, M. J. and Muhanna, W. A. (1986). The performance of multi-version concurrency control algorithms. *ACM TODS*, 4(4), pages 338–378. DOI: 10.1145/6513.6517.

Chan, A., Fox, S., Lin, W.-T. K., Nori, A., and Ries, D. R. (1982). The implementation of an integrated concurrency control and recovery scheme. *ACM SIGMOD Conference*, pages 184–191. DOI: 10.1145/582383.582386.

DeWitt, D. J., Katz, R. H., Olken, F., Shapiro, L. D., Stonebraker, M., and Wood, D. A. (1984). Implementation techniques for main memory database systems. *ACM SIGMOD Conference*, pages 1–8. DOI: 10.1145/602260.602261. 314

Graefe, G., Bunker, R., and Cooper, S. (1998). Hash joins and hash teams in Microsoft SQL server. *VLDB Conference*, pages 86–97. 313

Graefe, G., Lillibridge, M., Kuno, H. A., Tucek, J., and Veitch, A. C. (2013). Controlled lock violation. *ACM SIGMOD Conference*, pages 85–96 (Chapter 4). DOI: 10.1145/2463676.2465325. 314

Graefe, G. and Kimura, H. (2015). Orthogonal key-value locking. *BTW Conference*, pages 237–256 (Chapter 5). 305, 309, 310

Lomet, D. B. (1993). Key range locking strategies for improved concurrency. *VLDB Conference*, pages 655–664. 304, 311

Mohan, C. (1990). ARIES/KVL: A key-value locking method for concurrency control of multiaction transactions operating on B-tree indexes. *VLDB Conference*, pages 392–405. 304, 307, 311, 314

Mohan, C., Haderle, D. J., Lindsay, B. G., Pirahesh, H., and Schwarz, P. M. (1992). ARIES: A transaction recovery method supporting fine-granularity locking and partial rollbacks using write-ahead logging. *ACM TODS*, 17(1), pages 94–162. DOI: 10.1145/128765.128770.

Mohan, C. and Levine, F. E. (1992). ARIES/IM: An efficient and high-concurrency index management method using write-ahead logging. *ACM SIGMOD Conference*, pages 371–380. DOI: 10.1145/130283.130338. 304, 307, 308, 311, 314

CHAPTER 10

A Problem in Two-Phase Commit

Early lock release vs. controlled lock violation

Goetz Graefe

A common optimization in distributed databases lets read-only sites participate only in the 1st phase of a 2-phase commit. Upon receiving the request to vote from the commit coordinator, read-only sites release all their (read-only) locks, vote to commit and, with this optimization, opt out of the 2nd commit phase. The coordinator does not communicate with those sites in the 2nd commit phase. Unfortunately, there is a problem with this optimization if sites employ multi-version storage.

For a concrete example, let's assume four database sites with local concurrency control and two-phase commit for distributed transactions. Each site supports and employs multi-version storage.

Figure 10.1 shows a sequence of actions (time advances top to bottom). There are two transactions, coordinated from sites A and B (they could be the same site). Both transactions copy values between database item C1 on site C and database item D1 on site D. Eventually, both transactions commit. They use two-phase commit including the optimization of early lock release for read-only locks. On site C, database item C1 is read first by transaction T1 and then modified by transaction T2—thus, <u>transaction T1 precedes transaction T2</u>. On site D, database item D1 is modified by transaction T1. For some reason, the pre-commit of transaction T1 on site D takes a fairly long time. When transaction T2 attempts to read database item D1, transaction T1 is still in its pre-commit logic. Thus, transaction T2 reads the most recent committed version of item D1. Here, <u>transaction T2 precedes transaction T1—a contradiction</u>. The final result also contradicts what should be expected after committing copy transactions.

The culprit or cause is not multi-version storage but early lock release. If early lock release is replaced by controlled lock violation, transaction T1 does not release its S lock but retains it, albeit only weakly enforced. Before transaction T2 writes C1 := 4, its acquisition of an X lock violates the weak S lock and therefore succeeds with a completion dependency (which is weaker than a commit dependency). Thus, at this time and this place (site C) it becomes clear that

	Site A	Site B	Site C	Site D
Initial setup			Set $C_1 := 3$	Set $D_1 := 4$
T_1 and T_2 begin	T_1 begins	T_2 begins		
	T_1 requests to copy C_1 to D_1			
			T_1 reads C_1	
				T_1 writes $D_1 := 3$
T_1 begins two-phase commit	T_1 requests votes			
			T_1 votes yes, releases S lock	T_1 begins pre-commit (slow!)
		T_1 requests to copy D_1 to C_1		
				T_2 reads D_1 (last committed version)
			T_2 writes $C_1 := 4$	
T_2 begins two-phase commit		T_2 requests votes		
			T_2 pre-commits, votes yes	T_2 votes yes, releases S lock
T_2 commits		T_2 commits		
			T_2 finishes, releases X lock	
				T_1 pre-commits, votes yes
T_1 commits	T_1 commits			
				T_1 finishes, releases X lock
Final state			$C_1 == 4$	$D_1 == 3$

Figure 10.1: Early lock release in two-phase commit.

transaction T2 must commit after transaction T1. When transaction T2 requests votes, site C delays its response until transaction T1 has finished (either committed or aborted).

Figure 10.2 shows how controlled lock violation creates a deadlock. It will be detected by a distributed graph analysis or (more practically) it will be assumed after a timeout. Either transaction may roll back, which lets the other transaction commit. Note that both dependencies are completion dependencies, not commit dependencies, i.e., a dependent transaction does not care whether the other transaction commits or aborts, as long as it completes and completely releases its locks.

Controlled lock violation weakens not only shared but also exclusive locks. Controlled lock violation of a shared lock creates a completion dependency; controlled lock violation of an exclusive lock creates a commit dependency. Note also that a read-only participant using controlled lock violation (rather than early lock release) for read-only locks must participate in both commit phases of a two-phase commit, and thus both commit phases require communication with all participants (rather than only the read-write participants in the second round of communication).

The expected outcome is that one transaction aborts and the other commits. The worst case is that both transactions abort such that the original state persists. It is not possible that both transactions succeed in the interleaved execution of Figure 10.1. If one or both transactions restart and execute one after another, i.e., less interleaved, they may both succeed.

If sites A and B were actually the same site, the mutual (circular) dependency among transactions T1 and T2 could readily be detected, with no need to wait for a transaction timeout. Note that the cycle detection concerns only transactions, not individual locks as in traditional deadlock detection.

Figure 10.3 shows this course of events. With exactly one transaction committing, the final state has equal values in database items C1 and D1. Alternatively, transaction T1 could have been chosen as the victim in deadlock resolution. In that case, the final values of C1 and D1 would both be 4.

The source of the traditional database optimization seems to be R*: "We also exploit the read-only property of the complete transaction or some of its processes. In such instances, one can benefit from the fact that for such processes of the transaction it does not matter whether the transaction commits or aborts, and hence they can be excluded from the second phase of the commit protocol. This also means that the (read) locks acquired by such processes can be released during the first phase" [Mohan et al., 1986].

	Site A	Site B	Site C	Site D
Initial setup			Set $C_1 := 3$	Set $D_1 := 4$
T_1 and T_2 begin	T_1 begins	T_2 begins		
	T_1 requests to copy C_1 to D_1			
			T_1 reads C_1	
				T_1 writes $D_1 := 3$
T_1 begins two-phase commit	T_1 requests votes			
			T_1 votes yes, weakens S lock	T_1 begins pre-commit (slow!)
		T_2 requests to copy D_1 to C_1		
				T_2 reads D_1 (last committed version)
			T_2 writes $C_1 := 4$ with completion dependency on T_1	
T_2 begins two-phase commit		T_2 requests votes		
			T_2 delays its vote, informs site B of its completion dependency on T_1	T_2 votes yes, weakens S lock
				T_1 delays its vote, informs site A of its completion dependency on T_2

Figure 10.2: Controlled lock violation in two-phase commit.

	Site A–B	Site C	Site D
Initial setup		Set $C_1 := 3$	Set $D_1 := 4$
T_1 and T_2 begin	T_1 and T_2 begin		
	T_1 requests to copy C_1 to D_1		
		T_1 reads C_1	
			T_1 writes $D_1 := 3$
T_1 begins two-phase commit	T_1 requests votes		
		T_1 votes yes, weakens S lock	T_1 begins pre-commit (slow!)
	T_2 requests to copy D_1 to C_1		
			T_2 reads D_1 (last committed version)
		T_2 writes $C_1 := 4$ with completion dependency on T_1	
T_2 begins two-phase commit	T_2 requests votes		
		T_2 delays its vote, informs site B of its completion dependency on T_1	T_2 votes yes, weakens S lock
			T_1 delays its vote, informs site A of its completion dependency on T_2
Deadlock detection	Circular dependency among T_1 and T_2		
T_2 abort	Choice of victem: T_2	T_2 rolls back, releases locks	T_2 rolls back, releases locks
T_1 succeeds			T_1 votes yes, weakens X lock
T_1 commits	T_1 commits	T_1 commits, releases locks	T_1 commits, releases locks
Final state		$C_1 == 3$	$D_1 == 4$

Figure 10.3: Controlled lock violation with a single coordinating site.

10.1   REFERENCES

Mohan, C., Lindsay, B. G., and Obermarck, R. (1986). Transaction management in the R* distributed database management system. *ACM TODS*, 11(4), pages 378–396. DOI: 10.1145/7239.7266. 323

CHAPTER 11

Deferred Lock Enforcement

Weak exclusive locks for more concurrency and more throughput

Goetz Graefe

ABSTRACT

Within a database transaction, the longest phases execute the application logic and harden the commit log record on stable storage. Two existing techniques, early lock release and controlled lock violation, eliminate or weaken conflicts during the hardening phase. Two new techniques, deferred lock acquisition and deferred lock enforcement, do the same during execution of the application logic. Together, deferred lock enforcement and controlled lock violation minimize the duration of strict exclusive locks, maximize concurrency and throughput, yet ensure full serializability. The new techniques complement snapshot isolation and multi-version storage.

11.1 INTRODUCTION

Decades of unchanging industrial practice in database systems as well as recent focus on optimistic concurrency control for key-value stores and in-memory databases may leave the mistaken impression that further improvements to pessimistic concurrency control and locking will not be possible or worthwhile. The present chapter attempts to convince even the skeptical reader of the opposite.

In fact, there are multiple avenues toward fewer conflicts, more concurrency, and higher throughput. First, lock *scopes* can be fitted better to queries, updates, and other database operations. For example, while phantom protection with any traditional locking method locks at least an entire gap between two index entries, orthogonal key-value locking locks only a small fraction of such a gap. Second, lock *modes* can match more precisely the operation at hand. For example, increment locks are widely ignored but precisely fit the needs of incremental maintenance of materialized "group by" and "rollup" views, which are common in data warehousing and web analytics. Third, lock *durations* can be optimized for greater concurrency. For example, early lock release and controlled lock violation let new transactions read and modify database items before their latest versions are hardened, i.e., before their (commit) log records reach stable storage. Two new techniques introduced here, deferred lock acquisition and deferred lock enforcement, complement early lock release and controlled lock violation.

Transaction execution proceeds in multiple phases and commit processing comprises multiple steps. The longest phase in a transaction is either its read phase, i.e., executing the transaction's application logic, or hardening, i.e., writing its commit log record to stable storage. Traditionally, stable storage has been a pair of rotating magnetic disks; currently, it means flash storage; and eventually, it will be non-volatile memory. Early lock release and controlled lock violation focus on locks, concurrency, and contention during hardening. They may or may not remain relevant with recovery logs on non-volatile memory. Deferred lock acquisition and deferred lock enforcement focus on locks, concurrency, and contention during execution of transactions' application logic. Their importance will increase with any decrease in the importance of early lock release and controlled lock violation.

Figure 11.1 illustrates the phases of a transaction. The long-running phases are shaded in the header row. Instruction counts and durations are typical for a small transaction and today's software and hardware. Traditional locking holds and enforces all locks throughout all phases, from the first data access until the transaction's commit log record is safe on stable storage. Throughout this chapter, variants of this diagram illustrate the effects of alternative techniques. Commit processing in Figure 11.1 includes two auxiliary steps required in some of the new techniques. The diagram omits distributed transactions and two-phase commit.

Transaction phases → ↓ Techniques	Read phase = transaction and application logic 10^5 inst = 20 μs	Commit Logic			Hardening = force log to stable storage 1I/O = 200 μs
		Commit preparation	Commit log record 10^3 inst = 0.2 μs	Update propagation	
Traditional locking		n/a		n/a	

Figure 11.1: Lock enforcement durations in traditional locking.

This chapter introduces two new techniques, deferred lock acquisition and deferred lock enforcement. The former employs common update locks whereas the latter uses the semantics of two uncommon lock modes, reserved and pending. When combined with multi-version storage and controlled lock violation, the new techniques enforce exclusive locks for only an instant during commit processing, yet with full serializability. Traditional weak transaction isolation levels [Gray et al., 1976] are also possible.

The origins of deferred lock acquisition and deferred lock enforcement were the thoughts that

- any method of concurrency control must find true conflicts and should avoid finding false conflicts;

- therefore all methods of concurrency control should permit precisely the same concurrency;

- any performance advantage of optimistic concurrency control must have a different source;

- the source may be transaction-private update buffers, which optimistic concurrency control always requires;

- transaction-private update buffers are a form of multi-version storage;

- multi-version storage might also benefit pessimistic concurrency control; and

- a transaction with a transaction-private update buffer has no need for traditional exclusive locks during execution of the transaction's application logic.

In the remainder of this chapter, Section 11.2 reviews related work, both techniques to be used in implementations and complementary techniques. Sections 11.3 and 11.4 introduce deferred lock acquisition and deferred lock enforcement, respectively. Section 11.5 covers integration of deferred lock enforcement with a variety of other techniques in database concurrency control, logging, and recovery; Section 11.6 focuses on distributed operations including two-phase commit and log shipping. Section 11.7 summarizes and concludes.

11.2 RELATED PRIOR WORK

This section reviews prior techniques that contribute to deferred lock acquisition and deferred lock enforcement or that complement them.

11.2.1 MULTI-VERSION STORAGE

Multi-version storage enables efficient snapshot isolation for all read-only transactions. Thus, it complements all locking techniques. Concurrency control, e.g., locking, is needed only in read-write transactions. Chan et al. [1982] wrote about their implementation of this approach: "Read-only (retrieval) transactions, on the other hand, do not set locks. Instead, each of these transactions can obtain a consistent (but not necessarily most up-to-date) view of the database by following the version chain for any given logical page, and by reading only the first version encountered that has been created by an update transaction with a completion time earlier than the time of its own initiation. Thus, read-only transactions do not cause synchronization delays on update transactions, and vice versa."

With multi-version storage, read-only transactions can run in snapshot isolation without any need for concurrency control, e.g., locks or end-of-transaction validation. Only read-write transactions require concurrency control. Therefore, the remainder of this chapter focuses on read-write transactions, ignoring read-only transactions. It mostly ignores weak transaction isolation levels, because those only reduce read-only locks whereas the new techniques focus on exclusive locks.

Figure 11.2 summarizes the rules for choosing versions. Record-level locking, e.g., key-range locking in ordered indexes such as B-trees, ignores versions and instead focuses on index entries. One transaction's shared lock prevents another transaction from committing a new version but it does not prevent creation of a new, uncommitted version. While a read-only transaction reads the version appropriate for its start-of-transaction timestamp, a version creator reads its own updates, and all other read-write transactions read the most recent committed version. All new locking techniques must work with multi-version storage in this way.

Transaction Mode	Lock Mode	Version Access
Read-only	Snapshot isolation, no locks	Read the version appropriate for the start-of-transaction timestamp
Read-write	Shared lock	Read the most recent committed version
	Exclusive lock	Create, modify, and read an uncommitted version

Figure 11.2: Transactional data access in versioned databases.

11.2.2 TRANSACTION-PRIVATE UPDATE BUFFERS

Transaction-private update buffers are required in optimistic concurrency control [Kung and Robinson, 1981]. While executing their application logic, optimistic transactions prepare end-of-transaction validation by gathering sets of reads, writes (updates), insertions, and deletions.

Optimistic transactions with end-of-transaction validation must defer all forms of database updates until validation has succeeded. Propagating a transaction's updates from its transaction-private update buffer to the shared database, at least to the global buffer pool, is a distinct step in commit processing.

Figure 11.3 shows the most traditional form of optimistic concurrency control. Compared to Figure 11.1, it adds another period after commit logic and hardening. In backward validation, a committing transaction compares its own read- and write-sets with those of transactions already committed [Härder, 1984]. There is no concurrency control during a transaction's read phase. In backward validation, these sets must remain in place until the last concurrent transaction finishes, i.e., possibly long past commit processing and hardening.

Sets of insertions and deletions, although required in the original description of optimistic concurrency control [Kung and Robinson, 1981], can be avoided if all space management actions are delegated to system transactions. System transactions (also known within ARIES as top-level actions) modify the physical representation of database contents but do not modify the logical database contents as observable with queries. For example, insertion and removal, or presence and absence, of a ghost record (also known as pseudo-deleted record) cannot be discerned with a "count(*)" query or any other type of standard query. With all space management in system

Transaction phases → ↓ Techniques	Read phase = transaction and application logic	Commit Logic			Hardening = force log to stable storage	Beyond transaction completion
		Commit preparation	Commit log record	Update propagation		
Backward validation						

Figure 11.3: Exclusion enforcement in optimistic concurrency control.

transactions, user transactions only modify allocated space. For example, a logical deletion or insertion merely toggles a record's ghost bit and perhaps modifies other fields. With no physical insertions and deletions, a user transaction can capture all its database changes in its transaction-private update buffer.

Transaction-private update buffers are required and proven in many implementations of optimistic concurrency control but have not been combined with pessimistic concurrency control, i.e., with locking. Deferred lock acquisition and deferred lock enforcement, the topics of Sections 11.3 and 11.4, combine locking with either transaction-private update buffers or multi-version storage.

11.2.3 UPDATE LOCKS AND INTENTION LOCKS

Update locks are an example of clever lock *modes* that enable more concurrency, less wasted effort, and thus higher transaction processing rates than systems without update locks. Within Korth's theory of derived lock modes [Korth, 1983], Gray and Reuter describe update ("U") locks [Gray and Reuter, 1993] for upgrading from shared ("S") to exclusive ("X") modes. An update lock is a shared lock with a scheduling component: the transaction holding an update lock is first in line to convert its shared lock to exclusive mode. Only an exclusive lock permits modifying the shared database, e.g., in the global buffer pool.

Figure 11.4 shows the compatibility of these lock modes. The shaded entry reflects the fact that only one transaction can be first in line for an exclusive lock. The question mark indicates that some designs do and some do not permit an additional shared lock when another transaction already holds an update lock.

SQLite [SQLite, 2004] locks database files in shared ("S") mode while reading and in exclusive ("X") mode while applying updates. While computing database updates, it locks affected files with reserved ("R") locks. Commit processing holds pending ("P") locks while waiting for active readers to finish. While one transaction holds a reserved lock, other transactions can acquire new shared locks as if the reserved lock were a shared lock; while a transaction holds a pending lock, other transactions cannot acquire new locks as if the pending lock were an exclu-

Requested → ↓ Held	S	U	X
S (shared)	✓	✓	–
U (update)	?	–	–
X (exclusive)	–	–	–

Figure 11.4: Lock compatibility including update locks.

sive lock; yet the transition from reserved to pending is always conflict-free and instantaneous, because their only difference affects only subsequent lock requests.

Figure 11.5 shows the compatibility of these lock modes. The shaded field and its adjoining fields indicate that reserved and pending locks are forms of update locks. These two lock modes resolve the ambiguity indicated with a question mark in Figure 11.4.

Requested → ↓ Held	S	R	P	X
S (shared)	✓	✓		–
R (reserved)	✓		–	–
P (pending)	–			–
X (exclusive)	–	–	–	–

Figure 11.5: Lock compatibility including reserved and pending modes.

Also within Korth's theory of derived lock modes [Korth, 1983], hierarchical and multi-granularity locking [Gray et al., 1976] permit a fine granularity of locking for lookups and up-dates as well as a coarse granularity of locking for large scans. A prototypical example is locking pages in a file, with the possibility of locking an entire file or locking individual pages. Another standard example is locking an entire index (for a large query) or individual index entries (for a small transaction). Locks on individual granules (e.g., pages or index entries) require an informational "intention" lock on the coarse granule (e.g., the file or index).

Figure 11.6 shows the compatibility of traditional intention lock modes. The top-left quadrant is the standard lock compatibility matrix. Intention locks are always compatible, in-dicated in the bottom right quadrant, because a finer granularity of locking will find any actual conflict. The remaining two quadrants are simply copies of the top left quadrant. Figure 11.6 omits the traditional combined lock mode S+IX, which is compatible with any lock mode com-patible with both S and IX modes.

Requested → ↓ Held	S	X	IS	IX
S	✓	–	✓	–
X	–	–	–	–
IS	✓	–		✓
IX	–	–	✓	

Figure 11.6: Compatibility of traditional and intention lock modes.

11.2.4 ORTHOGONAL KEY-VALUE LOCKING

Orthogonal key-value locking [Graefe and Kimura, 2015] is an example of lock *sizes* or *scopes* that enable more concurrency and thus higher transaction rates than traditional lock scopes.

While both orthogonal key-value locking and ARIES key-value locking [Mohan, 1990] focus on existing distinct key values in ordered indexes such as B-trees, there are three significant differences. First, the gap (open interval) between two distinct key values has a lock mode separate from (and entirely orthogonal to) the lock for the key value and its set of instances. With separate locks for key and gap, phantom protection does not need to lock any existing index entries. Instead, it merely requires that a locked key value continue to exist in the index. While one transaction uses a key value for phantom protection, another transaction may lock the key value and logically delete it by turning it into a ghost entry. Subsequent transactions may use the ghost for phantom protection or may turn it into a valid index entry again.

Second, the set of all possible instances of a key value (e.g., the domain of row identifiers) is hash-partitioned and each partition can have its own lock mode. The concurrency desired in a system determines the recommended number of partitions. An equality query may lock all partitions at once but an insertion, update, or deletion may lock just one partition such that other insertions, updates, and deletions may concurrently modify other rows with the same key value but a different row identifier. More precisely, a concurrent transaction may update or delete a row with a different hash value and thus belonging to a different partition. Each individual row identifier has its own ghost bit such that two deletions may indeed proceed concurrently and commit (or roll back) independently.

Third, the set of all possible key values in a gap is hash-partitioned and each partition can have its own lock mode. An equality query with an empty result locks merely a single partition within a gap. Locking a partition achieves serializability yet permits other transactions to insert into the gap. Range queries may lock all partitions within a gap. With this recent refinement not included in earlier descriptions [Graefe and Kimura, 2015], orthogonal key-value locking can lock none, some, or all row identifiers associated with an existing key value plus none, some, or all non-existing key values in a gap between neighboring existing key values.

Figure 11.7 illustrates orthogonal key-value locking for distinct key value "Jerry" in a non-unique secondary index on first names. The column headings indicate points and ranges in the domain of index keys. In addition to the lock scopes shown, orthogonal key-value locking also supports any combination. For example, a range query can, with a single invocation of the lock manager, lock a key value and its adjacent gap. This lock covers all existing and non-existing instances of the locked key value as well as all partitions of non-existing key values in the adjacent gap. For comparison, the last line of Figure 11.7 shows the one and only lock scope possible in ARIES/KVL, i.e., a distinct key value with all instances and an adjacent gap.

Index Entries and Gaps	Entry (Gary, 1)	Gap			Entry (Jerry, 3)	Gap	Entry (Jerry, 6)	Gap			Entry (Mary, 5)
		Gary, >1	>Gary, <Jerry	Jerry, <3				(Jerry, >6)	>Jerry, <Mary	(Mary, <5)	
An entire key value											
A partition thereof											
An entire gap											
A partition thereof											
Maximal single lock											
ARIES/KVL											

Figure 11.7: Lock scopes available in orthogonal key-value locking.

Ancillary differences include application of key-value locking only in secondary indexes or uniformly in both primary and secondary indexes. They further include use of system transactions and of ghost records for insertion of new key values as well as system transactions creating and removing ghost space within individual records. Thus, system transactions perform all allocation and de-allocation operations in short critical sections with inexpensive transaction commits (no log flush on commit). User transactions merely modify pre-allocated space, including the ghost bits in each index entry. This greatly simplifies logging and rollback of user transactions as well as space management.

Orthogonal key-value locking is complementary to deferred lock acquisition and deferred lock enforcement. While orthogonal key-value locking is an example of a technique that reduces count and scope of locks, the new techniques focus on reduced durations of exclusive locks.

11.2.5 EARLY LOCK RELEASE AND CONTROLLED LOCK VIOLATION

Controlled lock violation [Graefe et al., 2013] is an example of improved lock *durations* that increase concurrency and thus transaction processing rates over prior techniques. Early lock release and controlled lock violation focus on the time when a transaction becomes durable by writing log records including the commit log record to stable storage. With today's processors and I/O devices, hardening a transaction may take much longer than executing a small transaction over an in-memory database, as is common now in online transaction processing. Logging on non-volatile memory may eventually reverse this imbalance.

Concurrency control and serializability must ensure that many interleaved transactions are equivalent to some serial execution. Once a transaction has a commit log record with an LSN (log sequence number) in the log buffer in memory, the transaction's position in the equivalent serial execution is final. The need for further concurrency control seems to end at this point. This is the central insight behind early lock release. Variants of early lock release relinquish either only the read-only locks or all locks at this point.

Controlled lock violation is similar to early lock release but also considers durability and write-ahead logging. It ensures that subsequent transactions cannot publish new database updates before the relevant update transactions are durably committed and logged on stable storage. It retains all locks until a commit log record is on stable storage but locks are weak during hardening. Other transactions may acquire conflicting locks, and query or modify data, but cannot complete until the first transaction is durable. If the second transaction is a read-write transaction and must write a commit log record in the same recovery log as the first transaction, then this dependency is necessarily satisfied. In two-phase commit, locks may be weak during both commit phases [Graefe et al., 2013].

When a transaction T2 requests a lock that conflicts with a weak exclusive lock held by a committing transaction T1, controlled lock violation grants the request but with a commit dependency. In other words, T2 cannot commit until T1 is completely durable. If T2 is a read-write transaction, this has little practical effect, since T2 will eventually need to write its own commit log record. If T1 is a local read-only participant in the two-phase commit of a global read-write transaction, then this commit dependency will cause a delay. Note that this delay in the read-only participant is no longer than the delay in read-write participants writing their pre-commit log records to stable storage.

Figure 11.8 contrasts controlled lock violation and two forms of early lock release. Controlled lock violation achieves practically the same performance and scalability as early lock release of both S and X locks but without the danger of premature publication of not-yet-durable updates. Controlled lock violation and early lock release of only S locks are correct but with large differences in performance and scalability.

Controlled lock violation requires management of commit dependencies. Hekaton has proven that this is possible with high performance and scalability [Diaconu et al., 2013]. A read barrier holds back result sets in the server until all commit dependencies have cleared. In the

| | Early Lock Release | | Controlled Lock |
	S Only	S and X	Violation
Trigger	LSN for commit log record		
Performance	Good	Best	Almost best
Consequence of a write-read conflict	Waiting	Premature publication	Commit dependency

Figure 11.8: Early lock release vs. controlled lock violation.

published description, it remains unclear whether transaction hardening, i.e., writing a commit log record to the SQL Server recovery log, is considered such a commit dependency.

Figure 11.9 compares the effective durations of locks in traditional locking and in controlled lock violation. With weak lock enforcement (shaded lightly) during one of the long-running transaction phases and with a commit dependency as only and almost meaningless penalty for violating another transaction's weak locks, controlled lock violation greatly increases concurrency and system [Graefe et al., 2013].

| Transaction phases → ↓ Techniques | Read phase = transaction and application logic | Commit Logic | | | Hardening = force log to stable storage |
		Commit preparation	Commit log record	Update propagation	
Traditional locking		n/a		n/a	
Controlled lock violation					

Figure 11.9: Lock enforcement durations with controlled lock violation.

Early lock release and controlled lock violation are complementary to deferred lock acquisition and deferred lock enforcement. While these prior techniques reduce lock duration at end-of-transaction, the new techniques focus on reduced durations of exclusive locks during a transaction's read phase.

11.2.6 SUMMARY OF RELATED PRIOR WORK

Multi-version storage and snapshot isolation free read-only transactions from concurrency control, e.g., locking. Transaction-private update buffers enable optimistic concurrency control and are proven in many implementations but they are new to pessimistic concurrency control. Deferred lock acquisition and deferred lock enforcement require transaction-private update buffers or multi-version storage.

Update locks are used in deferred lock acquisition; their refinement, reserved and pending locks, are not used explicitly in deferred lock enforcement but their semantics are. Finally, controlled lock violation relies on weak enforcement of locks during some transaction phase, as does deferred lock enforcement.

The next two sections combine these related prior techniques into new techniques.

11.3   DEFERRED LOCK ACQUISITION

The goal of deferred lock acquisition is to reduce each transaction's "lock footprint" during execution of the transaction's application logic. By deferring acquisition of all exclusive locks to commit processing, it eliminates all exclusive locks and their conflicts during execution of the transaction's application logic.

A transaction with deferred lock acquisition requests only shared locks until it commits. Thus, execution of the transaction's application logic can rightfully be called the transaction's read phase. Updates including insertions and deletions are cached in a transaction-private update buffer.

While it is sufficient, i.e., correct, to acquire only shared locks during a transaction's read phase, update locks are recommended for modified database items, e.g., changing key values in B-tree indexes. Update locks can co-exist with shared locks but not with other update locks. In this way, deferred lock acquisition detects write-write conflicts immediately when they occur.

Figure 11.10 illustrates lock enforcement in a transaction with deferred lock acquisition. During the first long-running transaction phase, all transactions acquire locks only in shared and update modes, thus running freely without lock conflicts except for write-write conflicts.

Transaction phases → ↓ Techniques	Read phase = transaction and application logic	Commit Logic			Hardening = force log to stable storage
		Commit preparation	Commit log record	Update propagation	
Deferred lock acquisition					

Figure 11.10: Lock enforcement durations with deferred lock acquisition.

Permitting only a single uncommitted version for each database item at any time ensures a linear history of versions, including no more than a single uncommitted version. In systems with multi-version storage, the uncommitted version can be stored immediately in its final place (and remain locked). This eliminates the need for a transaction-private update buffer from each transaction's state and for the update propagation step from the commit logic.

Deferred lock acquisition upgrades locks in an initial step during commit processing. If a transaction holds multiple update locks that need upgrading to exclusive locks, and if some of these locks must wait for reader transactions to release their locks, then upgrading and waiting occurs one lock at a time. While avoiding such serial waiting seems difficult in deferred lock acquisition, deferred lock enforcement naturally waits for all such locks and reader transactions concurrently, as discussed in Section 11.4.

11.3.1 TRANSACTION-PRIVATE UPDATE BUFFERS

In the past, transaction-private update buffers were used exclusively in implementations of optimistic concurrency control. In fact, it seems that transaction-private update buffers have been a distinct difference in the implementations of optimistic and pessimistic concurrency control. The present research started with this observation and the question what advantages transaction-private update buffers could enable in the context of pessimistic concurrency control, i.e., locking.

The introduction of optimistic concurrency control [Kung and Robinson, 1981] assumes that the transaction-private update buffer holds uncommitted database pages. At the time, page-level locking was common and page-level optimistic concurrency control seemed appropriate. In the 1990s, record-level locking became common [Lomet, 1993, Mohan, 1990, Mohan and Levine, 1992]. A modern transaction-private update buffer holds individual index entries.

As transactions ought to "see" their own updates, a transaction-private update buffer adds overhead to each database read. Instead of simply fetching data values from the shared database and its buffer pool, each read operation by a read-write transaction must inspect its transaction-private update buffer. In-memory indexes and bit vector filtering may reduce the effort but some overhead unavoidably remains.

Transaction-private update buffers also require an additional step during commit processing not required in traditional pessimistic concurrency control. Once a commit log record is formatted and has a log sequence number, i.e., once concurrency control against other transactions is complete, buffered updates must be propagated from the transaction-private update buffer to the shared database and its buffer pool. Thereafter, the transaction may free its transaction-private update buffer.

In spite of these overheads, transaction-private update buffers are a required and proven technology that may be transferred from optimistic to pessimistic concurrency control. In this case, exclusive locks are required only when updating the shared database, e.g., in the global buffer pool. Updates in the transaction-private update buffer do not require any locks in the database. Therefore, read-write transactions may defer acquisition of their exclusive locks from their read phase to commit processing, i.e., a step immediately before formatting a commit log record in the log buffer.

11.3.2 LOCK TIMING AND SEMANTICS

Nonetheless, a read-write transaction needs to lock during its read phase at least the database items it reads. This includes the database items the transaction modifies. For updates, it seems prudent to acquire an update lock. An update lock requires the same overhead as a shared lock, i.e., an invocation of the lock manager, and it identifies conflicts that doom a transaction, i.e., two transactions modifying the same database item at the same time. If such a conflict is detected, one of the transactions may abort immediately, which is the only conflict resolution strategy available with end-of-transaction validation, or the requesting transactions may wait, preferably with a lock time-out and with limited wait depth [Thomasian, 1998].

Figure 11.11 shows the lock compatibility in deferred lock acquisition for two transactions both in their read phases. Compared to Figure 11.4, it replaces the question mark with a check mark. Note that a transaction running with deferred lock acquisition in its read phase does not acquire exclusive locks; thus, Figure 11.11 could omit its last row and its last column.

Requested → ↓ Held	S	U	X
S (shared)	✓	✓	–
U (update)	✓	–	–
X (exclusive)	–	–	–

Figure 11.11: Lock compatibility in deferred lock acquisition.

If concurrent read-write transactions hold locks on the same data item, all reader transactions must commit first, i.e., the writer must wait when upgrading its update lock to an exclusive lock during commit processing. Deferred lock acquisition delays read-write conflicts until the updater's commit phase.

If commit preparation upgrades multiple locks from update mode to exclusive mode, sorting these requests might seem to prevent deadlocks. Unfortunately, this is not the case. Concurrent writers in commit preparation will not conflict, because write-write conflicts would have been detected earlier when these transactions acquired their update locks, with no further conflicts during their upgrade to exclusive mode. Regarding read-write conflicts, concurrent transactions in their read phases acquire shared locks as they access database items, i.e., they do not sort their lock requests for deadlock prevention. Hence, sorting locks before upgrading them from update mode to exclusive mode will not guarantee deadlock avoidance.

What does seem helpful is a change in the semantics of update locks according to the state of the transaction. While a transaction is in its read phase, i.e., executing application logic, its update locks should not prevent other transactions from acquiring shared locks. Once a transaction begins commit processing, i.e., lock upgrades to exclusive mode, new requests for shared locks should conflict with update locks. This issue is addressed in deferred lock enforcement.

11.3.3 INTEGRATION WITH MULTI-VERSION STORAGE

Transaction-private update buffers are a proven technique but nonetheless introduce overheads such as space management, look-aside searches during a transaction's read phase, and update propagation during commit processing. Fortunately, multi-version storage enables an elegant solution in combination with deferred lock acquisition and its early detection of write-write conflicts. Append-only storage such as log-structured merge trees [O'Neil et al., 1996] and partitioned B-trees [Graefe, 2003] are necessarily multi-version storage.

Concurrent transactions in their read phases conflict if two transactions attempt to modify the same database item. Their update locks conflict and one transaction must abort or wait. If the granularity of versioning is at least as fine as the granularity of locking, the proposed solution works. For example, if both versioning and locking focus on database pages, there can be only one uncommitted page version at a time. The same is true if both versioning and locking focus on key values. The proposed technique does not apply if the granularity of locking is a distinct key value and the granularity of versioning is a database page, or if the granularity of locking is an individual index entry and the granularity of versioning is a distinct key value and its list of index entries.

With only a single uncommitted version at a time, it can be stored immediately, i.e., while still uncommitted, directly at its final place, i.e., where update propagation would move it when copying it from a transaction-private update buffer during commit processing. In other words, read-write transactions require two versions. Of those, one is uncommitted and locked in update mode and the other one is committed and available to all read-write transactions. Read-only transactions may require multiple committed versions. The oldest active transaction governs removal of the oldest versions.

With no transaction-private update buffer, all transactions search only the database, not any additional data structure. A read-only transaction in snapshot isolation reads the version appropriate for its start-of-transaction timestamp. A read-write transaction reads either the last or the second-to-last version: a shared lock gives access to the last committed version and an update lock gives access (both for update and retrieval) to the uncommitted version. An update transaction naturally reads its own updates.

Figure 11.12 illustrates the effect of multi-version storage and removal of the update propagation step. This effect is more significant in combination with deferred lock enforcement introduced in Section 11.4.

While it is desirable that each commit succeeds, it is imperative that transaction abort and rollback must never fail. Fortunately, an update lock is sufficient to remove an uncommitted version. In case of transaction abort, there is no need to upgrade a lock from update to exclusive mode, just as there is no need to force the transaction's final log record to stable storage.

Transaction phases → ↓ Techniques	Read phase = transaction and application logic	Commit Logic			Hardening = force log to stable storage
		Commit preparation	Commit log record	Update propagation	
Dla plus multi-version storage				n/a	

Figure 11.12: Lock enforcement durations with multi-version storage.

11.3.4 SUMMARY OF DEFERRED LOCK ACQUISITION

In summary, deferred lock acquisition avoids exclusive locks during a transaction's read phase, i.e., while executing a transaction's application logic and thus during the first long-running phase in a transaction. Transactions in their read phase can run freely, without lock conflicts or waiting, until they begin commit processing. Only write-write conflicts are detected immediately when they occur, which prevents conflicting updates that cannot possibly both commit.

The absence of conflicting database updates ensures, for each database item, a linear history of versions as well as a single uncommitted version at any point in time. In multi-version storage, this single uncommitted version can be appended to the version chain in the database (or in the shared buffer pool) if it remains locked. A transaction-private update buffer is not required. The simple rule for version selection is that the transaction holding the update lock reads and modifies the uncommitted version, all other read-write transactions (holding shared locks) read the last committed version, and read-only transactions (holding no locks at all) read the version appropriate for their start-of-transaction timestamp.

11.4 DEFERRED LOCK ENFORCEMENT

The goal of deferred lock enforcement is to improve upon deferred lock acquisition. It eliminates update locks and their conversion to exclusive locks. Moreover, instead of upgrading lock modes one lock at a time, a transaction's commit preparation step waits concurrently for exclusive access to all database items modified by the transaction.

With deferred lock acquisition, a read-write transaction in its read phase acquires and holds update locks. In contrast, with deferred lock enforcement, a read-write transaction in its read phase acquires and holds exclusive locks, but only as weak locks. More specifically, deferred lock enforcement interprets exclusive locks as reserved locks during a transaction's read phase, as pending locks while a transaction is preparing for commit, and as exclusive locks while a transaction is committing. Importantly, the switch from reserved to pending is accomplished with a simple change in the transaction's state in the transaction manager. All pending locks drain conflicting reader transactions concurrently. Merely the verification that all conflicting reader transactions have indeed released their locks is serial.

11.4.1 LOCK SEMANTICS AND TRANSITIONS

The important difference to deferred lock acquisition is that deferred lock enforcement has no need for update locks. Instead, it employs only shared and exclusive locks. However, the semantics of exclusive locks depend on the transaction's execution phase. Whether or not a shared lock and an exclusive lock conflict depends on the state of the transaction holding the exclusive lock.

During a transaction's read phase, its exclusive locks are interpreted and enforced as if they were reserved locks. Recall from Figure 11.5 that a lock in reserved mode is compatible with existing readers (just like any update lock) and it permits new readers as well. Once a transaction begins commit processing, its exclusive locks are interpreted and enforced as if they were pending locks. With that interpretation, existing readers may finish their work and commit but new readers cannot acquire new shared locks. Eventually, when no reader remains, an exclusive lock attains the traditional exclusive semantics and the holding transaction may modify the shared database.

Of course, a transaction attempting to commit may also force active readers to abort. The policy governing this decision may consider the age and size of the transactions involved. Similarly, whether or not to grant a new shared lock may be controlled by policies based on age and size of transactions.

Figure 11.13 shows the same asymmetry as Figure 11.5. While one transaction holds a shared lock, another transaction may transition from working ("X as R", i.e., exclusive locks interpreted as reserved locks) to attempting to commit ("X as P", i.e., exclusive locks interpreted as pending locks). On the other hand, while one transaction is attempting to commit (holding an "X as P" lock), no other transaction can acquire a shared lock (or any other lock) on the same data item.

Requested → ↓ Held	S	X as R	X as P	X
S	✓		✓	–
X as R	✓		–	–
X as P	–			–
X	–	–	–	–

Figure 11.13: Lock compatibility in deferred lock enforcement.

Figure 11.14 illustrates lock enforcement in deferred lock enforcement. It is rather similar in appearance to Figure 11.10. During the first long-running transaction phase, all transactions acquire shared and exclusive locks, but the exclusive locks have the semantics of reserved locks until commit processing begins. Thus, transactions run with maximal concurrency until their commit is requested.

Transaction phases → ↓ Techniques	Read phase = transaction and application logic	Commit Logic			Hardening = force log to stable storage
		Commit preparation	Commit log record	Update propagation	
Deferred lock enforcement					

Figure 11.14: Lock enforcement durations with deferred lock enforcement.

A transaction acquires locks only during its read phase, i.e., while executing the transaction's application logic; it does not request locks while executing its commit logic. Thus, in deferred lock enforcement, a transaction's lock request for an exclusive lock is always processed as if it were a request for a lock in reserved mode, and only the left half of Figure 11.5 matters for lock requests under deferred lock enforcement.

The transition from reserved to pending semantics does not require any checks of lock compatibility, because the change affects only future attempts by other transactions to acquire S locks on the same database item. The transition is accomplished by a change in the transaction's state and takes effect immediately. The transition from pending to exclusive semantics occurs automatically when no concurrent reader remains, i.e., concurrent read-write transactions reading the database item. This transition requires a check that all concurrent readers have released their locks. In single-threaded transaction execution, these checks happen one at a time. However, in a transaction modifying multiple database items and thus converting multiple locks from pending mode to exclusive mode, all locks drain their readers concurrently. In contrast, deferred lock acquisition waits to upgrade one lock from update mode to exclusive mode and only then attempts to upgrade the next update lock.

In database systems with fine-granularity locking, transactions locking multiple items are as common as tables with indexes. In almost all database management systems, record-level locking focuses on one index at a time and maintenance of secondary indexes requires locks within each affected index. The only exception is ARIES/IM [Mohan and Levine, 1992], where the scope of a single lock is a logical row including the row's entries in secondary indexes as well as (in each secondary index) the gap to a neighboring index entry.

11.4.2 INTEGRATION WITH CONTROLLED LOCK VIOLATION

The principal idea of deferred lock enforcement is interpretation of exclusive locks as weak locks that permit concurrency in some controlled ways and circumstances. The same idea enables controlled lock violation. There are some similarities but also a number of differences.

Both deferred lock enforcement and controlled lock violation are based on shared and exclusive locks. Both techniques enable hierarchical and multi-granularity locking using intention lock modes. Both techniques interpret lock strength according to the transaction state. One technique may lead to a transaction abort, e.g., after a timed out lock request or due to limited wait depth, whereas the other one never leads to a transaction abort, only to a commit dependency. Finally, one technique applies to transactions in their read phase, i.e., before a transaction's commit point, whereas the other one applies to a transaction while hardening, i.e., after the transaction's commit point. Thus, deferred lock enforcement and controlled lock violation complement each other and use similar ideas, notably temporarily weak locks.

Figure 11.15 illustrates the combined effect of deferred lock enforcement and controlled lock violation. Exclusive locks are effectively removed from both long-running phases of a transaction, i.e., both from the read phase with the transaction's application logic and from hardening by forcing a commit log record to stable storage, with strict enforcement only during (all steps of) commit processing.

Transaction phases → ↓ Techniques	Read phase = transaction and application logic	Commit Logic			Hardening = force log to stable storage
		Commit preparation	Commit log record	Update propagation	
Both dle and clv					

Figure 11.15: Lock enforcement durations with deferred lock enforcement and controlled lock violation.

11.4.3 INTEGRATION WITH MULTI-VERSION STORAGE

Multi-version storage complements deferred lock enforcement in much the same way as deferred lock acquisition. Again, all append-only storage is automatically multi-version storage and read-only transactions can run in snapshot isolation without any locks. Early detection of write-write conflicts ensures at most one uncommitted version at a time and permits omission of transaction-private update buffers. Uncommitted new versions can be placed immediately and directly next to prior committed versions. Thus, there is no overhead for a transaction-private update buffer, for look-aside search to ensure that read-write transactions "see" their own updates, or for an update propagation step during commit processing.

Figure 11.16 shows the remaining enforcement period of exclusive locks. The contrast to traditional locking is as stark as can be. For the instruction counts of Figure 11.1, the duration of strict exclusive locks and thus their opportunity for conflict with shared locks shrink by three orders of magnitude. While traditional locking holds all locks throughout both long transaction phases, the combination of techniques enforces exclusive locks only during two steps of commit processing. If there is no lock conflict during commit processing, then exclusive locks are enforced only for an instant, independently of the size of the transaction. Concurrency during the two long-running transaction phases is practically unrestrained.

Transaction phases → ↓ Techniques	Read phase = transaction and application logic	Commit Logic			Hardening = force log to stable storage
		Commit preparation	Commit log record	Update propagation	
Traditional locking		n/a		n/a	
Dle, clv, multi-version storage				n/a	

Figure 11.16: Lock enforcement durations with three techniques combined.

11.4.4 TRANSACTION COMMIT LOGIC

With some transactions exploiting deferred lock enforcement and some not, and with some transactions exploiting controlled lock violation and some not, the complexity of the commit logic might seem daunting. In fact, it is a fairly simple process.

A read-only transaction in snapshot isolation can finish without commit logic. A read-only transaction not in snapshot isolation may have incurred commit dependencies by violating earlier transactions' weak locks. If so, it must wait for those transactions to become durable, i.e., their commit log records in the recovery log on stable storage. Thereafter, the read-only transaction can finish without further commit logic.

In order to enable other transactions to exploit controlled lock violation, a committing read-write transaction must indicate when controlled lock violation becomes acceptable, when completion dependencies are resolved, and when commit dependencies are resolved. These two forms of dependencies are resolved at different times, one at the start and one at the end of the committing transaction's final hardening phase. Finally, if the committing transaction has employed deferred lock enforcement, it must switch from weak enforcement of exclusive locks to traditional enforcement, i.e., it must take its exclusive locks from reserved via pending to traditional exclusive semantics.

Figure 11.17 shows the commit logic for read-write transactions with and without controlled lock violation as well as with and without deferred lock enforcement. Lines 1 and 11 frame the method. Line 2 terminates the transaction's read or working phase. If the committing transaction has acquired its exclusive locks with deferred lock enforcement, this change in the transaction status changes their semantics from reserved to pending. Therefore, concurrent transactions can no longer acquire shared locks in conflict with the committing transaction's exclusive locks. Line 3 is required only if the committing transaction has acquired its exclusive locks with deferred lock enforcement, i.e., if there could be concurrent transactions holding conflicting shared locks. In response to such a lock conflict, the committing transaction can wait, abort, or abort the other transaction.

```
1.  void TX::commit () {
2.    status = attempting;
3.    if (DLE) check for conflicting S locks
4.    status = committing;
5.    format a commit log record in the log buffer
6.    status = complete;
7.    flush the commit log record to stable storage
8.    status = committed;
9.    release all S and X locks
10.    status = done;
11. }
```

Figure 11.17: Commit logic for read-write transactions.

Line 4 indicates that a commit decision has been made and that any exclusive locks no longer have pending but traditional exclusive semantics. However, as the two bottom lines in Figure 11.5 equal each other, this change in lock semantics does not change any conflicts or concurrency. Moreover, the committing transaction becomes protected. For example, if another high-priority transaction has a lock conflict with the committing transaction, the higher-priority transaction cannot abort the committing transaction and must either wait or abort itself. Line 5 documents the committing transaction's place in the global sequence of transaction commits. Thus, the only remaining purpose of locks and concurrency control is to prevent premature publication of new database updates.

Line 6 is required only for the benefit of other transactions that exploited controlled lock violation in their lock acquisitions. It resolves read-write conflicts between the committing transaction (as reader) and those transactions (as subsequent writers). Line 7 hardens the committing transaction; this is the last phase shown in Figure 11.16 and similar diagrams. Line 8 resolves write-read conflicts between the committing transaction (as writer) and other transactions that are exploiting controlled lock violation (as readers). Line 9 winds down the committing transaction's concurrency control and line 10 releases its remaining resources, e.g., the transaction descriptor in the transaction manager.

11.4.5 SUMMARY OF DEFERRED LOCK ENFORCEMENT

In summary, deferred lock enforcement complements controlled lock violation, which effectively eliminates lock conflicts during hardening, as well as multi-version storage, which eliminates the update propagation step. Among transactions in their read phase, deferred lock enforcement preserves the high concurrency of deferred lock acquisition. Transactions can execute their application logic and access database contents freely, without lock conflicts or waiting, until they begin commit processing. Compared to deferred lock acquisition, deferred lock enforcement simplifies lock modes and lock management by eliminating update locks and their conversion to exclusive locks. More importantly, if a single transaction has updated and locked multiple database items, e.g., a row and its index entries, and if there are concurrent read-write transactions holding S locks on these database items, then a transaction with deferred lock enforcement waits concurrently for all these readers to finish and to release their locks. Figure 11.18 summarizes locks and their semantics in deferred lock acquisition and in deferred lock enforcement.

	Deferred Lock Acquisition	Deferred Lock Enforcement
Locks during execution	S, U	S, X
...and their semantics		S, R
Commit preparation	Upgrade U → X, one lock at a time	Concurrent waiting, check each X lock
Locks during commit	S, X	S, X
...and their semantics		S, P → X

Figure 11.18: Deferred lock acquisition vs. deferred lock enforcement.

11.5 DEFERRED LOCK ENFORCEMENT AND OTHER TECHNIQUES

This section sketches how deferred lock enforcement works when integrated with other techniques in database concurrency control, logging, and recovery.

11.5.1 SYSTEM TRANSACTIONS

System transactions are a mechanism to let user transactions delegate all space management within a database to short critical sections. For example, system transactions split B-tree nodes and remove ghost records, i.e., logically deleted data retained in the database for easy transaction rollback. System transactions do not modify user-visible contents, only its representation. Protected by latches, they only modify in-memory data structures. With no user-visible semantics, system transactions require no transactional locks and their commit log records can linger in the buffer pool until written with subsequent log records.

System transactions are the best mechanism for creation and removal of versions. For example, one system transaction may be programmed to erase obsolete old versions whereas another system transaction creates a new, locked, uncommitted record version that is initially a copy of the last committed version. With no user-visible change in the database, no locks are needed, and therefore system transactions interact with deferred lock enforcement no more than with controlled lock violation.

11.5.2 WEAK TRANSACTION ISOLATION LEVELS

There are two classes of transaction isolation levels weaker than serializability. First, industry-standard snapshot isolation divides each user transaction into two implementation transactions, one that does all database reads in snapshot isolation (as of transaction start) and one that does all database writes like a traditional transaction (committed and visible after transaction end). Second, traditional weak transaction isolation levels [Gray et al., 1976] reduce the scope or the retention period of read-only locks.

Figure 11.19 shows the standard lock compatibility matrix, just for reference and comparison. Figure 11.20 shows a lock compatibility matrix that approximates the effect of "read committed" transaction isolation. It differs from the standard compatibility matrix only in the case that one transaction holds a shared lock and another transaction requests an exclusive lock, i.e., a read-write conflict. In traditional read committed transaction isolation, a reader acquires a shared lock but retains it only while actually reading the database item. It does not hold the lock until end-of-transaction as required in repeatable read and serializability. Figure 11.20 assumes that a reader retains a shared lock but permits a writer to acquire an exclusive lock. Note that a reader must not read again once another transaction holds an exclusive lock, so this is merely an approximation, not precisely equivalent to read committed transaction isolation.

	S	X
S	✓	–
X	–	–

Figure 11.19: Standard compatibility of shared and exclusive locks.

Figure 11.21 shows a lock compatibility matrix that approximates the effect of "dirty read" transaction isolation. It differs from Figure 11.20 only in the case that a writer holds an exclusive lock and a reader requests a shared lock. Here, the shared lock is granted such that the reader may read "dirty," i.e., as-yet uncommitted, database contents. Put differently, Figure 11.21 and dirty read transaction isolation detect write-write conflicts but neither read-write conflicts nor write-read conflicts. Note that a writer transaction may modify an item twice; if a reader trans-

	S	X
S	✓	✓
X	–	–

Figure 11.20: Lock compatibility approximating "read committed" transaction isolation.

	S	X
S	✓	✓
X	✓	–

Figure 11.21: Lock compatibility approximating "dirty read" transaction isolation.

action reads the database item between those two steps, it reads database contents that was never committed, neither before nor after the writer transaction.

Figure 11.22 shows the lock compatibility matrix for transactions with deferred lock enforcement, with each transaction in its read or working phase. In a transaction's read phase, an exclusive lock is equivalent to a reserved lock, and reserved locks are compatible with shared locks. Figure 11.22 is equal to the top-left quadrant of Figure 11.5 but also resembles Figure 11.21. In other words, transactions with deferred lock enforcement run about as freely as in traditional dirty read isolation, but deferred lock enforcement ensures serializability whereas dirty read is far weaker. Deferred lock enforcement achieves serializability by the commit logic of Figure 11.17 and its very brief traditional enforcement of exclusive locks.

	S	X as R
S	✓	✓
X as R	✓	–

Figure 11.22: Lock compatibility of transactions working with deferred lock enforcement.

Transactions running in industry-standard snapshot isolation do not require any locks for their reads, just like read-only transaction in snapshot isolation as discussed above. The writes and their locks conflict with other writes, as they do in deferred lock enforcement. Put differently, for committing transactions, deferred lock enforcement detects all conflicts and thus ensures serializability; but for transactions executing their application logic, deferred lock enforcement eliminates conflicts between reads and writes. Thus, deferred lock enforcement eliminates most concurrency control conflicts and achieves most the performance advantage of industry-standard snapshot isolation over traditional locking. Of course, splitting reads and writes into separate implementation transactions with different commit points violates a core premise of transactions, namely that all actions within a transaction appear atomic, i.e., indivisible.

Traditional weak transaction isolation levels reduce scope or duration of shared locks. The difference between serializability and repeatable read transaction isolation is phantom protection, i.e., transactional guarantees for continued absence, e.g., by shared locks on gaps between existing key values in an ordered index. The difference between repeatable read transaction isolation and read committed transaction isolation is lock retention until transaction commit vs. lock release immediately after reading a database value. These differences in scope and duration affect only shared locks, whereas the difference between traditional locking and deferred lock enforcement affects strength and duration only of exclusive locks. Thus, the choice among weak or strong transaction isolation levels is orthogonal to the employment of deferred lock enforcement; deferred lock enforcement is compatible with repeatable read and read committed transaction isolation if weak transaction isolation is indeed desired.

11.5.3 INTEGRATION WITH HIERARCHICAL LOCKING

The discussion above focuses on shared and exclusive modes but real systems with mixed transaction sizes rely on hierarchical lock scopes and intention locks. In a way, one can even think of the lock scopes in orthogonal key-value locking as a three-level hierarchy with the combination of key and gap as top level, key and gap separately as middle level, and partitions of key or gap as bottom level.

Just as the update lock mode can be split into reserved and pending modes, the intent-to-update ("IU") mode can be split into intent-to-reserved ("IR") and intent-to-pending ("IP") modes. Lock compatibility follows in a straightforward way, i.e., repeating the construction of Figure 11.6.

Figure 11.23 shows the compatibility of lock modes including intention, reserved, and pending modes. Intention locks are always compatible, indicated in the bottom-right quadrant, because a finer granularity of locking will find any actual conflict. The top-left quadrant mirrors Figure 11.5. The remaining two quadrants are simply copies of the top left quadrant.

Figure 11.23 omits combination lock modes, e.g., SIX combining the S and IX modes and compatible with all lock modes compatible with both S and IX locks.

Deferred lock enforcement assigns the semantics of reserved and pending locks to exclusive locks during a transaction's read phase and its commit preparation step; in addition, it does the same with the respective intention locks.

11.5.4 LOCK ESCALATION AND DE-ESCALATION

Section 11.5.3 introduces mechanisms and lock modes for deferred lock enforcement combined with hierarchical locking. A transaction may, during its execution, change its granularity of locking within the hierarchy. For example, even if a transaction starts with record-level locking, it may switch to page-level locking or even index-level locking, typically in order to reduce the

Requested → ↓ Held	S	R	P	X	IS	IR	IP	IX
S	✓	✓	–		✓	✓		–
R	✓		–	–	✓		–	–
P	–				–			–
X	–	–	–	–	–	–	–	–
IS	✓	✓	–					
IR	✓		–	–		✓		
IP	–							
IX	–		–	–				

Figure 11.23: Compatibility of intention, reserved, pending, and intention locks.

number of its locks. Lock escalation of this kind is readily supported with deferred lock enforcement, i.e., X locks interpreted as R and P locks during transaction execution and commit preparation. It works precisely as it does with traditional X and IX locks, except that those are interpreted as R, IR, P, and IP lock modes (see also Figure 11.23).

Inversely, if a transaction employs a coarse granularity of locking, whether from its start or after lock escalation, it can switch to a fine granularity of locking, e.g., to enable more concurrency, to resolve a conflict, or to avoid a deadlock. Lock de-escalation works precisely as it does with traditional X locks, except that X locks are interpreted as R and P locks during transaction execution and commit preparation.

11.5.5 INCREMENT/DECREMENT LOCKS

With deferred lock enforcement about lock timing and orthogonal key-value locking about lock sizes, increment/decrement locks are about lock modes, the third dimension for improving locking and concurrency. Increment/decrement locks are more appropriate than exclusive locks for incremental maintenance of materialized views and their indexes, specifically views with a "group by" clause in their definition. Such a view is also known as a roll-up or a cube. Ghost records in those views and their indexes should be indicated not by a ghost bit but by a count equal to zero [Graefe and Zwilling, 2004]. System transactions can create and drop records with a count equal to zero without taking locks.

Figure 11.24 shows the lock compatibility of shared, increment/decrement, and exclusive locks. Since "I" is often used for intention locks, increment/decrement locks are indicated with a "D" here. Increment/decrement locks are compatible with one another (the shaded area) but neither with shared nor with exclusive locks. Note that increment/decrement locks permit neither reading a value nor setting a value; they only permit incremental, relative maintenance of counts and sums. This includes incrementing a count from zero and decrementing a count to zero.

	S	D	X
S	✓	–	–
D	–	✓	–
X	–	–	–

Figure 11.24: Lock compatibility including increment/decrement locks.

Increment/decrement locks require their own weakly enforced forms, equivalent to their own forms of reserved and pending lock modes. While one transaction holds an increment/decrement lock with weak enforcement, other transactions may read committed data (the last committed version) under a shared lock. However, an increment/decrement update cannot commit while an active reader may require repeatable read. This limit to committing one increment/decrement transaction at a time (per data item) is a more up-to-date description of the "commit-time-only exclusive locks" of earlier work [Graefe and Zwilling, 2004].

Figure 11.25 summarizes lock compatibility for increment/decrement and exclusive locks. Their conflicts with shared locks mirror the conflicts of exclusive locks with shared locks (see the row and the column labeled S). Their conflicts with exclusive locks mirror the conflicts of exclusive locks with other exclusive locks (see the three large blocks marked as conflicts). Conflicts among increment/decrement locks are limited to the commit point (see the shaded area), which makes them much more suitable than exclusive locks for incremental updates of summary rows in materialized "group by" views and their indexes.

Requested → ↓ Held	S	D as R	D as P	D	X as R	X as P	X
S	✓		✓	–		✓	–
D as R	✓			✓			
D as P			✓				
D	–			–		–	
X as R	✓						
X as P			–			–	
X	–						

Figure 11.25: Lock compatibility including increment/decrement locks and their weak modes.

11.5.6 DEADLOCKS

Unfortunately, deferred lock enforcement does not prevent deadlocks. Consider, for example, the following scenario:

1. transaction T1 holds a shared lock on item I1;

2. transaction T2 holds reserved locks on items I1 and I2;

3. transaction T2 attempts to commit and thus upgrades to pending for item I1 and exclusive for item I2; and

4. while transaction T2 is waiting on item I1, transaction T1 requests a shared lock on item I2, and thus also waits.

The usual mechanisms and policies for deadlocks apply, e.g., deadlock prevention by limited wait depth and transaction abort after a timeout. Either of these two policies would successfully prevent the deadlock in the example scenario. Limiting the wait depth to 1 would prevent transaction T2 to wait on transaction T1, because transaction T1 is already waiting; with respect to limited wait depth, it does not matter that T1 is waiting specifically on transaction T2. Transaction abort after a timeout would resolve the deadlock, albeit only after a delay.

The two policies differ in the options available for managing a concurrency conflict. With limited wait depth, either transaction may abort. If one transaction is attempting to commit and the other one is still acquiring locks, it seems reasonable to abort the latter transaction. On the other hand, if the committing transaction is small (few scans, few locks) but the other transaction is large (complex query, many locks), then it may be less expensive overall to roll back and repeat the transaction attempting to commit. Approximate deadlock detection by timeout does not identify the set of transactions holding conflicting locks. Thus, the only possible policy aborts the transaction that timed out while requesting a lock.

11.5.7 TRANSACTION ROLLBACK

An aborting transaction immediately weakens effectively releases its read-only locks. An X lock, once acquired and held, permits not only an initial update but also subsequent updates of the same data item. This includes in particular updating a database item back to its original value, as required for transaction rollback. Thus, with an R lock sufficient to create a new (uncommitted) version of a database item and to modify it again within the same transaction, partial and full transaction rollback works with R locks just as additional updates to database items already modified. Locks in reserved mode suffice for removal of uncommitted versions. Thus, an aborting transaction never creates new conflicts with any readers, neither with read-only transactions in snapshot isolation nor with read operations of other read-write transactions. *Mutatis mutandis* the same is true for D locks.

As in traditional transaction rollback, including partial rollback to a transaction save point, after a database item has been updated back to its original value, the transaction may release its exclusive lock on this database item or downgrade it to a shared lock. In other words, after the rollback logic updates a database item back to its original value (even if not its original representation), it may simply release the pertinent R lock. There is no need for an R lock to become a P or X (or D) lock for transaction rollback.

11.5.8 INSTANT RECOVERY

Instant recovery based on write-ahead logging [Graefe et al., 2016] assumes physical or "physiological" log records, i.e., each log record pertains to a specific database page. As long as concurrency control protects and enables transaction rollback, logging and recovery are not affected by lock durations or scopes. For example, multi-version records or index entries are page contents like any other for the purposes of logging and recovery logic. Thus, deferred lock enforcement is entirely orthogonal to all techniques in instant recovery including both single-page repair and single-transaction rollback. Together, on-demand single-page repair and on-demand single-transaction rollback enable many novel techniques, including self-repairing indexes, instant restart, single-phase (single-pass) restore, instant backup, instant restore, instant fail-over, and so much more.

Figures 11.26 and 11.27 summarize differences between ARIES and instant recovery. Figure 11.26 focuses on contents and format of write-ahead logs and Figure 11.27 focuses on techniques and performance of recovery. Light shading indicates minor differences in the formats of recovery log and log archive that enable major differences in operational capabilities. The format of the recovery log differs in the backward pointers of ordinary update log records and in rollback log records. The format of the log archive differs in sort order and indexing, yet log archiving remains a single-pass over the recovery log, comparable to run generation in external merge sort. These minor differences enable many instant recovery techniques from page repair to system restart, media restore, and node failover; as well as self-repairing indexes, backups without load on the database server or its network, and more. For example, instant restart after a system (software) crash enables new transactions and new checkpoints within seconds of restart (after log analysis and lock re-acquisition) whereas traditional ARIES recovery requires minutes for the "redo" phase (due to I/O in the database) and possibly hours for the "undo" phase (in case of long-running transactions that require detailed rollback). For another example, each root-to-leaf traversal in a self-repairing index can verify all index invariants along its path, and single-page repair of any inconsistent node accesses directly the minimal set of log records to construct a new up-to-date page.

During restart, pre-crash loser transactions do not re-acquire read-only locks; thus, there can be no read-write conflict among pre-crash transactions. In the context of deferred lock enforcement and multi-version storage, transaction rollback during restart requires removal of uncommitted new versions. New post-restart transactions may read the last committed version of any database item even before completion of a loser transaction's rollback. Loser transactions merely require R (reserved) locks during restart, just as they held before the crash. Note

Logging Techniques		ARIES	Instant Recovery
Backward pointers to log records	In recovery log	By transaction	By database page
	In transaction manager	Most recent log records	All log records
Contents versus representation	Invalid records	Pseudo-deleted records	Ghost records, ghost space
	...their usage	Record deletion	Deletion, insertion, records growing + shrinking
	Representation changes	Nested top actions	Systen transactions
	...their completion	Dummy commit log record	Commit log record or no separate log record
Logging transaction rollback	Log record	Compensation log record	Rollback log record
	Pointer in rollback	"Next undo" lsn	Original "do" lsn
	Contents in rollback	Original values	No values, just a pointer

Figure 11.26: Logging in ARIES and instant recovery.

that transaction rollback without a crash similarly proceeds with R locks only, as discussed in Section 11.5.7.

11.5.9 OPTIMISTIC CONCURRENCY CONTROL

Commit processing for optimistic concurrency control requires that each transaction's validation and write phases together are atomic [Kung and Robinson, 1981]. The write phase should include not only propagation from the transaction-private update buffer to the global buffer pool but also hardening the transaction and its commit log record in the recovery log on stable storage. Otherwise, premature publication can occur just as in early lock release [Graefe et al., 2013]. High-performance database servers cannot tolerate hardening one transaction at a time and therefore require concurrent commit processing for multiple transactions.

Concurrent commit processing for optimistic concurrency control requires a shared data structure very similar to a traditional lock manager. Lock acquisition, i.e., validation in the parlance of optimistic concurrency control, includes a check for intermediate data accesses by other transactions. Mechanisms for this validation include version numbers, timestamps, or transactions' read and write sets. Lock release should occur after hardening, perhaps with concurrency optimized using controlled lock violation. Many implementations of optimistic concurrency

Recovery Techniques		ARIES	Instant Recovery
Page failure and repair	Index consistency check	Offline	Continuous, online
	Single-page repair	Backup and log replay	Selective log records
System failure and restart	Log analysis	Forward log scan	Backward log scan
	"Redo" recovery	Forward log scan	Page-by-page on demand, in parallel
	"Redo" database I/O	Random reads + writes just for recovery	Only for new transactions
	"Undo" recovery	Backward log scan	Transaction-by-transaction on demand, in parallel
	Lock re-acquisition	Durin "redo" scan	During or after log analysis
	First new transaction	After "redo"	After log analysis and lock re-acquisition
	First new checkpoint		
Media failure and restore	Log archiving	Copy and compress	Run generation and indexing, "net change" aggregation
	Backup	Full or incremental copy	Instant, in multiple files; (remote) virtual backup
	Media recovery	Backup copy, log replay	Single-pass restore or instant restore
	First new transaction	After log replay	Instant
	First new checkpoint		
Node failure and failover	Stand-by nodes	Up-to-date database + log	Backup, log archive, log tail
	Failover	Instant	
	Failback, re-integration	Either log replay or full provisioning as new	Instant failback
	First new transaction	After log replay	Instant
	First new checkpoint		

Figure 11.27: Recovery in ARIES and instant recovery.

control employ early lock release (rather than controlled lock violation) without regard to premature publication. Optimistic concurrency control with a lock manager for commit processing also permits distributed transactions with two-phase commit and with optimistic participant transactions.

A single system may concurrently execute transactions under optimistic concurrency control and transactions under pessimistic concurrency control with deferred lock enforcement. All transactions may employ controlled lock violation. Validation of a transaction under optimistic concurrency control must consider locks in the lock manager, including those held by transactions under pessimistic concurrency control. Commit processing of transactions under pessimistic concurrency control with deferred lock enforcement must consider the read and write sets of transactions under optimistic concurrency control. The definition of conflicts follows the obvious interpretation: read sets and shared locks do not conflict but all other overlaps do. Put differently, conflicts between optimistic transactions (with read and write sets) and pessimistic transaction (with locks, and with or without deferred lock enforcement and controlled lock violation) assume conversion of read and write sets into locks (as required in optimistic concurrency control with concurrent validation) and then follow the usual lock compatibility rules.

If indeed end-of-transaction validation in optimistic concurrency control acquires locks and checks whether lock acquisition and retention would have been conflict-free, then optimistic concurrency control with a lock manager for concurrent validation appears to be a form of deferred lock acquisition. If so, how can optimistic concurrency control perform or scale better than pessimistic concurrency control, i.e., locking with deferred lock enforcement and controlled lock violation? Perhaps better performance and scalability requires compromises on atomic validation and write phases, e.g., atomic validation phases without the write phases. In other words, the atomic phase or critical section starting with the validation phase may fail to include writing the commit log record to stable storage and perhaps not even include propagation from the transaction-private update buffer to the shared database.

Figure 11.28 illustrates two forms of optimistic concurrency control in the format of Figure 11.1 and of Figure 11.16. Timestamp validation with concurrent validation also requires locks and a lock manager. It can benefit from controlled lock violation during the hardening phase. In other words, timestamp validation is competitive with the combination of deferred lock enforcement and controlled lock violation. Two differences remain due to early detection of write-write conflicts in deferred lock enforcement: first, optimistic concurrency control wastes effort on doomed transactions due to conflict detection only at end-of-transaction; and second, optimistic concurrency control requires transaction-private update buffers and thus update propagation from those buffers to the shared buffer pool. Further differences include optimistic concurrency control resolving all conflicts by transaction rollback whereas pessimistic concurrency control permits waiting for a lock, preferably with limited wait depth [Thomasian, 1998] and abort after timeout.

Transaction phases → ↓ Techniques	Read phase = transaction and application logic	Commit Logic			Hardening = force log to stable storage	Beyond transaction completion
		Commit preparation	Commit log record	Update propagation		
Traditional locking						
Backward validation						
Timestamp validation						
Dle, clv, multi-version storage				n/a		

Figure 11.28: Lock exclusion enforcement in optimistic concurrency control.

In some ways deferred lock enforcement is less restrictive than optimistic concurrency control. In pessimistic concurrency control, lock acquisition occurs during execution of application logic and typically not at start-of-transaction. In contrast, validation considers overlap (concurrency) of entire transactions, which is equivalent to lock acquisition at start-of-transaction. Timestamp validation is like lock acquisition because timestamps are inspected and recorded (within a transaction) during data access, not at start-of-transaction.

In some ways deferred lock enforcement is also more restrictive than optimistic concurrency control. Deferred lock enforcement prevents write-write conflicts before they occur and it prevents validation failures of shared locks. In other words, deferred lock enforcement permits at least as much concurrency as optimistic concurrency control except that it prevents conflicts rather than detecting them at end-of-transaction and wasting effort on transactions doomed to fail validation.

11.5.10 SUMMARY OF DEFERRED LOCK ENFORCEMENT WITH OTHER TECHNIQUES

In summary, deferred lock enforcement readily works with a variety of other techniques for database concurrency control and recovery. This includes recent techniques that optimize lock modes and lock sizes just as deferred lock enforcement optimizes lock durations. It also is compatible with traditional recovery techniques such as logged rollback and two-phase commit as well as recent recovery techniques such as single-page repair, single-phase restore, and incremental, on-demand, "instant" recovery.

11.6 DISTRIBUTED OPERATIONS

Distributed operations means, most importantly here, multiple local recovery logs, each containing not only log records about database changes but also transactions' commit log records.

The discussion below focuses on centralized two-phase commit; it does not consider distributed two-phase commit or non-blocking two-phase commit. Future research may address non-blocking commit protocols, appropriate termination protocols, and their interaction with controlled lock violation.

11.6.1 TRANSACTION COMMIT LOGIC

A local read-write participant in a global transaction may employ R and P locks, or an equivalent interpretation of X locks, during execution of the transaction's application logic. Locks must become traditional X locks upon the user's or the application's commit request, i.e., before the local participant transaction can submit its commit vote to the transaction coordinator.

By default, a transaction must retain its X locks (with traditional strength) while waiting for the coordinator's global commit decision. Controlled lock violation permits weakening lock modes not only during transaction hardening but also while waiting for the commit decision, with some restrictions and implications [Graefe et al., 2013]. In general, deferred lock enforcement affects a transaction and its lock modes before its commit process, whereas controlled lock violation affects a transaction during and after the commit logic.

In a distributed system, the commit logic of Figure 11.18 must integrate two-phase commit. While the local transaction writes its pre-commit log record to stable storage and then communicates with the transaction coordinator, controlled lock violation permits other transactions to conflict with the committing transaction's locks. If an exclusive lock violates a shared lock, i.e., in case of a read-write conflict, the violating transaction incurs a completion dependency on the committing transaction. If a shared or exclusive lock violates an exclusive lock, i.e., in case of a write-read conflict, the violating transaction incurs a commit dependency on the committing transaction.

Figure 11.29 shows the commit logic for distributed transactions including the steps required for two-phase commit. Figure 11.29 augments the commit logic of Figure 11.17 with the new lines 5–8.

Line 5 documents in the recovery log that the local transaction will abide by the centralized commit decision. Lines 6 and 7 contribute a vote and await the global commit decision. As both logging and communication can take considerable time, controlled lock violation permits other transactions to violate the committing transaction's locks at the expense of a completion dependency or a commit dependency.

```
1.   void TX::commit () {
2.     status = attempting;
3.     if (DLE) check for conflicting S locks
4.     status = committing;
5.     write pre-commit log record to stable storage
6.     send commit vote to coordinator
7.     receive global commit decision from coordinator
8.     status = decided;
9.     format the final commit log record in the log buffer
10.    status = complete;
11.    flush the final commit log record to stable storage
12.    status = committed;
13.    release all S and X locks
14.    status = done;
15. }
```

Figure 11.29: Commit logic for distributed read-write transactions.

Line 8 indicates that the transaction's final commit decision has been reached and now requires final documentation in the recovery log. The remaining steps are the same as in Figure 11.17.

Figure 11.30 adds two-phase commit to Figure 11.16. Lines 5–7 of Figure 11.29 map to the new step within the commit logic, which is shaded in the header as it may take more time than the hardening phase. Traditional locking enforces all locks throughout the transaction's entire duration. Controlled lock violation can become effective as soon as the pre-commit log record has a log sequence number and the transaction has a place in the commit history. Thereafter, other transactions can violate locks while the committing transaction flushes its pre-commit log record to stable storage, votes, waits for a commit decision, and logs it. The combination of deferred lock enforcement and controlled lock violation cannot weaken locks quite so early, because strong exclusive locks are required for update propagation from the transaction-private update buffer to the shared database or its buffer pool. Adding multi-version storage renders transaction-private update buffer and update propagation obsolete; thus, controlled lock violation has full effect and exclusive locks are strictly enforced only for the shortest possible duration, i.e., from data access to assignment of a log sequence number to the pre-commit log record.

The combination of deferred lock enforcement, controlled lock violation, and multi-version storage avoids the transaction-private update buffer and propagation of its contents to the shared buffer pool. Thus, strict lock enforcement is required only during commit preparation including formatting a pre-commit log record in the log buffer, i.e., comparable to the strict enforcement of exclusive locks in single-site transactions as shown in Figure 11.16.

Transaction phases → ↓ Techniques	Read phase = transaction and application logic	Commit Logic				Hardening = force log to stable storage
		Commit preparation	Two-phase commit	Commit log record	Update propagation	
Traditional locking		n/a			n/a	
Controlled lock violation						
Deferred lock enforcement						
Both dle and clv						
Dle, clv, multi-version storage					n/a	

Figure 11.30: Lock enforcement durations in distributed transactions.

11.6.2 LOG SHIPPING AND REPLICATION

ARIES-style "physiological" write-ahead logging requires rollback ("compensation") log records. Thus, a transaction rollback updates everything back, logs these updates, and then commits. Since a transaction "commits nothing" after rolling back, i.e., no logical database changes remain, there is no need to force the commit log record to stable storage. In log shipping from a primary site to a secondary site, the log stream includes either all log records, including rollback log records, or only log records of successfully committed transactions. The same choice applies to the log archive.

In either design, a primary site may execute database transactions, document their updates in the local recovery log, and ship the log records to each secondary site, which will apply them to its copy of the database. If a secondary site serves read-only queries, there must be some concurrency control between queries and transactions replicated from the primary site. Note that concurrency control among updates is not required because all required checks already happened on the primary site. Obviously, no concurrency control among read-only queries is required. Ideally, both the primary and the secondary sites employ multi-version storage. In that case, both sites may rely on deferred lock enforcement and its recommended combination with multi-version storage.

With read-only transactions in snapshot isolation never blocking update transactions and read-write transactions never blocking read-only transactions, a secondary site can process both its query workload and its log shipping workload concurrently without either workload interfering with the other. Nonetheless, some concurrency control is required such that read-only transactions can discern which versions are committed and which ones are still locked by incomplete transactions and thus must remain invisible to the query workload.

11.6.3 SUMMARY OF DISTRIBUTED OPERATIONS

In summary, distributed transactions benefit from the combination of deferred lock enforcement, controlled lock violation, and multi-version storage. Deferred lock enforcement also integrates readily with partitioning and log shipping from a primary site (for each partition) to one or multiple secondary sites.

11.7   SUMMARY AND CONCLUSIONS

With only modest software differences from traditional pessimistic concurrency control, deferred lock acquisition and deferred lock enforcement guarantee serializable transaction isolation but significantly improve concurrency in a transaction's read phase, i.e., while transactions execute application logic. In contrast to traditional locking, the new techniques let concurrent transactions run their read phase without lock conflicts and without waiting, with the exception of write-write conflicts. Exclusive locks are enforced with strong, traditional semantics only briefly during commit processing, i.e., for the minimal time to ensure full transaction isolation and serializability. With read-only transactions running unconstrained in snapshot isolation, the restrictions on read-write transactions are that

- a database item cannot have multiple concurrent updaters (as one of them would need to abort);

- an updater cannot commit with a concurrent active reader (to ensure repeatable-read and -count);

- a new reader must wait (briefly) while an updater commits (to prevent starvation of commits); and

- a reader of updates cannot commit until those updates are durable (to avoid premature publication).

These restrictions apply only in cases with lock conflicts. In a conflict, either transaction can abort or the requester can wait, best with limited wait depth and a timeout. Of course, precise lock scopes avoid many false conflicts. For example, orthogonal key-value locking lets two transactions lock the same key value; one transaction can commit an update to the key value, e.g., toggling the ghost bit for a logical insertion or deletion, while another transaction ensures phantom protection in an adjacent gap. If desired, weak isolation levels reduce shared locks and conflicts with committing updaters but also correctness guarantees.

Detecting write-write conflicts as early as possible has multiple advantages. First, by finding doomed transactions (that cannot possibly commit) as early as possible and not as late as end-of-transaction, it avoids wasted work. Second, it enables more conflict resolution options than end-of-transaction validation, e.g., waiting or aborting either transaction in a conflict. Third, it limits each database item to a single uncommitted version at a time. With multi-version storage, desirable in any case for read-only transactions in snapshot isolation, this eliminates the overheads of transaction-private update buffers including look-ups during all reads and update propagation during commit processing.

Deferred lock enforcement complements controlled lock violation: both enable more concurrency than traditional locking and both use weak lock modes during one of the two long-running phases of read-write transactions. Whereas controlled lock violation employs weak locks while a transaction hardens, i.e., while its commit log record goes to stable storage, deferred lock enforcement employs weak locks during a transaction's read phase and execution of its application logic. Deferred lock enforcement also complements multi-version storage: by detecting write-write conflicts as soon as possible and ensuring only a single uncommitted version for each database item, deferred lock enforcement permits efficient version storage in shared database structures and avoids the overheads of transaction-private update buffers. Finally, deferred lock enforcement complements non-volatile memory: as low-latency persistent memory replaces external devices for the recovery log, the importance of controlled lock violation decreases and that of deferred lock enforcement increases.

Figure 11.31 compares all techniques from traditional locking to the recommended combination of deferred lock enforcement, controlled lock violation, and multi-version storage. Traditional locking acquires and holds all its locks during both long-running phases. In contrast, deferred lock enforcement and controlled lock violation reduce the effective duration of exclusive locks to the bare minimum: concurrent waiting for truly exclusive access followed by formatting a commit log record.

ACKNOWLEDGEMENTS

Jeff Naughton suggested multiple improvements in the presentation. Caetano Sauer gave insightful feedback about deferred lock enforcement and its relationship to optimistic concurrency control.

Transaction phases → ↓ Techniques	Read phase = transaction and application logic 10^5 inst = 20 μs	Commit Logic			Hardening = force log to stable storage 1 I/O = 200 μs
		Commit preparation	Commit log record 10^3 inst = 0.2 μs	Update propagation	
Traditional locking		n/a		n/a	
Controlled lock violation					
Deferred lock enforcement					
Both dle and clv					
Dle, clv, multi-version storage				n/a	

Figure 11.31: Lock enforcement durations.

11.8 REFERENCES

Chan, A., Fox, S., Lin, W.-T. K., Nori, A., and Ries, D. R. (1982). The implementation of an integrated concurrency control and recovery scheme. *ACM SIGMOD*, pages 184–191. DOI: 10.1145/582383.582386. 329

Diaconu, C., Freedman, C., Ismert, E., Larson, P., Mittal, P., Stonecipher, R., Verma, N., and Zwilling, M. (2013). Hekaton: SQL server's memory-optimized OLTP engine. *ACM SIGMOD*, pages 1243–1254. DOI: 10.1145/2463676.2463710. 335

Graefe, G. (2003). Sorting and indexing with partitioned B-trees. *CIDR*. 340

Graefe, G., Lillibridge, M., Kuno, H. A., Tucek, J., and Veitch, A. C. (2013). Controlled lock violation. *ACM SIGMOD*, pages 85–96 (Chapter 4). DOI: 10.1145/2463676.2465325. 335, 336, 355, 359

Graefe, G., Guy, W., and Sauer, C. (2016). *Instant Recovery with Write-Ahead Logging: Page Repair, System Restart, Media Restore, and System Failover*, 2nd ed., *Synthesis Lectures on Data Management*, pages 1–113, Morgan & Claypool Publishers. DOI: 10.2200/s00710ed2v01y201603dtm044. 354

Graefe, G. and Kimura, H. (2015). Orthogonal key-value locking. *BTW*, pages 237–256 (Chapter 5). 333

Graefe, G. and Zwilling, M. J. (2004). Transaction support for indexed views. *ACM SIGMOD*, pages 323–334 (Chapter 3). Extended in G. Graefe: Concurrent queries and updates in summary views and their indexes. *Hewlett Packard Technical Report HPL-2011-16*. DOI: 10.1145/1007568.1007606. 351, 352

Gray, J., Lorie, R. A., Putzolu, G. R., and Traiger, I. L. (1976). Granularity of locks and degrees of consistency in a shared data base. *IFIP Working Conference on Modelling in Data Base Management Systems*, pages 365–394. 328, 332, 348

Gray, J. and Reuter, A. (1993). *Transaction Processing Concepts and Techniques*, Morgan Kaufmann. 331

Härder, T. (1984). Observations on optimistic concurrency control schemes. *Information Systems*, 9(2), pages 111–120. DOI: 10.1016/0306-4379(84)90020-6. 330

Korth, H. F. (1983). Locking primitives in a database system. *Journal of the ACM*, 30(1), pages 55–79. DOI: 10.1145/322358.322363. 331, 332

Kung, H. T. and Robinson, J. T. (1981). On optimistic methods for concurrency control. *ACM TODS*, 6(2), pages 221–226. DOI: 10.1145/319566.319567. 330, 338, 355

Lomet, D. B. (1993). Key range locking strategies for improved concurrency. *VLDB*, pages 655–664. 338

Mohan, C. (1990). ARIES/KVL: A key-value locking method for concurrency control of multiaction transactions operating on B-tree indexes. *VLDB*, pages 392–405. 333, 338

Mohan, C. and Levine, F. E. (1992). ARIES/IM: An efficient and high concurrency index management method using write-ahead logging. *ACM SIGMOD*, pages 371–380. DOI: 10.1145/130283.130338. 338, 343

O'Neil, P. E., Cheng, E., Gawlick, D., and O'Neil, E. J. (1996). The log-structured merge-tree (LSM-tree). *Acta Information*, 33(4), pages 351–385. DOI: 10.1007/s002360050048. 340

SQLite. (2004). File locking and concurrency in SQLite version 3. `http://sqlite.org/lockingv3.html` 331

Thomasian, A. (1998). Performance analysis of locking methods with limited wait depth. *Performance Evaluation*, 34(2), pages 69–89. DOI: 10.1016/s0166-5316(98)00025-x. 339, 357

PART IV

The End of Optimistic Concurrency Control

CHAPTER 12

The End of Optimistic Concurrency Control

Why good locking will always win

Goetz Graefe

ABSTRACT

This chapter argues that all database systems and key-value stores should remove any implementations of optimistic concurrency control, including those based on timestamp validation. For less contention and less wasted effort, for better performance and better scalability, they should replace optimistic concurrency control with a state-of-the-art implementation of locking.

12.1 INTRODUCTION

The promise of optimistic concurrency control, as opposed to pessimistic concurrency control or locking, is that it permits more concurrency, less contention, higher utilization, and more throughput. This turns out not to be true; in fact, with equally careful implementations, the opposite should be true except for higher CPU utilization due to effort wasted on doomed transactions.

In the discussion here, optimistic concurrency control means end-of-transaction validation. Validation of read- and write-sets means the usual backward validation, i.e., committing transactions intersect their own read- and write-sets with those of transactions already committed [Kung and Robinson, 1981]. The alternative is forward validation, i.e., committing transactions intersect their read- and write-sets with active transactions [Härder, 1984]. End-of-transaction validation of timestamps compares timestamp values in the database at the time of the data access and at the time of the commit request, in effect checking for interleaving updates by other transactions. In contrast, pessimistic concurrency control means lock acquisition before data access. While the duration of shared (read-only) locks depends on the desired transaction isolation level [Gray et al., 1976], transactions retain their exclusive (read-write) locks until commit in order to guarantee rollback without concurrency conflicts.

Carey found that it does not matter how transactions find no conflicts: in workloads and access patterns with no or very rare conflicts, locking is just as good as optimistic concurrency control [Carey and Muhanna, 1986, Carey and Stonebraker, 1984]. If there are no true conflicts and none of the techniques finds false (non-existing) conflicts, then all transactions can proceed without delay and a bottleneck other than concurrency control, e.g., I/O or processor bandwidth, will limit the system's transaction processing throughput.

If there are conflicts, however, then pessimistic concurrency control is superior to optimistic concurrency control. One of the reasons is that optimistic concurrency control lets all transactions run through all their application logic and data accesses, even transactions for which an outside observer can see that they are doomed to abort due to a conflict. Pessimistic concurrency control detects such conflicts as soon as they occur, not as late as end-of-transaction validation.

The remainder of this chapter repeats and introduces categorical reasons why locking must be superior if optimistic and pessimistic concurrency control are implemented with equal care. These reasons are more powerful than measurements of some system or another that may be tainted by implementation care or ingenuity, by semantic differences such as the quality or granularity of phantom protection, or by more subtle semantic differences such as concurrency control during transaction hardening.

12.2 EARLIER COMPARISONS

Kung and Robinson [1981] introduce optimistic concurrency control and assert that "these methods should be more efficient than locking" as "the hardware will be underutilized if the degree of concurrency is too low." (Text in quotes is from the cited papers.) The design focuses on serializable transaction isolation because "it has been shown in Kung and Papadimitriou [1979] that serialization is the weakest criterion for preserving consistency of a concurrent transaction system." Since end-of-transaction validation can fail, producing output belongs into the write phase: "returning a result from a query is considered to be equivalent to a write, and so is subject to validation." Note that the combination of validation and write phase must be atomic: "The simplest way to implement this is to place the assignment of a transaction number, validation, and the subsequent write phase all in a critical section" which was deemed "perfectly suitable in the case that there is one CPU and that the write phase can usually take place in primary memory" ("one CPU" then means today "one CPU with one core with one hardware thread"). Due to buffer pool faults and I/O during each transaction's read phase, "we expect the read phase to be orders of magnitude longer than the validation and write phases." Otherwise, validation in multiple stages or concurrent validation (called "parallel validation") seems required.

With respect to global data structures and their low-level concurrency control (i.e., critical sections), there is an implicit assumption that transactions publish their read- and write-sets for other transactions to inspect during their validation phases. There is a further assumption that the read- and write-sets are organized by transaction, not for index-search using key values or other identifiers within the database.

With respect to database contents and high-level concurrency control (i.e., transactions), the write phase consists of propagation of updates from the transaction-private update buffer to the global database in the buffer pool, but with respect to transactional durability, the write phase must include forcing the commit log record to stable storage. Subsequent transactions may publish recently updated database contents only after these updates are committed and safely logged on stable storage. Early lock release repeats this subtle mistake [DeWitt et al., 1984].

If a transaction is to "see" its own updates (as it does in serial execution without transaction-private update buffers), then each database look-up must first inspect the transaction-private update buffer or, perhaps more efficiently, in the transaction's write-set. There is an equivalent in locking: each database update must first check whether the required lock is already in place. In other words, checking for existing locks before each data access has an equivalent in optimistic concurrency control: checking the transaction's write-set or its transaction-private update buffer. Lock acquisition also has an equivalent: creating an entry in the write-set and a copy of an existing database object within the transaction-private update buffer.

A particular advantage of optimistic concurrency control is "that for query-dominant systems, validation will often be trivial:" if no database updates have been committed during a read-only transaction, validation of this transaction finds no write sets with which to intersect its own read set. In pessimistic concurrency control, it seems that such a transaction can set a read-only lock at the database granularity and retain more detailed information in transaction-private memory (very much like a read-set in optimistic concurrency control), to be used for lock de-escalation if an update transaction starts; note that lock acquisition during lock de-escalation is always conflict-free and therefore fast.

Härder's analysis [Härder, 1984] of optimistic concurrency control [Härder, 1984] zeroed in on many weak spots in optimistic concurrency control, e.g., phantom protection and the limited options for conflict resolution: "If a conceivable conflict is detected, a 'pessimistic' view has to be taken: this conceivable conflict is resolved by aborting the transaction. Hence, these schemes rely on transaction backout as a control mechanism."

Härder's analysis also comments on conflict resolution by waiting (for a lock) as opposed to only by transaction abort: "It is assumed that transaction wait normally diminishes the risk of conflict. Hence, a higher fraction of transactions has to be expected to be aborted by using optimistic CC schemes." An earlier analysis found 36% vs. 10% of aborts [Peinl and Reuter, 1983].

About phantom protection in optimistic concurrency control, Härder observes: "Since the records were originally missing, there are no tokens to validate, and therefore no way to catch that a logical conflict has occurred. This problem can be alleviated to some degree if page-level tokens are chosen and the insertion of a 'missing' record can be detected via the access path structures which it belongs to."

Härder's overall conclusions are:

1. "Hot spot data need controlled serialization.

2. If waiting situations and deadlocks are unlikely, locking is as good as optimistic CC.

3. Each system needs some control hierarchy in order to provide efficient read and write operations on large data sets. For example, operations like loading a file, deleting a file, searching a file sequentially can be supported appropriately by some hierarchical locking scheme.

4. Locking seems to be better suited to handle non-existence problems of records" [Härder, 1984].

Carey and Stonebraker [1984] developed an algorithm-independent simulation framework and used it to compare locking, timestamps, and optimistic concurrency control algorithms. "All were found to perform equally well when conflicts are rare. When conflicts are not rare, it was shown that blocking is the preferred tactic for handling conflicts, as restarts waste resources and consequently lead to poorer performance. Hence, locking algorithms appear to be the concurrency control method of choice for centralized database systems." For deadlock resolution, "our results indicate that better policies will choose transactions which have completed little work."

Carey and Muhanna [1986] describe "a simulation study of the performance of several multi-version concurrency control algorithms, investigating the extent to which they provide increases in the level of concurrency and also the CPU, I/O, and storage costs resulting from the use of multiple versions." They find that "each multi-version algorithm offers significant performance improvements despite the additional disk accesses involved in accessing old versions of data."

Mohan [1994] "expands" on Härder's analysis and discusses "support for access paths (indexes, hash-based storage), partial rollbacks, nested transactions, fine-granularity (e.g., row-level) conflict checking, different isolation levels, distributed transactions, and so on" in order "to increase awareness of the implementation aspects of OCC." Many of the practical problems occur in the context of insertion and deletion. For example, if entries in secondary indexes contain physical addresses of rows in a table's primary storage structure, then when are rows placed and physical addresses decided, and when is free space reserved? With respect to logging and recovery, when are log records created and appended to the write-ahead recovery log, and how does that affect the duration of the write phase? Mohan lists further open issues such as logging and guarantees in two-phase commit; concluding with surprise that there are numerous performance studies comparing optimistic and pessimistic concurrency control but no complete system design that addresses issues such as ANSI SQL compliance on difficult issues such as statement-level verification of integrity constraint, partial (statement-level) rollback, and distributed transactions.

Graefe [2016] focuses on timing of conflict detection and options for conflict resolution, but limits the analysis to single-version storage and thus short-changes locking by failing to recognize that transaction-private update buffers, which are inherently required in optimistic concurrency control, are a form of multi-version storage. The study attempts to unify optimistic and pessimistic concurrency control by using a lock manager to implement optimistic transactions. In optimistic concurrency control, the lock manager captures the read- and write-sets but with conflict checks delayed to end-of-transaction validation.

12.3   COMMON MISCONCEPTIONS

A common misconception is that locking is for single-version storage and that optimistic concurrency control is for multi-version storage. Actually, locking works very well with multi-version storage: a shared lock on a versioned database item freezes the most recent committed version, i.e., it prevents installation of a new committed version, and an exclusive lock on a versioned database item permits creation, reading, writing, and (in case of rollback) removal of a new version.

A related misconception is that with single-version storage in both cases, optimistic concurrency control performs better than locking. Note, however, that in optimistic concurrency control, each read-write transaction requires a transaction-private update buffer, and that this buffer makes any implementation of optimistic concurrency control implicitly a multi-version system. Thus, a comparison of single-version locking and optimistic concurrency control seems an apples-to-oranges comparison; their performance difference stems as likely from single-version vs. multi-version storage as from optimistic vs. pessimistic concurrency control.

Also related is snapshot isolation: if read-only transactions run "as of" start-of-transaction, they benefit from multi-version storage and are serializable without any concurrency control [Chan et al., 1982]. In this design, only read-write transactions require concurrency control. Removal of large, long-running (read-only) queries from concurrency control and contention is due to multi-version storage, not due to optimistic concurrency control.

"Industry-standard" snapshot isolation reads database contents as of start-of-transaction and writes as of end-of-transaction, i.e., each transaction runs as a read-only transaction plus a separate write-only transaction, with different commit points and different placements in the serialization sequence. Berenson et al. wrote: "Snapshot Isolation is non-serializable because a transaction's Reads come at one instant and the Writes at another" [Berenson et al., 1995]. Thus, such a "transaction" is certainly not atomic or indivisible with respect to concurrency control and transaction semantics. Serializable snapshot isolation requires a single commit point for all reads and writes, and thus all reads of a read-write transaction must be as of the commit point at end-of-transaction.

Another misconception is that optimistic concurrency control, in particular end-of-transaction timestamp validation, is cheap because data and concurrency control information are co-located, thus saving a lookup in a hash table and the associated low-level concurrency control in the lock manager. However, the same effect can be achieved if a lock manager and its lock information are distributed across the nodes of an in-memory data structure such as the page frames of a buffer pool. Thus, achieving these savings is orthogonal to the concurrency control technique employed.

Perhaps the most dangerous misconception is that optimistic concurrency control requires an atomic validation phase, when in fact it requires that validation and write phases together are atomic. Moreover, if the write phase ends when the transaction-private update buffer is empty, other transactions can validate and commit at this time, which permits premature publication of new data values before they are persistent. This is precisely the subtle correctness problem of early lock release [DeWitt et al., 1984] solved by controlled lock violation [Graefe et al., 2013]. It may be that implementations of optimistic concurrency control have benefited from lacking a solution to premature publication. In fact, this might be a reason why optimistic concurrency control has seemed faster in the past, i.e., faster than locking without early lock release or controlled lock violation. Another reason might have been a comparison of locking for serializability with optimistic concurrency control for a weaker transaction isolation level, with optional page-level concurrency control for phantom protection based on timestamp validation using PageLSN values [Mohan et al., 1992]. In any case, if each transaction's validation and write phases including hardening are atomic, serial validation means committing and hardening one transaction at a time, which makes serial validation utterly impractical and concurrent validation absolutely mandatory in multi-user transaction processing.

Finally, it seems a misconception that locks held while executing a transaction's application logic matter. Because hardening is by far the longest phase in small transactions, it seems that controlled lock violation after the commit point matters most, i.e., weak lock enforcement while writing log records to stable storage. This is true until recovery logs move from flash to non-volatile memory; at that time in the future, locks and lock enforcement during the application logic become more important again.

12.4 LOCKING IN OPTIMISTIC CONCURRENCY CONTROL

Even a database management system built strictly on optimistic concurrency control requires locking in some situations. Locking is required not only in low-level concurrency control to protect physical in-memory data structures by coordinating threads (critical sections, latches) but also in high-level concurrency control to protect logical database contents by coordinating user transactions [Graefe, 2010].

Most notable is concurrent validation, i.e., multiple optimistic transactions in their validation and write phases at the same time. These transactions must detect conflicts not only with committed transactions but also with each other. Thus, they must share a data structure that indicates which database items occur in which transactions' read- and write-sets. This many-to-many relationship between database items and transactions is precisely what a lock manager captures. Moreover, the low-level concurrency control (latching) requirements during concurrent validation are precisely the same as latching in a traditional lock manager.

This shared data structure serves not only concurrent validation but also serial validation. In optimistic concurrency control with backward validation, i.e., a committing transaction intersects its read- and write-sets with those of transactions committed earlier, a committed transaction must leave its read- and write-sets in a place where subsequent committing transactions can find them and compute intersections efficiently. A lock manager's hash table organized by database item is precisely the data structure required. While sorted set representations of read- and write-sets permit intersection algorithms similar to merge join, a hash table permits intersection computation similar to an index nested loops join. If concurrency conflicts are rare and if therefore non-empty intersections are rare, index nested loops join is a more efficient algorithm, assuming an efficient index structure such as an in-memory hash table. Moreover, when a transaction's last concurrent transaction finishes, the transaction's read- and write-sets must be removed from the shared data structure. Again, a lock manager's organization around transactions (organizing the many-to-many relationship between database items and transactions) is precisely what is needed. Figure 12.1 summarizes how optimistic and pessimistic concurrency control may employ a lock manager and the information it captures.

	Optimistic Locking		Pessimistic Locking (traditional locking)
	Backward Validation	Forward Validation	
Lock acquisition	Before each data access		
Lock strengthening	After commit decision	Before commit decision	During lock acquisition
Conflict detection	During 2nd commit	During 1st commit	
Lock weakening	After last concurrent transaction	After allocation of commit LSN	
Lock release		After transaction hardening	
Transaction end			

Figure 12.1: Lock management in optimistic and pessimistic concurrency control.

Finally, a lock manager is required for optimistic participants in distributed transactions and their two-phase commit (or any alternative, e.g., Paxos). Once the user or the application requests a transaction to commit, all participants either abort or promise to abide by the coordinator's commit decision. In other words, while waiting for the coordinator's decision, a participant transaction must not fail or be preempted in any way. This is equivalent to locking the database items in the transaction's read- and write-sets in shared and exclusive modes. Note, however, that database items locked in this way permit controlled lock violation [Graefe et al., 2013] by other transactions, i.e., concurrency with concurrency control and serializability during waiting and hardening.

12.5   ADVANTAGE: LOCKING

Without conflicts, locking is just as good as optimistic concurrency control, and optimistic concurrency control is just as good as locking. Therefore, the arguments below focus on conflicts more than on conflict-free situations.

1. Atomic validation and write phases, atomic together and including writing a commit log record to stable storage, requires concurrent validation. This in turn requires a lock manager with lock acquisition during validation and lock release when the last concurrent transaction exits the system (for backward validation). Forward validation and end-of-transaction timestamp validation also require atomic validation and write phases, concurrent validation, and a lock manager. In other words, optimistic concurrency control does not save the overhead of a lock manager but it adds the overhead of transaction-private update buffers for new and changed database contents.

2. If locking is needed in any case, e.g., for concurrent validation and for two-phase commit, then complete reliance on locking saves the effort to implement, maintain, test, and tune a second method for concurrency control, i.e., optimistic concurrency control.

3. Locking supports a wide variety of lock modes beyond shared and exclusive, or read-only and read-write. In optimistic concurrency control, there is no equivalent to update, reserved, and pending lock modes, or to increment, decrement, and escrow modes [O'Neil, 1986]. It is conceivable and it may be practical to add an increment-set to the read- and writes-sets of each transaction, but with only end-of-transaction validation, it is impossible to replicate the scheduling component of update, reserved, and pending locks ("first in line to upgrade to exclusive"). In any case, in spite of 35 years of optimistic concurrency control, there is no solid theory of derived modes and their concurrency similar to Korth's work on lock modes [Korth, 1983].

4. For decades, database systems based on pessimistic concurrency control have reduced overheads yet increased concurrency by means of hierarchical locking [Gray et al., 1975]. Many systems employ lock escalation and some even lock de-escalation. There is no equivalent for hierarchical locking in optimistic concurrency control, although it could be invented, probably with only moderate complexity. Optimistic techniques equivalent to lock escalation and de-escalation seem more difficult to invent, albeit probably feasible.

5. Intersection of read- and write-sets based on transactions' entire durations is equivalent to lock acquisition at start-of-transaction, not to incremental lock acquisition at the time of data access. If data accesses are distributed evenly throughout a transaction's read phase, then optimistic concurrency control enforces exclusion, on average, for twice the duration and will find twice as many conflicts, strengthening the argument that optimistic concurrency control is practical only if conflicts are exceedingly rare. This argument does not apply

to end-of-transaction timestamp validation, because timestamps are taken at the time of the first access to a database item.

6. In case of conflict and conflict resolution by transaction abort, lock-based systems can select a victim by transaction size, priority, etc. In contrast, in optimistic concurrency control (with backward validation), the only possible policy is that the first committer wins and the second committer fails. In other words, a small transaction can force rollback and restart of a large transaction. In a workload with a variety of transaction sizes, locking will perform better than optimistic concurrency control, assuming a reasonable policy for conflict resolution upon lock conflicts.

7. In optimistic concurrency control, even doomed transactions run to completion and eventually require rollback and restart. Not only in backward validation but also in forward validation, which requires that active transactions register their read- and write-sets incrementally such that committing transactions can intersect them with their own, conflict detection is delayed until end-of-transaction validation. In contrast, early conflict detection in pessimistic concurrency control avoids such wasted effort. In a workload with conflicts, locking will perform better than optimistic concurrency control.

8. Waiting is a valuable additional method of conflict resolution, in particular if tempered by limited wait depth [Thomasian, 1997, 1998] and timeouts. Transaction abort and rollback are often much more drastic than necessary but they are the only method for conflict resolution after end-of-transaction validation, which is the defining characteristic of optimistic concurrency control.

These arguments are really at the heart of the overall assessment that pessimistic concurrency control or locking is categorically superior to optimistic concurrency control. If every one of these arguments is erroneous or misguided, then of course the overall assessment is mistaken, too.

12.6   ANOTHER QUICK LOOK AT OPTIMISTIC CONCURRENCY CONTROL

If the reader accepts that optimistic concurrency control requires a lock manager for concurrent validation as well as for two-phase commit, then end-of-transaction validation can be reinterpreted in terms of lock acquisition. Specifically, end-of-transaction (backward) validation of read- and write-sets is equivalent to asking: for the shared and exclusive locks equivalent to the read- and write-sets, would there have been a conflict if locks had been acquired at start-of-transaction? Similarly, end-of-transaction timestamp validation is equivalent to asking: would there have been a conflict after lock acquisition at first access to a database item? Viewed in this light, optimistic concurrency control is a form of deferred lock acquisition.

For what it's worth, serializable snapshot isolation similarly requires that no other transaction may modify relevant database items between data access (reads) and end-of-transaction, similar to the validation of read- and write-sets. Thus, serializable snapshot isolation for read-write transactions, in whatever implementation, is equivalent to asking: would there have been a conflict after lock acquisition at first access? Of course, like all highly concurrent data management designs, serializable snapshot isolation is greatly aided by multi-version storage with semantics as described above, i.e., read-only transactions without locks, shared locks for the last committed version, and exclusive locks for creation, manipulation, and commit of new versions.

Figure 12.2 summarizes the argument. Putting it all together, what's really wanted is a locking regimen that exploits multi-version storage and detects conflicts early yet permits maximal concurrency during transactions' read phases, i.e., while executing their application logic. Controlled lock violation does something vaguely similar during transactions' hardening phases; the new technique would complement controlled lock violation during transactions' read phases.

		Optimistic Concurrency Control		Pessimistic Concurrency Control (locking)
		Backward Validation	Forward Validation	
Global data structure ...	Insertion	On commit	Before each data access	
	Deletion	Delayed by the last concurrent transaction	Commit end	
Conflict ...	Visibility	2nd commit	Before data access	Before data access
	Detection		1st commit	
	Resolution options	Abort 2nd transaction	Abort 1st or 2nd transaction, delay 1st commit	Wait for lock release, lock de-escalation in 1st or 2nd transaction, abort 1st or 2nd transaction
Related techniques		Track oldest active transaction		Hierarchical locking, "increment" locks, limited wait depth, timeout, commit-lsn

Figure 12.2: Optimistic vs. pessimistic concurrency control.

12.7 RECOMMENDATIONS

Based on these observations, conclusions, insights, and speculations, here are a few recommendations for the design and implementation of database management systems and of transactional key-value stores:

1. Remove optimistic concurrency control—instead, focus on a careful design and implementation of locking and of the lock manager.

2. Exploit multi-version storage and snapshot isolation for read-only transactions, like Chan et al. [1982] but perhaps at the granularity of rows and index entries.

3. For read-write transactions, exploit controlled lock violation [Graefe et al., 2013], both in local transactions and in two-phase commit.

4. Focus on the granularity of locking, e.g., key-value locking and key-range locking [Lomet, 1993, Mohan, 1990, Mohan and Levine, 1992] including their orthogonal variants [Graefe, 2007, Graefe and Kimura, 2015].

5. Focus on lock modes, e.g., increment locks in materialized "group by" views [Graefe and Zwilling, 2004, Korth, 1983, O'Neil, 1986].

6. Focus on lock durations, e.g., during execution of each transaction's application logic and during transaction hardening.

12.8 CONCLUSIONS

In summary, there is no advantage in optimistic concurrency control for transaction processing performance and system scalability, but many categorical disadvantages or, in a different light, advantages in locking. With two equally good implementations of optimistic and pessimistic concurrency control, locking will provide better efficiency, scalability, and performance, in particular in times of contention. Here, equally good means serializability including phantom protection, multi-version storage and snapshot isolation for read-only transactions, the same granularity of concurrency control, integration with distributed transactions and two-phase commit (or something equivalent, e.g., Paxos), careful implementation of data structures and algorithms, and thorough testing and tuning. Both models of concurrency control can benefit from controlled lock violation, not only in single-site databases but also during two-phase commit. Future work will offer a complement to controlled lock violation that affects not a transaction's hardening phase but execution of application logic in a transaction's read phase.

ACKNOWLEDGEMENTS

By carefully reading a draft and questioning some of its arguments, Jeff Naughton enabled multiple improvements, which is gratefully acknowledged.

12.9 REFERENCES

Berenson, H., Bernstein, P. A., Gray, J., Melton, J., O'Neil, E. J., and O'Neil, P. A. (1995). A critique of ANSI SQL isolation levels. *ACM SIGMOD*, pages 1–10. DOI: 10.1145/223784.223785. 373

Carey, M. J. and Muhanna, W. A. (1986). The performance of multi-version concurrency control algorithms. *ACM TODS*, 4(4), pages 338–378. DOI: 10.1145/6513.6517. 370, 372

Carey, M. J. and Stonebraker, M. (1984). The performance of concurrency control algorithms for database management systems. *VLDB*, pages 107–118. 370, 372

Chan, A., Fox, S., Lin, W.-T. K., Nori, A., and Ries, D. R. (1982). The implementation of an integrated concurrency control and recovery scheme. *SIGMOD*, pages 184–191. DOI: 10.1145/582383.582386. 373, 379

DeWitt, D. J., Katz, R. H., Olken, F., Shapiro, L. D., Stonebraker, M., and Wood, D. A. (1984). Implementation techniques for main memory database systems. *ACM SIGMOD*, pages 1–8. DOI: 10.1145/602260.602261. 371, 374

Graefe, G. (2007). Hierarchical locking in B-tree indexes. *BTW*, pages 18–42 (Chapter 2). 379

Graefe, G. (2010). A survey of B-tree locking techniques. *ACM TODS*, 35(3) (Chapter 1). DOI: 10.1145/1806907.1806908. 374

Graefe, G. (2016). Revisiting optimistic and pessimistic concurrency control. *Hewlett Packard Labs Technical Report HPE-2016-47*, May. 372

Graefe, G., Lillibridge, M., Kuno, H. A., Tucek, J., and Veitch, A. C. (2013). Controlled lock violation. *ACM SIGMOD*, pages 85–96 (Chapter 4). DOI: 10.1145/2463676.2465325. 374, 375, 379

Graefe, G. and Kimura, H. (2015). Orthogonal key-value locking. *BTW*, pages 237–256 (Chapter 5). 379

Graefe, G. and Zwilling, M. J. (2004). Transaction support for indexed views. *ACM SIGMOD*, pages 323–334 (Chapter 3). DOI: 10.1145/1007568.1007606. 379

Gray, J., Lorie, R. A., Putzolu, G. R., and Traiger, I. L. (1975). Granularity of locks in a large shared data base. *VLDB*, pages 428–451. DOI: 10.1145/1282480.1282513. 376

Gray, J., Lorie, R. A., Putzolu, G. R., and Traiger, I. L. (1976). Granularity of locks and degrees of consistency in a shared data base. *IFIP Working Conference on Modelling in Data Base Management Systems*, pages 365–394. 369

Härder, T. (1984). Observations on optimistic concurrency control schemes. *Information Systems*, 9(2), pages 111–120. DOI: 10.1016/0306-4379(84)90020-6. 369, 371, 372

Korth, H. F. (1983). Locking primitives in a database system. *Journal of the ACM*, 30(1), pages 55–79. DOI: 10.1145/322358.322363. 376, 379

Kung, H. T. and Papadimitriou, C. H. (1979). An optimality theory of concurrency control for databases. *ACM SIGMOD*, pages 116–126. DOI: 10.1145/582095.582114. 370

Kung, H. T. and Robinson, J. T. (1981). On optimistic methods for concurrency control. *ACM TODS*, 6(2), pages 213–226. DOI: 10.1145/319566.319567. 369, 370

Lomet, D. B. (1993). Key range locking strategies for improved concurrency. *VLDB*, pages 655–664. 379

Mohan, C. (1990). ARIES/KVL: A key-value locking method for concurrency control of multiaction transactions operating on B-tree indexes. *VLDB*, pages 392–405. 379

Mohan, C. (1994). Less optimism about optimistic concurrency control. *RIDE-TQP*, pages 199–204. DOI: 10.1109/ride.1992.227405. 372

Mohan, C., Haderle, D. J., Lindsay, B. G., Pirahesh, H., and Schwarz, P. M. (1992). ARIES: A transaction recovery method supporting fine-granularity locking and partial rollbacks using write-ahead logging. *ACM TODS*, 17(1), pages 94–162. DOI: 10.1145/128765.128770. 374

Mohan, C. and Levine, F. E. (1992). ARIES/IM: An efficient and high concurrency index management method using write-ahead logging. *ACM SIGMOD*, pages 371–380. DOI: 10.1145/130283.130338. 379

O'Neil, P. E. (1986). The Escrow transactional method. *ACM TODS*, 11(4), pages 405–430. DOI: 10.1145/7239.7265. 376, 379

Peinl P. and Reuter, A. (1983). Empirical comparison of database concurrency control schemes. *VLDB*, pages 97–108. 371

Thomasian, A. (1997). A performance comparison of locking methods with limited wait depth. *IEEE TKDE*, 9(3), pages 421–434. DOI: 10.1109/69.599931. 377

Thomasian, A. (1998). Performance analysis of locking methods with limited wait depth. *Performance Evaluation*, 34(2), pages S69–89. DOI: 10.1016/s0166-5316(98)00025-x. 377

Author's Biography

GOETZ GRAEFE

Goetz Graefe has been a professor, product architect, and industrial researcher since 1987. Like other database vendors, Microsoft SQL Server adopted his designs for query optimization and query execution. He has published tutorial surveys on query execution, sorting, b-tree indexing, concurrency control, logging and recovery, as well as numerous novel techniques and research results in query processing and transactional data storage. He is the 2017 recipient of the ACM SIGMOD Edgar F. Codd Innovation award.